REAL FOOTBALL

FOOTBALL

CONVERSATIONS ON AMERICA'S GAME

STEPHEN H. NORWOOD

UNIVERSITY PRESS OF MISSISSIPPI / JACKSON

www.upress.state.ms.us

The interview with Joe Washington Jr. is a slightly revised version of
my article, "The Making of an Athlete: An Interview with Joe Washington,"
Journal of Sport History 27 (Spring 2000): 91–145.

The University Press of Mississippi is a member of the
Association of American University Presses.

12 11 10 09 08 07 06 05 04   4 3 2 1
∞
Library of Congress Cataloging-in-Publication

Norwood, Stephen H. (Stephen Harlan), 1951–
  Real football : conversations on America's game / Stephen H. Norwood.
    p. cm.
  Includes index.
  ISBN 1-57806-662-X (alk. paper) — ISBN 1-57806-663-8 (pbk. : alk. paper)
  1. Football players—United States—Interviews. 2. Football—Social aspects—
United States. 3. Football—United States—Psychological aspects. I. Title.
  GV939.A1N67 2004
  796.332'0973—dc22   2004008106

British Library Cataloging-in-Publication Data available

CONTENTS

REAL FOOTBALL

THE APPEAL OF FOOTBALL

During the Battle of the Bulge in World War II, when the Germans were parachuting troops dressed in American uniforms behind Allied lines, U.S. sentries as a matter of course challenged men who approached them by demanding the answers to questions, often obscure, about baseball. Baseball was then considered a central part of an American male's identity. Yet, today, few U.S. soldiers would be able to answer the questions these sentries posed.

During the 1960s, professional football surpassed major league baseball, long the national pastime, to become the most popular spectator sport in the United States. Professional football is today one of the principal forms of entertainment for men. Enormous crowds gather every Sunday during the increasingly protracted season to attend National Football League (NFL) games across the country, with millions more watching on television. Televised Monday Night Football games, introduced in 1970, caused restaurant patronage, movie attendance, and even crime to drop during those evenings and led Tuesday to replace Monday as the day when Detroit's automobile plants recorded their highest rate of absenteeism. Monday Night Football has endured longer than any program on television in prime time.[1] Despite football's enormous popularity, however, the general public possesses relatively little knowledge of contemporary America's most complex sport or of the experience and feelings of the men engaged in it.

This book examines the making of the professional football player and how he approaches his sport mentally and emotionally. It focuses on eight men who played in the NFL (and one, also in the All-America Football Conference, AAFC) for at least ten years, as well as another who coached football for forty-five years. The interviewees have played nearly every gridiron position, and they explain in depth the requirements, responsibilities, and outlook that each involves. They describe the types of personality most suited to offense and to defense. As players in a highly specialized sport, they outline the significant differences within categories of position—for example, in the defensive secondary, cornerback, strong safety, and free safety and between outside and middle linebacker.

The men interviewed provide insight into big-time college as well as professional football. Nearly all attended the University of Oklahoma or Louisiana State University, two of the nation's premier college football programs. The interviewees analyze major college football recruiting and coaching methods, practice regimens, and the athlete's academic experience, as well as race relations in college sport.

The book examines the emotional meaning of sport over each stage of the life course, from childhood, through high school, college, and the NFL, to retirement. The players consider the long-term impact of receiving encouragement or a dressing down from a father or a coach and changing authority relations in high school and college. Two father-son combinations, Dub Jones and Bert Jones and Joe Washington Sr. and Joe Washington Jr., are among those interviewed. The men discuss their feelings about pleasing and disappointing the fans, personal antagonisms arising over competing for a position, being heavily recruited by big-time college football programs, becoming a first-round NFL draft choice and the very different experience of being drafted in a lower round, and being traded or cut. The players also describe how they handled the experience of being injured, sometimes severely, or watching teammates suffer serious injury. Bert Jones, for example, broke his neck in a game, the injury ending his career. Steve Zabel was on the sidelines with the New England Patriots when Oakland Raiders safety Jack Tatum broke the neck of his teammate Darryl Stingley, permanently paralyzing him—a fate Bert Jones narrowly avoided.

Football's appeal derives in large part from its peculiar combination of highly modern qualities—an emphasis on order and precision, coordination within a group, and split-second timing—with more primitive elements, sublimated in bureaucracies, the open display of violence and aggression, which are involved in every play—in the bruising contact on the line, in the blocking and tackling in the open field. No NFL team, or college team for that matter, would sell any tickets if it played touch football.[2] Fran Tarkenton, the quarterback who introduced scrambling at that position in the 1960s (a more spontaneous and unorthodox style that coaches feared threatened the coordination and precision they valued in an offensive unit), in a murder mystery drew a sharp contrast between the approaches in football associated with offense and defense. In an insight derived perhaps from observing football's mainstream from without,

Tarkenton has a character suggest that NFL coaches viewed offense as a "well-oiled machine," in that "the whole team [is] moving like the fingers of one hand." For an offensive play to succeed, "Every move has to be exactly in accord with the play as diagramed. The slightest deviation can cause [it] to fail. . . . A tenth of a second's mistake on anyone's part, and it will look like comedy night at the demolition derby." By contrast, defense is reactive and more improvisational. It is "loose, flexible," and almost never will "a whole team on defense act like a unit."[3]

Although football is very much a team game, and helmets and facemasks heighten player anonymity, it nonetheless involves a significant degree of individualism, even on offense, which is often overlooked. To be sure, All-Star games in football are far less meaningful than in baseball, since the former requires much more coordination among players. Baseball's All-Star game, marking the midsummer divide, occupies a central position in the sport's calendar and is associated with some of the game's truly legendary feats, like Carl Hubbell striking out five men in succession, including Ruth, Gehrig, and Foxx; Ted Williams hitting a home run off Rip Sewell's Eephus pitch; and Pete Rose barreling into Ray Fosse at home plate. By contrast, fans regard the NFL's Pro Bowl as far less significant, a minor postseason exhibition. And while the practice of according individual nicknames to baseball players is exceedingly common—the Georgia Peach, the Big Train, the Sultan of Swat, the Yankee Clipper, the Say Hey Kid, and so on—it is unusual in football, where nicknames are more often given to units—the Steel Curtain, the Fearsome Foursome, the Hogs, the Doomsday Defense, the Killer Bees.

Nevertheless, Jerry Kramer, the All-Pro Green Bay Packers guard of the 1960s and one of the most perceptive commentators on football, observed that at many positions a player must spend much of the game concerned with a particular opponent, whom he confronts directly again and again. Thus, as in a boxing match, one-on-one combat often becomes an important focus in a game, bringing some individual recognition even to an offensive lineman thought to toil in almost complete obscurity. Within the team framework, "there's a dramatic, and important, individual game within the game," particularly for the linemen, and for the pass receivers and defensive backs. A player can contribute significantly to the team by prevailing in his own personal match-up. As Green Bay's offensive right guard, Kramer each week studied the defensive left tackle he would face the next Sunday: "He dominates my thoughts and consumes most of my energy."[4] Thus, University of Oklahoma cornerback Tony Peters, one of the players I interviewed, first came to wide attention when he shut down receiver Lynn Swann of then number-one-ranked Southern California, a future

NFL Hall of Famer, covering him man-to-man the whole game and preventing him from catching a single pass. Indeed, Peters observes that the cornerback position "puts you out on an island, pretty much by yourself." Baltimore Colts tackle Sam Ball's inability to handle veteran New York Jets defensive end Gerry Philbin was a significant factor in the Jets' stunning Super Bowl III upset of the heavily favored Colts in 1969.[5] Like the National Basketball Association fans entranced by the dramatic duels between offensive star Wilt Chamberlain and defensive standout Bill Russell, football fans of the 1950s thrilled at similar confrontations between Cleveland Browns running back Jim Brown and New York Giants middle linebacker Sam Huff. As Ken Mendenhall notes, given the length of some NFL careers, such one-on-one match-ups, unlike in college, can regularly occur for a half decade or more, becoming deeply etched in fans' minds.

In combining thorough advance planning, synchronization of parts, specialization of roles, and hierarchy—the leadership of the coach and the quarterback, the subordination of line to backfield—with violence and individual confrontations, football resembles military combat, with which it is often compared. It is a sport in which danger is omnipresent. The quarterback is even referred to as the "field general," and a team's objective, scoring a touchdown, requires that it invade its opponent's territory. Like soldiers, football players wear helmets. Like war, football is played in any sort of weather, often cold and nasty. With their muddied faces and uniforms, football players sometimes seem to resemble combat soldiers. The U.S. Army once even sent officers to observe the Dallas Cowboys practice to help them learn how to conduct a training camp. And President Richard Nixon felt football supplied the most appropriate image for the massive B-52 bombing campaign he unleashed against North Vietnam in April 1972; he named it Operation Linebacker.[6]

Football coaches, sportswriters, and players themselves often use military imagery to describe various aspects of the game. Jerry Kramer entitles the sections of his book *Instant Replay*, a diary of his 1967 season with the Packers: "Preliminary Skirmishes," "Basic Training," "Mock Warfare," "Armed Combat," and "War's End." Famed NFL and AAFC quarterback Y. A. Tittle referred to the football field as a "battleground," where unrelenting attack was required, since in football few leads are ever safe: "Bomb the hell out of them no matter what the score is. That's my philosophy." Kickoff teams are called "suicide squads."[7] Joe Washington Jr. compares the kickoff returner to a "kamikaze pilot."

In his 1961 autobiography, Ty Cobb, once considered baseball's greatest player, lamented that pro football "threatens to replace baseball as our Number 1 sport" because those engaged in the national pastime no longer displayed the qualities associated with masculinity in his playing era, the first three decades of the twentieth century: courage, fierce competitiveness, the willingness to endure pain. In Cobb's Dead Ball era and in the 1890s, baseball was "no pink tea," and "mollycoddles" stayed out of it. He claimed that when his contemporaries went up to bat, they boldly confronted their antagonist on the mound, "making *him* fear *them*." There was "none of this plate shy bobbing in and out of the box, pulling away from curve balls." Players remained in the lineup "whether [they] were lame, sick, or half-blind from pain." Chicago Cubs infielder Johnny Evers ran out a triple with a broken leg, and Boston Beaneater Hugh Duffy played out the 1894 season with a "leg . . . slashed open by spikes from ankle to knee," compiling the highest batting average of all time. If a player "split a finger fifty years ago," he "stuck it in the dirt and kept going." [8]

But the Georgia Peach claimed the modern player was of a softer breed, lacking his contemporaries' fiery zeal and passion for the game: "The spirit of Mars has vanished." Rather than toughing it out, players sidelined themselves for even the most minor afflictions. "Develop a bit of indigestion," Cobb declared, "or a minor bone chip in his arm" and the player was "clamped into a bed at Johns Hopkins . . . fed by dieticians, and generally treated like a maharaja with the gout." [9]

However, the more traditional masculinity that Cobb valued is still emphasized in pro football, a very physical game in which collisions occur on every play, injuries are frequent, and players often continue to perform hurt. Dallas Cowboys coach Tom Landry recalled that when he played with the New York Giants in the 1950s, "the ability to take, or better yet, *dish out* physical punishment was often the mark of a man," and he emphasized that "a reputation for toughness was a high honor, hard sought." [10] Enduring pain is essential in football because, as former New York Giants head coach Allie Sherman declared, "In this game, a player aches from July to December." Legendary Cleveland coach Paul Brown noted, "You have to pay a physical price to dominate another team." [11] Green Bay Packers quarterback Bart Starr recalled fullback Jimmy Taylor in the 1962 NFL title game returning time and again to the huddle after absorbing terrible punishment from the New York Giants defense, "bent over holding his insides together." Although Ty Cobb a year earlier rued that major league baseball players had lost their "lust [for] battle," Giants quarterback Y. A. Tittle remembered hearing the New York defense before the game in an adjoining room "kicking chairs, stomping around like a lot of bull elephants and growling at each other." [12] Baltimore Colts quarterback Earl Morrall observed that "to a professional, pain is part of the game," noting that one of his linemen "played the last three games of the [previous] season with a broken bone in his forearm." [13] Hall of Fame center Jim Ringo of the Packers once played a game with fourteen boils on his buttocks. Afterwards, Ringo's "hip pads were smeared with bloody pus." Yet when the coaches reviewed the game films, they awarded him the highest grade a player ever received during Vince Lombardi's then seven-year reign with Green Bay. Ringo "had not missed a block." [14]

Tony Peters recalls that the Washington Redskins motivated members of their special teams, who might feel overlooked because they spent much of the game on the bench, by rewarding them when they "hit a guy during a game, and really KOed him." That kind of hit was called a "pancake," sending an opponent down on his back. For such a hit, the team would pay out $100 or $200, extra pocket money. Washington area merchants might also provide gifts like television sets or golf clubs. Obviously, "the spirit of Mars" survived in football.

In pro football, coaches and sportswriters often apply pressure to play when injured. Jerry Kramer recalled that Vince Lombardi told Packers defensive lineman Lionel Aldridge to "stop loafing" less than three weeks after he had broken his leg and demanded that he start running. Kramer declared that Lombardi had the "highest threshold of pain in the world" because "none of our injuries hurts him at all." [15] Steve Zabel observes that "The coaches' attitude was, if you don't have a cast on, if you're not in the hospital, scheduled for surgery, you should be out there." Zabel also noted that team management had little consideration for players' health. It installed artificial turf to save money on ground maintenance, a higher priority than preventing player injuries, which were less frequent on natural grass. Joe Washington Jr. recalled that after he suffered a serious knee injury that required surgery during the exhibition season of his rookie year with the San Diego Chargers, the San Diego press mocked him by claiming his "best move was a limp to the sideline."

Like baseball, where to succeed a pitcher must know how to throw inside, football is a game of intimidation, so a player's ability to suppress fear is often critically important. Y. A. Tittle noted that successful passing required that a quarterback have the ability to wait "until the last possible second" before throwing the ball, "even when it means getting flattened by a big defensive end." [16] Clendon Thomas, who played safety in the NFL, observes that pass receivers running crossing patterns and defensive backs are playing a game of chicken. Fearlessness, along with great moves and hands, made Raymond Berry, against whom Thomas played, one of pro football's all-time greatest receivers: "He'd wake up in the hospital, but he'd have the ball in his hands." Tony Peters states that a defensive back must "stick [his] face into a mass of humanity going three times the speed of sound."

The pro football player's resolve, like the prizefighter's, is regularly tested in an environment pervaded with violence, where he can suffer severe bodily harm and is often expected to perform hurt. Athletes who have published books on courage, notably Mickey Mantle and Frank Gifford, associate it with the willingness to confront potentially dangerous situations and to persist in the face of injury. In a 1946 title bout against Rocky Graziano, "Tough Tony" Zale, middleweight champion of the world, broke his right thumb in the second round but battled on, absorbing fearful punishment before scoring a knockout when, in the sixth round, "Rocky took a right in the stomach and promptly sat down." Tough Tony was "everybody's hero," while Graziano was considered "a bum," who had "quit when the going got rough." Graziano redeemed himself in the rematch when he fought on despite sustaining a bad cut over his eye in the first round. In the sixth round, his face "a crimson mask," his vision impaired, he battered Zale into the ropes and scored a technical knockout. Howard Cosell noted that "Graziano proved he had the courage to take a beating and not give up." [17] Similarly, Gifford's quarterback, Y. A. Tittle, returned to the 1963 NFL championship game after Bears linebacker Larry Morris had smashed his already injured knee, causing pain so searing "It was like somebody stuck a knife in [it]." Gifford remarked that many players "wouldn't have gone back into that game with a gun." [18]

Mickey Mantle, who himself played much of his career in pain as a result of osteomylitis in his knees, used Brooklyn Dodgers infielder Don Zimmer as a model in his book *The Quality of Courage.* Zimmer had been badly beaned in the minors, leaving him unconscious for eleven days. But he returned to action and won promotion to the majors, only to be hit in the face with a pitch and suffer a fractured cheekbone. Yet, he again came back, continuing to dig in at the plate, unfazed by knockdowns. When Detroit Tigers pitcher Jim Bunning decked him in a spring training game, he rose and hit the next offering out of the park. [19]

Sometimes a football player's determination to persevere when injured, often inculcated in childhood, can be carried too far, as Steve Zabel notes. Zabel, then with the New England Patriots, returned to action for the playoffs after missing six games with a knee injury, even though it had not healed. He remained in despite sustaining additional damage to the knee on the game's very first play, even as his performance deteriorated, because he had long learned to view quitting as shameful, no matter what the circumstances. Zabel observed, "There are things that are instilled in you as a young boy that carry over to your . . . pro career, and can hurt your performance rather than help it."

Tony Peters found little benefit in a junior college running-and-tackling drill called "The Hamburger," designed to eliminate players who shied away from repeated head-on collisions. The runner and his two offensive linemen, confronting three defenders, were not allowed outside a zone only five yards wide.

Peters notes, "It was the old Roman view of gladiators—they place you in a cage, and the strong survive." The coaches verbally abused players who performed in "a cowardly manner." But Peters concludes, "Having played in the NFL for eleven years, I don't think that drill improved your ability to function in a game." He observes, "It doesn't take a whole lot of intelligence to run and stick your head through a wall."

Physicality is only one part of football, a sport that also requires considerable mental insight and intense concentration and often involves deception and psychological competition. Tony Peters believes athletic talent is roughly even in the NFL, and that what separates the outstanding players from the mediocre is the "mental approach to the game." The successful player carefully studies his opponents, learning to "read" them in order to anticipate how the upcoming play will unfold, which he must do in two or three seconds. As a defensive back, Peters could detect from an offensive tackle's posture whether to expect a run or a pass. Quarterback Bert Jones, who often spent nights at the stadium reviewing film of upcoming opponents, could detect from how a defender lined up, staggered his stance, or positioned his hands, what he would do. The quarterback's task is made more difficult by defensive backs giving him "false reads" to disguise a defense, as Peters notes. Greg Pruitt, who compares football to a chess game, asserts that learning to make the correct adjustments, which involves mental insight as well as experience, separates the excellent from the ordinary running back. Through careful study, an opponent will develop the means to counter a running back who ran well in a game the next time they meet. If the running back is ever to repeat the performance, he must prepare for these changes and learn to react effectively to them.

Because mental acuity is so significant in football, coaching assumes greater significance than in other, less complex sports. Football's high degree of specialization requires that a head coach in the NFL or at a college with a major athletic program work with a staff composed not only of offensive and defensive coordinators, but various assistants expert in a narrower aspect of the game. Relations between coaches and players are more hierarchical in football than in baseball, reflected in football coaches wearing formal street attire on the field, while baseball managers dress exactly like the players. Football coaches must design and analyze plays that are generally more intricate than in other sports, evaluate player performance, teach various skills, and involve themselves in interpersonal relations to promote team morale, develop player talent, and enable units to cohere more effectively.

The men interviewed assess a wide range of approaches used in football coaching at the professional and major college levels, including those of NFL coaching Hall of Famers Paul Brown and Joe Gibbs; Forrest Gregg and Mike McCormack (player Hall of Famers who became head coaches), Ted Marchibroda, Tommy Prothro, Eddie Khayat, and Chuck Fairbanks, and at the college level Bud Wilkinson, Fairbanks, and Barry Switzer. Joe Washington Sr. also describes coaching at African-American high schools in Texas both during and after the Jim Crow era and playing at Prairie View A&M under legendary black coaches Pop Long and Jimmie Stevens.

Two of the men interviewed for this book played pro football during the 1950s (one of them also in the late 1940s), and another played at a black college and then coached high school football during that period. This study explores both the change and continuity in the sport since the late 1940s. Pro football was the "neglected stepchild" in American sports, lagging well behind major league baseball, college football, horse racing, and boxing in attracting spectators and in the attention bestowed by the media. Tom Landry described the Yankee Stadium crowds at his AAFC New York Yankees games in 1949, as well as those for NFL teams then, as minuscule compared to those who had turned out when he played at the University of Texas or to see the baseball Yankees. He declared that the pro football crowds of that era "often felt more like high school than the big time." Each winter after the pro football season ended, during the late 1940s and early 1950s, Landry returned to Texas only to have friends there ask where he had been.[20] New York Giants star halfback Frank Gifford had the same experience when he came home to southern California after his 1952 NFL rookie season. The popular game show "What's My Line?" was so confident panelists would fail to recognize Giants quarterback Charlie Conerly that it made him a contestant, even though he played the most glamorous position on the gridiron, in the nation's largest metropolis.[21]

By the 1930s, the quality of play in the NFL had probably surpassed that in college football, but the latter enjoyed considerably higher status and a larger audience than the pro game until the 1950s. Pro football had difficulty overcoming the damage to its reputation sustained during its early years because of franchise instability, player contract jumping, low pay, and a widespread perception that gambling on games was more common than in the colleges.[22]

Radio coverage of pro football games was sparse, reflecting the sport's inability to generate much of a following outside cities with NFL teams. No radio network carried the NFL title game until 1940, although there had been such a broadcast of baseball's World Series as far back as 1922. Nor did radio broadcast many regular season NFL games beyond the cities in which teams were located before the late 1940s. Movie theater newsreels only started weekly coverage of pro football games in 1949.[23]

Television contributed significantly to the expansion of pro football's fan base during the 1950s, helping to spread its appeal to areas of the country without NFL teams, in the South and Southwest, the Rocky Mountain states, the Pacific Coast, and New England. During the early 1950s, NFL teams discovered that they could significantly stimulate attendance by broadcasting their road games on television, and "blacking out" their home games, within a fifty-mile radius of their city. Football was a sport highly suited to television, unlike baseball, where cameras on many plays could not encompass all the action. By the 1950s, like radio, television networks had added color analysis to complement play-by-play broadcasters, capable of providing the audience with clear explanations of the most intricate plays in this highly complex sport. During the 1960s, television added slow motion and instant replay, making football plays even more comprehensible. The NFL's enthusiasm for television contrasted with the National Collegiate Athletic Association's much more cautious approach. Television exposed fans residing a great distance away from NFL cities to pro football, enabling teams to develop sizeable followings outside their localities.[24]

Pro football benefited from significant innovation in offensive play during the 1940s, as the introduction of the modern T-formation, replacing the single wing, resulted in much more passing and open field running. By 1945, NFL teams on offense passed about thirty-five percent of the time.[25] Fans considered this more balanced run-pass attack more exciting than the conservative, ground-oriented offense that continued to prevail in college football. The population craved a higher level of excitement as the pace of work and of life in general quickened dramatically in post–World War II America's continuously expanding bureaucratic, industrial, highly technological society.

The increasing sophistication of defenses, one of the most striking changes in pro football during the 1950s, also significantly enhanced its appeal.[26] The larger Cold War atmosphere of the decade, when the United States was determined to react vigorously to probing actions by the Soviet Union and Communist China designed to test the nation's resolve, probably contributed to the new emphasis on defense in football. The United States initiative in establishing the North Atlantic Treaty Organization in 1949, followed by several other similar mutual defense pacts in the 1950s formed to contain the Soviet Union and China, led to a heightening of the fans' emotional involvement with football defense, containing the other team's attack.

By permitting players to specialize only in defense, the two-platoon system, which had largely taken hold in the NFL by the 1950s, although not in college football, improved the quality of defensive play. Players could concentrate on mastering a narrower range of skills, and those unable to perform effectively on offense were no longer eliminated. Fans now perceived the defense as a fully autonomous unit, entirely distinct from the offense, requiring different personality traits. Defensive play seemed more instinctual, encouraging an unbridled aggression that was unsuitable on the tightly coordinated offense.

Television helped glamorize football defense when CBS broadcast "The Violent World of Sam Huff" in October 1960, wiring the New York Giants middle linebacker with a miniature microphone and filming him for several weeks in training camp and during a preseason game. The close-ups and the sound of violent contact as Huff led the Giants defense in containing the opposing offense electrified male viewers all across the nation. The Giants had been the first NFL club in the 1950s to introduce the defense rather than the offense prior to a game. Defensive end Andy Robustelli recalled, "Until then football belonged to the offense, and so did all the cheers." But now, Yankee Stadium rocked with fans bellowing "De-fense!" and "Huff, Huff, Huff!" Sportswriter Paul O'Neil noted that the Giants fans "roar as gleefully as the Roman mob sighting lions when New York gives up the ball and the defensive team trots ominously to take over." [27]

By 1960, defense in the NFL was far more advanced than in college. In describing his transition from Louisiana State University, which had a top-flight football program, to the Baltimore Colts in 1973, Bert Jones recalled that the NFL game was "much more complex than in college." He observes that "Today in a college game, you can look out on the field and tell what defense they're in, whereas in the pros you never knew. You saw so many different coverages and so many different fronts."

Like the Western film, pro football also benefited from its image of rough masculinity that many found appealing in the 1950s, because of anxiety that affluence, unprecedented leisure, and rampant consumerism had softened American men, making them unfit to meet the challenges of the Cold War. The pro football player, muddied, grizzled, and scarred, called upon to surmount repeated crises that appear whenever third down is reached, contrasted sharply with the decade's dominant male symbols at work and leisure—bland and sedentary—"The Man in the Gray Flannel Suit" and the paunchy suburbanite in Bermuda shorts.

At the same time, football appealed to many middle-class men in corporate management and the professions, an increasingly sizeable segment of the American labor force by the 1950s, because it appears to replicate their own bureaucratic work environment. No sport emphasizes the specialization of tasks and cooperation among players as much as football, and the clock is as central in it as it is to modern bureaucracy. A clearly defined hierarchy is also significant in football, as coaches design the plays the athletes execute, and the quarterback gives the signals that set the offense in motion and often calls the plays himself. Yet, football also encourages physicality and aggressive impulses that bureaucracy stifles, providing these middle-class fans the opportunity to experience them vicariously.[28]

Because the chances of being hurt are significant in football, medical treatment assumes greater importance than in most sports, and many of the players discuss how club management handles player injuries. Sports medicine in the NFL was primitive during the 1950s. Tom Landry recalled an experience not so very different from Ty Cobb's having his tonsils removed without anesthetic by an incompetent hotel physician in the first decade of the twentieth century. Landry remained in a game despite having split his lip wide open, with blood gushing onto his uniform. But later in the locker room the Giants team physician, who had been hired largely because he was the coach's brother-in-law, determined the wound needed to be stitched. He then began stitching Landry's face without using any anesthetic, inflicting "burning pain." After a time the doctor stopped, realizing he had forgotten to put any surgical thread in the needle. He proceeded to search for some thread, having Landry sitting nearby with the needle still stuck through his lip: "That was sports medicine in the early fifties." [29]

While sports medicine in pro football certainly had improved by the 1970s, several of the interviewees express strong dissatisfaction with the inadequate treatment provided by management and team physicians. Tony Peters, whose ruptured navicular ligament was misdiagnosed by the Cleveland Browns physician as a severe sprain, asserts that many team physicians "are so caught up working for an NFL team, with all that prestige, that they don't look as deeply into things as they should." Joe Washington Jr. learned he was to have major knee surgery his rookie year from the press; his club, the San Diego Chargers, had neglected to inform him. When the problem persisted after the surgery, his coaches resisted allowing him to seek a second opinion. Jerry Kramer joked that a team physician would probably tell you that you were all right "if you broke your neck during a close game." [30]

Probably the most striking contrast between the 1950s and the 1970s and after is the dramatic change in player salaries, attributable largely to lucrative television contracts and to player unionization. During the late 1940s, the AAFC's competition with the NFL as a second major pro football league had pushed player salaries up somewhat. But when it folded after the 1949 season, monopoly returned to pro football, drastically reducing player leverage in bargaining. NFL management never considered playing in Canada, the only alternative for the pro player, as a viable threat. As in major league baseball, pro football players needed to find other employment during the off-season.[31] Clendon Thomas notes that even in 1957, when he signed his first contract with the Los Angeles Rams, as their number-two draft choice, pro football was not "serious money." As late as 1960, not a single NFL lineman, offensive or defensive, made as much as $15,000 a year.[32] Dub Jones recalled that when he played in the NFL All-Pro game in the early 1950s, the participants were not even told what they would be paid.

Pro football players in the 1950s had almost no opportunity to earn money through commercial endorsements. Dub Jones, who still shares the NFL record for most touchdowns scored in a game, six in a 1951 game against the Chicago Bears, received only one endorsement offer after that exploit, for $500 from the Quaker Oats Company. By contrast, his son Bert, one of the NFL's premier quarterbacks in the 1970s, was presented with far better endorsement opportunities, including a contract to model Ralph Lauren Chaps line of slacks.

The 1970s and early 1980s, when six of the interviewees played, was an era of dramatic upheaval in pro football's labor relations. Football players were at a serious disadvantage in negotiating contracts, even after they began using agents in the late 1960s. As Joe Washington Jr. notes, management can count on selling out the stadium every week, regardless of losing any particular player. The public quickly becomes frustrated when games are delayed or canceled by strikes, tending to blame the players, who earn far more than most fans and are thus perceived as "spoiled brats." The 1970s and early 1980s were nonetheless marked by labor conflict that produced two major leaguewide walkouts, in 1974 and 1982, along with a significant wildcat strike in 1975. Several of the interviewees participated in these strikes.

In 1974, the players concentrated on what they defined as freedom issues, notably overturning the Rozelle Rule, which gave the NFL commissioner the right to compensate a team whose player became a free agent.[33] Steve Zabel believes that the players' youth and lack of maturity caused them to neglect their long-term interests, such as the pension plan, associated with a stage of life that then seemed very remote. The players tried to project an image of strength with macho imagery, flexing their biceps in T-shirts carrying their strike slogan "No freedom, No football!" but they were badly overmatched and could not prevail.

During the next exhibition season, the New England Patriots initiated a wildcat strike, again drawing on the imagery of machismo and raising the slogan "No freedom, No football!" The players and owners had still not achieved a collective bargaining agreement. Steve Zabel describes the wildcat beginning on the practice field's fifty-yard line. Those who favored a strike were invited to step across, and all forty-six did: "It was the Alamo all over." The Patriots stood fast, despite threats from Coach Chuck Fairbanks that all of the participants would be black-balled from the NFL, and were joined by several other teams. The owners managed to persuade the players to return, promising to bargain in good faith. But Zabel contends that they failed to do so and undermined the players' momentum. According to Zabel, rather than seriously try to resolve the issues, the owners proceeded to encourage the formation of the World Football League as a potential strikebreaking pool for the future.

In 1982, the players staged another strike, lasting fifty-seven days, marked by impressive solidarity. Never before had professional athletes staged as long a work stoppage. Their initial demand was that fifty-five percent of the clubs' gross revenue be used for players' salaries. The players were at a disadvantage in having no strike fund, but organized exhibition games between striking teams to build one. The players again failed to win their main demand, but did achieve higher minimum salary levels and a lucrative, graduated severance plan.[34]

Besides examining in depth the experience of negotiating contracts, several of the players also analyze the behavior of head coaches and team management during these strikes, the role of the player representative, and friction among players. They assess both the achievements and the limitations of the NFL Players Association and compare their cohort's labor conditions with those of more recent players.

Significant changes occurred in race relations in football during the 1960s and 1970s, although Tony Peters emphasizes that blacks' opportunities for coaching and front office positions in both pro and college football continue to be greatly restricted. For Joe Washington Sr., pro football was not really an option after he graduated from Prairie View A&M, and the major white college football programs did not show any interest in the high school athletes he coached until the late 1960s. Black scholastic and intercollegiate football, which produced some excellent players and coaches, some of whom he discusses, remained a largely self-enclosed world, which received little or no attention from the mainstream press until the 1960s. Yet when his son, Joe Washington Jr., played for him in the early 1970s, he was deluged with recruiting offers from the nation's top college football programs, and he visited about thirty-five campuses. Of course, not all programs were equally receptive to black athletes. Barry Switzer's rapport with black players and his willingness and ability to recruit them when few college programs in the South and Southwest were as interested, were a significant factor in the University of Oklahoma's football success during the late 1960s and 1970s.

Joe Washington Sr. provides keen insight into the role of sports in black community life during the Jim Crow era and in the southern black college. He also astutely assesses the challenges of coaching in the black high school during that period and the impact of desegregation. The African-American players of the next generation also discuss sports in black community life and analyze their experience in the period of school desegregation as well as adjusting to playing in a big-time college football program and to the NFL when blacks constituted a minority.

One of the most striking changes in football in the 1970s was the radical transformation of player conduct on the gridiron, notably the emergence of antics designed to call attention to one's self after a play has been completed—dancing and finger waving, a boasting about one's personal prowess that simultaneously humiliates the opposition. This represents a complete overturning of the traditional conception of sportsmanship—reflecting, some might say, a new "culture of narcissism." When Elmo Wright, a Kansas City Chiefs wide receiver, performed the first end zone dance in the NFL in 1971, "a simple two-step," his behavior so angered the opposing Oakland Raiders that one of them broke his nose, as a "lesson in humility." Yet within a few years, such dances, many far more elaborate, had become the norm in the NFL. Moreover, many defensive players wildly celebrated when they sacked a quarterback, leaping and pumping their fist in the air. Increasingly, they did so even after just making a solid tackle.[35] Young boys, who often view pro football players as role models, quickly imitated this behavior, and it filtered down even to elementary school playgrounds.

Bert Jones strongly disapproves of such " 'Look at me' taunting," which he believes "removes team unity from a team sport." Successful plays in football require cooperation among several teammates; no single individual deserves all the credit. His center Ken Mendenhall agrees that pro football "has lost a lot of class" because of the showboating on the field: "It's unprofessional to draw attention to yourself." He notes that Hall of Fame receiver Paul Warfield always just handed the ball to the official when he scored, nothing more, since "he wanted everybody to know that he had been there a lot of times before."

Most of the players discuss their feelings about retirement, a difficult, often traumatic experience for an athlete or coach. A man used to enjoying considerable public recognition and acclaim, often conveying significant authority because of his standing in the sports world, can plunge rapidly into obscurity, overwhelmed by a sense of powerlessness. Paul Brown described the period immediately after his firing as head coach of the Cleveland Browns as the "low point" of his life. Brown stated revealingly that he "felt like Napoleon on the isle of Elba." He removed any object from his home that served as a reminder that he had ever been a football coach.[36] Jerry Kramer noted that all of his Green Bay Packers teammates of the 1960s missed the applause after leaving the game, some more than others, and refers to the "void" of retirement.[37] Tony Peters observes that a successful pro player is treated "like an icon throughout the community." This results in "special favors": "You go to a bar or restaurant, and the owner knows you, and there's no charge." Peters concludes, "As a player, you lose sight of reality."

Most men, of course, have difficulty in adjusting to retirement, but professional football players face an additional set of problems. They must make the transition at a much earlier age, thirty or thirty-five as opposed to sixty-five or seventy. They must find another line of work at an age when many other men are well ensconced in a career.[38] Tony Peters notes that the NFL provides no support to players trying to make the shift to retirement. In addition, injuries accumulate over the course of a football career, so that many players, as retirees, live with chronic pain or with some disability. Some require surgery years later as a result of an old gridiron wound.

The men interviewed, however, seem to have made the transition to retirement from football with less difficulty than most players. None of them is currently associated with college or professional football. They have found new challenges and stimulation in a wide range of endeavors, which they describe in some depth. Together, they provide considerable insight into an array of social, cultural, and political issues and thoroughly explore the physical, mental, and emotional dimensions of America's most popular sport.

NOTES

1. Jack Clary, "The Third 25 Years," *Coffin Corner*, Winter 1995, 5; Allen Guttmann, *Sports Spectators* (New York: Columbia University Press, 1986), 140; Randy Roberts and James Olson, *Winning Is the Only Thing: Sports in America Since 1945* (Baltimore: Johns Hopkins University Press, 1989), 122.

2. Ed Linn, "Ray Nitschke: The Hard Road to Respect," *Sport*, November 1965, 83.

3. Fran Tarkenton with Herb Resnicow, *Murder at the Super Bowl* (New York: William Morrow, 1986), 107, 122–23. Tarkenton did not care to be called a "scrambler," a term he maintained had never been adequately defined. But he conceded that when he entered the NFL in 1961 he "must have looked like some kind of lunatic loping around" in the backfield, compared to other quarterbacks, "most of whom were about as mobile as sixteen-inch shore batteries." Fran Tarkenton, *Broken Patterns: The Education of a Quarterback* (New York: Simon and Schuster, 1971), 51–55.

4. Jerry Kramer, edited by Dick Schaap, *Instant Replay: The Green Bay Diary of Jerry Kramer* (New York: Signet Books, 1969), 104.

5. William Phillips, "A Season in the Stands," *Commentary*, July 1969, 68.

6. Tom Landry with Gregg Lewis, *The Autobiography of Tom Landry* (New York: Harper Collins, 1990), 217–18; James S. Olson and Randy Roberts, *Where the Domino Fell: America and Vietnam, 1945–1995* (New York: St. Martin's Press, 1996), 245–46. On the military parallel to football, see also

Allen Guttmann, *From Ritual to Record: The Nature of Modern Sports* (New York: Columbia University Press, 1978), 121–25.

7. Y. A. Tittle, *I Pass!* (New York: Franklin Watts, 1964), 148–49, 208; Linn, "Nitschke," 85.

8. Ty Cobb with Al Stump, *My Life in Baseball: The True Record* (Garden City, N.Y.: Doubleday, 1961), 56–58, 238, 276, 280.

9. Cobb, *My Life*, 55, 198.

10. Landry, *Autobiography*, 92.

11. Dave Anderson, "Pride and Pain in Pro Football," *Sport*, January 1966, 45; Paul Brown with Jack Clary, *PB: The Paul Brown Story* (New York: Atheneum, 1979), 155.

12. Cobb, *My Life*, 198; Tittle, *I Pass!*, 234, 236.

13. Earl Morrall, *In the Pocket: My Life as a Quarterback* (New York: Grosset & Dunlap, 1969), 146, 154.

14. Anderson, "Pride and Pain," 45, 78.

15. Kramer, *Instant Replay*, 97.

16. Tittle, *I Pass!*, 148–49.

17. Mickey Mantle, *The Quality of Courage* (New York: Bantam, 1965); Frank Gifford, *Gifford on Courage* (New York: M. Evans and Co., 1976); Howard Cosell, *Great Moments in Sport* (New York: Macfadden-Bartell, 1964), 56–58; Jacquin Sanders, "Tough Tony Zale," *Sport*, March 1966, 86.

18. Tittle, *I Pass!*, 256–57; Gifford, *Gifford on Courage*, 171.

19. Mantle, *Quality of Courage*, 51–54.

20. David Maraniss, *When Pride Still Mattered: A Life of Vince Lombardi* (New York: Simon & Schuster, 1999), 158; Landry, *Autobiography*, 86, 109.

21. Benjamin G. Rader, *American Sports: From the Age of Folk Games to the Age of Televised Sports*, 2nd ed. (Englewood Cliffs, NJ: Prentice-Hall, 1990), 262; Bob Carroll, *When the Grass Was Real* (New York: Simon & Schuster, 1993), 13.

22. John M. Carroll, *Red Grange and the Rise of Modern Football* (Urbana: University of Illinois Press, 1999), 101–2; Michael Oriard, "Home Teams," *South Atlantic Quarterly* 95 (Spring 1996), 477. In the 1930s, the legendary Red Grange, and many others in the NFL who had also played college football, maintained that the caliber of play in the pro game far surpassed that of the colleges. Carroll, *Red Grange*, 176–77, 183.

23. Michael Oriard, *King Football: Sport and Spectacle in the Golden Age of Radio and Newsreels, Movies and Magazines, the Weekly and the Daily Press* (Chapel Hill: University of North Carolina Press, 2001), 202; G. Edward White, *Creating the National Pastime: Baseball Transforms Itself, 1903–1953* (Princeton, NJ: Princeton University Press, 1996), 208; Oriard, "Home Teams," 493.

24. Carroll, *Red Grange*, 188; Oriard, "Home Teams," 492–93; Ronald A. Smith, *Play-by-Play: Radio, Television, and Big-Time College Sport* (Baltimore, MD: Johns Hopkins University Press, 2001), 94.

25. Bob Carroll, Pete Palmer, and John Thorn, *The Hidden Game of Football* (New York: Warner Books, 1988), 26–27.

26. Paul O'Neil, "The Giant Defense Is Triumph of Mind," *Life*, 5 December 1960, 122.

27. Carroll, *When the Grass Was Real*, 117–118; Robustelli quoted in Norm Miller, "Glory Days: Andy Robustelli and the Giants Popularized the 'D,'" *Coffin Corner*, November 1992, 9; Landry, *Autobiography*, 110–11; Jack Clary, "The Second 25 Years," *Coffin Corner*, Late Fall 1994, 7; O'Neil, "Giant Defense," 122.

28. Rader, *American Sports*, 267–68.

29. Landry, *Autobiography*, 93–94. On Cobb's tonsillectomy, see Cobb, *My Life*, 54–55.

30. Kramer, *Instant Replay*, 151.

31. Landry, *Autobiography*, 94.

32. Chuck Bednarik, "Who Says Pros Can't Play 60 Minutes?" *Saturday Evening Post*, 25 November 1961, 54.

33. Donald Kennedy, "Football Players Strike of 1987" in Ronald L. Filipelli, ed., *Labor Conflict in the United States: An Encyclopedia* (New York: Garland Press, 1990), 179–80.

34. Kennedy, "Football Players Strike of 1987," 80; Rader, *American Sports*, 338; *New York Times* 17 November 1982.

35. Michael Oriard, "Muhammad Ali: The Hero in the Age of Mass Media" in Elliott J. Gorn, ed., *Muhammad Ali: The People's Champ* (Urbana: University of Illinois Press, 1995), 9; Oriard, "Professional Football as Cultural Myth," *Journal of American Culture*, 4 (Fall 1981), 36.

36. Brown, *PB*, 288.

37. Jerry Kramer with Dick Schaap, *Distant Replay* (New York: Jove, 1986), 7.

38. Michael A. Messner, *Power at Play: Sports and the Problem of Masculinity* (Boston: Beacon Press, 1992), 111.

DUB JONES

RUNNING BACK, FLANKER BACK, DEFENSIVE BACK

—Miami Seahawks, 1946
—Brooklyn Dodgers, 1947
—Cleveland Browns, 1948–1955
—Offensive Coordinator, Cleveland Browns, 1963–1967

Dub Jones was a key member of the most formidable pro football team of the early post–World War II era, Paul Brown's legendary Cleveland Browns. The Browns boasted the best passing offense in football until that time, with quarterback Otto Graham throwing to Mac Speedie, Dante Lavelli, and Jones, the original flanker back. Jones holds the all-time National Football League (NFL) record for most touchdowns scored in a game, with six, a record shared with Ernie Nevers and Gale Sayers.

Jones begins by discussing his childhood in northern Louisiana during the Great Depression, the significant influence his high school football coach had on his development as an athlete, and his experience playing wartime college football for Louisiana State University and Tulane, while also serving in the U.S. Navy.

In 1946, Jones joined the Miami Seahawks of the new All-America Football Conference (AAFC). The next year, after the Seahawks folded, Jones became single wing tailback for the Brooklyn Dodgers, another AAFC franchise, playing in

Dub Jones. Courtesy of Dub Jones.

Ebbets Field. The year after, he was traded to the AAFC's perennial champion Cleveland Browns, where he played until his retirement.

Jones describes the pleasure and the challenge of playing both offense and defense in the same games, in a period before the introduction of free substitution, which occurred about midway through his pro career. He analyzes Paul Brown's approach to coaching. Jones discusses the historic confrontation between the Cleveland Browns and the defending NFL champion Philadelphia

Eagles, scheduled to open the 1950 NFL season after the AAFC disbanded and the Browns entered the NFL.

In 1963, Jones returned to Cleveland as offensive coordinator for Blanton Collier, and he discusses Cleveland's dramatic upset of the Baltimore Colts in the 1964 NFL championship game. He contrasts pro football when he was playing and coaching with the contemporary game.

STEPHEN NORWOOD: *Let me begin by asking who your parents were, where you come from, and how you got involved in sports as a child.*
DUB JONES: My parents were farmers. There were a few doctors and lawyers and merchants, but nearly everyone was a farmer. It was pretty tough farming in the hills of north Louisiana.

SN: *Were you born here in Ruston, Louisiana?*
DJ: I was born eighteen miles from here, in Arcadia. My father was killed when I was three years old, and my mother was left with four young boys. I was the youngest. After my father died, we moved to Ruston, which is a little bigger than Arcadia. We grubbed for a living through the Depression.

SN: *How did you manage?*
DJ: Well, my mother was just tough, that's all. Everybody talks about how hard the times were. I really don't think of them as being hard times, even though we burned oil lamps because we couldn't pay the electric bill. I still never thought of myself as poor. My mother was just a terrific lady who raised those four children.

SN: *How did she support you?*
DJ: She supported us by working. During the Depression, the best job she had was with a Works Project Administration sewing circle. Later, she got a good job as a registrar of voters. My oldest brother graduated from high school with honors, but the best thing he could do was go to the Civilian Conservation Corps (CCC) camp. He sent money back for us to eat on. I have a soft touch for the CCC, I'll tell you. Not only did they plant pine trees and build roads, but they fed families.

SN: *When did you start getting involved in sports?*
DJ: As a child. I was raised when you would stay glued to the radio, listening to a baseball game or a fight. It was just a great era for sports. There was nothing I looked forward to more than playing. So, it started at an early age with baseball.

SN: *Did you have an organized Little League? Or just play sandlot?*
DJ: I played on the first organized Little League in Ruston. I was nine when it was organized, by a political science professor at Louisiana Tech, in Ruston. He also coached the American Legion team. He was a great coach who devoted a lot of time for no pay for the youth of Ruston.

SN: *Was anyone else in the family an athlete before you?*
DJ: Yes, I had three older brothers, and they were all athletes. They all played American Legion baseball and high school football. The two oldest were good athletes, but they didn't play college ball. But the brother just older than me went to Louisiana State University (LSU) on a football scholarship. I was four years behind him. So, my three brothers gave me a lot of motivation to play.

SN: *Was there anything going on in the way of professional sports? And did you go to Louisiana Tech games? Did they have a football team?*
DJ: Yes, I went to every football game, baseball game, and boxing match at Louisiana Tech. I lived just off campus in a little shotgun house, and there was never an activity there that I didn't know about. I knew the college play-ers as well as I knew my grammar school playmates.

At Ruston High School, from 1938 to 1941, I was lucky to play football under an outstanding coach, Hoss Garrett. He was a young coach and had just arrived in Ruston, but, oh, he was a great coach. We won the state championship my senior year, the first time Ruston High School had ever done it. We were in the next-to-top high school division, as far as size of school. That same coach, Hoss Garrett, also coached my son Bert when he was in high school. He was a factor in my career, and he was certainly a factor in Bert's career, too.

SN: *How did he relate to the athletes? Did he encourage you when you did something well? Is that an important factor in coaching?*
DJ: Oh, that's a *big* factor. When I entered high school, I was very small. It was doubtful I'd be able to contribute a lot to the football program. But this coach had a knack for making the smallest, most unlikely to succeed kid feel he was part of the team. I didn't make the first team until my senior year. But I felt like I was just as important as the biggest star on that team.

SN: *So you consider him an important influence on your development as an athlete.*
DJ: Without question. There were many coaches then throughout the United States like Hoss Garrett. Back then, teaching and coaching was not a bad job.

But now, it's hard for a teaching and coaching job to compete with other jobs available to college graduates. So, I would guess we don't have quite the quality of teachers and coaches that we did back then. I hope I'm wrong.

SN: *You played all the different sports in high school?*
DJ: I played football, baseball, basketball, and boxed in high school.

SN: *Did you have any thoughts at that early stage about playing at a big-time college?*
DJ: Never dreamed that. I was the last player on the football team that you'd expect to play in college. Of course, inwardly I had that desire.

SN: *So it wasn't apparent that early that you were going to be that good a player. You developed later on.*
DJ: I developed as a football player my senior year in high school, and ended up being an outstanding high school player. But it didn't happen until then.

SN: *Were you a starting player all through high school?*
DJ: Oh, no, no, no. I sat on the bench. I never started until I was a senior.

SN: *What kind of football were you playing? This was the late 1930s and early 1940s.*
DJ: We used the Notre Dame box. We would line up in a T-formation and shift one way or the other to a box. I played left halfback or tailback.

SN: *Did you play defense, too?*
DJ: Oh, yeah. We played defense and offense. Stayed in the game the whole time.

SN: *How long did you continue doing that?*
DJ: We continued that even into pro football. My first year in pro football we played both ways. But that was the end of it.

SN: *Did you undergo any particular training for playing both ways? I imagine endurance would be especially important. You could have a real strong first half and then run out of gas.*
DJ: If you're not conditioned. That was a big factor.

SN: *What kind of things would they do for conditioning in high school?*
DJ: Mainly run.

SN: *Did they have weights?*
DJ: No weights.

SN: *What kind of facilities and equipment did they have in high school?*
DJ: We began to get excellent equipment. We had an excellent playing field.
We had a great family in Ruston who built us a stadium and an athletic
complex—a football field, a baseball field, and a basketball court. And they gave
us forty acres to build a new high school on. That high school was built when
I was a senior. They're still using that building for the high school today.

SN: *Did you get scouted by colleges?*
DJ: By my senior year in high school I was a good enough player to be scouted
by LSU and the local smaller colleges. LSU knew about me because I had a
brother who played football there.

SN: *How did you decide which college to go to?*
DJ: I went to LSU because I had decided that I wanted to play at as big a level
as I could.

SN: *Did LSU present it like you would play a major part in their program?*
DJ: No, no, no.

SN: *How would they approach a high school player then? How did they present
their offer?*
DJ: Well, their offer was a full scholarship, which meant tuition and books,
room and board, laundry, and fifteen dollars a month for spending money. Of
course, that was just a great, great offer, and there was no hesitation from me.

SN: *Was LSU recruiting primarily in Louisiana?*
DJ: No, no, no. LSU was really big-time football, and they recruited nationally,
any and everywhere.

SN: *As I understand it, the university had been moving forward. Huey Long
had been putting emphasis and money on it.*
DJ: I entered LSU a little after Huey Long was gone, but there were remnants
of Huey Long still there. He had put a lot of emphasis on the athletic program.
He tried to run that like he did a lot of things. But, yes, he was very active in
every facet of LSU, particularly in the athletic part of it. He built an Olympic
swimming pool, probably the largest in the world. And we had a great stadium
at that time. There was heavy recruiting in all phases of athletics.

SN: *Was there an athletic dorm?*
DJ: Yes, except the freshmen stayed in the barracks with the other students. We called them the barracks because they had been set up for ROTC. Sophomore year, you moved into the athletic dorm. I really don't recommend that. Of course, the athletic dormitory had a great cafeteria and great food.

SN: *Why do you not recommend it?*
DJ: I think it's preferable to stay with the regular students, because you're with the other players enough on the football field, four hours a day or so. It's best that you room with some political science student, or engineer, or pre-law student, or pre-med student, or whatever. It's better for the football player, and it's better for the student body.

I was at LSU for one year, and then I went into the navy, and they sent me to Tulane University. I was in the V-12 program and attended classes and played football at Tulane for two years, 1943 and 1944. During the war, the college athletes were all dispersed. Some of them ended up at another college like I did, playing football with a bunch of strangers.

Wartime college football was not as good football as before the war, because not all the good players ended up in a school playing football. We had some good players, but we had a lot of inferior players, too. You had very little time to practice.

SN: *Were you developing as a football player during this period?*
DJ: Oh, yeah. I was eighteen. I had a good experience at Tulane, filling out and playing under a great coach, Monk Simons, who was an old Tulane standby. He was a fine, fine coach and remained a friend to me for years and years to come. When I went to LSU, I was just a spindly kid, six foot two and 158 pounds.

SN: *Did that just happen or were there training methods? Did they tell you that you needed to fill out?*
DJ: They would have loved for me to fill out. My first year as a pro, with the Miami Seahawks in the AAFC, they debated where to play me, at quarterback or at fullback. I ended up playing fullback. And they said, "Boy, when that boy fills out, he's going to be a real fullback." Well, ten years later I was about ten pounds lighter. We used to debate who was the skinniest ballplayer, Mac Speedie or me.

SN: *So at Tulane, was there anything you learned about football?*
DJ: The basics that I learned from my high school coach carried me through at Tulane. Football hasn't changed much. It's still a run and hit game.

SN: *You had the rise of the T-formation in the 1940s, from the single wing.*
DJ: More strides were made in football in a shorter time in the early 1940s than at any other time. Clark Shaughnessy, who introduced the T-formation, probably did more to change the game of football than any other coach. He had been the coach at the University of Chicago when they disbanded football. I think he sat out for a year. In the meantime, Stanford was on a real binge to hire a new coach and really do something with their football team. And Clark Shaughnessy got the job. Some of the alumni said, "Who in the world is this Shaughnessy?" Boy, they had some disgruntled alumni.

But he came out to Stanford. And he took Norm Standlee and put him at fullback, and took Frankie Albert and put him at quarterback, and changed this guy and that guy. Then he put in the T-formation and the man in motion, and the lateral and quick opening play, and the pitch out, and just throwing the ball all over the field. He just had a fantastic year with a mediocre team and went on to the Rose Bowl. Later, he put in the T-formation with the Chicago Bears.

SN: *So, you played at Tulane for a couple of years in the navy, and you played both offense and defense. What was your defensive position?*
DJ: Halfback or safety.

SN: *Did you prefer offense to defense?*
DJ: Not really. Back then defense was really part of the game. I mean, football is a hit game. And if you just play offense, you miss out on so much of the game. I feel that the present-day players, who play only offense or only defense, miss out on so much of the game. I liked playing both. I didn't prefer one or the other. Of course, you get a little more press coverage on offense.

SN: *I imagine that late in the game it was hard to send guys out on long pass routes. You'd get tired being in the whole game. Did that affect the game?*
DJ: Fatigue was a factor. You just needed to be in shape.

SN: *There was no free substitution until 1950, so you couldn't move guys in and out. That change occurred right in the middle of your pro career.*
DJ: There's no question about it, free substitution permits a lot of different boys to participate in football who wouldn't be able to do it otherwise. Maybe they ought to change the rules back and not have free substitution.

SN: *Then you move toward a strong emphasis on specialization, where you can only do one aspect of the game. In your period there was a lot more versatility.*

DJ: The fact of the matter is, I can't even think of a great offensive player who wasn't a good defensive player. Otto Graham was a great defensive player. In his first year with Cleveland, he played safety. Mac Speedie, the greatest end that I know of that ever walked on the field, a great offensive receiver, was a tremendous defensive end. And you probably can't have a great defensive player unless he'd be a pretty good offensive player, too. This specialization has taken a lot away from the game.

SN: *Today the extreme is the placekicker. You get these guys from Europe who've never played football; they've played soccer. And they can kick. They come into the NFL and break all the kicking records. But they can't do anything else. You played with Lou Groza, who was a great placekicker and also played a position.*
DJ: Right, he was a great offensive tackle.

SN: *How did you move from Tulane to the pros?*
DJ: I was eligible for the pro draft in 1946, and I was drafted by the Chicago Cardinals of the NFL. I think I was their number-one draft choice.

SN: *Were you aware you were going to get drafted by a pro team?*
DJ: No, not really. You did get correspondence from pro teams back then. They sent letters saying they were interested.

SN: *Did you follow pro football yourself?*
DJ: I had never followed pro football, just local college ball. I ended up not signing with the Cardinals. I had asked for a $10,000 salary. Jimmy Conzelman, the Cardinals' coach, said, "Oh, that's unheard of! We can't pay that!" So I said, "Well, I don't want to play pro football anyway. I want to go back and finish college." I hadn't finished, and I still had a year of eligibility left, because the war years didn't count. So, I wasn't chomping at the bit to play pro football.

I didn't think much about it until the Miami Seahawks contacted me a few weeks later, in this new league, the AAFC. They offered me a salary of $12,000 a year. I told them I had said to Jimmy Conzelman that I would let him know if I changed my mind about playing. I called him up and told him that the Sea-hawks had offered me $12,000. I really wanted to go to the Cardinals, who had a great team. But Conzelman said, "No, that's too much money." So I called Miami back and said I'd sign with them. In the meantime Conzelman checked it out and found I was telling the truth. He called me back and offered me another $2000. I replied that I'd already told the Seahawks I'd sign with them. I had just told them on the phone, but I figured that was the contract. That shows you how different it is from today.

But, I soon thought going with Miami was the worst thing I ever did. After a year, the team couldn't even meet the payroll, and the league had to step in and pick it up. I did have a great coach at Miami, Jack Meagher, who had been the coach at Auburn University. But because we had a losing season, he got fired. When you lose everybody gets excited, and they point fingers at any and every thing, so they pointed the finger at him. He didn't deserve it. It was just an inferior team. He was a short-lived pro coach, but he was a great one.

I had played in the College All-Star game in 1946 against the Los Angeles Rams, and we'd beaten them. Otto Graham was our quarterback, Pat Harder was the fullback, and Crazylegs Hirsch, Elmer Angsman, and I were the halfbacks. We just had tons of stars on that team. Because of the war, this 1946 College All-Star team spanned two or three years of college football players. Most of those players went to the AAFC.

SN: *Why did they go to the AAFC?*
DJ: Because it paid more money. It was just like the American Football League, with Joe Namath. This new league was getting the talent because the old league was holding down the salaries.

SN: *What was the caliber of play the first year in the AAFC?*
DJ: Well, it was a really unbalanced league. They had fantastic teams, like Cleveland. The good teams in the AAFC compared favorably with the good teams in the NFL. We had the worst team at Miami. Miami had signed a lot of prewar players that had been good ballplayers three years before. But they came back after the war out of shape—a big, fat tub, not the player of three years ago. There were only three players who came off that Miami team who continued to play pro ball, and I was the only one to play any length of time. Monk Gatford and Lamar Davis only played a short time.

SN: *Did you draw significant crowds in Miami?*
DJ: No, not at all. Most of our early games were played away. We played Cleveland, and San Francisco, and Brooklyn, and by the time we got down to Miami, we had already suffered tremendous losses to those teams. That put a dampener on the crowds, even before we got home. So, that team folded after the first year, and I went on to the Brooklyn Dodgers. They wanted a single wing tailback to replace Glenn Dobbs, who was a superstar at the time. But he was having medical problems, and they wanted to get rid of him.

They thought I could replace him as a tailback, which I did. I had played in the T-formation at Miami, but Brooklyn used the single wing. It was back to what I had played in college.

We opened the season against Cleveland, and Bill Willis got to me before the ball was even centered to me. Oh, man, it was a rough, rough game. I ended up with a wrenched knee, a separated clavicle, and a hip pointer. I was just practically in the hospital after that game. I was out of football for a few weeks.

SN: *Was that the first time you got seriously hurt playing football?*
DJ: Yes. Well, I wasn't really seriously hurt. Yeah, it was serious enough to keep me out of football for about four weeks. And then when I came back, I broke my hand when I was tackled returning a punt.

I couldn't play offense, tailback, with my hand in a cast, so I played defense. That's when Paul Brown first became interested in acquiring me for Cleveland, watching me play defense against the Browns. We almost beat Cleveland in 1947. I think I intercepted a couple of passes against them. And during the off-season, Paul Brown called me and asked if I would be interested in playing for Cleveland. Of course, I said, "Heck, yes!" I was exuberant to have the chance to play with them.

SN: *Did you play in Ebbets Field in Brooklyn?*
DJ: Ebbets Field, yes.

SN: *Brooklyn was a big baseball town, with fans very attached to the team. Did they turn out for the football Dodgers?*
DJ: Yeah, they turned out for the football games, too, reasonably well. We had pretty good crowds. It was very different from Miami.

SN: *Was there community involvement with the Brooklyn football Dodgers? The baseball Dodgers were very involved with the community. The people would recognize the players on the street.*
DJ: Oh, yeah! Even though it's a huge city, the circle the football team circulated in was the same the baseball team circulated in. I mean, you'd get a corned beef sandwich at the same joint that the baseball player went to. The sandwich shop or the corner beer joint was the same as the one the baseball players went to. I did get to know a couple of the baseball players pretty well—Pete Reiser of the Dodgers and Yogi Berra of the Yankees. I had become a friend of Yogi's when I was in the navy. After I left Tulane I ended up at the submarine base at New London, Connecticut.

SN: *How did you get there?*

DJ: That was part of my navy career after I left Tulane. I finished submarine school just as the war ended. I played football there for a while, and Yogi was the equipment manager. And he and I became great friends. I would see him at the football games. He loved football. Later on, his son played with the Baltimore Colts with Bert. Anyhow, that's how I got to know Pete Reiser.

SN: *He was a baseball player with football-player-type injuries.*

DJ: Yeah. But I always knew that Pete Reiser was the best baseball player ever, according to Yogi. He was all-everything, best fielder, best hitter, best runner. He never showed up in the record books because he got hurt, but he was that kind of player.

SN: *How did you get traded from Brooklyn to Cleveland?*

DJ: In 1948, Paul Brown traded his first-round draft choice, Bob Chappius, for me. And boy, that made me feel really worth something, for Cleveland to trade its first-round draft choice for me. Paul Brown told that story many times, that the greatest trade he ever made was when he traded Chappius to Brooklyn for Dub Jones. But it wasn't until years later, when I read Paul Brown's book, *The Paul Brown Story* (Atheneum, 1979), that I learned of the real trade. And the real trade was that he had traded Chappius to Brooklyn for Dub Jones plus $25,000. He never told me about the $25,000. Twenty-five thousand dollars then was like $200,000 or more now. He probably would have traded Chappius for the $25,000 without Dub Jones.

SN: *As a second-year pro player with the Brooklyn Dodgers, you'd shifted back into the single wing and were a tailback. You also played defensive halfback and safety . . .*

DJ: Because of a broken hand. And that's why I went to the Cleveland Browns. I was traded to Cleveland as a defensive back.

SN: *Paul Brown had looked at you as a defensive player because he had been impressed with your play with Brooklyn.*

DJ: Yeah. And they were pleased with me to begin with, through the exhibition season, until we played Baltimore in an exhibition game in Akron, Ohio, the week before the regular season opened. That game was the lowest point of my career.

Y. A. Tittle was Baltimore's quarterback, and he had a receiver named Lamar Davis, who'd played with me at Miami. We were leading just before the half when Tittle called a pass play. I was playing right defensive halfback, and the flow came my way, and I took the outside back, which was my coverage. In the meantime, Lamar Davis came down and broke on a post pattern. Our safety, Cliff Lewis, never dreamed that Y. A. Tittle could throw a ball as far as he could, and that little Davis could run as fast as he could. All that Paul Brown could see was Tittle throwing a sixty- or eighty-yard touchdown pass to Lamar Davis just before the half.

Brown figured the whole world would know they were going to throw a big, deep pass. He jerked me out of the game, which he was notorious for. He was right on the spot, demanding to know, "What happened?" And I replied, "Well, I think it was a flow this way, and I took the outside man, and that's the way I thought it was." He said to me, "You're killing our football team!" And I sat on the bench the rest of the game.

Paul Brown wasn't really sure what had happened with the coverage, but somehow he blamed me for it. Our defensive coordinator, Blanton Collier, was away scouting at the time. That's when the coaches scouted the other teams. But when they got the movies, they realized it wasn't my coverage, it was Cliff Lewis's. So, they had to put me back on defense.

I opened the season against the Rams as a defensive back, but Paul Brown had already made up his mind that he wasn't quite satisfied with me as a defensive back. He had Otto Graham playing safety instead of Cliff Lewis, and the Rams would send a man in motion and then they'd send Lenny Ford down and he'd catch the ball. They'd pick up ten or fifteen yards, time after time. Brown would jerk me out of the game, and demand to know, "What happened? Get over on the phone!" So I'd get on the phone, and I'd have nothing to say. I mean, I was doing what I'd thought I was supposed to do. He benched me for one game.

During that time, Dick Gallagher, our assistant coach, who had great faith in me, told Paul, "This guy's too good of a ballplayer to sit on the bench. Put him on offense." And Paul said, "Well, he can run, but I don't know if he can catch a pass or not."

So, I got switched to an offensive back only because Paul Brown got disgusted with me as a defensive back. The first game they put me in, I caught a touchdown pass. And from that time on, I was an offensive back.

SN: *You had talked of yourself as a running back. This is the first time pass receiving has come up. You became an outstanding pass receiver.*
DJ: Paul Brown had confidence in me as a runner, but not as a pass receiver. But I developed into one. We had the two ends, but after I got to playing, they started setting me out as a flanker. That was when that position first developed.

SN: *That's when it first developed, the pro set, with the flanker back, instead of four men in the backfield?*
DJ: I think that's when it developed, and Paul Brown thinks it is. We used three receivers, and I was the third end.

SN: *You had a quarterback who liked to throw.*
DJ: Oh, yeah. But still, through the years, I ran a little, too. Of course, they ran Marion Motley most of the time.

It was sort of an accident that I became a receiver. When I came to Cleveland in 1948, the Browns had already been established as a fine football team. They had two great receivers in Mac Speedie and Dante Lavelli, and a great running back in Marion Motley, who would be equivalent to the Jim Brown of his day. When he was in shape, he was a great running back, and he was in shape at that time.

SN: *What happened later?*
DJ: Later he gained too much weight, and blew up to 250 or 260 pounds. But back then he weighed 230. The Cleveland Browns could win all the games they wanted to by just throwing the ball and then handing off on a draw play to Marion Motley.

SN: *Could Otto Graham stand with the best quarterbacks of today?*
DJ: Our quarterback, Otto Graham, was just way above any other quarterback. He could stand with the best of today's quarterbacks. He didn't look all that great. But he had that indefinable ability to bring out the best in a lot of players. In his era, nobody could compare with him.

SN: *Your coach, Paul Brown, called the plays. Was that unusual?*
DJ: Well, yeah, that was unusual at the time. Today, it's routine.

SN: *Do you think that's a good idea?*
DJ: Yes. The coach is in so much better a position to direct the game than the quarterback, who has just gotten the hell knocked out of him and is flat on his back. He's not thinking. The quarterback is busy executing the play or recovering from the play, whereas the coach can be thinking ahead. He has so much more information to direct that game with.

SN: *Paul Brown used to send his guards in with the plays. Did Otto Graham work well with Paul Brown? Did they ever have any conflict over what to do?*
DJ: No. Paul Brown and Otto Graham were pretty much in sync, always.

SN: *What else can you say about Paul Brown's coaching style?*
DJ: We had a lot of talent on the Cleveland Browns, but I don't think Paul Brown was interested in furthering any one particular person. He was a team man. He'd rather see Mac Speedie catch a ball, and Dante Lavelli catch a ball, and me catch a ball, than to see Speedie catch three balls and me and Lavelli none.

Paul Brown drew a lot from his players. I was a student of the game, and I would like to think that Paul respected me. I wasn't the only person he respected. He consulted with the players regularly, although not with all of them. I doubt that he ever made a decision that he didn't consult with a core of his team. And when he made a decision it was usually right. That's why he had the discipline that he had. Paul had a real talent for reading players, and knowing what to depend on from a player. The key is knowing what information is good information. And he had a knack for that.

SN: *How did the Cleveland players react when the AAFC disbanded in 1949? Did you know there was going to be a merger of some teams into the NFL?*
DJ: I think we all knew [the situation]. The AAFC never did get competitive balance. So, the three best teams—Cleveland, San Francisco, and Baltimore—joined the NFL for the 1950 season. The AAFC's New York Yankees merged with the Giants, and Buffalo merged with us. I think the Los Angeles Dons merged with the Rams. We were happy that we got into the NFL, and that it was all one league.

SN: *When the Cleveland Browns joined the NFL in 1950, they scheduled you to play the reigning NFL champions, the Philadelphia Eagles, in the season's opening game. How did the Browns prepare for that game, and what was it like?*
DJ: Cleveland had been champions every year in the AAFC, but when we merged into the NFL in 1950, we didn't know if we could beat the best of the NFL. Before we played the Eagles, we played either two or four exhibition games and wiped out the NFL teams. We just wiped them out. There was no contest.

SN: *Was Cleveland then confident it could beat the best of the NFL?*
DJ: Well, no, we didn't know. We watched films of Philadelphia, and they had a defense that you just thought you couldn't penetrate at all. Their coach Greasy Neale was one of the fine coaches of that era. I don't know whether he deserves full credit for this 5-4 umbrella defense or not, but his team perfected it. The Eagles had the great defensive unit of that era. And looking at the films, they did look tough. They were huge. But we prepared for them.

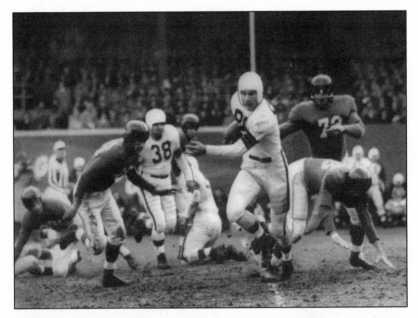

Dub Jones of Cleveland Browns (86) starting off on a sixty-eight-yard touchdown run; Tom Landry of New York Giants is closest player on left, November 18, 1951. Courtesy of the Cleveland Press Collection, Cleveland State University Library.

It was the opening game of the season, but it was almost like a Super Bowl. It was the Super Bowl of its day. We'd played in the AAFC championships, but they just weren't anything like this. This was *the* game. We played in Memorial Stadium in Philadelphia. The stadium was packed. It met all the requirements of an exciting game. Early in the game I caught a touchdown pass on their great defensive back, Russ Craft. He was an All-Pro back and a fine ballplayer.

SN: *It was a convincing win for Cleveland. When did it become clear that was going to happen?*
DJ: It was still a ball game on into the third quarter. It was one of those games where we were hitting on all cylinders. Every facet of our team was working— our punt return teams, our coverage teams. Our offensive line was blocking people that we thought couldn't be blocked. And we were catching passes on people the whole world thought were the best in the business. It was just one of those games where you planned to do certain things, and you went out and did them. And we beat 'em, 35-10. I just can't tell you the emotional experience that that game was.

Dub Jones admiring the football that Cleveland Browns' head coach Paul Brown presented to Jones after he tied Ernie Nevers's NFL record of six touchdowns scored in one game (a record that has since been tied by Gale Sayers but never surpassed); Blanton Collier, Cleveland assistant coach, standing at far right; quarterback Otto Graham and team captain Tony Adamle standing in back; the Browns defeated the Chicago Bears 42-21, November 25, 1951. Courtesy of Corbis.

The next year, 1951, I scored six touchdowns in a game against the Chicago Bears, which tied the record for most touchdowns in one game. It was just a lucky event. I mean, I played many games as well. But it just happened to be one of those days.

SN: *It's only been done three times in the history of pro football.*
DJ: I'm proud it happened against the Bears, a great team, in a game that meant something. They were leading their division, and we were leading ours. It was a hard-hitting game, a tough game. Even though I scored six touchdowns, it wasn't against a team that was broken, where we were scoring at will. It was a hard fought game. I'm proud of that, too.

Paul Brown, Cleveland Browns head coach, December 4, 1951. Courtesy of the Cleveland Press Collection, Cleveland State University Library.

By 1953, we were getting some pretty bad publicity, because we had lost two or three championship games, 1951, 1952, 1953. We were mad at the press, and mad at Paul for some of the press we were getting about being an "over the hill" team. So, the offensive players had a meeting, and we determined to take the game against Detroit under control ourselves if it got off on the wrong key. If we were going to lose the game, we were going to lose it ourselves. So, we opened the game—and oh man, we played the greatest game we ever played. We just blew Detroit off the field. So, we never had to take over the play-calling. I don't know how far we would have gotten with it. But we had been determined to do it if we fell behind.

SN: *Pro football became a lot more popular during the 1950s. In 1950, they started televising NFL games. . . .*
DJ: It was about 1952 that people down here began to get pro football on television. A combination of things contributed to pro football's rising popularity—*Sports Illustrated* came out and television. And I have to give Howard Cosell credit and other commentators who glamorized pro football.

I played in the NFL All-Pro game in the early 1950s, and we didn't even know what we'd get paid for the game. Years later, in the 1960s, I was visiting with Glenn Davis about this when I was coaching in the Pro Bowl game. He was working with the Los Angeles *Times*, and was the promoter of the All-Pro game. Glenn said, "Remember, Dub, when we played, we could hardly get paid." He said that they tried to sell the television rights for the game, and they couldn't sell them for anything. And this was just about ten years later, and they sold the television rights for millions of dollars for the one game. Well, it was the same game. What changed was the market.

SN: *The Cleveland Browns would sell out Municipal Stadium, which seated over 80,000, even in the AAFC.*
DJ: Right. What I'm saying is that the game of 1950 was as big or bigger to the fans and players as it is to the fans and players of 1995. The Cleveland Browns would sell out Municipal Stadium, which seated over 80,000, even in the AAFC. Those people enjoyed that game and were just as enthusiastic as the fans at the games today. The only difference is that now there are millions of television viewers out there pumping money into the game that you didn't have then. Television laid a lot of money on the table, and that's why the scramble is there today. And it's pitiful.

SN: *Well what was it like, in the late 1940s and early 1950s, before television, earning a living as a pro football player? Would you also have to have a job during the off-season?*
DJ: Playing pro football when I played, you made a lot more money than you could make at another job. Of course, you'd also have to work in the

off-season. But if you had not been playing football, you could have been getting experience at another job. So, you ended up hurting yourself.

SN: *Plus, there was no commercial endorsement money, was there? Did some-body like Otto Graham even get any of that?*
DJ: Very little. I was the only player on the Cleveland Browns, other than possibly Otto Graham, who got an endorsement. When I scored six touch-downs in one game, Quaker Oats paid me $500 for this endorsement. It was a newspaper or a magazine ad. And oh man, I thought that was out of this world, $500. I asked Paul Brown if it would be all right for me to take that $500, and he said yes. I felt I had to have permission to take it.

SN: *Was football in the 1950s a rougher game than it is now? You think of guys like Hardy Brown, the 49ers linebacker, considered an extremely violent, even dirty, player. Has there been any change in that aspect of football?*
DJ: One of the worst things that has happened to the game of football is that they have glamorized what we considered a cheap shot. Cheap shots are when you deliberately hit the head. You're supposed to hit the body and hit hard. But a head shot—that was almost unheard of in my day. It wasn't some-thing you admired. Now you talk about Hardy Brown. He was a cheap-shot artist back in our era. But there were very few like that.

If we'd had as many cheap shots back when I played as you do now, you'd have had some dead people. Plenty of dead people. Of course, we put face-masks on during my career, but I played without facemasks, too. We didn't do cheap shots. There were many times you could take a cheap shot at a man with no facemask, and they could have been killed. We had three fractured cheekbones on the Cleveland Browns in one year—me, George Young, and Lenny Ford—and all of them were cheap shots. But that was very unusual. Well, it happened. And after that, Paul Brown had the facemask introduced for the whole league.

SN: *When you broke your cheekbone, how did that happen?*
DJ: I was tackled, and a fellow with Buffalo slammed his knee into my jaw.

SN: *Deliberately?*
DJ: Yeah, deliberately. And Pat Harder, when he was blocking on a punt, just caught Lenny Ford with his elbow and just crushed him. It's a wonder he didn't kill him.

SN: *Isn't there a danger of retaliation when a player does something like that to one of your teammates?*
DJ: It was hard to retaliate when you were only playing offense, because a guy like Hardy Brown was playing linebacker. It was hard for offensive people to get to those guys.

SN: *When you were coaching in the 1960s, did you see more cheap shots than when you were playing in the 1950s?*
DJ: Oh, yeah. More so than in the 1950s.

SN: *And partly because television glamorized them?*
DJ: No question about it. When I was a coach, I fought Howard Cosell and everybody for glamorizing that great hit with a forearm to the head.

SN: *They did that on replay films all the time.*
DJ: Now you see Pittsburgh on television, with Mel Blount taking a cheap shot, and the commentator says, "Boy, what a great hit that was!" It was a no good hit. That wasn't part of our game. But it sells viewers. It will probably stay that way as long as they got the money on the table. I love a good hit. But a cheap-shot hit to the head?

SN: *Cheap shots are when you deliberately use a forearm?*
DJ: When you deliberately hit the head. Nor is a knee shot a part of the game, but you see a lot of them today. There are a lot of cases where a quarterback is in a tough position, and an onrushing player knows his knee is in bad shape and deliberately gives him a low hit at the knee. We would never do that. We would never think of getting a man's knee, under conditions where you had a choice.

SN: *What were the helmets like when you played?*
DJ: Early in my career, we had inferior helmets. But in the early 1950s, they went to an improved helmet, which was not very different from the one they use today. It was a suspended helmet and a very good one. Paul Brown had a lot to do with introducing it. Paul Brown was responsible for a lot of equipment improvement besides the facemask.

SN: *You decided to retire as a player in 1955.*
DJ: I had actually retired in 1953. My children had gotten up to school age, and I felt that it was time to quit. Eight years is a long time to play football,

when you're away from home. So, I retired after the 1953 season, and I went back to see an exhibition game in 1954, out of Dallas. And after the game, Paul Brown came up to me and asked me to come back. He said they needed me. So, I went back for 1954, and we had a good year, and then I came back for 1955.

But I got hurt in 1955 at the beginning of the season, and the injury hampered me all year. I started the season feeling I was in as good shape as I had ever been. But in hot, humid weather, George Ratterman overthrew me on a pass pattern, and I stretched and pulled that hamstring. The injury affected me all year, and that was just the end of it. I was out of football for seven years.

SN: *What did you do in those seven years?*
DJ: I was in business here in Ruston. In 1963 I went back to Cleveland as a coach, offensive coordinator, thinking that I was just going back for a few months to help some old friends. All of the Browns' coaches—Blanton Collier, the head coach, Howard Brinker, and Fritz Heisler—had been my coaches when I played.

SN: *What had Blanton Collier's position been under Paul Brown?*
DJ: Defensive coach. He never did play ball. It was just a wonderful experience for me, and that one year led to another and another and another. I was a coach for Cleveland for five years, 1963 to 1967.

Because Blanton Collier was hard of hearing, he just couldn't handle the situation during game time, and he depended on me to direct the team during the game. We directed the game from the press box when I was coaching. Whereas, when Paul Brown was coaching, he did most of the directing right where he was standing.

That first year was a great experience, as Cleveland really turned around. The year before the Browns had had a mediocre season. But we started the 1963 season by beating the New York Giants in the opening game. They were the team that year, and they later played the Chicago Bears for the NFL championship. We won our first six or seven games just going away. It was the most fantastic span of games that I've ever witnessed. We had a receiver, Gary Collins, who had caught just two passes the previous year. In 1963, I think he caught thirteen *touchdown* passes. Jim Brown had just an unbelievable season. We lacked one thing—we didn't have any speed at receiver. And we didn't have a speedy cornerback. We made a run at it, but we faded out at the end of the year.

But we added that speed at receiver the next year when we drafted Paul Warfield. Actually, we saw our number-one priority as getting a defensive back,

so we had drafted Warfield to play that position. At rookie camp Howard
Brinker, the defensive coordinator, and I both watched him. And I said,
"Howard, do you think that Warfield ought to play defense?" And he said,
"No." So we went to Blanton Collier, and I said, "Blanton, Howard thinks
Warfield will do more good on offense." And we moved Warfield to flanker.
He had never caught a pass in his college career.

And we just made a fantastic team just like that, which went on to win the
world championship in 1964. Of course, we had Gary Collins on the other
side, and we had Jim Brown. We were so powerful.

SN: *What about Frank Ryan, the quarterback?*
DJ: He had a great arm. We were *way* out in front in the pass offense.

SN: *Cleveland played Baltimore in the 1964 NFL championship.*
DJ: It was like the game in 1950 when Cleveland played Philadelphia, in that
we went in with a real concise game plan, and it really worked. It was really
a satisfaction to see those things unfold. Baltimore had a fine team. Johnny
Unitas was probably over the hill by that time, but he was still a fine quarterback. And Baltimore had a great defense. They played a zone defense and
could get away with it because they had two great defensive ends, including
Gino Marchetti, and a great rush from their front four.

We won the championship because we used Jim Brown in the pass offense
and because our defense really played over its head. We were probably the first
team that won a championship game with a mediocre defense. I shouldn't say
that about our defense, I love them, but they were players who really played
beyond their abilities. We didn't have any great, super defensive man like a
Bruce Smith, who can lift the whole team. But our defense played an exceptional game, and it was an overall team effort. We would have won the championship in 1965, too, if Warfield hadn't gotten hurt, although Green Bay was
getting stronger and stronger.

SN: *You had played both offense and defense as a player. Did that help you as a
coach? Today coaching is so specialized. You have a secondary coach, a defensive
line coach, and so on.*
DJ: Well, we had that then, too. The best tool I had as an offensive coordinator was our defensive coordinator, Howard Brinker. During the early part of
each week, he was strictly involved with the defense, and with our upcoming
opponent's offense. And I was completely involved with our offense and the
opposing defense. But Howard and I would have dinner every Thursday night.

We would sit, just the two of us, and look at a movie. This would be the first time that Howard had seen our opponent's defense. But on Thursday night, he was involved with helping me. We'd run that movie, and we'd stop, and he'd say, "I don't understand how they can do this, when we tried that and we can't do it." I wouldn't have taken anything for that quiet night with our defensive coach, looking at our opponent. And that's why I never really had a game plan until Friday. You had to have a game plan on Tuesday, but after that Thursday night session, I'd have a revised, revamped game plan.

SN: *Since you left coaching, what are some of the major changes in football?*
DJ: The biggest difference between football now and when I was coaching in the 1960s is the prevent defenses, which have taken a lot out of the game. You don't have as pretty a pass game now as when I was coaching or when I was playing. We had a prevent defense in the late stages of the game, but now they use it during the regular course of the game. On almost any passing situation, a good quarterback is faced with an eight-man secondary. When you put eight people back there, it's tough to have a precision-like pass. All you can do is a little shuffle, and a little slice, and a little dinky pass here, and a little dinky pass there. You don't see a real pass pattern. Occasionally you do in a blitz situation. But other than that, it's just a garbage dinky dunk pass. I think they ought to make a rule that you have to have four defensive men on the line of scrimmage, like the requirement now that you have to have six men on the offensive line. That would give the pass game a little bit of a break.

SN: *I want to ask you about your son, Bert, who grew up in this environment of pro football. How did that affect him?*
DJ: I was an unusual coach, in that I had my family come and stay with me at training camp, and my son Bert warmed up the quarterbacks there, Frank Ryan and Jim Ninowski. I had a verbal understanding with the club that my family would come with me. We stayed in an apartment at Hiram College, where the Browns trained. So, Bert's been close to football since he was a child.

Being exposed to the football world didn't have a great deal to do with Bert's success as a ballplayer, but it had a bearing on it. He heard a lot of football conversations. I hope some of them gave him some insight into the good things of football. But Bert was just a natural; he was obviously a ballplayer.

SN: *Did you notice that pretty early?*
DJ: Yes. He could pick up a rock and hit anything he threw at. He could pick up a bow and arrow, and hit anything he shot at. He could beat you at

marbles. He was just a real fine athlete. And he had a great temperament. He would set his mind to do something, and he'd get it done some way.

Bert would be a great coach. He has such a great feel for the game. He could move a football team, when nobody else could even think about it. He had that indefinable talent to put the ball in the end zone. And he had a great arm and a great release.

SN: *What quarterbacks would you compare him to?*
DJ: I would compare Bert to Joe Namath, when he had his knees and was in his prime, or to Dan Marino. When Marino throws passes, it's beautiful, it's great. But Bert could do the same thing sixty yards—boom! Marino is one of my favorite quarterbacks, don't misunderstand me. He, John Elway, and Joe Namath in his prime. In my era, Y. A. Tittle probably had the best arm. But he didn't have the release that Bert, Marino, or Elway had. But he didn't have to.

Today's quarterbacks have a tough row to hoe. They've got to get rid of the ball in a hurry. You've got to throw any way, and that's what they do. And that's what Bert could do—throw off of this foot, or that foot, or any foot.

It's a shame Bert got hurt. He had two injuries. The first was a three-quarters shoulder separation that he sustained in a game in Dallas. That really hurt. They should have operated on him then. He tried to play with that separation three different times during the course of the year. It was bad judgment on his part.

Having done that and realizing what a tough situation he had, he was more cautious the next year. He still had that shoulder separation. It never would close. But he built it up, worked his muscles, and overcame that separation. But then he hurt his shoulder again in the opening game in Kansas City. So, he said, "I'm not going to play until it gets well." He went to the other extreme. The team was depending on Bert, because without Bert they didn't have diddley squat. That's when the coach started yapping at him. He had played the year before after hurting his shoulder and then had hurt it again. He realized that this old college try likely killed him.

The next year the Colts traded Bert to the Rams. He wanted to be traded. Irsay was a pitiful owner. He was just a drunk, pitiful.

But Bert had some great years at Baltimore, with a mediocre team, and he had a fine coach there in Ted Marchibroda. They had a great relationship. Then he got hurt, and it went to pot—his relationship with the owners, the press, everything. Anyway, he ended up getting traded to the Rams, and I've never seen him play better. I saw him in his opening games with the Rams, and he was fantastic.

But then in a game in Atlanta, a guy came in and took a cheap shot at him after he'd been tackled and was falling. The guy hit him and dislocated his jaw.

The doctor put that back in, and Bert went back in and played the rest of the game, and went home and played the next game, too.

But Bert's left side became numb, and they had a CAT-scan made, and found out he had a vertebra that was severed—a piece about as big as your little finger, and it was lodged up against his spinal cord. The doctors said he could have turned his neck and become a paraplegic. He played two games like that. Then, of course, they had to operate on him, and he stayed on the operating table for six hours.

He had to quit. The doctor didn't rule out any playing, but he said he would be crazy to play. You can't play thinking about your neck. And Bert doesn't ski, he doesn't play tennis, he doesn't do a lot of things now that he normally would do. He never complains about it, but he came just that close to being a paraplegic.

QUARTERBACK

—Baltimore Colts, 1973–1981
—Los Angeles Rams, 1982

Bert Jones was one of the National Football League's premier quarterbacks in the 1970s and early 1980s. His father was a prominent NFL player and coach, and Jones discusses his childhood exposure to pro football, which included being the Cleveland Browns ball boy in training camp. He explains how he developed as a quarterback in high school in northern Louisiana, and at Louisiana State University. He also discusses the recruiting process in college football. An All-American at LSU who went to three bowl games, Jones discusses the college athlete's football and academic experience.

Jones was the Baltimore Colts' number-one draft choice, the second player selected in the NFL draft. He discusses adjusting to pro defenses, which were far more complex than in college. Quarterback is the most important position in football, and Jones provides an in-depth analysis of what is involved in playing it. He identifies the qualities of a good quarterback, and discusses the importance of how the quarterback and the center handle and time the snap. Jones describes the differences in outlook and in what is required in playing offense versus defense. He also explains why there is a significant home field advantage in football.

Bert Jones, Baltimore Colts quarterback. Courtesy of Bert Jones.

In addition, Jones discusses the labor issues and player walkouts during his period in the NFL, including his leading a wildcat strike on the Colts, called to protest the firing of head coach Ted Marchibroda and his staff. He describes his disenchantment as the Colts owner's meddling pushed a team that had won division championships into decline and his trade to the Los Angeles Rams. Jones discusses how players handle getting hurt, and the career-ending injury he sustained when he broke his neck in a game. Finally, Jones examines the changes in pro football since his retirement in 1982, expressing his displeasure with the narcissistic end-zone dances, "the pointing the fingers and the taunting."

STEPHEN NORWOOD: *You must have had a very interesting childhood, given that your father was a very prominent professional football player with a legendary team, the Cleveland Browns of the All-America Football Conference (AAFC) and later the NFL, and then became a coach in the NFL. He was telling me a little bit today about how you grew up in the training camp. He made it a provision that he would be allowed to bring his family to training camp. What was it like having him as a father, and could you describe your early connection to sports?*

BERT JONES: The first question is, you have kind of a unique background. From other people's eyes that may be true, but for me, having a father who was a professional football player and coach, going to an NFL training camp while I was growing up, and being a ball boy for an NFL team didn't seem unusual to me. Nor did knowing my father's good friends—the Otto Grahams, the Lou Grozas, the Dante Lavellis, the Mac Speedies, and the Marion Motleys. That was just the way I grew up. It seemed the norm. Everybody else who didn't have a father who was a professional football player seemed abnormal to me.

Because we lived in an environment in north Louisiana where my parents and generations back grew up, the mystique of being a professional athlete didn't seem as grandiose as it might seem now. My father's job was to go away from August to right after Thanksgiving to play football, and then to come back and run the lumberyard.

SN: *Did the other boys who went to elementary school with you envy you? Did you want to become a pro football player?*

BJ: Football was certainly big to a lot of us, but you did not have the constant exposure to professional sports then that you do now. Because of my background, as a child I didn't think of anything else except aspiring to play professional sports. A lot of people wanted to play high school ball. I thought that was all right. A lot of people wanted to play college ball. I thought of that as the only way to get to pro ball. The norm for me was to be a professional football player.

SN: *Well, at what age did you become aware of this? How young are you when it begins to dawn on you that . . . ?*

BJ: The stories have been told of my first grade teacher asking everyone, "What do you want to be when you grow up?" The proper thing to say would be a policeman, or a fireman, or an accountant, or a lawyer. My response was that I was going to be a professional football player. And the retort to that was, "Well, what if you can't?" And I said, "Well, I'm going to be!"

SN: *Were your brothers the same way?*
BJ: I have four brothers—there were seven children in our family—and I don't think my brothers were as adamant about being a professional football player as I was. That means that I've always been about a half bubble off.

SN: *You're not the oldest.*
BJ: No, I'm the middle child of the seven—the neglected child in my family. My mother still does not know my name. She calls roll, and I happen to be the fourth one down. But three of my brothers did play college football—one at LSU, one at Arkansas, and one at Louisiana Tech.

SN: *Did your father work in the off-season, or was he home all the time?*
BJ: Well, growing up, I didn't remember him playing ball, because he had retired. I was born in 1951, and he retired in 1955. I did not know my father as a professional football player, other than just a few snapshots of my memory when he was playing. I remember going to Cleveland, and I remember all of his friends. But I don't remember him playing football, other than through the memories of film. We used to have a sixteen-millimeter review of the Cleveland Browns' 1951 season, when he scored six touchdowns in one game. That was pretty prominent in the film. But we didn't watch it much, since we didn't have a film projector. I probably saw the film five or six times.

But in 1963, my father decided to go back to Cleveland as the offensive coordinator for the Browns. As a matter of fact, I was at the grand opening of the Canton Football Hall of Fame. The Cleveland Browns played in the inaugural game, and I was there as a ball boy.

That was a truly unique environment to live in, because in the summers the whole family, all seven children, would go up to Cleveland from Ruston, Louisiana, and live in the Browns' training camp. That was highly unusual. Since then, there probably hasn't been another woman in training camp ever. My mother was the only one that I knew of. My father would farm different boys out to live with different players, because there weren't enough apartments and rooms. My best friends were the Frank Ryans, the Jim Ninowskis, the Paul Warfields, the Clifton McNeils.

SN: *Were these guys good role models for kids?*
BJ: Oh, yes, and if they weren't, we didn't know it. I used to hide in Jim Brown's locker all the time, and jump out and pretend that I had scared him,

and he played along with it. He was a very personable guy. He was not a good role model, but he was a good friend. I knew Leroy Kelley like he was my brother, for five or six years.

SN: *Tell me about your father's role in the 1964 NFL championship game between Cleveland and Baltimore, the game where the Browns upset the Colts 27-0.*
BJ: The Colts were heavily favored. My father was offensive coordinator for the Browns. He called all the plays in the second half of that game, because Frank Ryan, the Browns' quarterback, sustained a hit to the head in the first half and couldn't remember the plays. As we used to say back then, he was dinged. Today, we need to have an MRI and a CAT-scan done before we reenter. But back then, as stupid as it sounds, it was kind of like a badge of courage to say, "I played the game, and don't remember any of it."

SN: *That second half, Cleveland used the pass quite effectively.*
BJ: Right. Gary Collins caught two or three touchdown passes in the second half.

SN: *So even with Ryan in that condition, he connected.*
BJ: It's kind of funny. Your thought process is okay sometimes when you're dinged. But your long-term memory or your short-term memory from five minutes ago is gone. With the score 0-0 at halftime, the Browns came back in the second half, and won 27-0. It was great to be a child and know that not only did you know all the guys who had won the NFL championship, but that I was their ball boy in training camp.

SN: *When did football begin in the school system?*
BJ: Seventh grade.

SN: *And you started playing then?*
BJ: Yes.

SN: *Was that something your father encouraged?*
BJ: My father was the exact antithesis of what you would think a professional athlete would be, as it relates to his son.

SN: *You think of Mickey Mantle's father teaching him to switch hit when he was five years old.*
BJ: My father was the opposite. His theory was, if you haven't got anybody to throw to, I'll catch for you. But never once can I ever recall him saying, "Hey, you need to go throw the football, so you can become a good thrower and be a

player." If anything, he was a great equalizer as it related to his children and sports. He invented what we called "crazy Football," in which the younger players were a more valuable commodity, since they could run and throw backwards or forwards, anytime they got the ball, while the older ones were more limited in what they could do.

SN: *What was junior high school football like? Was it taken very seriously?*
BJ: Football in Ruston was taken seriously, but it was not a religion, and it was not the single focus of the community. I began playing organized football there in seventh grade. I also played baseball and basketball and ran track.

While my father was in Cleveland during the football season, I had a brother four years older playing high school football and a brother a year older than me playing football, and I was playing in junior high, and my mother would go out and chart a game.

SN: *Did you have a favorite sport? Was it football, because your father had been a football player?*
BJ: I don't know whether it was because of my father, but football was my favorite sport. And the truth be known, I'm just not sure it was where my abilities were best. I was a talented baseball pitcher. But for some distorted reason, I made the conscious decision that I did not want to choose between football and baseball. And so I stopped playing baseball when I was a sophomore in high school. I think that was probably the maddest that I can recall my father ever being as it related to any sport. He asked me, "Why do you want to quit baseball? You're a good baseball player, play it." My answer was that I quit because I wanted to run track, so that I could get faster in order to play football better. Yet, my abilities in baseball were far superior at the time to my abilities as a football player.

SN: *Did you become aware you had unusual talent? I was surprised your father told me that although he became a very, very good player by his senior year in high school, up until then he wasn't really a starting player. How about you?*
BJ: I was like my father in that I did not become a starter until relatively late in high school—in my case, not until my junior year. We're pretty late bloomers genetically. I didn't physically mature until relatively late. I didn't shave until my rookie year in the NFL. Ken Mendenhall and I tried to grow mustaches, and neither of us could.

At Ruston High School, I played under the same coach my father had, a tremendous coach.

SN: *Did he compare you?*

BJ: No, he did not make comparisons.

SN: *It must be difficult to be the son of a famous player.*

BJ: See, I've never felt the pressure of being "the son of." I didn't feel the pressure within the family. I didn't feel the pressure from a coaching staff growing up, in junior high and high school. I did feel the pressure of being a Jones, but it didn't have anything to do with being the son of Dub Jones. It was that your brother Bill hit hard, your brother Schump hit hard, and you better hit hard too, or you won't be like them.

SN: *Did you play quarterback in high school?*

BJ: I did. I was a defensive back also until I became not good enough to play with the other ones. I played both ways—very limited in junior varsity, because I didn't start until my junior year in high school. On junior varsity I played defensive back, but I was beaten deep often.

SN: *So what influence did the coach have in developing you as a quarterback at the high school level? What kinds of things did you work on then?*

BJ: Well, my coach was not that good at developing a quarterback. The motor skills of being able to go out and throw the football are not very teachable. I could always throw. I could throw well, and I could throw hard, and I could throw long, and I could hit what I was throwing at. So, we utilized that on third down if we had to.

SN: *How about things like release time, being able to make a quick decision under pressure, who's open, who's not open?*

BJ: I think it's taught more now. Back then, if my brother wasn't open over here, I threw to my first cousin over there. It wasn't too difficult. I didn't have but two receivers.

SN: *A lot of people who follow football would ask what it's like—how do you stand in there when someone's going to hit you?*

BJ: It happens all the time. You're just a piece of spaghetti. You just have to play with the punches.

SN: *What about your mother? Did she take notice of you?*

BJ: Well, my mother is probably a better athlete than my father, and her father was a phenomenal athlete. He played at Louisiana Tech and at Tulane, to go through medical school. He was ambidextrous. He was a pitcher and a half-back. He pitched one game of a doubleheader right-handed and the next game left-handed.

SN: *Did you know him?*
BJ: Oh, yes. He taught me to throw a knuckleball when I was nine.

SN: *Did you ever get hurt playing football in high school?*
BJ: My mother would not let me. She just didn't allow it. She didn't want to hear about it. Getting hurt was not an option. I sprained my ankle a couple of times, and my mother told me that if I sprained it again, I would have to quit playing. She wasn't going to let me play anymore. As opposed to "Are you okay?" Our tendency when we got hurt was to go to the corner and get well.

I'm sure that my parents were happy that I played and proud that I did. But without a shadow of a doubt, I feel that there was no question that it would not have mattered one way or another if I had played.

SN: *Let's talk about the college recruiting process. How were you recruited? When did you begin getting signs of interest?*
BJ: I wasn't that good a football player in high school, and I didn't have a whole lot of signs of interest from college recruiters. I also came out the same year that Joe Ferguson came out of high school. He was a phenomenal high school player, and continued on to be a phenomenal college and pro player also. He was highly recruited and regarded as probably the best quarterback in the country. And he was just fifty miles down the road. So, they drove by me to get to see him, and justifiably so—he was a better player at the time.

So, the recruiting process with Bert Jones was not real difficult. I only had a few schools that offered me a scholarship opportunity. I took the one that played the toughest football there was, and that was LSU.

SN: *Which was a major program. Was that the only major program that was looking at you?*
BJ: There were other places that I could have pursued, but none that just jumped off the walls for me. Tulane and LSU offered me scholarships, and all the local colleges would have offered me a scholarship.

SN: *You didn't go on recruiting trips out of state?*
BJ: I went on just two recruiting trips—Tulane and LSU. Ara Parseghian, the coach of Notre Dame, was a good friend of my father. My father asked me if

I wanted him to pursue that for me, and I really did not want him to. I don't know why.

When I hadn't signed anywhere by March or April, Coach Eddie Robinson of Grambling came down to visit me, and he said, "Look, Bert. You're fixing to put a lot of pressure on me. If you don't hurry up and go sign with somebody, I'm going to have to recruit you and sign you." And I said, "Don't offer it unless you mean it."

Eddie Robinson, of course, is the winningest coach in the history of football. My father, when he was playing pro ball, had helped him set up the Grambling offense, and he'd worked out at Grambling. When Eddie Robinson changed from a Notre Dame box or a wing-T or whatever, my father gave him the system to implement it. They've been good friends for years and years and years. And Eddie Robinson has been my dear friend all my life.

In fact, when I played with the Baltimore Colts, I would work out at Grambling and would hold workouts for their team. We had full seven-on-seven workouts. I'd have all their defensive backs and all their receivers, and I'd just run the show. We'd run pass routes, and I'd have somebody to throw to all day long. I worked with Doug Williams and with Matthew Reed when they were in college there. And still to this day, I'm the emcee at Coach Robinson's football banquet. But I wanted to play football in a major college, and Grambling was not the big arena.

I did not regard college as anything other than the next step to get to pro ball. So, going to college wasn't a big deal to me. I just wanted to play in the big show, and go where I could. Education was something that was looked on very seriously by my family. I'm kind of the black sheep. I have brothers and sisters who have achieved levels beyond. My brother was an honors graduate in animal husbandry from Louisiana Tech, while he played football. He went on to graduate from LSU Law School number one in his class, and he was chief of the law review. I have two brothers who are engineers. I have a sister who has a degree in medical technology. I have another who's an accountant. I have another brother who has a master's degree in theology. I was not a good student in college. I graduated with a 2.7 or 2.8 grade point average from the School of Business at LSU. But towards the end, I realized how important academics was.

SN: *You had seen Frank Ryan, who had a Ph.D. in mathematics, who was quarterback for the Cleveland Browns when you were following them in the training camp. So, it indicated you could have outstanding academic credentials combined with football.*

BJ: We had a very controlled environment at LSU, and I never cut class. It was more controlled back then than it is now. My roommate was Tommy Casanova, who is an M.D. We lived in an athletic dorm, and we had a ten thirty curfew every day, all the way to my senior year.

SN: *Did the players observe that?*
BJ: I did. The players observed that curfew.

SN: *Today they have external constraints. Athletic departments have people who accompany players to class to make sure they get there.*
BJ: Well, I know there is not a tougher job on the campus than being a student athlete. I had a twelve o'clock meeting every day about football for thirty or forty minutes, and then we went to practice at two thirty. We got back at seven thirty and had supper. You're talking about six hours every day of a really intense work environment, fall and spring semesters. Now the NCAA has mandatorily reduced it.

SN: *Was there a certain grade point average you needed to maintain?*
BJ: Yes, you needed to keep a 2.0 grade point average.

SN: *How did the faculty treat athletes in class?*
BJ: Well, I can only tell you what I experienced. In the LSU School of Business, the athlete was not winked at by the professors; you were considered just another student in the class.

I thought I was getting a break when I walked into my advanced statistics class on the first day of my sophomore year. The professor got up in front of the class, and asked, "Are there any football players in this class?" I always kept a low profile, but I thought, "Hey, this may be my chance. This might be what I've been hearing about all these times." So I slowly raised my hand, and he nodded his head. And then he said, "Are there any Kappa Sigs?" That was a fraternity at LSU, of which I was a member. I slowly raised my hand, and I said, "Man, I've got a double dip here. I'm in good shape." And the professor said, "Son, I want you to know right now, there is only one thing that I hate more than a football player, and it's a Kappa Sig." He went on, "I can tell you right now, that you need to *get out* of my class and never come back." He was as serious as he could be.

Unfortunately, I didn't have any other way to go. I said, "Sir, I've got to have this class." He replied, "I'm just telling you, you need to transfer, and get another instructor, because I'm not kidding you." I said, "We'll see." And I came back to the next class, and he told me, "I wasn't kidding you the other day, when I told you that you needed to leave my class." He said, "I've had threats from football players, and I hate Kappa Sigs," because of whatever reason it was. He told me, "You need to leave." And I said, "I'm not leaving. I'm taking this class." And I took it.

Needless to say, I worked my tail off in that class, made As, and because of it, we became great friends. I took three more classes under him, and I considered him my best professor. He became dean of the school, and he told me, "Hey, you won. You won me over."

SN: *I would have thought at LSU, a big football school, some of the professors might have been star struck.*
BJ: Well, I wasn't that big a star. But I went by my middle name in a lot of classes, just to keep from being known as a football player.

At LSU, I lived in the athletic dorm, and most of my associations were through the athletic department, but I joined a fraternity to be exposed to normal people. Football players are not really normal.

SN: *How are football players not normal?*
BJ: They're stuck on their tails, and they think that their position in life is a little more important than it really is. I just like normal people, who like to hunt and fish, and say hello to momma, and that kind of stuff, as opposed to "Hey, look at me!"

SN: *Did you feel the coaching staff at LSU was sophisticated to the point of just going by merit, or did they play favorites?*
BJ: The LSU coaching staff was not sophisticated at all. They were old school, and not very smart at either understanding or adapting.

I think one of the main attributes of a good coach is that he has the ability to adapt his team, or his system, to the players that he has. Take Bear Bryant. He had Joe Namath, Kenny Stabler, and Scott Hunter, and he was the passingest coach in the whole nation. Then he ran out of passers, and he ended up with a whole bunch of running backs. So, what did he do? He went to the wishbone. And then, all of a sudden, he got a quarterback who could throw again, and he goes back to throwing. He adapted his system to his players.

Whereas, at LSU, I was in a system that adapted the players to the system. They were playing two quarterbacks all the time, primarily a run-option type quarterback. That just wasn't conducive to my style. They did some things that were not copasetic. They told me that I would be calling the plays, and then I didn't. But that wasn't any big deal. I played only half the time while I was at LSU.

SN: *What was their logic there? What were their arguments in favor of doing that? Were you just shuttling in plays from the bench?*

BJ: No, you'd go in for a series, and then come out for one or two, and then go back in. It was a weird deal. I may have one NCAA record. I'm the only quarterback in the history of 1A college football who only played half the time and was second string, who made consensus All-American, and who was a first-round NFL draft choice. We had one quarterback who could throw the ball and one quarterback who could run. So, they threw the guy who ran and ran the guy who threw.

SN: *What kind of seasons did your team have?*

BJ: We were very successful, and we were probably ranked in the top ten during my three years.

SN: *Did you go to bowl games?*

BJ: We went to the Orange Bowl my sophomore year, the Sun Bowl my junior year, and the Bluebonnet Bowl my senior year.

SN: *Is there a big break between high school and playing in a program like LSU's?*

BJ: Playing football is no different from high school to college to the pros, in that you get hit just as hard in high school as you do in college and in college as in the pros. It didn't hurt any more in high school or in the pros. It was all pretty much the same.

My family came to all of my games at LSU, because it was within driving distance. But my father would never interfere with what I was doing. Never did he critique me on my play. He never said, "You should have done this, you should have done that." I'm sure he was just crying in his beer, even though he doesn't drink. But he never second-guessed, and he never injected what he thought should have been done.

SN: *Did you play any other sports in college?*

BJ: I tried to play other sports at LSU, just so I could get out of spring training. I tried to throw the javelin for the track team. I tried to play tennis on the tennis team.

SN: *Did you ever get hurt playing football in college?*

BJ: Yes, I got hurt my sophomore year, when I tore a cartilage in my knee in practice, a week before the season started. It exploded every day. It swelled up. They would drain it every day, and inject cortisone every day. They didn't know any better about drugs back then. We used to get radiation for psoriasis. I don't think it was malicious. They were trying to get you ready to play, but I don't think there was any conscious irresponsibility. I'm still friends with the doctor and the trainer to this day.

SN: *Were you concerned about this injury?*
BJ: The day after the season ended, I had my knee operated on. I wasn't really concerned about my injury. I was just getting it fixed to continue on. Why do you think they call them punch doctors? They just punch them and put them back together.

SN: *There's the question that when you're twenty years old, you have one way of responding. When you're thirty, you've been banged up maybe ten more times, and there's an accumulation of different injuries. I just wonder . . .*
BJ: My response to injury never changed during my career. It should have changed, but it never did. My pro career ended because I broke my neck. But my response to that—this makes me feel and seem ignorant now—but my response was, "Hey, look. It doesn't even hurt! I have numbness, but I don't have pain. Why are we making such a big deal over this?" I hurt my neck in the first quarter of the game, and then played the rest of that game, and then played over half of the next game.

SN: *Which guys from your LSU teams made it to the pros?*
BJ: Only a few of the players from my teams at LSU went on to play in the NFL. Tommy Casanova was a great ballplayer. Once he got his medical degree he stopped playing ball. Bo Harris probably played four or five years for Cincinnati as a linebacker. My first cousin, Andy Hamilton, whom I grew up with, played four years. And that's it.

SN: *I thought Oklahoma sent more.*
BJ: Well, Oklahoma always had the best team that money could buy. It was said that they'd go to the pros and take a pay cut.

SN: *They had that reputation?*
BJ: I think it's pretty factual. At LSU, we didn't get any perks on the side. The only perk I had the opportunity to get in college was selling the complimentary tickets the players were given for the games. Most of the players sold them. My mom and daddy came to the games in Baton Rouge, so I didn't have the opportunity to sell them.

When I came out of my four years of eligibility at LSU, I still lacked six hours to graduate. So, after my rookie year, I went back to LSU to get my degree, which I did.

SN: *Could I ask you about the NFL draft process? You were a number-one draft choice. What was it like? Were you looking to a particular team, a favorite like the Cleveland Browns? Did you think you'd be a number-one choice?*
BJ: Yeah, I knew I would.

SN: *But you said you didn't have a stellar college career.*
BJ: Right. It was because my motor skills were superior to anyone else's. I was the second player picked in the draft.

SN: *Did the Baltimore Colts just call you up and say you were their number-one draft choice?*
BJ: Yeah, they called me on the phone.

SN: *Did they say they'd start you?*
BJ: No, they didn't say anything, other than come up and see if you can make the team. That's kind of the perception that I had.

Houston had the first pick, and they had drafted Dan Pastorini two years before, so they didn't need a quarterback. New Orleans had had the second pick, but they traded it to Baltimore for a defensive lineman, whom they thought was real good, but who turned out to be a journeyman. That was one of the major sins of the New Orleans Saints. They weren't in a position to need a quarterback, because they had Archie Manning, who was in his second year.

I played in the College All-Star game in Chicago. My good buddy from Shreveport, Joe Ferguson, and I did the same thing we did when we played in the High School All-Star game. We got in the car, drove up together, and roomed together again.

SN: *So you got a late start in training camp?*
BJ: I got no training camp.

SN: *Was Otto Graham still coaching the College All-Stars?*
BJ: No, John McKay was the coach. The College All-Star game was the first time I had ever experienced what I would regard as not necessarily a football-working environment. It was an eye-opener.

SN: *What do you mean?*
BJ: It was the first time that I had ever been exposed to a non-enforced curfew. People were out having a good time. Players were burning the candle at both ends, which was not the style at LSU.

SN: *Did you play in that game?*
BJ: Yeah. We almost beat the Miami Dolphins in that game, and we should have beaten them. They had been undefeated in the NFL the previous season, the first undefeated team in NFL history.

SN: *Did you notice anything about them that was different from college-level play?*
BJ: Yeah, they were much more sophisticated than the college teams I had seen. They knew what they were doing, and they played as a unit. They were a far superior team. I found it challenging to play against them; it was the arena I had been looking for. I played most of the game. Joe Ferguson was the other quarterback who played.

SN: *What was it like moving from Louisiana, the Deep South, to Baltimore?*
BJ: It was not that big a deal for me, because I'd been used to Cleveland as a kid. I'd gone to the deli there, and I knew Shaker Heights and Cleveland Heights, and the East Side and the West Side, and the North Side, and downtown and uptown. And Baltimore was a very personable city.

I was not awestruck with the environment of the NFL, because that's what I grew up with. There was no mystique. It was just, "This is where you're supposed to be, and it took a long time to get here."

I knew everybody in the NFL. I got a playbook from the Baltimore Colts that was a Paul Brown derivative, because it came through Don Shula and Weeb Ewbank, who was on Brown's staff. If you grab a family tree of the NFL, you have Vince Lombardi and Paul Brown. And past that, who else is there?

As a matter of fact, my playbook used the same terms and the same numbers as my father's. The system that I ran for the Baltimore Colts had been developed by the Cleveland Browns. My father can tell you how they made up the names Dig, Dag, and Dog, and different pass routes like that.

SN: *Who was your first head coach at Baltimore, Schnellenberger?*
BJ: Howard Schnellenberger, a great guy and a fabulous coach.

SN: *What was his coaching style like?*
BJ: He was pretty intense, an overworker. It was his first year there as head coach. Howard was the new coach of a new ownership that had just fired

every Baltimore Colt who was known, including John Unitas. They unloaded every player who had been great in the past. There were not two people on that 1973 team who survived the 1971 Super Bowl.

Of course, I didn't know a thing. I came in there as dumb as a rock, with just a lot of motor skills. Actually, I was not dumb as a rock, but I was not adept at playing what it was that we were fixing to do. The strategical level of play was so far advanced beyond what I had been exposed to in college, that it was not apples and apples. It was not an easy transition for me to make.

SN: *In terms of a lot more plays that you run, a lot more defenses that they throw up at you?*
BJ: And what you're supposed to do in certain situations.

SN: *Just the complexity of things.*
BJ: Exactly. Everything in the NFL was much more complex than in college. Today in a college game, you can look out on the field and tell what defense they're in. Whereas in the pros, you never knew. You saw so many different coverages and so many different fronts. You really had to be adept at understanding them. I think my first year in the NFL, I played on motor skills.

SN: *You had a good shot at the starting quarterback position. Were there veterans close to the other quarterback, Marty Domres?*
BJ: There was an obvious difference in abilities between him and me. There was no question which of the two was going to be the real player. He threw an end over end, Billy Kilmer pass, and I threw a pretty good zinger.

SN: *Did he try to help you out in any way?*
BJ: No. He did everything to my detriment. I was going to be his biggest nightmare. I was going to be the guy who took his place.

SN: *Did he just retire then?*
BJ: No, he continued on and played as my backup.

SN: *Did Johnny Unitas loom as a presence? Did you compare yourself to him? Baltimore fans had seen one of the all-time greats at quarterback.*
BJ: Oh, it was everywhere. But being compared to him, or having people say I wasn't as good as him, didn't really matter to me. In their own unknowing way, by making that comparison, people were giving me one of the greatest compliments that I could receive. "Hey, you're not quite as good as John Unitas."

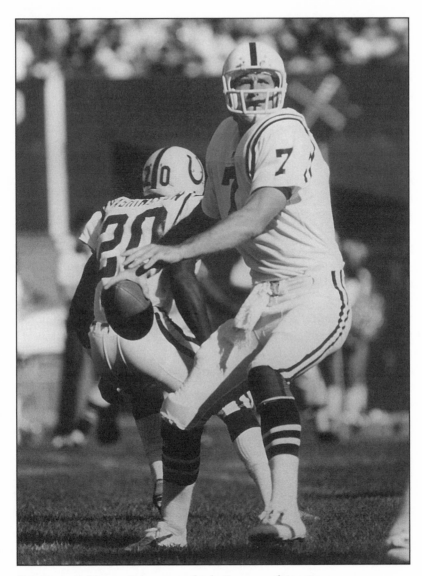

Bert Jones, Baltimore Colts quarterback. Courtesy of Bert Jones.

"Thank you. Give me a break. He was one of the best that ever was. I appreciate that you put me in the same sentence with John Unitas."

I'll never forget my first professional football game, which was against the Cleveland Browns. One of my best friends in the Browns' training camp when

I was growing up was Gene Hickerson, a tremendous pulling guard. Gene was an old-school kind of player, in that his warm-up consisted of walking out on the field and leaning against the goalpost, and then going in and coming back and playing the game. I'll never forget that when I went out there to play in my first game, he was doing what he always did, leaning against the goalpost to get ready for the game. And I went and leaned up on the other side, and he said, "Oh my goodness! It's time for me to quit, isn't it? I am too old!" He had known me as a kid, and now I was coming to compete against him.

It was just a strange sensation competing against the Browns, to whom I had been so attached as a kid. My father's best friend was the defensive coordinator for the Browns. I didn't know whether to root for the team I was playing for or for the Browns.

SN: *Baltimore was a good football town, right?*
BJ: It was a very good football town. We were well received there, and when we won, we became better received. I like a good, educated fan.

SN: *Are there many of them?*
BJ: Oh, yeah. I love Eastern Seaboard towns. The fans there are just more attentive to what's going on. I do not like a Dallas, I do not like a Houston, I do not like Atlanta. I detest Los Angeles. Give me a Philadelphia, give me a Washington, give me a New York, give me a Boston, give me a Cleveland, give me a San Francisco. I think old towns and old cities have character. They have an ethnic background and different characters within their own neighborhoods.

SN: *Who succeeded Howard Schnellenberger as head coach?*
BJ: Joe Thomas, the general manager, became the Colts' head coach, and that was total disarray. Half the coaching staff quit. I love Joe, and he had a great ability to find a ballplayer. But he wasn't a coach. It was a scary deal. That was the year of a strike that went through preseason, and so I didn't go to training camp that year either.

SN: *What did you think about the strike? What issues were involved?*
BJ: I supported the strike because I was a team kind of guy, but I didn't relate to the strike issues. The labor union issues were never of that much importance to the star players. They were actually to the detriment of the stars, because what they tried to do, in theory, was to establish a single class called "professional football player." But the star's elite status provides him with an opportunity to make more and do better.

The NFL Players' Association adhered to a salary cap, which is like this: "Okay, General Electric, I know you're too stupid to run a good business, and you're going to pay your people so much that you'll make yourself noncompetitive, and you'll lose money and go out of business. So, as a labor union, I'm going to keep you from doing that! I'll say that you can't pay us but five dollars an hour, no matter what you do. So, we can keep you making all the money that there is to make." That's not your typical labor union position.

SN: *Did you have any receiver who you want to point out as highly talented?*
BJ: The most gifted receiver I had at Baltimore was Roger Carr, who was from Louisiana Tech. He was the best receiver I ever played with, a phenomenal player. He was the one breakaway guy I had. I also had Glenn Doughty, who ran a 5-flat forty-yard dash. If I told him to get inside that cornerback, let me hit him on his right breast, and keep the defender on his left, it would happen. That's the way I threw. Give me a side to throw to and I'll keep it away from the defender. Lydell Mitchell and Don McCauley were both very gifted receivers coming out of the backfield. They were not fast enough running backs to be outside running threats, and so to get outside, instead of running, we would throw it around the corners.

I had a good tight end, Raymond Chester, but his style was not as conducive to our style of play. He was a great talent, and we had a lot of good years together, but we didn't utilize him as well as he could have been utilized. He was kind of a breakaway tight end. But he didn't have great hands, so you couldn't use him as just a gut inside possession receiver.

At the end of my career, the best running back I played with was Joe Washington.

SN: *He was a pass receiver, too. He led the NFL in pass receptions one year.*
BJ: Oh, yeah. And a good passer.

SN: *Right. He threw a touchdown pass in that game against New England on Monday Night Football.*
BJ: Oh, yeah. He ran a kick back for a touchdown, ran a punt back for a touchdown, scored a touchdown, threw a touchdown pass, and probably caught a touchdown pass. It was a one-man show.

SN: *He was one of the smallest guys at running back in that period, wasn't he? Greg Pruitt told me he was the pioneer of small running backs.*
BJ: Yeah. Greg and I came into the league together. Oh, what a great talent. Joe Washington and Greg Pruitt were so much alike you'd think their gene pool was

the same. Greg's upper body might have been a little heavier. But they were just alike—quick scat backs with phenomenal power. And they both ran sideways faster than they ran forward, which is really a talent.

SN: *Even at that size they were able to take all that pounding.*
BJ: They delivered a lot of the pounding also.

SN: *How about going into the playoffs? You played with three American Football Conference (AFC) division champions.*
BJ: We had to play Pittsburgh twice and Oakland once. The first year we were certainly outclassed. We were talented in that we worked well as a unit, but we were green. Our offensive line did a good job, but they were too small. We were not, man for man, capable of handling our opponent, although we often beat them strategically.

SN: *Did you bring film home?*
BJ: Did I come home sometimes is more like it. I would spend nights at the stadium, just sitting on the training room table, studying film.

SN: *Just constantly preparing, studying?*
BJ: Yeah. That was our strength. But outside the quarterback position, it was not that common to do that. But it should have been, because pictures don't tell lies. Jack Lambert was the best middle linebacker in the world, and we only beat Pittsburgh once when they were in their strength. But the only reason we did was because I had tips on him and on Jack Ham. For example, I knew that if Jack Lambert had his right hand on his thigh pad, he was blitzing. If Jack Ham staggered his stance a certain length, he was coming.

When Steve Zabel was playing linebacker with New England, I could read him like a book. When he lined up on the tight end, if he was eyeball to eyeball, he was going to do one thing. If he got a shade to the outside, he was going to do something else. If he got a shade to the inside, he was going to do something else. If he got a shade to the outside and had his feet square, he was going to do one thing. If he got to the outside and had his feet staggered, he was going to do another.

If our opponent was stupid enough to signal in defensive coverages from the sideline with hand signals, I would read them, too. I'd switch sides in the huddle just so that I could look at the defensive team and see what the coaches were doing.

SN: *Would teams you met in the playoffs be that unwise?*
BJ: No, not playoff teams.

SN: *When a guy came over in a trade, you would draw on him for information about his former team. Zabel said he set up the New England Patriots for you.*
BJ: He did. He helped us beat New England. You just do the things you have to do. It's not cheating. It's grasping the knowledge that's available to you.

SN: *What was your experience negotiating contracts at Baltimore?*
BJ: Negotiating a contract wasn't too difficult. My brother, who was practicing law in Houston, was my agent. My daddy would just get on the phone with Paul Brown, who was then the owner of the Cincinnati Bengals, and say, "Tell me what they're getting paid." So, it wasn't too difficult a task.

When the Colts went from being a losing team to being a playoff team, management did not compensate me accordingly—nor did I ask them to. I had negotiated a contract, and I'm a man of my word. If I told them I was going to play for this amount, that's what I was going to do. I buy and sell lumber in a business environment today, and my word is my bond.

SN: *When you were playing, how common was it for teams to put incentives in contracts?*
BJ: Incentives were very common, but I didn't like them. For one thing, if I had an incentive to have x number of completions, I could have done it. But I might not have had the team's best interest in mind. I would have thrown the ball more, when I didn't need to throw it. The only incentives I had in my contracts were the simple ones. If we got to the playoffs, then I would get paid more. Back then, you had a set pay scale, where when you played in the playoffs, you were going to get $5000 or $10,000, whatever it might have been. But that was a significant pay cut from what my normal game check was. So, I just added that I needed to get a game check plus whatever it was. The incentive was to get to the playoffs, to win as a group. But I never had an individual stat that related to paying me more money at the end of the year.

SN: *Did you do commercial endorsements?*
BJ: I did get to do some, but not too many, since Baltimore was not a media Mecca. I did a national commercial for Ivory Soap. When Ralph Lauren developed a clothing line called "Chaps," I was the model for the ads "Bert Jones, the Quarterback, Wears Chaps by Ralph Lauren." They ended up paying me for three years not to be photographed anywhere else.

SN: *You led a wildcat strike. How did that happen?*
BJ: There were some serious difficulties on the Colts during Ted Marchibroda's second year as head coach, as a conflict developed between him and the general manager and owner over who had jurisdiction over what. In our first year with Marchibroda, we had turned it around on the Baltimore Colts, and won the AFC Eastern Division championship. But the next year, a week before the season started, they fired Marchibroda and his staff, as a result of this turf battle.

It was improper for them to remove our coaching staff one week before our opening game, and our team just said, "Whoa!" I went public and said, "We've come to the conclusion that there are no grounds to remove this coach from the football team. He brought the team from last place in the division to first place, and whatever difficulties there are shouldn't supersede the fact that he should be the coach."

I called Pete Rozelle, and told him we probably weren't going to play. He said, "What?" And I said, "We're not going to play. We just have a real bad deal here. They're going to have to reinstate our coach." We called a press conference and shut her down.

SN: *Did the whole team stand behind you?*
BJ: Yes. I guess I was in a bulletproof state at the time. I was the quarterback, and I was the guy who had led the team back from the doldrums to prosperous times. Everybody else on the team was vulnerable. And it was done. A day and a half later, they brought the coach back. We came back and we won the AFC Eastern Division championship again.

SN: *Did the owner hold it against you?*
BJ: The general manager, Joe Thomas, did.

SN: *He was calling all the shots?*
BJ: Yeah, as it related to the players. Joe Thomas did it all; the owner was a nonexistent drunk.

SN: *Let's examine what's involved in playing quarterback.*
BJ: The quarterback is the most important player on the team, bar none. If you don't have a quarterback who can get the job done, you're not going to win consistently.

SN: *Is that true in college, where there's less emphasis on passing?*
BJ: Probably less so. But if you have a good quarterback there, you're in much better shape. A quarterback is just as good as the other ten men out on the

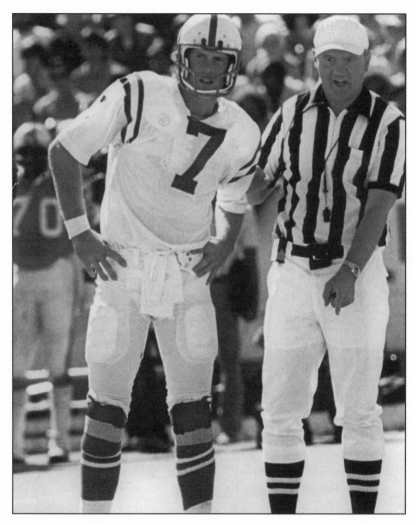

Bert Jones, Baltimore Colts quarterback. Courtesy of Bert Jones.

field with him. The motor skills are the norm. The other aspects are what makes one very good. And if you've got a good team, you can be a very good quarterback. If you're an average quarterback, and your team is not that good, you can't ride your team above. But if you're a great quarterback, and you have an average team, it is the most important position. You can make your team leap ahead, more so than at any other position on the field. If you have a great team, you can win with an average quarterback. If you have an average team, you can't win with an average quarterback.

SN: *What are the ingredients of a good quarterback?*
BJ: The ingredients of a good quarterback are, first, to have a tenacity on the field. You have to be able to get things done. Meaning doing whatever it takes to get there. Being a good player, leading the team.

SN: *People have to respect your leadership.*
BJ: Well, I think you develop leadership through doing, as opposed to through telling.

SN: *There is this stereotype of, you're behind, with two minutes to go, and the quarterback, on his own twenty, says, "Okay, guys, we're taking it down, we're going to score." And they have to believe you're going to do it.*
BJ: Well, if you're not good enough to get it done, they're not going to believe you can do it. But, if you're good enough to do it, they'll believe you, and you'll be a leader.

The things that most people think are the most important ingredients of a good quarterback are what I regard as the norms. You have to be big enough, and tough enough, and strong enough to withstand playing the game of football. You have to be able to throw the ball, and you have to be able to think. Those are the norms. Everybody's got to be able to throw the ball to the guy who's in the open.

As it related to my game, the most important facet of being a good player was the strategic aspect of the game, and calling the correct play, and having the players perform in the best manner they could, to beat the defense I was looking at. It's always a game of cat and mouse, and it was so much fun. That was the game. The motor skills of getting the ball to that guy there was just the norm.

I don't regard the importance of a quarterback to be just a great thrower. If I had my choice, I would probably only throw fifteen or twenty times a game. I mean, I love to throw, but I would rather dominate somebody than play a game of chance. Run the ball down their throats, and passing dinks and dunks, and not having a third and fifteen.

Just because you have the motor skills to play the game, doesn't mean you're going to be a good quarterback. I'm sure that Randall Cunningham one day will come on. But here's a guy who has phenomenal motor skills, but is just an average player, at best, because for some reason he doesn't have the tenacity on the field to get it done. He doesn't have a will to get it done, or he hasn't been in a circumstance where he could get it done.

The antithesis of that is you get a guy named Billy Kilmer, who couldn't throw a pass the length of this pickup truck. Yet he plays and he wins, and he has his team following him and believing in him. So, what is it that makes him so good? I think it's just the blood and guts of wanting to be the best, and wanting to beat people, and making sure that it gets done.

I think you have to be quite confident, verging on cocky. Probably being cocky. A controlled cockiness needs to be there.

SN: *I was at a game in Washington where Chris Hanburger hit Don Meredith as hard as a quarterback can get hit. I don't think Meredith ever saw him coming. And on the very next play, the last play of the game, Meredith threw a touchdown pass and won the game. How do you get up and do that?*
BJ: You have to be pretty resilient. The adrenalin is probably the greatest rush a man has ever known. I'm not saying this is right; I think it's foolish. But I played when, physically and medically, it was damn near impossible to do what I did. You can't throw the ball and have a separated shoulder. But I did. And the reason I did is I didn't know why I did. I didn't know any better, I guess.

SN: *You have to have a high pain threshold, I would think.*
BJ: I played one whole year with every rib broken. I played another year with an arm separated. I broke my nose two or three times. These are things that you just don't really worry about.

SN: *Do you take painkillers so as not to feel the pain?*
BJ: No. Adrenalin is the best painkiller in the world. There's nothing that touches adrenalin. And through those periods, I've had different ways to combat pain, through injections or what have you. I wasn't much on oral painkillers. I think it's stupid. But hey, look. I'm here to play, I want to win, and right now I have a broken rib and it hurts like a son-of-a-gun. And I don't want it to hurt. So, what do you do? You fix it. You spend half an hour before the game marking little Xs on to your rib cage with a sharpie, to tell them where it hurts the most so that when you go in there it doesn't hurt as much. But that's when you have no recourse.

But that's not the norm. Drugs and painkillers were not a necessary aspect of playing the game. As a matter of fact, it was a minor deal. I did it when I had to do it. But I never shot up joints, and I never did other things. I had a bunch of broken ribs that weren't life threatening, and they used to take X-rays between quarters to make sure it wasn't.

Being a quarterback is like not really being a player. The physical requirements are not nearly as radical as at other positions.

I was pretty intense in my training. I ran and threw the football. I was not a big weight lifter. I lifted a little bit. The bruisers have to be bruisers, the finesse guys have to be finesse guys, and quarterbacks have to have their arms in shape. So, I threw a lot. I used to go out before the game for two hours and work out. I'd run around and play catch. The ball boy would throw it to me. I'd play games—throw at the goalposts.

You have to know your receivers, but that comes pretty much naturally. I think it's a little overemphasized. Look, the guy's going to be open right here, if the defense is correct, and you get the ball to him. If he does the job, he's supposed to be right there.

SN: *With baseball pitchers, even the best sometimes, there are some days when they just don't have their stuff. With a quarterback, do you go out there, and sometimes your throwing doesn't click?*
BJ: Not really. I don't recall ever having those days. The margin of error as it relates to a baseball pitcher and as it relates to a quarterback are two different things. Your target range is a little bit bigger in football. Plus, major league batters are good. If you make a mistake, they park it. They don't just hit it, they knock it out.

SN: *Did you have any weaknesses as a quarterback?*
BJ: I didn't have many. I don't want to sound ugly, but I was probably faster than any other quarterback, and I was bigger than any other quarterback. I threw as well, if not better, than any other player. The motor skills were not weak. A weakness was probably that I was real intense.

SN: *That's a weakness?*
BJ: I think it can be, in that sometimes you can get a little carried away. And I did. I was a linebacker in a quarterback's position. I don't think that really worked against me that much, other than that it shortened my life a few years, just because of the race of the heartbeat. But I controlled it.

SN: *How important is blocking by the running backs, for protection of the quarterback?*
BJ: Blocking by the running backs is vitally important.

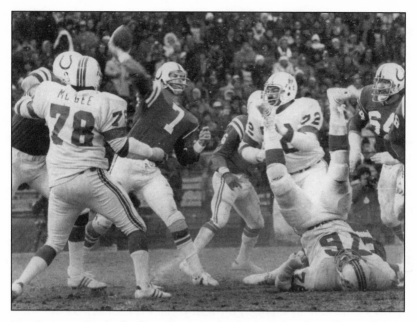

Bert Jones passing in the face of New England Patriots' rush. Courtesy of SunStaff, The Baltimore Sun.

SN: *It's an often-overlooked aspect of the game.*
BJ: It's often overlooked, except by the quarterback. (Laughs) If you have two running backs who can block and run, you can kill anybody. But if the defense can lock in on one running back and know that the other guy is a blocker, then basically you're one-armed going into a fistfight.

Having a running back who can block is really truly an asset, especially with the mobility of the linebackers in today's game. If you've got somebody who can contain a linebacker one-on-one, then it's a home run. Because that means it's one-on-one downfield, and if you can stop that guy getting to you, you win. "Please blitz me," is what I used to say. I walked up to the line of scrimmage, and I knew where I was uncovered and where my vulnerable spot was. So, I would avoid it, whether through fading, or rushing, or putting another man over there. But please blitz me, because then we have three receivers and three defensive backs, or we have five receivers and five defensive backs.

I did get sacked zillions of times; I even set an NFL record in one game, when I think I was sacked fourteen times. When that happens, you just hit them harder the next time. Or you help them up. That really aggravates them.

SN: *I want to ask you about the relationship between the quarterback and the center. Do quarterbacks function better with a center they're comfortable with? Does it make a big difference in terms of how you handle the snap, the timing of the snap?*

BJ: It makes a huge difference. Everybody takes for granted the exchanges between the center and the quarterback, when, in reality, it's not always that easy. Often you see fumbles at that time, all the way through. It's terrible to say, but I knew what Ken Mendenhall's rear end looked like probably better than his wife, simply because I spent nine years under his ass. And vice versa. He knew that when I flinched it was time to snap the ball. And he knew that most of the time I didn't know when the snap count was—so if I flinched, to give me the ball!

I don't know why, but for some reason I never remembered the snap count. So, consequently, I would generally ask my center. He would actually walk up to the line of scrimmage looking back, because he knew the question was coming because that was the last thing I was thinking about. And he would tell me at that point.

I had an excellent handling of the ball with my center, Ken Mendenhall. As a matter of fact, we never lost a snap in a regular season game in the whole time that we played. I don't think you could find that anywhere else. It's difficult, because the quarterback is always running around forgetting the snap count, and the center is always having to either pull down the line or reach down the line. Consequently, the snap is often not automatic. But with us, it pretty much was automatic.

SN: *How about longer snaps, when you were in the shotgun formation?*

BJ: We never did the shotgun. I'd like to have done the shotgun, but we did not use it much. I wish we had. It would have been a lot of fun. It would have saved my legs, too.

SN: *Did you work with other centers after Ken Mendenhall?*

BJ: I had one more center after Ken Mendenhall, Ray Donaldson, who was a great center and who became a very fine player. He came out of Georgia and was just a prince of a fellow. But it took a little time to reestablish that continuity between quarterback and center. For one thing, he couldn't remember the snap count either, and that really created a problem. Then both of us had to go to a guard to remember it. And it wasn't because either of us was stupid, because Ray Donaldson is a very intelligent and gifted athlete. Ultimately, we became very proficient in the snap. But I don't think our snap exchange and understanding and feel was ever like it was with our offensive line earlier in my career.

SN: *Is halftime a key period in a game?*
BJ: Absolutely. You have to make adjustments. I'm sure the rah-rah works on some people, but you didn't have to rah-rah me. At the professional level, needless to say, that doesn't have to occur. The only thing you had to do with me was just keep me on the floor. I was pretty jacked to go. Many times, people used to say, "You're so crazy, you've got to be on bennies." But I didn't take bennies. I said, "I'm just crazy."

SN: *What did you think about having the goalposts on the goal line, instead of ten yards back in the end zone? Some receivers used to get banged into those posts.*
BJ: Oh, yeah. I loved them on the goal line. You could hide around them. There were plays designed to use them as stationary blockers. They prevented lateral movement of the linebackers and stopped flow. It was just like the sidelines. The defense uses the sidelines as another man, like the offense did with the goalposts. Slide in between the goalposts, and you got this man blocked, and he can't get you.

SN: *Is there a big difference playing on your home field?*
BJ: I don't think there's any question. Each field is different. Playing on your home field, you know how it operates. We played on a baseball field in Baltimore. Some parts of the field were strong turf, some parts were dirt, and some parts were cinder.

SN: *Is the crowd a factor?*
BJ: If you're winning, your home-team crowd is certainly a factor, because you can hear when you need to hear. It's the opposite when you're away. The crowd drowns out audibles all the time.

SN: *So what else gives you a home-field advantage?*
BJ: Just knowing your own turf. We played on a flat field. Other fields, with artificial turf, had big crowns—meaning from the middle of the field to the sidelines, from some places there is a variation of from eight to twenty inches. They're almost two feet high in the middle, a mound that slopes off both ways to remove the water from the artificial turf. That will affect how you throw the ball. You have to know about all these variations to throw an accurate pass. If you're throwing from the middle of the field, the pass may be eighteen inches higher at the sideline than it was when you released it.

SN: *Does jet lag take something out of you physically when you're on the road?*
BJ: The break in routine when you're on the road affects you more than the jet lag. In Baltimore, you lived at home. You got up and went to practice Saturday morning. Then you got on an airplane in the afternoon, and it was a forty-minute flight to New York. It's an hour flight to Boston, an hour and a half flight to Miami, forty-five minutes to Buffalo, so what's the big deal? You drive to Washington.

SN: *Did you ever say anything on the field to disrupt an opponent's concentration?*
BJ: There are weird psychological games that you play out there, if given the opportunity. And it's rude. I had a defensive lineman who played for a very good team in Pennsylvania that won a bunch of Super Bowls. But I could make him so mad that he couldn't play. Because of that, we could do some things.

SN: *How would you make him mad?*
BJ: I'd call him an ugly name or anything. Then I had a defensive back on Buffalo whose skin I could get under. I used to do it intentionally. I'd walk up to him before the game and just really get his goat. From that point on I won, because he had lost focus of what he was going to do. I had a defensive back who got so mad and frustrated at me that just out of the blue, he just came to tackle me, just blitzed to tackle me, and didn't have anybody else covering. Well, needless to say, here we go. Let's have fun. I know that's probably tacky, but you do those things.

Finally, I couldn't stand it any longer, and I just told the guy from Buffalo, "Look. I know you think I'm crazy, but let me tell you what I've been doing for years. I just really feel you need to know."

SN: *There's a stereotype that defense is more animalistic, instinctual, sheer aggression.*
BJ: It is.

SN: *And that offense requires much more precision, coordination—people working in concert.*
BJ: Yeah. Well, all defense is is reaction—react and get the ball—whereas offense is orchestrated. Defense is a disciplined position also, but not nearly to the degree that offense is.

SN: *Is it true that the defensive unit and the offensive unit don't have much to do with each other? On your team, would you fraternize with guys on defense?*

BJ: Probably so. I had a defensive back that I was real good friends with. My defensive linemen typically were a little bit off the beaten path. Linebackers are always nuts.

SN: *You're not the first person to say that. Greg Pruitt told me that linebackers are a totally different breed. Nobody else hangs out with linebackers.*
BJ: They shouldn't. Of all the positions, linebacking is the most animalistic. It takes a little bit different kind of guy to want to go around hitting people hard with a full running head start as often as you can.

Ray Nitschke was crazy. I knew him well, very well. He played against my father [when he coached]. He was a great guy. But he came from the old school—the old, old school, which is great. I love it. I used to really love to pick on him, saying, "Ray, I really appreciate you doing what you did." And he said, "What's that?" And I told him, "Making the game liked so much that we could make all this money!" It drove him crazy. He said, "I got one more damn hit in me, one more coming, *and it may be you!*" But he was a great guy. I'd hate to see him when he used to drink. He was sober for thirty years. But back when he was a drinking man, I know he was really crazy.

SN: *Who did you room with on the road?*
BJ: I typically lived with offensive linemen.

SN: *Why? Because they were the guys who protected you?*
BJ: No. Offensive linemen and myself had more in common than any of the other players on the field. Their ideals and philosophies were similar to mine. And they're smarter than any other players. Offensive lineman is without question the most mentally trying position on the field.

SN: *How is that?*
BJ: They have to make so many spontaneous adjustments. At least, they used to. Now it's just a mass of humanity, where all we're doing is forming a wall and nobody gets past us. But back when we were playing, offensive linemen weighed 235, 240, 245. They were all small-statured people, who could run, and pull, and do the things you had to do. They had to make adjustments, because we used our offensive line.

SN: *Football is a complex game. How many sportswriters really follow what's going on?*
BJ: There are not many well-educated sports journalists who know what's going on. To give you an example, there was a tag line late in my career

where, hey, Bert Jones is not hitting the man in the seam of the zone. What a buzzword! Sounded great. Give me a break!

So I confronted the writers about it at a press conference. I said, "Look, gang, I've come to my wits' end about this. I tell you what. Y'all say that I can't hit a man in the seam of the zone." I told them, "I'm really coachable. So, please show me what I'm supposed to do." I went on, "I won't answer any other question until you all give me what it is that I'm doing wrong." Nobody said a thing. And I called each one that I'd seen had said it on the air or wrote it. You know, it gets to be a buzzword. I said, "Here's a blackboard, we're in our coaching room, let's figure it out." I told them, "Draw me up an offense and a defense, and show me what it is."

Well, I shamed one of them to come up to the blackboard. But he only got ten men on offense, and he couldn't figure out where the eleventh man went.

And then the next guy got up there. And I said, "All right, what is it that I'm doing? Show me a zone coverage, and show me where it is that you want me to hit the man in the seam." And I started going down the line. I said, "Look, gang. It's obvious that one of us is missing the point here." Finally, I got one man who finally drew up eleven men on defense. And I said, "Show me a strong zone. Can anybody in this room show me the rotation of a strong zone?" I told them, "It's obvious that you all know, because you all are saying that I can't hit a man in the seam of the zone." Not a soul could.

I told them, "The first thing I learned, the first day that I ever put on a pair of pads in my first organized football game in the seventh grade, was how to run a strong zone. I mean, the most fundamental thing on defense, and none of you in the room could do it."

Well, needless to say, the next day I wasn't getting the secondary receivers very well. So, it didn't win the war.

Still, I got along with the writers very well. The beat writers were good guys. They might get on your case, but they were on your side. They were supposed to write you as the good guys. There were a couple of them, though, who wouldn't give up the torch of the old school and John Unitas. They really despised me for being the guy who took Unitas's place. Of course, when you lose, the writers are always hostile. But it didn't bother me.

The writers lived in our locker room. They had free access all the time, which has been changed now.

SN: *Didn't the Baltimore owner, Bob Irsay, begin meddling with the team on the field? What impact did that have?*

BJ: Two years after our wildcat strike, the Colts got rid of the general manager, and the owner became involved in the games. And from that time on, the team became noncompetitive.

SN: *And the coach, McCormack, succumbed to the owner.*
BJ: Oh, absolutely. Mike McCormack became the head coach at Baltimore, and he had no backbone at all. That was unfortunate, because he was a smart man. He had been a tremendous ballplayer and had played with my father. But when he was head coach, the owner, Bob Irsay, got in the press box and started calling the plays.

McCormack was really a weak person; he was just a survivor. You have two kinds up there—the ones who are going to do something and the survivors. It reminds me of a shorebird. They're always running around next to the water, but they're never going to get in, and they're never going to get out.

The Colts didn't have a general manager at that time. Well, there was a general manager, but he was just a figurehead. Actually, you have to have some intelligence to be a figurehead. He was just a dummy.

It was quite apparent that the Colts were going downhill. They kept getting rid of players. Look, you lose John Dutton, you lose Joe Ehrmann, you lose Lydell Mitchell, you lose Joe Washington, you lose Roger Carr, you lose all those players who were anything. . . .

Of course, it was a disincentive to want to win in the NFL. What does it take to make a good football team? It takes good players, and good coaches. And good players require more money. Good coaches do also.

The problem is that every team in the NFL gets an equal share of the money from television. The Super Bowl winner and the last place team in the league make the same exact amount of money off of TV. It's different in baseball, which is why it's an entirely different system there. That's why I always said that if you wanted to establish incentive, establish incentive to win. That is, the Super Bowl team gets a whole lot more money, and the last place team gets a whole lot less.

The only difference in team income is with the concessions, what the city gives them, the luxury boxes. That's why everybody wants luxury boxes, because they get the rent on them, and that's not split.

SN: *You moved from Baltimore to the Rams. What was involved in that?*
BJ: As the Colts went downhill, I told team management I would not be back. I moved from Baltimore to the Los Angeles Rams because I walked into

the huddle, and I realized that I didn't know anybody in there. They were all just a number.

I forced the issue of being off the team, and the Colts contacted me and told me they had traded me to the Rams. Through whatever they do among the owners, they negotiated a trade. It happened right before the draft. I was doing a Nike promotion, as it related to "field generals," where we took a poster of all the NFL quarterbacks who were on the Nike staff. And I was in Los Angeles taking that photo shoot when I had to sign papers giving my approval in order to make it valid for me to be traded. It all happened quickly and efficiently.

SN: *What did you do in the off-season?*
BJ: I came back to Louisiana and worked in the lumber business that I'm in now. I started it in 1979.

SN: *How about the year with the Rams. What was it like?*
BJ: It was a great experience. It was the first time since Joe Thomas left the Colts that I felt that I was in with a franchise and organization whose intentions were to win. Carol Rosenbloom's wife, Georgia Frontiere, was the owner of the Rams, Carol having passed in a drowning accident. Her intentions were picture pure, just what I would have liked. I wanted somebody who would spend money and do the things necessary to make an NFL franchise win. The only problem was that she didn't have somebody who could figure it out. And because of that, they kind of floundered.

SN: *Was this a veteran club?*
BJ: Yeah, pretty much. It was a vets and young guys coming around.

SN: *And your receivers?*
BJ: The receivers were average, but they had a lot of the "Look at me" attitude, which I don't like. They wanted to be able to dance after they got the ball.

SN: *So, what happened that year?*
BJ: I played a very abbreviated season with the Rams, because after two games there was a strike.

SN: *Were you involved or interested in the strike issues?*
BJ: Once again, the strike was certainly to my detriment. I was sitting on top of the world as it related to a contractual agreement and salary. There wasn't

any problem there. Of course, the rest of the team was very involved in the strike.

SN: *Does having been out on strike affect your performance when you come back?*
BJ: Sure. There's no question about it. If it had not been for the strike, I would have played six or seven more years. I wouldn't have had the career-ending injury. Ten minutes into the first game after the strike ended, my center missed the nose tackle, and he got a hold of me. I had the ball in my right hand, and the nose tackle was holding me by my left arm, and he fell behind my legs. Their linebacker, Fulton Kuykendall, saw what was happening and he got to running at me. I saw him coming, but I was like a punching bag. He hit me with a long running start with a guy hanging onto me. He had about a ten-yard running start. I guessed right, and he guessed left, and his head hit me right on the chin.

That would never have happened without the strike, because never would my center have lost the nose tackle on his first step. He was just out of practice. He hadn't blocked in five or six or seven weeks.

And so I blew my jaw out, and I called time and told them to fix my jaw, to pull it back in place.

SN: *And then?*
BJ: And then I went back in and finished that game.

SN: *You played another game too?*
BJ: Yeah. But during that week I noticed a lot of loss of feeling and numbness, and weird symptoms in the left side of my body. I thought maybe I had a heart condition, but I knew that my blood pressure was about 110 over 70, and my pulse was okay.

I didn't think I was having a problem, but I asked the doctor about it, and he asked me how my neck was. I said it was a little stiff, but I had fractured my jaw, so it was the old theory that if you have a headache, hit yourself in the stomach. Don't worry about it too much. But about half way into the next game, I started noticing that I just couldn't feel a lot of my left side.

That's when the doctor said, "You need to come on to the sidelines," and they took me and did a CAT-scan. That was before MRI testing. They did that on a Monday. On Tuesday I was going out to practice for a Thursday night game against San Francisco, and they called me in and told me I had to come to the hospital.

In the hospital they put me in traction for a couple weeks. They told me, "We've found a real discrepancy here, and we need to see if we can relieve the problem." And I said, "What's that?" And they told me, "We don't know."

Then they told me I was going to need a surgical fusion. I said, "Well, let me go home first." And I got in my pickup truck and drove from Los Angeles to Ruston. I went and planted a couple hundred acres of pine trees, and I went quail hunting. Then I got on an airplane and flew back to Los Angeles. I got there at ten o'clock and was operated on the next morning.

The operation took a long time. It will, anytime you're plucking a ruptured disc from in and amongst your spinal cord. They didn't realize it was as bad as it was, or they would never have let me out of the hospital.

SN: *Steve Zabel saw Darryl Stingley get paralyzed and said it affected his play from that point.*
BJ: It was traumatic for all of us. My injury was very similar to Darryl Stingley's, but it had a different result. It's just that when I ruptured and exploded the disc in my neck and fractured the cervical, it didn't interrupt my spinal cord. It was exploded like a little hand grenade, and floating around in there everywhere, but it just didn't cut the spinal cord. I had to retire because of the injury, at age thirty-one.

SN: *Did you always know your career could be over in a minute?*
BJ: Oh, yeah. I was one of the few who knew that the swinging door was going to hit you in the butt sometime. You just didn't know when it was going to be.

SN: *How are you physically today?*
BJ: I remember being in the hospital bed, looking up at that white light, and not being able to move. And I said, "If I ever get out of here, I'm going to get in shape." So when I got out, I started running. I haven't been running lately. But I ran and finished the New York City marathon a few years ago. It was a great experience.

SN: *Nothing bothers you particularly?*
BJ: My neck is a little stiff, but I think that's more a result of talking on the telephone eight hours a day.

SN: *What was it like adjusting to retirement?*
BJ: It wasn't hard. I had seen it. My daddy had done it twice. What was so unusual about it? Of course, times had really changed. When I first went to Baltimore, I went in a car and pulled a four-by-six U-Haul trailer, with

everything I owned in it. When I came home ten years later, it took two moving vans. I had a wife and four children.

SN: *Do you still wish you were out there playing sometimes?*
BJ: For a bunch of years, being retired from football wasn't any problem, because I remembered what it had been like in the hospital. I remembered the doctor saying, "I don't know why you're not suffering some kind of permanent paralysis." And I said, "Like what?" And he said, "Like breathing, or moving from the chin down." I said, "Hello. There's a real world out there, and this is not part of it that I need right now."

But those things go away. There's still the desire to compete. I played a lot of sports, and I don't think that there's any that gives you the satisfaction that football does. Why, I don't know. I enjoy reminiscing, but I'm not like so many of them. I reminisce about the people I was with, not the things that we did.

SN: *Do you still stay in touch with any of them?*
BJ: I still have good friends from football, whose ideals are similar philosophically. Joe Washington and I still communicate. He was gone last week when I was in Baltimore, but I talked to his wife, Meadow Lark, and saw her. My wife is friends with Meadow Lark, because they're both very conscientious about their health, and how they handle things, and they like good-looking clothes, and they're both well educated. Meadow Lark has a master's degree in sociology. My wife has a master's degree in exercise physiology and a master's in physical therapy and is a physical therapist. So, like kinds attract each other. Joe and I are friends because I think we're both devoted to our wives, love our families, and enjoy having fun.

I'm still friends with Bruce Laird, a defensive back, and three or four offensive linemen. Unfortunately, it's hard to communicate and to stay in close contact if I live in Ruston, Louisiana, and have four children and a job.

I'm in the lumber business now that I set up back in 1979. I have a treating plant and a planing mill, and about fifty guys who wait for me to tell them what to do at six thirty in the morning. I ship my lumber to places like Chicago and Pennsylvania.

I also do a little outdoors TV show that's shown on ESPN, kind of for fun, not as a job. And one of the things I do for that is to go hunting and fishing around the country.

SN: *You also coach a Little League team. Tell me about that.*
BJ: I get everybody who was left out when they picked the teams. They rank the players, and when they go through eight players, I get the last one on "A,"

and when they go through "B," I get the last one, right on down the line. My team learns how to play baseball, but first, they have fun. Every player on the team wants to pitch or catch, so they all get to. Everybody gets to play the position he wants to play. I don't have any starters. Everybody plays exactly the same amount of time. We had thirteen players, and they give you jerseys numbered one through thirteen. The first game, the player with jersey number 1 bats first, and the second game the one with number 2 bats first, and number 1 goes to last up. We go straight on down the line, until the last batter bats first, and the first batter bats last. That was my batting order. And because of it, I didn't even let them keep score for the first half of the year, when they were really bad. Children shouldn't feel defeated.

Having fun is what it's all about. You know, football, baseball, basketball— it's all a game. You can have fun. But a lot of people don't believe that. It's ridiculous how seriously some people take it. That's unfortunate, to place unbelievable pressure on children to play ball. I don't want a parent aspiring to do through his kid what he didn't do in sport. So, I'm there for a wake-up call, to let these other coaches know that this is not the top of the mountain.

SN: *You see the other coaches taking it too seriously?*
BJ: Oh, it's ridiculous. I think the other coaches just think that I'm crazy, because I don't think this is the most important thing in the whole world. My team is having fun. They shouldn't do that.

SN: *How has football changed since you retired? And what do you think about those changes?*
BJ: Since I retired from the NFL in 1982, the game has changed in a lot of ways. For one thing, the pay is different. I was the highest paid player in the league for a little while, and I wasn't receiving what a second-string offensive lineman would be getting now.

The game itself has become more exciting. The players are bigger and faster. They're stronger, and they hit harder. When I played, my offensive linemen averaged 245 pounds. Today, they're 295. There is less finesse in offensive line work, and there is more throwing.

The rule changes make it easier to do certain things, which have made the game more exciting. There's less combat in the defensive secondary, where it's more cover and less hit. That makes throwing the ball easier. There are more rules, which restrict the ability of the defense to attack a quarterback. And if a quarterback is less vulnerable to injury, you can certainly have a more reckless abandon in your overall game plan.

The substitution rules also allow the game to be more specialized. You have a first-and-ten defense, you have a first-and-ten offense, you have second-and-five offense and defense, a third-and-ten offense and defense, a third-and-one offense and defense, and so on. They had that when I played, but everybody just used the same people.

There is something that I'd like to see different. I'd like them to implement rules that would not only discourage, but would stop, the "Look at me" taunting in the NFL. I think it's rude; I think it's ugly. It isn't a team concept. It's horrible. It's filtered all the way down to high school and junior high, even to grammar school. The lewd actions on the field, the taunting, and the showboating have no place in football. It removes team unity from a team sport. It's a jerk approach.

SN: *They could apply a penalty to that.*
BJ: If you do it, you should be thrown out of the game. You're out of the game, and you don't get paid.

There's nothing wrong with genuine excitement. It's great, and everybody needs to have enthusiasm if you want to play. Jump up and down when you make a touchdown, "Yes, we did it!" or throw the ball down, "Yes, we did it!" That's a natural reaction. But what you're seeing today is "Look at me," the prancing and the dancing, the pointing the fingers, and the taunting.

That's what I'd change most about the game. And I'd change the desire of the players. I would change it so they all wanted to play to win. They shouldn't care who received the acclaim. It's great to be complimented, and it's great to be rewarded, but that should not be the end and the goal. It should be a team function and a team result.

The "Look at me" attitude is one of the things that made me not miss the game as much when I had to retire. They don't play, "Hey, I want to beat you" today. It's more, "I want to go out there and show them what I am." I really despise "Look at me."

CLENDON THOMAS

RUNNING BACK, SAFETY

—Los Angeles Rams, 1958–1961
—Pittsburgh Steelers, 1962–1968

Clendon Thomas was an All-American running back who played on two national championship teams at the University of Oklahoma, in 1955 and 1956, coached by the legendary Bud Wilkinson. These teams compiled a winning streak that had reached an astounding forty-seven games when it was finally broken in 1957. In 1956, Thomas led the nation in scoring. He provides an in-depth analysis of Bud Wilkinson as a coach and recruiter. Thomas was strongly influenced by his father, an excellent industrial league pitcher for Oklahoma City baseball teams, who coached him as a child.

Thomas was the number-two draft choice of the Los Angeles Rams in 1957 and played eleven years in the National Football League, for the Rams and Pittsburgh Steelers. Early in his pro career he caught a pass from Rams quarterback Bill Wade that, at the time, was the record for the longest pass reception in the Los Angeles Coliseum. He was converted to safety, where he spent most of his pro career. Thomas compares the "altogether different" strong and free safety positions. He describes the experience of covering such outstanding receivers as Raymond Berry, Gary Collins, Paul Warfield, Mike Ditka, and Jackie Smith and of playing behind talented defensive linemen like Ernie Stautner and

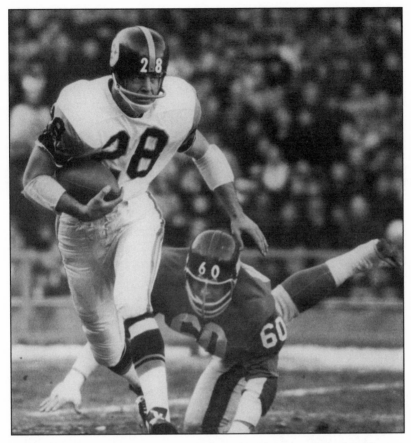

Clendon Thomas (28) with the Pittsburgh Steelers. Courtesy of Clendon Thomas.

Big Daddy Lipscomb. He believes that Lipscomb's 1962 death of a drug overdose was not an accident, but murder.

Thomas also discusses how NFL players negotiated contracts in the late 1950s and 1960s, and he compares football on the field in that era with the contemporary game.

STEPHEN NORWOOD: *Let me begin by asking you about your background. When and where were you born?*
CLENDON THOMAS: I was born in Oklahoma City in 1935. My dad worked for Cities Service Oil Company, in the oil field.

Roy Thomas, Clendon's father, pitching for the Cities Service Oil Company industrial league baseball team, Oklahoma City. Courtesy of Clendon Thomas.

SN: *How did you get interested in football?*
CT: I grew up playing baseball. Football wasn't even in my thoughts. There was no Little League football. I became involved with baseball through my father, who was an excellent player and loved the game. I played YMCA baseball, which came along when I was twelve or thirteen and was the only organized activity to do in the summer. My father coached me.

There were a lot of commercial league teams in Oklahoma City, sponsored by the oil companies and packing plants, and my dad played on them up through the time I was in high school. He was good enough that even when he was in his forties, the twenty-year-olds were calling him to come pitch for them. I'm convinced my father could have pitched in the big leagues.

SN: *Did he have any aspirations ever to play professionally?*
CT: Yes. At one time he was approached by the New York Giants, back when the starting pay was not enough to make a living playing ball. He was married

by then and couldn't consider it. After I joined the Rams, I took him out to Los Angeles to watch the World Series, when Don Drysdale and Sandy Koufax were there. He sat in the stands for a while, and then he said, "I always wondered if I could have played in the big leagues, and now I know." He knew he could have, and I knew he could have. He could throw a ball so hard. His fastball had a huge jump at the plate. I could barely catch him in high school, and I was a pretty decent player. When I was eighteen years old, and ran a 21.2-second 220-yard dash, in order to keep this God-given gift in perspective, he took his shoes off and outran me in front of my friends.

Like most kids, I dreamed of playing big league baseball. I wanted to play in Yankee Stadium. I wanted to stand on the left side of home plate and hit one like Babe Ruth had done.

SN: *You followed major league baseball as a kid?*
CT: Oh, yeah. I wanted to play in Wrigley Field, Forbes Field, Tiger Stadium, Comiskey Park, and the other major league parks. And I did get to play in them—only I played football there, not baseball!

My father taught me the fundamentals of baseball, and we hunted together. He was a great guy to be around.

SN: *What position did you play?*
CT: He was a pitcher. He wouldn't let me pitch as a youngster, because I had a good arm and he wanted me to save it. So, I played in the infield and outfield, and caught a little bit, in the YMCA league and in high school. I learned to be competitive, and I disliked losing.

SN: *Did he talk about sports, major league baseball, with you?*
CT: Sure. My father and I used to go watch the Oklahoma City Indians together, the minor league baseball team, back when they had Al Rosen and some other quality players who eventually went up to the majors.

SN: *Pro football wasn't as popular in the 1940s as baseball. Did you follow pro football?*
CT: Pro football wasn't popular until television came along in the 1950s. I didn't begin to watch pro football until I was in college.

SN: *So, at this point it's just baseball.*
CT: Back then we followed baseball on the radio.

SN: *You did play high school football. How did your high school coaches influence your development as a player?*

CT: I benefited greatly as an athlete from having been coached in high school by two former professional players. My football coach, at Southeast High School in Oklahoma City, was George Franck, who had played in the NFL for the New York Giants. He came to Southeast from the service and had been a Marine pilot. Cecil Shaw, my basketball coach, had played that sport professionally in San Francisco. I had only known Mr. Franck a week, when he said something that had a lasting effect on me. I was a six foot two, 155-pound freshman, just a beanpole, practicing football against some juniors and seniors. Mr. Franck had watched me for about a week, when he called me aside. And he said, "Clendon, would you like to play professional football some day? If you don't get hurt, you will." I thought about what he said that day a thousand times. He didn't ask me if I'd like to play for Oklahoma or Oklahoma State. After watching me practice for one week, he told me if I would work hard enough and wanted it enough, I had the talent to play professional football some day.

It really was fortunate for me that I was coached in high school by experienced, well-educated professionals, because they had insights and knew things that most coaches, even at the college level, weren't privileged to know. The instruction I got from George Franck in football and Cecil Shaw in basketball was exceptional. It definitely helped me later on in my career, because I learned the good habits of winners right off the bat. For example, I was never a fumbler in the pros. Even today, there's not much written, and most coaches give poor advice, on how to keep from fumbling. But Mr. Franck knew the fundamental technique of why you did and why you didn't.

SN: *What was the college recruiting process like? How did you end up at Oklahoma?*

CT: I was an All-State high school football player, but because I played for a small school with a losing record, not many colleges were interested in recruiting me. The University of Tulsa finally made an offer, and Central State University in Edmond, Oklahoma, tried to get me. Oklahoma State said I could walk on, but didn't offer a scholarship.

Fortunately, Hal Mix, a reporter for the *Daily Oklahoman*, the Oklahoma City newspaper, got the University of Oklahoma interested in me. He wasn't an assigned sportswriter. On occasion he filled in for the designated writers when they had scheduling conflicts. He was just a great guy, a fan, who watched me play at Southeast High School and told the coaches at Oklahoma about me, again and again. He made them interested in me. He got Pop Ivy, one of the Oklahoma coaches, to come to my high school and see me play. Still, I had the feeling that I was one of the last players Oklahoma recruited.

SN: *Bud Wilkinson was Oklahoma's head coach. What were your impressions of him when you came to Oklahoma?*

CT: Coach Wilkinson personally came to my home and recruited me to come to the University of Oklahoma on a football scholarship. I don't know how he ever found time. I've asked a lot of my former teammates that question over the years. Did he come to your house as well? Did he come and sit in your front room and discuss the opportunity with your family and make a commitment to you? In most instances, the answer was yes. How a man that busy could go to thirty or forty kids' homes, and still manage to get everything done, is amazing. But Coach Wilkinson did come to my house, and he told my parents what he expected of me in football and what he expected of me in class. He explained what the rewards would be, if I did certain things. He laid all that out, and then he kept his word to the *n*th degree.

In my life, I've met a handful of men who if they said they'd do something, they'd do it. Art Rooney, the owner of the Pittsburgh Steelers, was one of them. Coach Wilkinson was one of them. And my dad kept his word. You could write it down in stone.

For example, Coach Wilkinson made sure a player kept his scholarship if he got hurt. Most players are painfully aware of the fact that they only have value to the university if they perform. Gerald McPhail hurt his back when he was a junior. And Coach Wilkinson called him in and told him he didn't want him to play anymore, because he might suffer serious injury. He told him he'd arrange a part-time job around the chow hall, just to let him keep his scholarship. Coach Wilkinson was man enough to walk in and say, "I don't want you to cause permanent damage. Don't worry about it. You're still on scholarship until you graduate."

Today, it's different. Many kids are recruited falsely. Universities hang this big, wonderful dream out in front of you. But in reality, if you can't cut it, you're not going to stay, because you're too expensive. But when Coach Wilkinson committed to a scholarship, he kept his word.

SN: *Were you recruited as a running back?*

CT: We played both offense and defense in high school and college, but Coach Wilkinson never recruited anyone who couldn't play defense. He was going to build a team that could play defense. Then he'd find out if you could play offense. The simple fact is that if your opponents can't score, they can't win. You should be able to get twenty-one points out of your offensive unit, so if you can hold the other side to fourteen points, you win. It's just that simple.

I was a big, fast kid. And if you're big and fast and you're willing to hit somebody, you can be taught to play defense.

SN: *What position did you play on defense at Oklahoma?*
CT: I played a number of positions on defense as a professional, because I was big enough. But I wound up as a defensive safety at Oklahoma.

SN: *What was freshman year like? You didn't play very many games?*
CT: Freshman year, 1954, was pretty boring; it was a learning period spent doing drills. You learned all the plays, so that when you walked out as a sophomore, you were ready. You played both ways, so you had to learn offense and defense.

We didn't scrimmage much because the coaches were concerned about injuries, and there's nothing more dangerous than an intrasquad scrimmage. When I watch you move everyday, and run your patterns, and get used to your habits, I can really nail you. I can be over exactly where you're going to be, and I can meet you and kill you. Plus, on any team, there are always cases of guys who don't like each other, and that animosity will come out in a scrimmage. One player wants to teach another a lesson or get even, and all he has to do is step in the place he's coming and put a forearm up against his chin. When you play another team, you usually don't have those hidden agendas. You just play to win.

When I was with the Pittsburgh Steelers, Bill Austin ruined our ball team for the year by ordering an intrasquad scrimmage. When he assumed the head coaching position, he said, "I've heard about this great defensive team you have at Pittsburgh. I want to see it."

That day, Bill Saul, our middle linebacker, tore his knee up, Ken Kortes, our left defensive tackle, broke his leg, and three backs went to the hospital with brain concussions. It was idiocy. And it was almost idiocy on our part to do it, because we were the ones dealing out the punishment to each other. We didn't have any replacements for the guys we lost. It really hurt us that year. And all because a coach said, "I want to see it."

SN: *Was Port Robertson in charge of the academic side for the Oklahoma foot-ball program then? Can you describe his approach?*
CT: Port Robertson was the coach at Oklahoma who monitored whether you were in class and how you were doing. He made it clear from the beginning

that you were going to be disciplined. There wasn't all this Mickey Mouse stuff. He said, "If you miss class, you're going to run stadium steps." No questions. "You're going to get up at dawn." And we were going to make our beds. He said he'd come in and look at our rooms, and if he didn't like the way the room looked, we were going to run stadium steps. He meant it. And he had very little trouble with the guys. He ruled with an iron fist.

SN: *Did Oklahoma recruit mostly from in state at that time?*
CT: Oklahoma didn't recruit nationally at that time. Most of the players were from Texas and Oklahoma. Today, I don't think a coach could survive who didn't recruit from all over the place.

We had such phenomenal talent on the varsity at Oklahoma that Coach Wilkinson introduced what they called alternate squads, that is, two units that each played about half the game, both offense and defense. It was the start of that fast break offense where we began to see whether we could wear people out. Your unit would stay in if you were on a scoring drive, and it would stay in if you were holding the other side on defense. But basically, we played seven and a half minutes, and then we'd come out and the other unit would go in.

SN: *Sophomore year you were with the varsity unit. How did that differ from freshman football? Was that a big jump?*
CT: It was a drastic change, a big step up, but I did well. I scored my first touchdown against Pitt. It was all over after that. It was like, now I know I can. Like my dad's comment at the World Series, "I always wondered. Now I know." Still, I never dreamed that the next year, 1956, I'd lead the nation in scoring.

I played on two national championship teams at Oklahoma, in 1955 and 1956. The best team we had was that 1956 team, my junior year, which had depth everywhere. Ankle deep, just player after player sitting there who could all come up and start. We were just loaded with guys who went on up to pro ball.

SN: *Who was on those teams?*
CT: We had Tommy McDonald, who played with the Philadelphia Eagles; Jimmy Harris, who played for the Rams; Billy Pricer, who played for the Baltimore Colts; Jerry Tubbs, who played for the Dallas Cowboys; Bill Krisher, who played for the Pittsburgh Steelers; and Bob Harrison and David Baker, who both played for the San Francisco 49ers. Many others played in the Canadian Football League. We had so much depth that our third unit had guys like Prentice Gautt, who played for the St. Louis Cardinals, and Bobby Boyd, who went to the Baltimore Colts.

SN: *How would you describe Bud Wilkinson's coaching style?*
CT: Coach Wilkinson was unlike any other coach I ever had; I never saw another one with his interpersonal skills. I played for Sid Gillman, a marvelous coach for the Los Angeles Rams, and I played for Buddy Parker, who won the title with Detroit and was my coach with the Pittsburgh Steelers. Buddy Parker was a brilliant guy and a good coach. And I had some other coaches mixed in there. Those guys were all terrific coaches. But Coach Wilkinson was unique. I never saw him correct one of his assistant coaches on the field, in front of players. He would cover for them. Now, whether or not he talked to them or corrected them in the locker room afterward, I don't know. He understood that people are human and will make mistakes on occasion. This created intense loyalty and support from his staff and pride, admiration, and respect from his players.

Coach Wilkinson would on occasion also talk to each of his players individually for a minute or two during practice. It was usually a pump-up deal, where he's patting you on the back, and really encouraging you. But sometimes it was to redirect your attitude.

When you messed up, he didn't get frustrated or angry with you. One day, he caught me loafing in practice, and he called me over. He did that because that way the other players didn't know whether you were getting chewed out, or whether he was telling you what a great job you were doing, or what. He got me over, and he asked me, "Are you having trouble in class? Are you having any trouble at home? I noticed you're not having a good practice. Is there anything wrong? Are you having girl trouble? Are you having grade trouble? Can I help you?" Well, he and I both knew that I wasn't having any trouble. I was just loafing. All I could do was answer, "No, I'm not having all this trouble." And he said, "Well, let's go. Let's have a good practice." I started hustling after that, and I had a good practice. I don't know of any other coach who would have handled it like that.

SN: *He would talk to his players individually. Did the players see him as approachable?*
CT: Not like his assistant coaches. He always kept his distance to a point. I think he did that intentionally. It was a coaching technique. Too much familiarity and the first thing a kid will do is begin to take advantage. He understood all those dynamics, and never let us get that close. It was always, "Mr. Wilkinson," it was always, "Coach." Even to this day, I always refer to him as "Coach" or "Mr. Wilkinson." Even at my age, I still have that kind of respect for the man.

SN: *If you were losing, did he ever become agitated?*
CT: Well, you've got to understand, we didn't lose. (Laughs)

SN: *You worked with the assistant coaches at Oklahoma more directly than with the head coach?*
CT: Oh, yeah.

SN: *If you're playing both offense and defense, you're working with several.*
CT: Well, they all had their function. Coach Wilkinson had a talented group of assistant coaches, and part of his method for preparing for a game was to get them all together and have each of them put an offensive and a defensive game plan on the board. Every coach that worked for him put a game plan up. I don't know when they got together, but they'd be ready when we walked on the field. He also asked each assistant coach to bring in one of those crazy plays that we always tried. Somebody was always coming up with a Statue of Liberty, or a Swinging Gate, or some surprise play that always worked. What was amazing about Coach Wilkinson was that his ego never got in the way. If Pete Eliott had a better game plan than his, he'd use Pete's. Or if he liked certain parts, he'd use them.

That was a way for Coach Wilkinson to let his assistants know they were important. It was a key ingredient in his success. Of course, they were phenomenal people to begin with. Pete Eliott went on to do a great job coaching at Illinois, and Pop Ivy wound up coaching with the New York Giants. And Sam Lyle in the Canadian Football League, and he was probably as good a recruiter as anyone ever.

SN: *You went to bowl games?*
CT: We went to two Orange Bowls, in 1955 and 1957. We could only go to a bowl game every other year, due to some rule.

SN: *How did you prepare for them?*
CT: Coach Wilkinson put us through the hardest workouts you could imagine. They killed us. My first bowl game, we had taken a bus to our hotel, the Bal Harbor, and there was a wide and long traffic island in the middle of the street there. Wilkinson told us to put our shorts and shoes on, meet out on that traffic island, and we were going to loosen up. We'd been home for Christmas for a few days, so we hadn't practiced. He had us go out on that traffic island, and he ran us for what seemed like eternity. We were gasping

Clendon Thomas (35) at the University of Oklahoma. Courtesy of Clendon Thomas.

for breath. We were looking at each other, asking, "What on Earth is going on?" And then Wilkinson called us up, and he said, "I owe it to you, and I owe it to the university, and I owe it to the state of Oklahoma to get you ready for this ball game. And if you do what I ask you to do this week, you're not ever going to have any bad memories, and you'll win." I've often reflected on what he said that day, and the intense work and pain we went through. Most fans think of going to bowl games as a reward, a vacation. It's not. That week was the hardest workout in my life. It was worse than two-a-days, because it was at the end of the year. You've had a long year.

SN: *Was your father interested in your going into the NFL? Did he talk to you about it?*
CT: No, we didn't talk about it. I did enjoy my family attending the bowl games. My mother had initially not liked football. Mothers are all alike—they don't want you to get hurt. By that time my mother had become a pretty good fan, but she was as concerned about me hurting someone else as getting hurt.

My senior year, the team voted not to go to the Orange Bowl, but Coach Wilkinson overturned our decision. It didn't take a Rhodes scholar to figure out why we didn't want to go. We didn't want to go through those workouts again.

SN: *Wouldn't you get national television coverage?*
CT: I could care less. Nobody in his right mind would want to go through that. I don't know where anybody ever thought that Wilkinson was this nice guy. He was nice off the field. I would not trade places with anyone for my exposure and bowl experiences.

SN: *But you do think that conditioning does make a difference.*
CT: Of course, physical conditioning makes a big difference, and we did win both bowl games, against Maryland and Duke. You can take great athletes and let them get out of shape, not be mentally prepared, and they are not going to win.

SN: *Did you do weight training at Oklahoma?*
CT: We didn't do weight training in the 1950s. The theory then was that lifting weights would tie you up to the point of making you ineffective. And I think if you did lift wrong, that was a possibility. Today, weight training is heavily emphasized, and it makes a difference in how well you perform. If you can pump 350 or 400 pounds, you can handle a pretty good-sized man in front of you. And lifting also makes you faster. Rocky Bleier, whom I played with at Pittsburgh, wouldn't have been the player he was without weights. He was slow when he came into the NFL. He ran only a 4.7 forty-yard dash. Then he went to Vietnam and was wounded, and his rehabilitation, which involved weights, made him not only stronger but faster. He was able to do a 4.5 forty-yard dash, which took him from ordinary to excellent.

Weight rooms didn't come into vogue in the NFL until about the middle of my career, when I was with Pittsburgh. The Rams didn't have one when I came into the league. Some players had their own free weights, but nothing special. I toyed with weights a little bit, and it helped me toward the end of my career, even the small amount that I did. I never did get really serious about it. And it was probably wise at this stage of my career, because if you don't use safe equipment and the proper procedure, you can mess yourself up.

SN: *What kind of mental preparation did Coach Wilkinson emphasize? Did you do a lot of film sessions and analysis of different plays? Did he repeat the film if mistakes had been made the previous week?*

CT: Mental preparation is important, too. I don't think you can win with dummies. You don't have to be a Rhodes scholar, because I think through repetition and the right attitude you can learn. College offenses are pretty simple, but you still have to practice plays over and over again to do them consistently correctly in games. There's also some memory work involved. Most teams used live colors to indicate what the play would be on an automatic at the line of scrimmage. If the live color is red, and the call is "red 22," it means the play is going to be 22. If the call was "blue 22" or "yellow 22," you didn't pay any attention to it. And you've got a list of numbers, maybe 1 to 100, on passes—red 12 or red 28 or red 36 are all different pass plays. So, you have to memorize those and think quickly at the line of scrimmage. Repetition and the will to study allow your team to make instant changes without errors. This effort can be the difference between winning and losing.

Coach Wilkinson always emphasized how important it was not to make mistakes. I remember one time he asked us if it would be all right for a player to make three or four mistakes in a game. And of course, we all answered no. Then he asked us, "How about two mistakes?" Again, most answered no. Then he said, "How many of you people think it's okay to make one mistake in a ball game?" Well, we all held our hand up. But he explained to us why that was unacceptable. If a team makes three mistakes in a game, it will generally get beat. You only get the ball thirteen times. And if you fumble it twice, and if you have a pass intercepted, if you make three mistakes, you'll generally lose, certainly in key ball games against good talent. That's enough to beat you. He made his point, you can never make a mistake. There are eleven guys on the field—eleven guys on offense, and eleven guys on defense. If each player makes just one mistake, that's twenty-two mistakes! He just rammed that through our heads.

Wilkinson emphasized particularly how important it was for us to stick our noses in the playbook, because mental mistakes are the ones that do the most damage. You can make a physical mistake and make up for it by being aggressive. If you get knocked down, you can get up and get another guy. You can make up for it by hustle, by second effort. But you're not allowed the luxury of a mental mistake.

SN: *How would he deal with that in a film session?*
CT: He pointed out our mistakes but he didn't dwell on them, because the player would usually know he had screwed up. "Clendon, you know what you're supposed to do here." "Yes, sir." Sometimes defensive teams could really get you confused, and there were legitimate reasons why you blocked the wrong guy. But if you didn't know what to do or who to hit, you'd better find

out and adjust. Coach Wilkinson focused on effort; we always had confidence the adjustments would be made. If you got the wrong guy, you better be getting somebody on the ground. He wouldn't tolerate lack of effort.

Coach Wilkinson really loved second effort. One time Billy Pricer, on a single play, took two or three guys down at the line of scrimmage. Then he got up and got somebody else and got up and got somebody else. When the play was over, he had taken seven guys to the ground. Wilkinson loved that play. He must have run that thing on film for us thirteen times, back and forth—the most reruns ever.

The first thing you know, he's got everybody on that ball team trying. It was obvious that if you did something special—not just what you were supposed to do, but if you did something extra—you were going to be pointed out in those film sessions. You play for lots of reasons, one is self-satisfaction, but it is a team sport, and the things we accomplished were as a unit or as a family. I wanted the respect of my peers, and I think everybody else was the same way.

That was the reward, for one of my teammates to come pat me on the back and say, "You had a great day." I certainly wasn't out there for money. I really wasn't out there to read my name in the newspaper. I rarely read the sports page all the time I was in college.

Coach Wilkinson even gave the third unit an important role in preparing for games by having them run our opponents' plays in practice. They would be the University of Texas, and they'd have charts of Texas's plays, and they would run those plays at us to get us ready. They gave us a picture of what Texas did. The way their line split. The ability to emulate these teams was an important contribution. They did a great job.

SN: *Did you expect to play in the NFL?*
CT: Even though I was on two national championship teams at Oklahoma, I really hadn't thought much about playing professional football.

SN: *Did Coach Wilkinson ever talk to you about playing professionally?*
CT: No. I never discussed it with any of the assistant coaches either. And I didn't talk about it with my father. I did have some inquiries from NFL clubs, beginning in my junior year. But I was in engineering school at Oklahoma and was primarily thinking about playing college ball and then becoming an engineer. Of course, you weren't talking about money in those days. Even at the very best, when I finished college in 1957, professional football wasn't serious money.

By draft time, though, having gotten inquiries from NFL teams, I thought it might be fun to go into the pros. I really wanted to know if I could do it.

My dad had always wanted to know if he could play big league baseball. I don't think I would have wanted to go through life not knowing if I could or couldn't, given the opportunity.

SN: *There must have been several players on your team at Oklahoma who got drafted.*
CT: There were several of my teammates from Oklahoma who had already gone into the NFL, whom I had talked to. Bill Pricer was with the Baltimore Colts, and Jimmy Harris was playing defensive back with the Rams, and there were others.

SN: *Did they come back to Oklahoma after they'd been in the NFL and talk about what it was like?*
CT: Sure. But no one can ever tell you what it's like until you've experienced it first-hand.

SN: *For some guys, draft day is a very tense time, when the family gathers by the telephone and you try to speculate which team it's going to be.*
CT: Although I had had some inquiries from NFL teams, I didn't have a clue as to which one would draft me.

SN: *Were you interested in going to a particular team, or did you pretty much not care?*
CT: Being from Oklahoma and not having an NFL team in this part of the country, it didn't matter much to me where I went. I did have some preferences, including the Rams, so I was pleased when they drafted me as their second choice.

SN: *What was negotiating with the Rams like?*
CT: Negotiating with them was pretty simple, because salaries were basically standardized by position. Today there are about twenty teams, so I would have been a first-round draft choice now, because there were only twelve teams in 1957. I signed a two-year, no-cut contract for $24,000, which was a very good salary in those days. When you graduated from college then, a pretty good job paid $8000. Pete Rozelle was the Rams' general manager, before he became commissioner of the NFL. I negotiated pretty hard with Pete to get the contract I signed for. It took me about an hour.

SN: *Was there a bonus?*
CT: I got a little bonus—a 1957 Chevy. No incentives. I understood from
Pete Rozelle that I signed a better contract than the one they gave to their
number-one draft choice, Jim Phillips.

SN: *You played in the Chicago All-Star game before you went to the Rams'*
training camp. What was that like?
CT: I stepped in a divot in the ground running a punt back against Detroit
and cracked a bone in my left leg. I hadn't suffered any serious injury in college, and this one healed in about six weeks. But because of the injury, I
missed training camp.

SN: *Were you worried that this might hurt your chances?*
CT: No, because it wasn't a serious injury.

SN: *How did the veterans treat the rookies?*
CT: The veterans do sometimes test the rookies on the field to find out
whether they have what it takes to stick. I remember when I was at Pittsburgh,
later in my career, I tested a rookie running back named Rooster Fleming. The
first day he was out there, he ran a sweep, and I was playing safety, and I just
killed him. I just took the air out of him. I was on top of him, and he was gasping for breath. It may sound horrible, but I did it. I just wanted to see what he
was made of. When he finally got his breath, he said, "Damn, Mr. Thomas."
That's all he said. And he went back to the huddle. I couldn't help but break
out laughing. He had watched me play in Pittsburgh and knew my name. The
very next play, he came right back at me. I walked over to our defensive coach,
Torgy Torgeson, and I said, "I don't know anything about the kid, but I can tell
you one thing, he's tough. I gave him a shot that would take anybody down,
and he came back for more." He had earned my instant respect.
   The next day, Rooster became the team favorite when we were going
through the ritual of having the rookies stand up and sing their school fight
songs. They'd have to stand on top of the table or on their chair and put
their hand over their heart and sing. And you really had to make them do it,
because most of them couldn't sing. We had kids from Notre Dame and Ohio
State, and they sang, and they were terrible. One or two of them didn't even
know all the words. You knew these guys were going to have trouble with
plays. We'd throw biscuits at them and boo. Then we asked Rooster to get up.
He'd only been with us for two days, and nobody knew where he'd come
from. He jumped up, climbed on top of a table, stuck his hand over his heart,

and you could have heard him for five miles. He let out this song, "On the banks of the Monongahela, . . . on high stands my alma mater, Gladstone Junior High." That's as far as he'd gone. At least that was his story. He was this city kid that had come out of Pittsburgh, and Mr. Rooney had let him come try out. He was a gem, a really tough kid. We did end up cutting him, but he went up to Canada and played four or five years there. He had what it took, and I respected him for making the most of his God-given talent.

SN: *When you recovered from the injury, did you start?*
CT: Yes, after my broken bone healed, the Rams started me as a running back. By that time, somebody had gotten hurt, and a couple of guys had been cut, and I just replaced one of the injured guys. I caught a pass from Bill Wade, our quarterback, which I was told was the NFL record for longest pass reception in the Coliseum. I think it was seventy-nine yards. I do remember the ball going up into the lights, into the dark, and down out of the lights.

But I didn't stay on offense long. I scored a few times. And it was interesting, because I could play offense in the NFL. But we had a whole group of veteran running backs on the Rams, including Jon Arnett and Joe Marconi.

I switched over to defense that year in part because of a conversation I had with Les Richter, our middle linebacker. Les played middle linebacker for thirteen years for the Rams. One evening, he took me to dinner and he told me, "Rook, you're big and you're fast, and you'll hit people. You get your rear end off that offensive team and over on that defensive team. You won't read your name in the papers much, but you'll be able to play ten or twelve years before retiring." He said, "If you play defense, you'll be able to walk out of here. Otherwise, you're going to get carried out of the tunnel after two or three years, all broken up."

SN: *So, it was your choice to switch to defense?*
CT: Yes. So, I became the free safety and played that position for a lot of years. When I began to slow down a little bit, I moved over to strong safety.

Les was right about what he said. It's a rough game in the pros, and running backs, even today, generally don't last long—usually not more than three to five years. There are exceptions, but it's rough to be a survivor. Players do not want to cripple anyone, but they roll into you and there are serious injuries.

SN: *Were you ever seriously hurt playing in the NFL?*
CT: I was able to get through my NFL career without suffering any really serious injury. I busted some ribs in Philadelphia, where I got flipped in the

air and a guy stuck his headgear in my back, and I had to miss a couple of games. And you get the normal bumps, bruises, and knocks. But I was very fortunate. I never had anything serious in all the years I played pro ball.

SN: *Was there much dirty play in the NFL?*
CT: No, because it all gets straightened out. Most is just players losing their poise. If somebody does something wrong, the referees tend to look the other way and let you correct it.

SN: *If a guy develops a reputation for being dirty, there'll be retaliation.*
CT: You can get him. You can hurt him. NFL players have the physical ability to hurt you, and they despise dirty play.

The players knew the fine line between what was legitimate and what was dirty. For example, some holding went on all the time, but there was a point where it crossed the line and became dirty. To be sure, some of the rookies were dumb enough to let you hold and not do something about it. I used to laugh—it would get funny. But the veteran players knew where that line was. It's not like in today's pro basketball. I have a lot of trouble watching, because there's so much pushing, banging, and slamming going on all the time that I don't know what a foul is.

SN: *How did playing defense in the NFL differ from playing defense in college?*
CT: I had played safety on defense at Oklahoma and had good coaches. But playing in the NFL was a lot different, in that they threw a lot more—more, in fact, as the years went by—and you needed complex multiple defenses. You see every play imaginable in the pros. Also, in college we had played a lot of zone, and you don't have that luxury in the pros. You can only cover man to man with good athletes. But the techniques of using reads in the line and backfield were consistent with what I had done in college. Of course, in the pros you played only offense or only defense, not both, so you were able to concentrate on becoming more adept at a particular position.

SN: *How would you compare playing free safety and strong safety?*
CT: They're altogether different positions. It was a lot easier for me to play free safety than strong safety. At strong safety, you've got to be willing to force the line of scrimmage. You're playing tight ends who weigh 240 pounds or more, that are stronger than you are. And you've got to be willing to come in and meet two guards and a tackle pulling. You can't back away. You've just got to go in and take one or two of them down.

Some of those big, tough fullbacks, like Jim Taylor, Joe Marconi, and Alan Ameche, were really tough to go up against. I didn't mind the halfbacks. But those big guys would hurt you. They had no problem taking a divot or two out of your face.

Jim Brown was a different kind of fullback. It didn't beat you up to play against him. He used his speed effectively. Most people didn't realize it, but he could run a 4.4 or less forty-yard dash. That's as fast as anybody.

S N : *He combined straight-ahead power with the moves of someone much lighter.*
CT: If you go back and look over the films on the Cleveland Browns, you'll see that Jim Brown was never caught from behind. Bobby Mitchell was Big Ten sprint champion, and Jim Brown could outrun him. They were unbelievable together. But we heard Mitchell couldn't handle it, because Jim was so big and fast. Psychologically, he just had trouble handling that.

S N : *Being in Jim Brown's shadow?*
CT: Yes. But my goodness! I wouldn't ever have broken up that combination. They were so dangerous. And Cleveland also had Gary Collins and Paul Warfield. Warfield, Collins, and those two guys—Jimminy Christmas! Why would you ever trade Bobby Mitchell away? You couldn't catch him.

At strong safety, you've got to be a good tackler. You're key support, because if they cave your linebackers in, if you're not in there stopping it up, then they're down to a 200-pound or a 185-pound cornerback. I was a good tackler, and I think fairly effective at strong safety. I played it a lot of years. But at the end of my career I was one-tenth of a second slower than when I started, and that made the difference. It was time for me to stop.

S N : *What, specifically, is involved in playing free safety?*
CT: Free safety was a great position, particularly when I was at Pittsburgh and playing behind guys like Big Daddy Lipscomb, Myron Pottios, Ernie Stautner, and John Reger. Not many people came through those guys, so I didn't have to tackle much. They'd stop 'em at the line of scrimmage. So, I was free to roam and look for balls. In 1963 I came in second in the NFL in interceptions. And it was because of the pressure I was getting from up front.

At free safety or any position, playing smart is essential. You've got to play with your head. That's how I lasted as long as I did. As years go by, you learn to play smarter and eliminate mistakes.

One of the first things you learn to do is expand your field of vision. You don't just watch one person. You watch two or three guys on the line and two or three guys in the backfield. And the longer you play, the more people you pick up. I want to know not only what they do—whether they stand up and block or pull and block—but I want to know what direction they're going. If they go certain directions that means my end is going to run in a certain direction, he's going to run an in-move or an out-move, and I'm going to take an inside shoulder or an outside shoulder when I first position myself. You know the minute the line moves whether it's going to be a run or a pass. Simple basics.

The first step I take can get me beat. If I take an outside shoulder and the receiver is going to run an inside move, then I've given away an advantage the minute I lined up on him. The first step I took, I helped him beat me. But if I can pick up on a running back and that running back does a flare pattern or runs wide, if I've done my homework, I know my end's going to run an inside move. So, immediately, when I take my first step, I take his inside shoulder away from him. If I can maintain that position the rest of the time, I've got him beat.

It doesn't always work, because the other team knows what you're keying off of after they watch you a little while, and they try to counter key in a game. When we had some of our bright teams, we could come off the field and say, "Hey, guys, they went counter-key on us five times. They know what we're reading, so they're going to do just the opposite." So we would adjust. Many times this meant throwing the week's preparation out the window. But if you got a bunch of bright guys on your team, you are able to adjust. That was fun, playing with guys who were that smart. When I was with the Steelers, Brady Keys, Johnny Sample, and Dick Haley made it look easy.

Veteran linebackers wouldn't play with a rookie defensive back behind them. They depended on the defensive back to call crack blocks, where they could get hurt. Literally go to the hospital. You let a guy come down the line and hit the linebacker in the back, and you don't yell, "Crack!" the linebacker is in big trouble. These blocks are no longer legal. The defensive back can see the guy coming, and the linebacker can't, since he's meeting the guard coming out of the line. I yell, "Crack!" and he turns and takes the guy on. He'll forget that guard coming at him, and he'll turn and protect himself. Or he'll throw his right arm down to protect his knee.

That's the reason you put rookie linebackers and rookie defensive backs all together. If a veteran linebacker plays in front of a rookie, he doesn't depend on him to call a crack block. He'll just ignore those guards and tackles coming, and he'll watch himself. He'll never trust a rookie, because with one mistake his career is over.

SN: *Do you think pro football was a rougher game when you played it than it is today?*
CT: The game was rougher when I played in that they used to crack block more than they do now and because they could pick. You could come down and pick people. An end could just go run over a defensive back who was covering another guy and didn't see the end coming. Picks were always semi-illegal, but they allowed a lot of it. It's kind of like some of the pushing and shoving in basketball today.

SN: *Who was the best pass receiver that you covered? The toughest guy to cover?*
CT: That's tough. There's a group of great ones, like Pete Retzlaff of the Eagles and Ray Berry of the Colts. Ray Berry was a great receiver, but Ray was outside, and most of the guys I covered came inside. There were a lot of fabulous outside guys, including Gary Collins and Paul Warfield. A lot of guys could beat you. They were all slightly different. One would have speed, another would have hands and speed, and so on. I just don't know how you pick the best.

One of the most talented receivers I played against was Jackie Smith, tight end of the St. Louis Cardinals. He was not just quick, but fast—really fast. Great, pure speed. He was big. The only thing that saved me for five years was that I had a little initial in my little black book that I kept on receivers, and it was "TT" for "terrible temper." When we played St. Louis during the season— I wouldn't touch him in the preseason—I'd flip him with an elbow, and I'd get my linebacker to slap him and do anything dirty to him. Just do something that would make him mad. And he would instantly go crazy. Then he'd spend the rest of the afternoon trying to hurt me. He'd yell and scream at the referees. And I'm hitting him in the facemask with my elbow. I wasn't going to hurt him. But it just infuriated him that I did that. As a result, that afternoon he would only catch three passes for seven yards or five passes for three or four yards. I'd have a great day, and he'd score no touchdowns.

But my final year, he got wise to me. When I pulled that routine on him, I saw him grinning. And he caught three touchdown passes on me, and I retired that year. He figured it out. It took him a long time to figure out what I was doing to him. I couldn't cover him. He was faster and bigger than I was. Maybe I'd have been fine in the earlier half of my career, but at the end, I couldn't stay with him. Jackie Smith could run away from a lot of people.

There were some other great tight ends, like Aaron Thomas of New York and Pete Retzlaff of Philadelphia. Retzlaff might be one of the best tight ends who ever played. I'd want him on my team. I might even pick Pete over Jackie.

But I'd hate to pick between those guys. I was quick enough that I had decent days on Pete Retzlaff. But not many people did.

SN: *How about Mike Ditka?*
CT: In his early days, when he first hit the field, I don't know that anybody could cover Mike Ditka. It wasn't his speed, although he had good speed. His size and strength made him tough to cover. But, thank goodness, he got crippled up a little bit and slowed down. Oh, he was awful! Once, when we were playing in Pittsburgh and Mike was with Dallas, late in his career, he ran a post pattern. And, while trying to catch a pass, I hit him and knocked him off line, and he hit the goalpost. I just cold cocked him. That's when they had the post close to the goal line. He was down on his knees mumbling, because it had really stunned him, and he'd thought I'd cheap-shotted him, not that he had hit the goalpost. I admit I was laughing and taking credit for it, warning him not to run in the middle again. He let out this terrible string of language, this whole group of you "blankety blank," and ended it with "You Fellowship of Christian Athletes SOB." That was the meanest thing he could think of at the time.

We played Dallas again two weeks later, and by then he'd seen the film of the play. And Mike walked over to me, during our warm-up time, and laughed and said, "You son of a gun, you took credit for that."

But boy, Mike was tough. Big, strong. I've still got a dent inside my skull from a forearm blow he gave me in 1963, when he stuck that little cheek piece inside my head. Man, I thought he broke my jaw. Someone else nicknamed him "Iron Mike," but I know why.

SN: *Who was the best quarterback you played against?*
CT: Probably Sonny Jurgensen, who had unbelievable talent. Some of it was instinct, things that you can't teach. A lot of it was hard work.

SN: *What were some of the things he did that you can't teach?*
CT: He could ad lib. He knew instantaneously what to do and how to keep from throwing an interception. I remember one play, when somebody was tackling him, and he threw a ball behind his back, drilling a fullback right in the chest with the ball as he was going down. How do you teach a guy to do that? That's just instinct and smarts. And Sonny could do that all the years I played.

SN: *I saw him a lot of times bring a team in to score in the last two minutes when they really needed to score.*

CT: Sonny could bring in a team to score in the last two minutes. Sonny knew it, and his team knew it. Teams he played against knew it. He was a very bright guy, and a great passer who loved to pass.

SN: *How long did you play for the Rams?*
CT: I played four years for the Rams, and we had everything you'd look at in a player, in guys like our quarterback, Bill Wade, and our end Del Shofner.

SN: *How would you describe the Rams quarterback, Bill Wade?*
CT: Bill Wade was a remarkable talent. He threw the ball as long and hard as anybody ever. I think you could have won multiple championships with Bill Wade, if the team had been there. After being traded, Bill took Chicago to the title. Bill was unselfish, a team player.

SN: *What led you to become dissatisfied on the Rams?*
CT: I had a little problem with some of the stuff that went on in Los Angeles, with the lifestyle there. I wasn't raised that way. But there are great people everywhere, and I have made lifelong friends there.

We had a good ball team at Los Angeles, but that big trade, where we sent thirteen guys away for Ollie Matson, destroyed it. That was a horrible trade. They gave the team away. Ollie Matson was a great player, but not for all those guys.

SN: *Did that trade demoralize the team?*
CT: I don't know about demoralize. But with that trade, they got rid of our older veterans who had stabilized our team. In their places we had all these new faces, and it took our team a couple of years to adjust. They traded the nucleus of our offensive and defensive lines. Coach Gillman was fired, and we got a new coach, Bob Waterfield, who inherited that deal. There was one system under Sid Gillman and it was successful. And when he was replaced, here comes another set of coaches and another system.

Because of that trade and the change in coaches, I tried to get traded. I really wanted to get traded to Dallas, which wasn't two hundred miles from home. I had called Dallas and asked them "If I can get out of here, do you want me?" and they had said yes. I could see them getting better and having a future. It would have been more stable, because they had hired a coach for life there, Tom Landry.

In those days, the two worst places they could think of to trade you were Green Bay and Pittsburgh, because they weren't winners.

SN: *Green Bay, because it was cold?*
CT: It's just that they weren't winning. To be sure, Green Bay was hitting its stride just about that time. But Green Bay had been a dumping ground for troublemakers. A lot of what Vince Lombardi inherited was that group of troublemakers. Guys who had said, "Trade me," had been sent to Green Bay.

SN: *And it was a small town, and you didn't get much attention there.*
CT: The place players wanted to go was New York, where you got the ad money, and the television shows, and the extra income.

So they sent me to Pittsburgh, to get even with me. They'd do that if you had enough guts to ask to be traded. I saw it on the news that the Rams had traded me to Pittsburgh. They didn't have the courtesy to call me. When I found out, I got in my car and drove home to Oklahoma City and had no intention of reporting to Pittsburgh. I was going to go back to school and finish my engineering degree.

SN: *So what led you to join Pittsburgh? Did they call you and persuade you to come?*
CT: After about two weeks, Buster Ramsey of the Steelers called me. I told him I wasn't going to come to Pittsburgh. I had a building business in Oklahoma City at that time, and I'd done real well in the off-season. I was making more money building houses than I had been playing football.

I also had heard all kinds of bad things about the Steelers—that they were a bunch of drunks and rabble-rousers. There had been some magazine articles about Bobby Layne, their quarterback, and some of his exploits. And again, I hadn't been raised that way. I had no intention of endorsing or participating in that kind of lifestyle.

But Buster Ramsey kept working on me, and I finally did decide to join the Steelers for the 1961 season. I was still single, so I didn't really have any obligations. I learned quickly most of the stories and reputations had been embellished to the ridiculous. I learned to love Pittsburgh, the people, the owner, and his family in particular. I felt like an adopted son of the local Pittsburgh community.

SN: *What were your impressions of the Steelers when you joined them?*
CT: The difference between the Rams and the Steelers was night and day. As I said, in Los Angeles we had everything that you'd look for in a player. When I got to Pittsburgh, I looked at the quarterback, Bobby Layne, and he's this portly guy, who was about halfway out of shape. John Henry Johnson, the

Clendon Thomas with the Pittsburgh Steelers. Courtesy of Clendon Thomas.

fullback, looked like a big, knock-kneed kid. They really didn't look like football players. But man, did they play on Sunday!

I learned a real good lesson right then. You can never look at a guy and tell what he can do on the football field. It doesn't matter what he looks like. You'd think that he'd need to be big, tall, and fast to get the job done. But there are some guys who can just get it done without having all the physical attributes.

There was terrific talent on the Steelers. And many of those guys could play today, including Johnny Sample, Brady Keys, John Henry Johnson, Ernie Stautner, Buddy Dial, Eugene Lipscomb, and Myron Pottios. The difference is the big men would be pumping iron all year long, and they'd weigh twenty-five pounds more, and they'd be faster.

SN: *How would you describe Bobby Layne's personality and style of playing quarterback? Was he a team leader?*
CT: Bobby Layne was a team leader who showed up on Sunday afternoon to play. He despised losing. He never had a great arm; he certainly didn't have the arm Bill Wade had. Bobby threw an old, wobbly pass that we always laughed at and teased him about. But the ball got to where it was supposed to be. Somehow it would wobble its way down the field to where an end had the chance to catch it. Bobby was smart, played smart, and called good ball games. He made the most of what he had. We won a lot of ball games with him. Unfortunately for Bobby, drinking cost him a lot of years and took some talent away from him.

SN: *How about John Henry Johnson, the fullback?*
CT: John Henry Johnson was unbelievable, a really great fullback who—because of the Pittsburgh-Cleveland rivalry and the direct comparison with Jim Brown—always had a great day when we played Cleveland. When we prepared to play Cleveland, our offensive team would line up and emulate the Browns for the defense. I don't think anybody could ever imitate Jim Brown, but John Henry could. He's a Hall of Famer, and he deserves it.

In 1963, we nearly won the NFL title, coming closer than any Pittsburgh team until the 1970s. And we should have won it. We finished second in the eastern conference, but we beat both teams that ended up playing in the NFL championship game, the Chicago Bears and the New York Giants. It was a shame, because if Big Daddy Lipscomb, our great defensive tackle, had not died before the season began, and if Bobby Layne had not retired—if we'd had both Bobby Layne and Ed Brown at quarterback—we'd have done it. We lacked the depth to get the job done.

With the constant change going on, the Rams never did fit me, but I wound up finding my home in Pittsburgh, in great part because I enjoyed the owner, Mr. Rooney, so much. Pittsburgh was the team I was comfortable with.

SN: *How would you describe Art Rooney?*
CT: I respected Mr. Rooney. Even though he was a multimillionaire, he was very down to earth. He took the time and made the effort to learn the names of my

mother and father and sisters. He knew family members' names for most of the Steelers' players. And that's amazing. I never worked for anybody ever, who showed enough interest to learn my family's names. And I truly liked his family. Mr. Rooney took the time to take me out to his farm, because he knew I enjoyed looking at horses and his foal crop.

Art Rooney made his money with a variety of companies he owned. But most people are unaware that after he paid his coaches' and players' salaries, he gave most of what he made from the Steelers to charity. You never read about it.

SN: *At Pittsburgh, you played with Big Daddy Lipscomb. How would you describe him?*
CT: Gene "Big Daddy" Lipscomb was a fabulous defensive tackle for us, a big, rangy guy who pushed 300 pounds, but who was as quick and as fast as anybody on the team, even the little guys. He wasn't fat at all, he was just huge, and looked like a big basketball player.

When I was with the Rams, I played with Deacon Jones and Lamar Lundy, who were fabulous defensive linemen, so I had something to measure Big Daddy by. Deacon, particularly, had such great speed. But Big Daddy was right up there with those two guys.

SN: *You rank him as good as Deacon Jones?*
CT: Oh, yeah. And I put Ernie Stautner right there with him.

SN: *Stautner was smaller, though.*
CT: Ernie was smaller, but absolutely like a cat and unbelievably strong. Ernie would never loaf. When he played, it was just 100 percent. So, Big Daddy would stay up there. They were a great combination.

SN: *Big Daddy Lipscomb did have a drug problem, didn't he?*
CT: No, he didn't. Big Daddy Lipscomb died of a drug overdose, but I think he was murdered. Gene was a joy to be around. He was a good-looking black man with money, and there was always an entourage hanging around him. They wanted to share in his good fortune. In some of the areas he was in, drugs were present, and they were always trying to get somebody with money to spend it on drugs. So, Gene was a target. Gene would drink a little Scotch—shouldn't have, but he did. As far as we understand it, he got drunk, passed out, and somebody gave him some drugs.

They said they found needle marks on Big Daddy's arm, but he couldn't stand needles. You couldn't get close to him with a needle. In the locker room, when something was hurting, doctors couldn't do anything with him. You couldn't shoot him in a muscle, and there was no way you could get anything deadened. He wouldn't take a vitamin shot. He certainly wasn't going to let anybody stick a needle in his arm. You'd have to have him handcuffed to a telephone pole. I think what happened is that when he got passed out, they thought they could shoot him with drugs and get him started.

SN: *Get him addicted so they could sell him drugs, rather than want to kill him.*
CT: Yeah. If they can get you on it, then you're hooked. But because he weighed 300 pounds, they probably gave him twice the dosage they should have, and that killed him.

SN: *Another great defensive player from your era was Ray Nitschke of the Green Bay Packers. How would you describe him?*
CT: I used to watch Ray Nitschke and wonder how in the world he wasn't a paraplegic. He used to hit people so hard. He knew no fear. If he ever hesitated, it didn't show. He'd run at guys and not give any quarter and never back away. He would stick his head right in somebody. I never thought of Nitschke as being vicious. I just thought of him as being tough. He'd hit you with everything he had. I can never understand how he could keep from backing off just a little bit, just out of sheer desire to take care of his own body. But he didn't. There are a few guys in pro ball who you watch come in and make a tackle, who never slow down. They just go as hard as they can go and go through somebody. I tip my hat off to them, the guys who can do that.
 The thing they forget about Jack Tatum, the defensive back who hit Darryl Stingley, is that he too could have been a paraplegic. Believe me, it takes guts to hit like that.

SN: *You say that Tatum, when he hit Stingley, could have gotten hurt, too?*
CT: When you hit a guy that hard, what makes you think it's just him taking a lick? He took a lick, too.
 I saw John Reger, our linebacker, pass out and go into convulsions after tackling Theron Sapp of the Eagles, sticking his head in his thigh. I walked to Dick Haley, and said, "He isn't going to make it; he's broken his neck." When you see a guy who goes into convulsions and passes out, quits breathing and turns black, then it's obviously serious. I'd thought he'd gotten killed. And Theron went down and couldn't get up, because Reger hit him so hard in

that thigh pad. He had driven through him so hard, that even with the thigh pad, he'd put a huge knot on Theron's thigh.

I saw film of other guys get seriously hurt making tackles. David Baker tore the inside of his headgear out tackling Jim Brown. It's nearly impossible to do. A defensive back from Minnesota, a safety, hit a guy so hard he ruptured a blood vessel in his head. They took him to the emergency room, where they saved his life by drilling a hole in his head to relieve the pressure. Had the Minnesota trainer not been on the ball, they would have lost him.

SN: *Intimidation must be a factor in pass coverage.*
CT: When pass receivers run crossing patterns, it's a game of chicken, with two guys running into each other as fast as they can go. Usually, when an end is running as hard as he can go, and I'm running as hard as I can go, one of us gives a little. I tended not to back off. That's the reason there are so many injuries on kickoffs, because they're both running at each other as hard as they can go.

As a defensive back, I wanted that reputation as a hitter. I would never, ever, want to hurt somebody intentionally. But I wanted the receiver to think about number 28 when he ran a post pattern—to think that I would be over there, and that he would pay a price. That if he came into the middle part of the field, I was going to take his head off. I'll do it legally, but I'm going to hit him. If he came into my territory, he was going to come out of there skinned up a little bit. I'd like to take his breath away, to where he'd be gasping for air, looking back and saying, "Who was that Mack truck who ran over me? Oh, number 28, that's Thomas." There were certain guys that couldn't handle it, who could be intimidated. Bob Hayes, with Dallas, did not want to run post patterns against Pittsburgh. But the great receivers ran their patterns, caught the balls, took their licks, and came back hard again and again.

Now Ray Berry, it didn't matter if you killed him, he was going to run a post pattern and catch the ball. He might wake up in the hospital, but he had the ball in his hands. He'd be hanging on to it. It was amazing. He'd run a slant, and the middle linebackers, like Nitschke, Butkus, Schmidt, and Pottios, were going to meet him. It didn't matter, he'd catch it anyway.

SN: *Did the money situation in football change during your NFL career?*
CT: All my dealings with management were straightforward and fair. I got paid as well as anybody got paid then. The Steelers told me that I was the highest paid defensive back in the NFL. I was making about $35,000 a year then. Larry Wilson of the St. Louis Cardinals was probably making about the same.

But it was a convoluted time, because there were guys just coming into the league who were signing for $200,000 bonuses and were getting paid $85,000 a year. They were mixing in with players who were still playing for $18,000 or $20,000 a year. Dick Butkus signed for a $200,000 bonus.

As older veterans, we were never going to improve our position. They were never going to pay us more, because it's like a depreciating racehorse. You start out with value because you're a rookie or a young veteran, and you become more valuable for a short period of time. Then, for about the next four or five years, if you don't get hurt, you're very valuable to them, because you're as good as you're ever going to be. And then you begin to tail off. It's a rough game, and you're going to accumulate injuries. In most instances, you slow down a step, and then you're no longer as valuable. And they know you're going to quit at some point. You only have a short period of time left.

SN: *How important were incentives in contracts?*
CT: Contracts were pretty straightforward then, with less emphasis on incentives than today. They'd throw in a few little bonuses for some guys. I didn't care for those, and I didn't fight for them. Today they have all these incentives clauses, based on things like how many interceptions you make, and you have to be real careful with that. Pretty soon you got a guy hunting a ball, who should be covering a man. It would have been real easy for me to quit covering a guy— get out of position, in order to gamble and get more interceptions.

SN: *The contemporary athletic scene seems very different from when you played in a lot of ways. You've got a lot of people who . . .*
CT: Seem selfish. Thank goodness there are still some guys who are putting back, and not just taking. But there is some selfishness.

SN: *There's a lot of ego involved today.*
CT: People are lying if they don't think ego plays a part in athletic success, because you didn't get there without ego. Ego helps drive you to excellence. But some of the guys make it difficult, where they're trying to draw so much attention to themselves. Selfish behavior is contagious and will destroy a team. And I don't like it.

SN: *Did you have any particular goal in football toward the end of your career?*
CT: I had one goal the last few years of my career, and that was to be on a championship football team. I had almost gotten there in 1963. That was a frustrating deal, not to ever win one. I think the only thing worse would be if

I'd been on a team that had played for the championship and had lost. That would drive you insane—to get that close and then not win.

SN: *Why did you decide to retire?*
CT: I decided to retire because the Steelers had a losing club that would win only one or two games. Mr. Rooney asked me to go back for what would have been my twelfth year. I went back, and stayed a few weeks, and worked out. Then I met with the new head coach, Chuck Noll, and told him that it wasn't going to work. I was an older veteran, so I knew the talent it took to win, and the Steelers didn't have it. I knew when we had John Henry and Ernie and Big Daddy, and some of those guys, and what it took. I'd been there with the Rams, when we came in second. Noll didn't particularly like it, but I told him, "You may as well find out what these rookies can do, and let them get experience." It would have been different if I could back up or play an important role for a real good ball team that had a chance for the title. But I knew I would be real frustrated there. I told him they were going to get beat all year, and I didn't want to be a part of it. I didn't want to be part of a loser. As it was, the Steelers only won one game that year.

SN: *You didn't want to get traded to another team?*
CT: No. The Chicago Bears did call me, and I went and played one preseason game with them, just for the heck of it. My wife, whom I had met in Pittsburgh, was a stewardess instructor with United Airlines in Chicago. But the Bears weren't going to win either. So, that's when I retired. I didn't feel good about playing for another team. I really loved Pittsburgh. That's where I had been comfortable and that had been home. That was my team.

SN: *What was it like, adjusting to retirement?*
CT: Adjusting to retirement was easy. I had a building business to come back to in Oklahoma City. I had gotten involved with Chet Leonhardt and Leonhardt Enterprises. They were developers. It was time for me to settle down. So, my wife and I came back to Oklahoma City and settled there.

SN: *How do you look back on your experience playing football?*
CT: I wouldn't trade it for anything. The people I met, from the steelworkers in Pittsburgh, the corner policeman, actors of Hollywood, Congressmen in D.C., the average fan, lifelong friends, opportunities. I got to do everything I dreamed about. But I won't say it was easy. It's a rough game. At the very best, it's rough. I feel very grateful that I got to walk out of it as healthy as I did.

Other than a few calcium deposits on my shoulders and a few little bumps and bruises and aches that show up once in a while, I'm really all right.

It was great meeting all these neat people and friends. Through the years I made good football friends whom I still stay in touch with. It's a special and very limited fraternity. The NFL tournaments allow me to stay in touch with an unlimited number of former players and teammates. I couldn't ask for anything more.

JOE WASHINGTON SR.

—Prairie View A&M, 1948–1951
—Head Football Coach, Hilliard High School, Bay City, Texas, 1951–1965
—Head Football Coach, Abraham Lincoln High School, Port Arthur, Texas, 1965–1995

Joe Washington Sr. spent forty-five years as head football coach at black high schools in Texas, first in Bay City and then in Port Arthur. He starred as a running back and defensive back on armed forces teams in Hawaii and then at Prairie View A&M in Hempstead, Texas. Several of his players, including his son Joe Jr., went on to careers in the NFL.

Washington describes growing up during the Jim Crow era in the small south Texas town of Rosenberg and discusses World War II's impact on race relations. He talks about his adjustment to armed forces football from the sandlots, as well as the tensions he experienced and his assertiveness when he returned to the Jim Crow South after several years of military service in multiracial Hawaii.

Washington played football at Prairie View for legendary African-American coaches Pop Long and Jimmie Stevens, and he discusses their coaching methods, enforcement of discipline, and strong commitment to education. He also analyzes the distinctive style of early black football.

Washington discusses the challenges of coaching at an underfunded black high school during the Jim Crow era, and changing race relations in south Texas during the 1950s and 1960s, including their impact on college football recruiting

Joe Washington Sr. (right), as head coach at Lincoln High School, Port Arthur, Texas. Courtesy of Joe Washington Sr.

practices. He also compares coaching today's youth with the players he worked with early in his career.

STEPHEN NORWOOD: *Let me begin by asking you to talk about your personal background, when and where you were born. And tell me about your parents, who they were, and what they did.*
JOE WASHINGTON SR.: I'm a native Texan, born in a small town named Rosenberg, twenty-four miles from Houston, on June 10, 1929. When I left Rosenberg to go into the army in 1946, its population was 3552.

SN: *Were there any industrial jobs there?*
JW: There were really no industrial jobs, and if there were they were manned by whites. If you were black and you were not a farmer, you did domestic or service work, or you worked in the rice fields out around Wharton. My mother,

Josephine Washington, did domestic work. My father, Henry Washington, could do quite a few things—he was a cook, he could do dry cleaning, and he even worked with a funeral home. I have a brother and a sister living, and one sister passed very early at birth.

SN: *Were your parents from Rosenberg originally, or had they come from somewhere else?*
JW: My father came from down the road in Wharton, and my mother was from Rosenberg.

SN: *How much formal education did your parents have?*
JW: They had seven or eight years of schooling, which was probably the norm for most blacks at that time. My parents separated when I was twelve, and my father moved to Houston and remarried. He owned a little cleaning and pressing shop there.

SN: *Could you talk a little bit about Rosenberg and social life in it? How were the neighborhoods set up?*
JW: Everything in Rosenberg was rigidly segregated. In any Southern town, the railroad track separated the blacks from the whites. Rosenberg is fifty-six miles from the Gulf of Mexico, and there were a great deal of Latin Americans there as well. The Hispanics lived in the black section, but they went to the white schools. But the Hispanic kids did not attend school as regularly as the black kids.

SN: *Do you think that had to do with language?*
JW: It could have.

SN: *They didn't have separate parochial schools for the Hispanic children?*
JW: Not in Rosenberg, a small town.

SN: *Did you ever go to Houston to visit anyone?*
JW: My first visit to Houston was with my Aunt Tena and her husband Uncle Johnny, who worked for the railroad company, when I was six, seven, eight years old, and it made quite an impression, since it was so busy. I remember the streetcars, and all the people going across Main Street. I was all dressed up for the occasion, and I had a little white straw hat on.

SN: *Did the older black people socialize you in any way to learn how to protect yourself in the Jim Crow society—how to survive? Did they have streetcars that were segregated?*

JW: Not in Rosenberg. We had no transportation. Growing up in that era, as a child you perceived that there were things that blacks couldn't do. If you got on the bus to go to Houston, you went with your mother and sat in the back. Those things became habit-forming. I can remember being lectured by my mother or my father, "Son, you don't do this." Visiting my mother where she worked was the biggest lesson. She'd say, "Son, do you know where Mrs. so-and-so lives? Well, come around to the back door." Well, you came around to the back door.

SN: *When did you first become involved in sports?*

JW: I became aware pretty early that I had good athletic ability. I ran a little faster than most of the kids and jumped a little farther than most of them. And when teams were chosen, I was the first to be picked. Whether you were eight, or nine, or ten, you knew there was something special in that.

We came up playing softball, and running, and playing basketball, but not football, because black youth were less exposed to it. We only became aware of how it was played, the elements of the sport, by watching Rosenberg's white high school team play.

SN: *Was your father ever involved in any kind of sports?*

JW: Yes, he played baseball. That's about all.

SN: *Semi-pro, pickup?*

JW: Just baseball around the community.

SN: *Were the adults in the black community in Rosenberg involved in sports? Did they follow sports in the outside world? Did they talk about certain players?*

JW: The biggest sports among the African-American adults in Rosenberg were boxing and baseball. They'd listen to the fights on the radio. Everybody talked about Joe Louis. Satchel Paige, Jesse Owens. My father played some baseball in the community. A man named George Howard managed a little African-American team, and was the catcher as well. He saw that I had some athletic ability and took an interest in me.

SN: *What kind of team was this?*

JW: A little semi-pro team.

SN: *Did they draw significant crowds?*
JW: Of course. They played on Sunday evenings on a little diamond in Rosenberg, and they traveled to other towns.

It was George Howard who really exposed me to football by taking me to watch the white high school games on Friday nights. Rosenberg High School. We would climb up in a tree, look over the fence, and watch them play football. Hey, that was what I wanted to play.

SN: *Climb a tree and look over the fence? They wouldn't let you in?*
JW: No.

SN: *This was for whites only?*
JW: That's right.

SN: *Even for spectators?*
JW: Oh, yeah. It was a white high school.

SN: *There's got to be a lot of hostility in a town that's segregated. Can you recall any specific incidents of hostility from whites there?*
JW: Oh, yes. Oh, Steve, sure. I was literally, totally aware of black-white prejudice. For example, Mr. Howard and I were in a tree one time, looking over a game in Richmond, three miles from Rosenberg. We had to get out of the tree and leave, because white kids started throwing rocks at us. Mr. Howard and I were really enthused over the game, but the rocks were flying. It got so bad that we had to get out of the tree and leave the game.

There was one time when I got a little bolder, at a football game in Rosenberg. Mr. Howard was not available to go with me that time. Somehow, very late in the game, I managed to get into that game.

SN: *In the seats?*
JW: Not in the seats, but into the stadium. The ticket seller had left, and I eased in by the end zone for the remaining few minutes of the game. Then the football players came running off the field to the dressing room. One of the real good players came by me, and somehow, his muddy, grimy hands rubbed across my face, and I could taste and feel the sand, and I thought, "Hey, man, this is football!" That was as close to a real football game that I got. But I knew it was the game for me. I wanted to play football.

My dearest friend James Simpson, whom I called "Killer," and I would play football one on one in my yard.

SN: *How did he get the name "Killer"?*
JW: We called him "Killer" because when he played basketball, he'd foul and such. "Hey, man, you're going to kill somebody." Killer and I would just line up with the ball and go—one running and the other tackling. We used my mother's oatmeal container as our football. Finally, Killer got a football for Christmas.

SN: *So as a kid, you didn't even get a toy football or baseball mitts?*
JW: A football as a toy wasn't nearly as common then as it is today. I didn't buy myself a football until my junior or senior year in high school. But we would play with the little oatmeal boxes.

In 1943, when I was fourteen, I got my first football equipment. The kids in Rosenberg would play the kids from Richmond in sandlot football after school. When the fall came around they preferred to play basketball, and I had to negotiate with them to get them to play football. We'd line off the field, and one or two parents would come to watch, or just a few people who liked the game. I had never owned a pair of football shoes; they weren't available. The black high school in Rosenberg didn't have a football team. The shoes we would get from the high school might be a right size 9 and a left size 10.

Then I saw some shoes advertised in the Sears catalogue. They weren't football shoes, but they were athletic shoes. I got on the bus and went down there and bought me a pair of those high-topped black shoes with ribbed soles. And I also bought an old red helmet that the guys in the armored tanks used. They were selling them for recreation. When I came back—boy, I was the talk of the town! I was the dude who had a helmet and some football shoes. I played in those a long time.

In these pickup games, I was the coach. I was the guy who'd tell them what to do—you play here, and I called the plays.

SN: *Was football the favorite sport of many of the other kids you grew up with?*
JW: Some of them. They liked football, but not as much as other sports. I played against some great athletes in college and in the service, but the toughest tackler I've ever confronted was a guy named Cecil Horton, who played with us in high school. This rascal—man, you talk about racking my brains, he did it. Clotheslined. I'd never been clotheslined ever, but this guy

did it to me. But he was the nicest guy, not at all a bully. As a matter of fact, he's a preacher now.

SN: *Did you ever worry about getting hurt playing football?*
JW: No, because the game meant too much to me. And if I did get hurt, I found out as a young kid that you'd get well. I used to see kids with broken collarbones—that was so prevalent when I was a boy. And guess what? I always wanted one. I never had one. But if I got hurt, I knew that I'd get well.

SN: *When did you put on your first football uniform?*
JW: I didn't get a full uniform until my senior year in high school, when a cousin who was a master sergeant in the tank corps brought his uniform to my house and gave it to me. He had played football in the tank corps. Helmet, shoulder pads—he said, "Take this." He knew I loved football. The uniform was too big for me. But it was real football stuff. Unfortunately, I never got a chance to play in it, because I was a senior and the football season was over.

Once I was in Houston on a Saturday, and I happened to pass by Rice Stadium, on Main and University. I looked through the gate for a few fleeting seconds, and I could see action. Golly! The next day at school, I told the kids I had seen Rice and Tulane play! On Saturdays, when Rice was playing football, I would chart the games listening to the radio broadcasts.

SN: *How did you do that?*
JW: I'd take a sheet of paper, draw me a football field, draw some of the lines. I'd start off, "Tulane kicked to Rice" and "Rice moved five yards," and so on.

Every year, I would buy *Street and Smith's Football Book*. Man, that was my bible. And I kept scrapbooks on football. My senior year in high school, I left a page blank—I said, "One of these days, I'm going to get my picture in this scrapbook."

I learned about the black colleges from working as a paper-boy, selling the two black newspapers, the *Informer,* published in Houston, and the Pittsburgh *Courier.* That's where I learned about Southern University, about Bishop, about Prairie View, and about Wiley College. And I read about Negro League baseball there.

SN: *So these newspapers were very important in expanding your horizons.*
JW: Very important.

SN: *The* Courier *had some good sportswriters, like Wendell Smith and Ric Roberts.*

JW: That's right. [And] my high school principal, A. W. Jackson, had a tremendous influence on me. When he would go to deliver speeches at schools and churches, I would go with him. He had confidence in me, and gave me a lot of encouragement. He emphasized how important it was to get an education. It wasn't a lot of counseling. He *told* you what to do. "You study. You go to school." He didn't negotiate with you on anything. Those were mandates. "Study your lessons! Go to church!"

SN: *Today kids don't respect authority like that. And it's much more difficult to get across to young people. But back then, you say this is someone who impressed you, and you would listen to him.*

JW: That's how I handled my sons, Joe Jr. and Ken. Now I have two little grandboys and two little grandgirls. Just the other night, I told the older grandboy, "You've got to be a leader. You're older than your little brother." This is the way I handle my boys. I don't try to compromise with them. I leave that to the grandmothers and the mothers and the fathers of those kids. I say, "I want you to do this. I want you to do that." I don't go through all that psychology.

There were a lot of things that I would not do as a youngster because of my respect for Mr. Jackson. For instance, one time during Halloween, the guys said, "Hey, man, let's go and do this." I told them, as an excuse, that I didn't get off from work in time. I had an after-school job in a restaurant then. Well, the fact was, that I didn't want to get involved because I knew that if Mr. Jackson found out about it, I'd be in trouble. And I felt the same way about my mother. I wasn't an angel, by any means. I was probably the cussingest little kid you've ever seen in your life.

SN: *How did Rosenberg change during World War II?*

JW: It seemed that after World War II started a curtain was raised, a door was opened, and light came in. I'm not a sociologist or an historian, but I think World War II helped race relations socially and economically. It was a turning point. There were more jobs, not just picking cotton and handy jobs. People from Rosenberg began commuting to Houston and Freeport. Those guys who were not employed went into the service.

SN: *Tell me about going into the military and playing football there.*

JW: In June 1946, Killer and I put our age up to get into the service. We said we were seventeen, and we weren't quite seventeen. After I was inducted, I was sent to Fort Sam Houston for a week or so, and then to Fort McClellan in Alabama for basic training, which ended in September. After that, I was sent home for a month and then to Camp Stoneman in California. That's where everybody stopped on their way to the Pacific.

I played a little sandlot football at Camp Stoneman, since it was October and November. You ran up against some mighty good athletes in the service, especially during that time. I wasn't really fully aware of what I could do or what I couldn't do. But give me a chance, and hey—after the game was over, there was always a guy walking up to me. And the next time we played, they were looking for me. We beat big guys. And I earned a reputation there.

All of us were thinking they were going to send us to Okinawa as occupation troops. But instead we were stationed in Hawaii, at Wheeler Field. My best friend Killer was assigned to Schofield Barracks, which was within walking distance, so we could visit each other. There were a couple of other homeboys over there with us. The big thing was the boxing matches at Schofield Barracks. They had great fighters there.

SN: *The army was still segregated in 1946.*
JW: Yes, but while we were at Fort Sam Houston, we would go
to the gym, and whites and blacks would start playing basketball together. And fights would start. Things would start popping. All the fights started at the damn gym. Still, I was seeing whites and blacks slowly moving together. Fort McClellan was totally segregated. Camp Stoneman, where everybody was running through, was a little less so—at least the guys who might be over you were white. Corporals leading a squad of guys to get their shots, or something like that. I saw some intermingling and some scraps.

I've always said that athletics is the most natural event to man. He's there instinctively. He doesn't have time to think, he reacts. You see his true attitude, whether it's aggressive or whatever. At Camp Stoneman, things became even more aggressive. Guys were coming from overseas, and they were hardened, black and white. One night at the gymnasium, we were playing basketball, and two Marines, one black and one white, got on a mat and went after each other—golly, man. Blood, you know. But it often wasn't racial. Two white guys would go at each other or two black guys.

Going on a truck down to Wheeler Field, I could see the football field. Hey, hey. This was November, and football season was just about over. But I had decided to go out for the base football team the next season. There were so many guys that I was so impressed with, that I just didn't know what to do. But my name would always come up.

SN: *What position did you want to play?*

JW: I went out for quarterback. Quarterback was all I knew how to play. But even at quarterback, I showed running ability. I could see the open man and throw to him or run with the ball. There must have been at least eight or nine black guys out for football.

Those of us going out for the football team met in a room, and you could see a lot of guys' forms there. Joe Blow, experience University of the Redlands, California, Southern Methodist University (SMU). It being the air force, a lot of the guys were college graduates. I was very honest about myself. Rosenberg, football player. That's all I had played, that's what I said.

We worked out in the gym for a month, and I don't think anybody knew who I was. I was the earliest bird in there and got my uniform, which was too large. But when I put that uniform on, hey, hey, hey! It was the first uniform I played in.

One day I was sitting on the sideline with my helmet between my legs, just looking at the guys the coach had out there playing. The coach was Sergeant Austin, who was a real hell-raiser. He had played for the Pittsburgh Steelers from 1938 to 1940. Some guy went wrong, and Coach Austin said, "Give me a back who knows what to do!" I had been a quarterback, and it was a halfback who had screwed up. So, I got out there. "Get your helmet!" Well, that brought chuckles from the guys. I had to go back and get my helmet. I wasn't accustomed to playing with a helmet.

The first thing the guy asked me to do was to block the defensive end. I went into him and blocked him, and he didn't get in. The next play I caught a pass over the middle with one hand, ran two or three yards, and fumbled it. The next time, I ran with the ball twenty or thirty yards down the sideline, made moves, and fumbled again. I had had no training and just ran naturally. After the workout, the coach asked me where I was from, and I said Rosenberg. And he said, "Where did you learn to run like that?" I told him, "Rosenberg."

That Wednesday they were going to put the names down for the major team, and I was going to go down and turn my uniform in. I saw a name on the list, Washington, but I thought it was another guy in our company with that name, a big fullback. Then Coach Austin walked over and asked me, "What's your first name?" I said, "Joe." He didn't even know my first name. He said, "You know, you made the team." I was amazed. But the guys in my company were not surprised. They figured I'd made it.

SN: *So you were a starting player on the base team?*

JW: Yes.

SN: *As running back?*
JW: That's right.

SN: *Were you playing T-formation or single wing?*
JW: We were shifting. Single wing was the big thing; the T-formation was young. I was a single wing tailback and loved it. I was a flashy-type runner and had the ability to go where I could cut in or throw the football. And then sometimes we would shift into the T. We were a dead head T across the front; there wasn't any flanker. Then I was the left halfback.

SN: *So this was the first time you had any formal coaching.*
JW: That's correct. Hold the ball, things like that. I was the first one at practice, and with my enthusiasm I improved each day, each day, each day. The first scrimmage game we had was against a semi-pro team we later played in the regular season. I was just elated over playing the game; I really didn't think much of what I did. It was a tough ball game. But the newspaper had complimentary things to say: "Joe Washington was a really outstanding back. He did a good job on both sides of the football, going from offense to defense."

SN: *What position did you play on defense?*
JW: I played defensive halfback and would tackle from one side of the field to the other. I could come up from anywhere. I was a tackling little rascal. You played three-deep at that time, a safety and two halfbacks. So, I did well, and most of the raves I received in that game were for defense, running guys down. My speed was much faster chasing a guy than running a straight 100-yard dash.

As a coach, I developed this philosophy: if a guy runs a 4.5 and wants to make a tackle, he'll make it. If a guy runs a 4.1 and doesn't want to make the tackle, he'll never get there. So, with a little speed but great enthusiasm, I could always wind up being there and making a tackle.

SN: *This was a racially mixed team, then. Whites and blacks were playing together on the base teams?*
JW: Yes. We played mixed semi-pro and air force teams, like Schofield Barracks and Hickham Field.

SN: *Was there any racial tension on the field? Football is a rough game, and it allows the opportunity to slip in unnecessary hits. You think of what happened to Paul Robeson.*

JW: Oh, yeah. Hey. But I was too naive to even assume that this was the case. A friend of mine, a homeboy, who was stationed at Schofield Barracks, told me, "Joe, they're going to get you. You shouldn't play." Well, golly, what did that mean to me? Don't play football? I was too naive.

We started off with one of the classiest teams on the island, but the early season buildup hurt us. My first ball game—headlines. Oh, man, I wasn't accustomed to that. And I really don't think that helped us. We didn't win all the games we should have. As a result, Coach Austin, a fiery coach, was removed and replaced with one of his assistants. And I was injured in midseason, in November, and I took a tailspin. A hip injury put me in the hospital for about a week. It took me about a month to really recuperate.

SN: *How long were you in the military?*
JW: Two years. Played on the base football team one year.

SN: *This was even bigger than the white high schools in Texas, wasn't it?*
JW: Oh, yeah. The crowds were good. We played in Honolulu Stadium. There were crowds that I never imagined before.

SN: *After your discharge from the military, you used the G. I. Bill to attend Prairie View A&M. What led you to decide to go to Prairie View?*
JW: I had wanted to attend either Southern or Wiley, which were the good black football schools at that time. They made the *Courier* and the *Informer* more than Prairie View. Prairie View was an academic school. But Killer said, "Let's go to Prairie View." And we rode over there, and boy, I'm ready to go. We entered college in June 1948, summer school.

Killer and I were like that—that close. I can't speak of anything in my life without mentioning Killer. I associated with Killer more than with my older brother. His mother and my mother were real good friends.

SN: *You went into the service with him and to college with him. Are you still friends with him now?*
JW: Oh, yeah. He lives in Washington, D.C., where he was a lieutenant colonel in the Pentagon. He was in ROTC at Prairie View, and then went into the Korean conflict. Whenever I'm in Washington, we get together. He was down here a month or so ago. We both admire each other's careers.

SN: *Where is Prairie View A&M located?*
JW: Hempstead, Texas. But now it's Prairie View, Texas, which is six or eight miles from Hempstead.

SN: *Had any of your teachers gone there?*

JW: Most went to teachers' colleges. The big black colleges in Texas for training teachers were the state schools, and Prairie View was a state school. And those who could go to Prairie View were something. Prairie View was the greatest teachers' college in Texas. Right now, if you go into their graduate school, you'll see as many whites getting teacher certification at Prairie View as at any other place. Sam Houston, Tilson, Bishop, Wiley, and Mary Allen were private schools where a lot of kids had an opportunity to get an education. You could get into the private schools a lot easier than into Prairie View, because so many churches would help you get into them.

SN: *What was it like, adjusting to college from the military?*

JW: Coming to Prairie View from Hawaii was a really big change for Killer and me. College seemed too tame, we had seen too many things. It was really tough adjusting. I was an eighteen-year-old veteran, and I was still wild. I went everywhere I could in Honolulu. My dear mother, may she rest in peace. But, man, I used to go to the little place where the girls did the burlesque shows. And at Prairie View, we were in town every night.

When I saw my little hometown, Rosenberg, again, I couldn't believe it, it looked so small. When I had left to enter the service, things there had looked large to me. But now when I got back, the little block that I used to run from Killer's house to mine was the shortest block I'd ever seen in my life! The little town was just too small.

But I began to settle down, and my grades went from Cs and Ds to Cs and Bs to Bs to As. Junior and senior years, I was on the dean's list. I made the dean's list as an athlete. I'm real proud of it, and my mother was very proud. She received a letter from the president of the college informing her that her son was on the dean's list, and for two weeks, there wasn't a house in Rosenberg that wasn't aware of it.

SN: *How about coming back to Texas from Hawaii? You had played for mixed teams in the service. Having been out in Hawaii and seeing the changes going on there, how did you adjust to a Jim Crow situation in Texas? Did you think things would be changing?*

JW: Returning to Texas after two years in the service, my aggression, my assertion, was coming to a focus, as far as going to places, demanding certain things. I understood what my rights and privileges were. It was being brought to light that I, too, had a place in the sun. I was not getting in the back of the bus. Many times I rode the bus home from college.

I remember a situation where a bus driver told me to get in the back. I told him, "Hey, there's no room in the back there." That may have saved the situation. I stayed in the middle of the bus, although I was standing. Bus drivers were different. Some were more sensitive to the issue than others. There were times when the bus would be more than half filled with blacks, not only sitting in their section, but moving farther up. There were times when blacks had to give up their seats as whites moved backwards. And there were times when we would sit in "their" section and they were standing. It was a volatile situation. There were some youngsters waiting for someone to tell us to move, and we're not going to move. But again, it depended on the bus driver.

While there was as much segregation in Texas as in any southern state, in my opinion, there was not as much violent race hatred as in some of the others. To be sure, there were strikes in Beaumont in the early 1940s—real bloody strikes. And you can look through the pages of history and see lynchings of Texas blacks. But the numbers of lynchings will not compare with those of other southern states.

At Prairie View, a black institution where you were training to teach black kids, you found yourself dealing with two different worlds. At school your head teacher was black, your president was black, your counselors were black. When you left the campus, you'd find that the owner of this place is white, the owner of that place is white, the manager of this place is white, the bus driver is white. Many times as a college student, when I went home on weekends, I found myself feeling, "I really can't wait to get back to Prairie View." There I felt much more comfortable. I had black role models, and I didn't have to submit to white leadership.

I wanted to play football at Prairie View, not to become a star, not to become an All-American—just because I loved the game. As a matter of fact, I had no aspiration for Joe Jr. to be an All-State, All-American, All-Pro, or anything of that sort. I wanted him to play the sport because I loved it, and I wanted to coach him.

SN: *What was your objective in going to college?*
JW: I went to Prairie View to get an education.

SN: *And your high school principal had really impressed on you the importance of that, and your mother also?*
JW: Yes. Our professors, our coaches, were trying to prepare us for the future—not of desegregation, that came later—but to compete. And education was the only way we were going to survive. They told us, "To make it in tomorrow's

world, son, you are going to have to have the best education you can get."
When you left Prairie View, you could teach many subjects.

SN: *Any idea of what you wanted to be when you finished college? Any particular aspiration?*
JW: Oh, sure. When I was in the service, working as a file clerk, I spent a lot of time looking at the brochures from various schools, and I thought of becoming a chemical engineer or an electrical engineer. Then I looked at becoming a C.P.A., business administration, because the work I was doing in the armed services was related to that a little bit. I enrolled in college with that in mind.

SN: *Did you decide to become a coach when you were at Prairie View?*
JW: I did. Coach wasn't anything that as a little kid I wanted to be. I coached kids, I coached my teammates, I read books, never thinking that I was going to coach. Until that freshman year, that summer when I enrolled for classes. Jimmie Stevens, who later became our head football coach, when he was registering students, turned me to something different. He asked me, "Well, what do you want to take, son? What do you want to be?" I said, "Look, coach [he was then assistant coach], I want to play football." And he answered, "Well, if you want to play football, son, you're going to take your P.E. course." He didn't know me from Adam.

Now, I began thinking about coaching, and if you wanted to be a coach, then you needed to major in physical education. By September, I was a P.E. major. Teaching and coaching were our alternatives at that time. Playing with the Chicago Bears or the Green Bay Packers was not much of a possibility.

At Prairie View, we knew there were black schools, and they needed teachers. Our professors tried to prepare us to teach that black child the very best that he could be taught. That was the way we looked at the future and the way out of things, a way to accomplish things.

SN: *Jimmie Stevens didn't know about you, even though you'd played football in the service?*
JW: After all, I hadn't come in from a high school, and I hadn't made All-State. I didn't play in Dallas or Fort Worth. So, naturally they didn't know me.

My freshman year at Prairie View, the head football coach was the legendary Pop Long. In the annals of black college history, Pop Long was one of the greats. He was known all over black America as a great coach. He was what you'd call the Bear Bryant, the Barry Switzer, the Jimmy Johnson—those guys

Jimmie Stevens, Prairie View A&M coach, 1949. Courtesy of Special Collections/Archives, Prairie View A&M University.

had the reputation. Pop Long was a great coach like Mumford was at Southern, just like Eddie Robinson. He had previously coached at Wiley College and Texas College. When I was an eighteen-year-old freshman, Pop Long had had a career of coaching. He was in the twilight of his coaching career.

SN: *Did Pop Long produce any famous players?*
JW: At Wiley, he had produced one of the greatest football players, as far as I was concerned, Shirley Ross. "Jap" Jones had also played under him at Wiley.

Pop Long did a great job of teaching. We met in a classroom in the Educational Building every day at noon, and Pop would have his playbook. We'd go over plays, and we'd talk strategies. He'd have highly organized practices.

Prairie View A&M coaching staff including head coach Fred "Pop" Long (second from left) and Jimmie Stevens (far right), late 1940s. Courtesy of Special Collections/Archives, Prairie View A&M University.

Pop Long left after my first year to coach at Texas College, and he was replaced by his assistant coach Jimmie Stevens, who was also a great head coach. He'd coached at Texas College before and at Wiley, maybe a couple of times. I played against Pop, because we played Texas College my sophomore year.

SN: *Did the Prairie View students come from Texas as a whole or from all over the South?*
JW: Most of the students at Prairie View came from in-state. We had a quarterback from Miami, and we had track kids from out-of-state. But most came from Texas.

SN: *How would you describe the athletic facilities when you were playing at Prairie View? You had been in the service, where you'd had real good equipment.*
JW: I wouldn't have cared what the athletic facilities were like at Prairie View, because I was playing football. That's what I cared about. I played tailback and some defense. Prairie View's facilities were good compared to the private black schools in the South that we played.

SN: *Did you just play black schools?*
JW: We didn't play any white schools. We did play Wilberforce in Ohio, and they had some white kids there.

SN: *It was illegal then in Texas for whites and blacks to play together on the same athletic field, wasn't it?*
JW: Certainly. We played in a segregated conference, the Southwestern Athletic Conference; the white schools, like Texas and Texas A&M, were in the Southwest Conference. Texas and Texas A&M had the biggest football programs in the state at that time, although SMU had the best.

SN: *Did the Prairie View games get any attention in the white press?*
JW: Yes, our games were written up in the Houston *Chronicle* and the Houston *Post.*

SN: *How common was it for an athlete at Prairie View to graduate?*
JW: During my era, if you were an athlete, you graduated from college. Of the athletes, the percentage of those graduating was astronomical. You were a college student first. It was nothing unusual for an athlete to make the dean's list. We prided ourselves on making good grades.

SN: *Did your coaches hold you to account on that, too? Did they want you to do well academically?*
JW: Well, do you know who the instructors were? Our coaches were also teachers, and they wanted you to do well academically.

I left Prairie View well prepared academically, with teacher certification and twelve hours of almost everything. Although I was a physical education major, I could teach math, English, and science courses. I had zoology, anatomy, and physiology with nurses. And Prairie View nursing school was the best in the state.

Today the attitude of college coaches toward academics is very different. They're so pressured to win by the fans. Now, Pop Long and Jimmie Stevens both wanted to win. They were fiery competitors. But they were tough enough to see that kid and put him first. In those days, the coaches knew what they were there for. They were education oriented. Instinctively, they were educators and disciplinarians. We have great coaches and winners in athletics today, but the disciplinarians were left somewhere way down there.

Discipline was something we were accustomed to, and that was the case in all the black colleges. To be sure, some kids were rebels, renegades. But the number of kids on the extreme was much smaller then. They didn't last long. You'd have to be a heck of an athlete for Pop Long or Jimmie Stevens to put up with anything unusual.

We had some kids who were bad guys, who would smoke or drink. I had two or three roommates I had to literally take under my wing. One of them was one of my best friends, Pick Brown, one of the greatest natural athletes you ever saw. He could throw a baseball ninety miles an hour, and he played fullback on our football team. He threw a ball to me once from the fifty-yard line, and I was in the end zone, and he threw it so hard it knocked me flat on my back and went right through my hands. He was later killed in a car accident.

If you were in one of Coach Stevens's classes—and that was also the case with the other coaches as well—you were a good citizen in the classroom. This coming in with hats on, we never heard of that.

SN: *What were the practices like?*
JW: Tough, tough, *tough.* Coach Stevens had been a captain in the infantry, and he was a tough disciplinarian as a coach. I was on the track team, too, and he was also our track coach. When we'd be on the track—maybe walking when we should have been sprinting. And we'd see him coming up the highway in his white-and-green Lincoln. Hey, mister, we were shaking in our boots. That's the kind of man he was.

SN: *Maybe it was easier for you to adjust because you had been in the military.*
JW: Oh, yeah. But the practices were still really tough. One of the biggest games of the Prairie View Panthers was what we called the Prairie View Bowl, which we played on New Year's Day at the old Buffalo Stadium in Houston—a big money game. It was just like the Cotton Bowl was for Texas. We really practiced hard for it. We'd get one day off for Christmas, and then report back the next day. We'd get up at five o'clock in the morning to practice, and there'd be frost on the ground. Even the lover of football, Joe Washington, would be crying in his coffee.

SN: *Did you win any championships at Prairie View?*
JW: No. The team that was beating us was Southern. We were second to Southern for my junior and senior year. My freshman year, Grambling was the champion.

When I played at Prairie View, I'd run into guys I'd played against in the service. I remember going to Grambling, and every time I'd run the ball and somebody would tackle me, I'd hear "Hey Joe!" It turned out to be a guy who'd been at Schofield Barracks when I was at Wheeler.

Joe Washington
(Freshman)
Rosenburg, Texas
Arts and Sciences

Joe Washington Sr. as a freshman at Prairie View A&M University. Courtesy of Special Collections/ Archives, Prairie View A&M University.

SN: *You say you met your wife in college. When did you get married?*
JW: I met my wife, Phyllis, at Prairie View the summer before she was a sophomore and I was a junior. We got married before she graduated. I was out a year and coaching in Bay City. I graduated in three years.

I believe that if I had played another year in college, and had I been just a little bigger, a little faster—I couldn't have gotten any quicker, but a little faster—maybe I could have really made it into the limelight. Soaking wet, I weighed 160 pounds when I graduated. I wasn't big, and I wasn't blindingly fast. But people thought I was fast, because I ran fast on the football field. I've run down guys who have beaten me in the 100-yard dash.

SN: *Was there any difference in the style of football that the black schools played, as opposed to the white schools? You could say there's a somewhat different style in basketball.*

JW: There was a certain distinctive style in football, too. Black coaches threw the ball a lot, rather than taking the ball and driving two or three yards in a pile of dust. There was more razzle dazzle, with reverses and sweeps. Coaches like Willie Ray Smith of Lufkin and Beaumont, Texas, had a lot of tricks in their bag. He had an accident that prevented him from playing the game of football, but he was a great coach, an imaginative coach. In black football, the secondary coverage might have been man for man, putting your best man against their best man, and staying with that from the start of the game to the end of the game.

SN: *To what do you attribute these differences?*

JW: The distinctive nature of black football derived in great degree from blacks not having been in the sport as long.

SN: *So if you have a smaller school and fewer players, the passing game is easier to work on.*

JW: It's easier to utilize a great passer and a great receiver than it is to teach anything else. Techniques might not have been wide and varied. Blocks might have been simple shoulder blocks and a hip block. White coaches had different draws, screens—more tools at their disposal.

Of course, the kind of football any team plays, black or white, depends on the kind of players it has. If you have a good quarterback and good receivers, you throw the ball a lot. If you have good runners and big, strong linemen, you're going to have two yards and a cloud of dust. If you've got flashy backs with good outside speed, you're going to run that kind of offense. If you've got four good linebackers, you're going to have a defense that emphasizes four linebackers.

Now, when you talk of a black team in 1928, I have no concept of what and how they did things. I don't know many black high school coaches who were coaching in 1928. Never heard of any. Can't name one.

SN: *How about Pop Long?*

JW: I knew Pop Long only as an early college coach. He might have been coaching back then in a little normal school.

SN: *Do you remember Fritz Pollard?*
JW: Just read about him. Most of the black football that you read about in the history books is black football played at a white school.

My first encounter with football was a mixed deal. I went to Prairie View and had a good knowledge of the game as a player. I played in the service with whites, and a lot of my coaching clinic experience was in white situations. And when I coached, I wasn't as razzle dazzle, as bag-of-trickish as Willie Ray Smith was.

SN: *What did you do after you graduated from Prairie View?*
JW: I coached at Hilliard High School, a black school, in Bay City, a small town in south Texas. In the early 1960s, the population of Bay City was about 8000 or 9000.

SN: *What proportion of Bay City's population was black?*
JW: Probably twenty to thirty percent.

SN: *How long were you there?*
JW: From 1951 until 1965.

SN: *How big was Hilliard High School?*
JW: When I was hired there were about 150 boys and girls in the school, and when I left, there were about 300.

SN: *What was Bay City like? How were people employed there?*
JW: Bay City is about thirty miles from the Gulf of Mexico, and most people farmed, worked in the rice fields or in the oil fields.

SN: *Were the rice fields big plantations?*
JW: Yes. There were large rice fields between Wharton and Bay City.

SN: *Did any blacks own their own land to farm, or was it still sharecropping?*
JW: By the 1950s, sharecropping had been much diluted. The rice fields were large, and people were hired to cut the rice and haul it, but as hired hands. There were farming areas in small towns outside Bay City, but no one had big cotton farms or big cornfields. As a whole, blacks worked in restaurants, grocery stores, around homes and schools, and in trucking and moving companies.

I was hired at Hilliard with a friend from Prairie View, James Solomon, the son of Dr. Solomon, the registrar at Prairie View, who had come South from

Detroit. James was a great little athlete, a basketball player. I'd just turned twenty-two. I became the head football coach, and he was the assistant football coach. He was the head basketball coach, and I assisted him. I was the head track coach, and he assisted me in track.

SN: *You were a teacher there, too?*
JW: Right. I was a teacher as well as a coach.

SN: *What subjects did you teach?*
JW: My first year or two, I taught math and English. I didn't teach physical education those years; James did. But when James left to go to Temple, Texas, I took over as basketball coach as well as football and track coach, and I taught P.E. until I left in 1965.

   We were all teachers first. You were hired as a teacher, and then you coached after school. None of us were hired as coaches at that time.

SN: *What schools did you play?*
JW: Most of the schools that we played in football were about the same size, although they shifted frequently. For two years, you might be in a league with Silsbee or West Orange, and the next year it might be Wellington in place of Silsbee and Jasper in place of West Orange. Some schools were larger, like Victoria, which was in a city of 30,000 or 40,000. When I first got to Bay City, Victoria was whipping tail. And I said, "We're going to catch up to Victoria," and we did.

SN: *What were the high school athletic facilities like in Bay City?*
JW: Our facilities were very poor. We didn't have a gym, and our dressing area the first couple years was a little room. There were no showers. We'd play our basketball games in a town called Van Vleck that had a gym. About 1956 they built a gymnasium at our school.

SN: *And how did that compare with the gymnasium at the white high school?*
JW: You could put our gym inside of theirs. It was just a scaled-down version of what they had at Bay City High School, the white school. It had a little itty-bitty dressing room for physical education. We had a football field, and James and I would line it off. I ruined some good shoes with that watery lime. But we were so caught up in this business that we made a vow to put the place on the map.

And we did turn the place around. When I arrived at Hilliard, the athletic department owed money to the local sporting goods dealer. I had to overcome that. We made sure we paid him so much money out of the gate receipts every week. We got the school out of debt. Instead of scrabbling, we were able to requisition the equipment we needed to outfit more of the kids. We had a field house built. Hilliard High School became one of the most feared and talked about athletic programs in the state.

SN: *What was it like being a rookie head coach, at the young age of twenty-two? You had obviously been in a position to observe some pretty good coaches and learn from their methods.*
JW: Coaching was quite a challenge, since I had never had any formal experience, never having been an assistant coach. But I emulated the coaches I had played under. I remembered those great coaches I'd had. I said, "What would Jimmie Stevens, or Pop Long, or Wayne Austin want me to do?"

I had closely observed the coaches I had played under. Wayne Austin and Jimmie Stevens to me were two peas in a pod. A white guy and a black guy—I thought they had the same personalities. Pop Long was different. I never heard Pop raise hell with anyone. Later on, I talked to some of my teammates from Prairie View, and I said, "You know, Pop used to coach the meeting with his socks turned down to his shoes?" And they'd look at me surprised. I noticed everything about Pop Long. I noticed everything about Wayne Austin, my first coach, even before he knew my name.

Those of us who had graduated from Prairie View and were coaching would go to the Prairie View games on Saturday, and Monday we were running Prairie View's plays. We loved them, and they respected us. We were big wheels. When we came to the Prairie View campus, we were treated just like the $200,000 donors at the University of Oklahoma.

SN: *There was one white high school and one black high school in Bay City?*
JW: Right. My white counterpart at Bay City High School, Don Hailey, helped me with coaching as much as anyone.

SN: *When did that start?*
JW: Mid-1950s. I had a great deal of respect for him. He was from Philadelphia, Pennsylvania, and was a Baylor product. I could talk with Don and with his whole staff. He and I became real good friends. Don had attended a coaching clinic at Rice run by its head football coach, Jess Nealy. I asked Don if I could go, and he suggested that I apply. This was in 1954 or 1955, and I was accepted,

Joe Washington Sr. at the University of Oklahoma football stadium.
Courtesy of Joe Washington Sr.

although I had to stay at the black hotel, the Ajapo, in Houston. I was realizing a childhood dream, because Rice and Tulane had always been my favorite
schools. I've always been the type of guy who sat in the front row, and Don
sat near me. Most of the other guys there didn't say anything to me. The
first thing that Coach Nealy said was, "Good morning, gentlemen," in that

Southern drawl of his. And then he looked at me straight in the face, and he made a special greeting and salutation to me. He said, "Coach, we're so happy to have you with us." Coming from Jess Nealy, I thought that was great.

SN: *You were the only black person there?*
JW: Yes. I dare say I was the first black to attend that Rice clinic.

SN: *Did that open the way for more black coaches to attend?*
JW: I think that's right.

SN: *Was this set up as a teaching clinic where high school coaches could learn more about football?*
JW: Right. Texas has always been a football state, and one of the ways they improved the quality of high school coaching was by the colleges putting on these clinics.

Now Prairie View also had a coaching clinic that I attended right after I graduated. Bear Bryant spoke at it. Certainly, when I started coaching, I was going to come back to my old school's clinic. In fact, I came back as a guest lecturer one year, after we had won the state football championship at Hilliard. That was Prairie View's modus operandi, they recognized their own.

About 1959, I campaigned for our high school to get a field house like Don Hailey had at Bay City High School. I asked the school board to come down and look at our facility. I had my whole P.E. class in that little dressing room when they arrived. They could hardly get through and had to struggle to get out the door. So, they saw we needed a field house. I made a replica of Don Hailey's field house for them, but they cut it somewhat. But we were able to get a field house, a nice facility.

At Hilliard, we played football on our own field, but it was inadequate. They did upgrade it, adding bleachers and lights, but it wasn't enough. We did not have a track. I had to use the track at Bay City High School. I wanted to get the same funding and the same facilities as the white school.

SN: *Now, in Bay City, the political office-holders were all whites, right?*
JW: That's correct. All the school board members in Bay City were white, all the city council members were white, and the mayor was white.

SN: *Blacks had no representation at all in city government then?*
JW: Not while I was in Bay City, up through the mid-1960s.

SN: *What was the voting situation for blacks in Bay City? Could you vote at all?*
JW: Almost nonexistent until the Voting Rights Act passed [in 1965]. Nonetheless, I pleaded the case of getting tax dollars to fund our facilities and equipment.

SN: *Bay City's black leaders must have been interested in supporting the school.*
JW: Oh, yes. Hilliard High School was named after one of the early black educators.

SN: *Where was the black leadership in Bay City drawn from?*
JW: They were physicians, the preachers, the teachers, the undertaker, and the Smith family that owned the grocery store. We had two black doctors. They came to Bay City a little after I began coaching there. One was the brother of my teammate on Prairie View's track team. The other one became our team physician and performed wonders for us. The black professional class, which made up much of the leadership, had grown considerably since World War II. In my age group, it was almost a revolution. This age group went to college more than any group before them. The G.I. Bill put more young black guys into colleges, which gave a new slant to things, opening job opportunities. They were going into teaching and other professions.

SN: *What were the town's hospital facilities like?*
JW: They were segregated. Prior to the black doctor coming, we had to rely on the white doctor. If a player were seriously injured, he'd be sent to the black section of Mantagorda County Hospital.

SN: *Having served in the military, I'm sure you knew what good facilities were. How would you compare the county hospital with what you saw in Hawaii?*
JW: The Mantagorda County Hospital offered the best medical facilities the county could. But the black facilities left a lot to be desired. There was never adequate room—that might have been the number-one drawback. The next thing was the sensitivity of the doctors and nurses. That depended upon the individual doctor or nurse.

The pecking order was really important to whites then. The biggest thing that whites were concerned with then was who's on first, who's in charge. And once it was established that they were in charge, things sort of drifted along in a smooth fashion. You might have worked at a job for forty years, and they brought in a white employee, and this white employee felt that he or she was in charge.

Having been in the military in Hawaii, I couldn't conform to that. That's why I had to get away from Rosenberg, because I wasn't conforming. Hawaii gave you a sense of things that were not available to you, but should have been. Later on, I was driving with my kids in Houston and we passed a horse stable on South Main. My kids said, "Hey, Daddy, we want to go ride the horse!" I pulled my little ole '57 Chevy into there, ready to go inside. And this guy says no, there is one on so-and-so and so-and-so. I was upset. My daughter asked, "Why can't they ride those old stinking horses?" She didn't want to ride, but wanted to know why her brothers couldn't. I told them, "Come on, get in the car, we'll go to another place." But we would take the kids to places; we wanted them to do what other kids were doing.

Another time in the early 1950s, when my kids were very young, they brought a youth baseball team to Bay City from a town farther down in south Texas that had integrated sooner than anyplace in Texas. There was one black player on that team. Being head coach, one of the town's citizens came to me and asked to have the kid stay with me, and they'd take care of the expense. I didn't want to be a part of that. But somebody had to take the kid, because they wouldn't let him stay with the white kids. Now that bothered me for a long time. My conscience really bothered me. I was contributing to that situation. At the time, I didn't want the kid to be exposed to too many bad things. In reality, though, I might have been adding salt to the wound. We talked about that a long, long time after it happened.

SN: *I imagine you sent some of the students you coached during your first few years to different colleges.*
JW: Not different colleges. Just one—Prairie View. At that time, the black college coaches used their ex-players as recruiters. If we had a player who was real good, we would get on the phone and call our college coach. Texas Southern, Southern, Bishop—all of us did that. They'd say, "Send him up, coach."

SN: *You mentioned that Pop Long coached at Prairie View, but then he left and coached elsewhere. So, you would send a player to an institution, not to a man?*
JW: Right. You'd send the kid to the school, not to the coach. If the coach left the school, you still sent the kid to your school, not the one the coach went to. Whoever became the coach learned where the networks were.

I had one kid, Richard Parker, a great thrower, who didn't want to go to Prairie View, because his girlfriend was at Wiley. I told him he was going to

Prairie View. Consequently, he didn't do well. After that, I wasn't going to force a kid. I was going to tell him the benefits of Prairie View, and if he didn't want to go there, I was going to try to get him someplace else. I had another boy named Barney Allen, a big, good-looking athlete, six foot three, 190 pounds. Joe Jr. at one time thought he was his brother, because he was one of those kids that we took in. And Barney wanted to go to Texas Southern. At first I tried to talk him into going to Prairie View, but he said he was really impressed with Texas Southern, and wanted to go there.

The most recruited player I had in Bay City, Sammy Lee Clark, ended up going to Prairie View. He was recruited by mostly black schools, but some white schools were interested, like Texas Western in El Paso. He played for us from 1956 to 1959, but if he had played five years later, he would have been highly recruited by the white schools. He was a hell of a football player, five foot ten, 190 pounds, who ran a 9.9 100-yard dash and threw the shot put forty-some feet. I won my first state championship with Sammy Lee. We played Hamilton Park High School of Fort Worth for the championship and beat them 22-14. Sammy scored all twenty-two points, playing with a bad knee. That shows what kind of a back he was. He hobbled out there and would score a touchdown for us. We'd get the ball close in or in a crucial spot, third and something, or fourth and goal, and Sam would go in. That's the way you played him. If Sam had started that game, we'd never have won, because they would have taken him out. He went on to Prairie View, but sustained a knee injury there as a freshman.

SN: *What schools would you play when you were coaching at Bay City? What was the orbit there?*
JW: We were in a segregated conference. But I wanted to play good schools, with good programs, even if it meant taking some losses. I felt my fans wanted to see good teams play, and my players would benefit from going up against top-level competition. The first great program that I played was Baytown. They had a hell of a coaching staff and very good facilities. My wife's parents knew the principal, and I arranged a game with them. So, we went to Baytown, and they beat us like a drum. Their facilities and the big crowd wore us to a frazzle. But the next year, they came to Bay City and we beat them. And from then on, I scheduled every good team I could. We would schedule teams out of Houston, San Antonio, Corpus Christi, as nondistrict teams.

SN: *So, you were willing to risk taking losses to set up a challenge, where you would be able to improve the program by testing your players against top-level competition.*

JW: I brought that same philosophy to Port Arthur, where I've coached at Lincoln High School since 1965. For the last ten years, we've scheduled schools three times my size. If I've scheduled three of those schools, I've scheduled three losses a year. But we never ran from a challenge.

SN: *And you think in the long run it helps players.*
JW: But it does not help me as a favorite or a great coach in the eyes of the fans.

SN: *All they look at is the won-lost record.*
JW: That's right. They want to win. I found this out, and it's sad. You could schedule Notre Dame, and if you lose, you're a poor coach. You could schedule Slippery Rock and win, and you're a great coach.

SN: *You had the job security where you could take chances on losing games?*
JW: No, no, no, no, no. I wish. But I did not let that bother me, even in my younger coaching days. You're on a one-year contract for your first ten years, and then a two-year contract, and then you get to three years.

In Bay City, we were fortunate enough to win on a consistent basis. I left Bay City with a hundred or so wins, thirty losses, two or three ties, in thirteen years. That's not so bad.

SN: *What changes took place in Bay City in your years there, from 1951 to 1965?*
JW: Between 1951 and 1965, when I left to go coach at Port Arthur, racial changes were evident in Bay City, including in sports. When I first arrived in Bay City, you didn't go across town for anything, other than working. But after a while, we were able to get our football games scheduled at the white high school stadium. Before that, when the games were played on our campus, I can't remember seeing any white fans at my football games. None. Absolutely none. But when we went across town and played on their turf, the whites started coming. And when I left Bay City in 1965, that stadium was packed for our games. We'd fill up our side, and it would overflow to the other side. Many times, there were as many white fans as black fans at our games. Both sides, with the same seating capacity, were full.

I also saw the public facilities, the restaurants, and the theaters becoming more liberal. When I first came to Bay City, we sat up in the balcony in the theater. We called it the "Crow's nest." And then we found ourselves sitting down on the floor, out of the balcony. I can't say this change was all over southeast Texas, but it was taking place in some towns.

SN: *Was there any organized pressure by the black community in Bay City against segregation?*

JW: There was no marching. There was none of that. There was nothing violent, and nothing real demonstrative. It was people talking, people associating together. Things that occurred in Mobile and Birmingham impacted us, because of the media.

There was a lot of unrest. Heck, I can remember situations in Bay City on an individual basis where words were exchanged, where people were saying, "Go here," or "Get in the line," "I don't have to get at the end of the line," things of that sort. Now there were many of those. But not the masses demonstrating.

Most people assumed a look-wait-and-see attitude. What happens there, we're going to do it here. That's why I say it happened slowly, because we waited to see what happened over there. Now again, different people would assume certain postures. Those who were stern segregationists, then you still had to follow the old order of laws in their place. Then one around the corner—open arms.

We were never ever satisfied with the way things were. People weren't demonstrating, but they were waiting for things to happen. Had we been subjected personally to the things that some of the blacks in other Southern cities were, we could have easily had a demonstration or riots. But it just did not occur. Numbers were probably the reason. People in a small town are more able to talk things over.

SN: *Why did you leave Bay City and go to Port Arthur?*

JW: I left in part to coach at a larger level and in part because the desegregation of schools was imminent. And when that happened, the tendency was to downgrade the black head coach to assistant coach, especially in football, because it was a high-profile sport.

SN: *Has Abraham Lincoln High School in Port Arthur, where you went to coach, always remained predominantly black?*

JW: It was 100 percent black when I first went there, and remains today over 90 percent black. There are many predominantly black high schools in Texas.

SN: *What part of Port Arthur does it draw from?*

JW: The west side.

Winning did not come as rapidly in Port Arthur as it did in Bay City because we tended to play larger schools. And as desegregation proceeded,

Joe Washington Sr. Courtesy of Joe Washington Sr.

we got smaller, as more black kids were going to white schools. When I came to Port Arthur on June 22, 1965, I had to get a staff ready, and we didn't have much time. We played in a black league. We were competitive, finishing 4-6. There weren't many schools smaller. We played schools from Houston, from Tyler, and the two black schools in Beaumont. But the next year, 1966, playing virtually the same schedule, we went to 6-4 and were cochampions.

In 1967, we went into a desegregated league, playing white schools that played black kids on their teams. We had losing records in 1967 and 1968, before going to 6-3 in 1969, finishing number two in the district. In 1970, our student body at Lincoln went from 1700 down to 1200. I started out in 1970 with kids on my team in August who in November, because of the zoning, were lining up against me, having been shifted to other schools. We finished 5-5 in 1970, but in 1971, with a school of 1200 kids, competing against everybody else with numbers almost twice our size, we finished 10-0. Joe Jr. was a junior, and he made All-State. In 1972 we were 10-1 or 11-1, and in 1973, 8-2 and won the district also. We were still the smallest school in our district, and these numbers started catching up with me in 1975. We struggled through until the early 1980s.

SN: *Because of your schedule, and your going up against really tough competition, I imagine more of your players were ready to play high-level college and even pro ball, than were those from schools where the coaches just played lesser schools to take the wins. How do you learn if you don't face good competition?*
JW: That's the way we looked at it. What you're saying is true, because during a ten-year period, we had at least two kids playing at the same time in the pros. At one time, we might have had three. We sent guys to San Diego, Miami, the 49ers, Joe with the Redskins.

SN: *Who were some of the players at Lincoln High School who went on to play in the NFL?*
JW: There were about half a dozen, including Leroy Leopold, Michael Green, Tim McKyer, Ronald Haliburton, and Joe Jr. A couple of other kids went into the Canadian League. Coaches would say, if you played for us, you'd become a pretty good football player.

It was difficult for us to win on a consistent basis, because we were a small school and numbers rule the world. In football, especially, numbers count. Because of the nature of the game—the physical contact—you've got to replace kids who go down. We could place eleven good football players on the field who could play with anybody. But lose one, and we were in trouble.

I had a player in Port Arthur who broke his neck in a football game, was paralyzed, and died within two years. The rest of that season I was just like a man who had amnesia. I was just going through the motions. Had it happened earlier in my career, I wouldn't have been able to handle it; it would have devastated me. I'm grateful that the Lord saw fit to put me in a situation where I could handle it.

SN: *I know that the University of Texas was slow to recruit black players. When did mostly white schools from out of state start looking at black high school players in Texas?*
JW: The recruiting of black kids by the major white colleges started in the late 1950s and early 1960s. They were really coming down and getting the

black Southern boy. Scouts came down to the games, although we weren't talked to as much as the bigger schools, like the ones in Beaumont. But by playing them, our kids were exposed to the scouts, too.

I'm using Aaron Brown as a guide. He went to Minnesota. Bubba Smith went to Michigan State.

SN: *You knew Bubba Smith?*
JW: Yeah, I know Bubba Smith's father. We're good friends. He first coached at my wife's hometown, Lufkin. Then he went to Orange and from there to Beaumont.

It was easier for the coaches at the northern schools to recruit a black kid. The guy from Michigan or Ohio State didn't have to look over his shoulder. But the Southern coach did. There were too many people he had to get an okay from. And this slowed them down tremendously. And we certainly cannot ignore the fact that there was a great deal of prejudices on coaching staffs. But the whole shooting alley came to Port Arthur after a while.

SN: *What are the problems you see coaching and dealing with the youth of today in the high school, as opposed to when you were starting out?*
JW: Today's athlete is bigger, he's faster, and he's stronger. He's as intelligent about the game as any athlete of any period. But he is a victim of modern times. He's a victim of money, material things that in earlier days kids weren't accustomed to. Today's athletes see games as avenues to different things than yesterday's kids. Yesterday's kids used sports as a way to enjoy life, association, character building. Now, it's more an avenue to businesses.

The high school athlete's personality was much different then. Then, other people dictated and controlled it and changed it. There are not many personality changes that a kid is undergoing today. What he came with, he's sticking with. I am who I am, and nobody changes me.

SN: *How does that work with a football team?*
JW: Yesterday's kid was "Help me, change me," and consequently the coach played a bigger role in the molding of his personality than he does today.

SN: *The player is just less willing to listen now?*
JW: It's not necessarily the case that all of today's players are less willing to listen, but that we are less willing to make him listen, because of outside factors. We're too aware of the consequences. Yesterday, there were no consequences. Just, "Don't kill my child," says mother and father. "When you beat

him up, let me be able to recognize him." No, it wasn't that bad. But you see the point.

SN: *You had more leeway to impose discipline.*
JW: Of course.

SN: *Who intervenes now?*
JW: Society. Society intervenes. Look at the recent case where the mother slaps the kid, and she's *arrested*. It was a little different yesterday.

Hey, you know how I'd spend my young days as a coach during the football season? Checking on my football players. Calling, if they had a phone, or driving around in my car to see if they were in on game night during the season. Today, we're concerned with society, and we don't do it as much as we should, or could, or would do it.

Peer pressure is a real problem for the kids now, too. Peer pressure has never been such a reality as it is today. You do it—because they're doing it. Majority rules. They rule, but that doesn't make them right. I think people get mixed up with that.

JOE WASHINGTON JR.

RUNNING BACK

—San Diego Chargers, 1976–1977
—Baltimore Colts, 1978–1980
—Washington Redskins, 1981–1984
—Atlanta Falcons, 1985

"Little Joe" Washington was born in Crockett, Texas, in 1953, the son of Joe "Flash" Washington, a legendary figure in Texas football. The senior Washington was an outstanding running back at Prairie View A&M and head football coach at high schools in Bay City and Port Arthur, Texas, for forty-five years. Joe Jr.'s father coached him when he played high school football in Port Arthur.

Joe Washington Jr. was an All-American running back at the University of Oklahoma, where he played on two national championship teams coached by Barry Switzer, in 1974 and 1975. He was the number-one draft choice of the San Diego Chargers, the fourth player selected in the draft. He played ten years in the NFL, with the Chargers, the Baltimore Colts, the Washington Redskins—on two Super Bowl teams—and the Atlanta Falcons. Bert Jones, his quarterback at Baltimore, described him as a "quick scat back," who, although weighing only 175 pounds, could take a lot of pounding, "and delivered a lot of pounding." Jones noted that like his Oklahoma teammate Greg Pruitt, he "ran sideways faster than [he] ran forward, which is really a talent." Washington was also an expert

Joe Washington Jr. with the Washington Redskins. Courtesy of Joe Washington Jr.

pass catcher and kickoff and punt returner. In 1979, as a running back, he led the NFL in pass receptions.

Washington talks not only of his early exposure to sports, as a six-year-old standing on the sidelines with arms folded, in imitation of his father, watching him run high school football practices, but of his perceptions of the Jim Crow system and black community life in Bay City, and how he later experienced school desegregation in Port Arthur. He critiques H. G. Bissinger's depiction of Texas high school football, *Friday Night Lights: A Town, a Team, and a Dream* (Addison-Wesley, 1990), providing a different perspective. Washington describes the college recruiting process, playing in a big-time football program at the University of Oklahoma under Chuck Fairbanks and Barry Switzer, whose coaching style he compares, and the college athlete's academic experience. The son of two schoolteachers who emphasized the importance of education, Washington graduated from Oklahoma in four years. Washington also explains the technique of the running back, on natural and artificial turf and in different weather conditions, and that of the kickoff and punt returner. Washington's adjustment to the NFL was complicated by a serious knee injury he sustained during the exhibition season. He later suffered two detached retinas, as well as further knee damage. He provides considerable insight into how players cope with injury and pain, and the pressure to play when hurt.

Washington served as player representative for the Chargers and participated in the 1982 NFL players' strike with the Redskins, and the interview examines pro football's labor situation in depth. Washington astutely analyzes not only strike issues and strategy, but contract negotiations, being traded, and relations between coaches and players. He also examines how athletes adjust to aging and retirement.

STEPHEN NORWOOD: *Why don't we begin by talking about your family background. When and where were you born, and who are your parents?*
JOE WASHINGTON: I was born in a little town called Crockett, Texas, in 1953. My parents are both educators. My dad coached me in high school. He's been coaching at least forty years. My mother was a schoolteacher. Her parents were schoolteachers in Lufkin, Texas. Her dad was the principal of the high school she attended. At that time, of course, there weren't many professions open to blacks. So, if you were a teacher, you were considered in the upper echelon, the cream of the crop.

Normally, I would have been born in Lufkin, Texas, my mom's hometown. But we had relatives in Crockett, and I think my parents were up there visiting at the time, plus the doctor there was the one to see. Crockett is about thirty-five or forty miles from Lufkin. In Texas at that time, blacks were not able to use certain hospitals.

At the time I was born, my parents were living in Bay City, Texas, a town about seventy-five miles west of Houston. It had a population of about 12,000. My dad was coaching there at the black high school. My sister was born there in 1954 and my brother in 1956. We lived there until I was in the sixth grade.

My dad had been a fantastic athlete, and he was a big influence on me. He played everything. I've looked at his scrapbook. He was referred to as Joe "Flash" Washington in all the newspaper clippings. As a kid, I remember him having real good speed. He was also a running back and played defensive back, and he said he was probably a little quicker than I was. He started playing in the air force, in Hawaii, where he was stationed. He made a pretty good name for himself there. Then he went to Prairie View A&M, and played football there.

My dad was from a little city called Rosenberg, Texas. So, we're all Texans. I know my mom's grandmother, my great-grandmother, was Indian, Comanche. So, I guess I have a little Indian blood running through me.

During the summers in Bay City, my dad worked for the city, taking care of the swimming pool that was right across from the high school. So, we learned to swim at an early age. I had no idea how much money he was making or if he needed the second job. As far as we were concerned, we never needed anything. I guess it was really due to the fact that my dad worked as hard as he did. We sort of took things for granted.

Everything was segregated at that time, and the city pool for whites was on the other side of town. They had their swimming pool, and we had our swimming pool. I do recall busloads of kids from surrounding towns—like Sweeney, which was thirty miles away—would come in during the week to swim in our pool.

My first exposure to athletics came from pickup games in the neighborhood. We had football games, and I always played with much larger kids. I had pretty good athletic talent, and they didn't mind choosing me on their teams. I also started to play Little League baseball in the first grade.

SN: *Were there any adult games in Bay City that you watched, an industrial league, or anything like that?*
JW: No, I don't remember any of that.

SN: *So your first exposure to athletics came from pickup games with kids. Did your father say anything about his involvement with sports in the past?*
JW: I didn't think that much about it, until I was in fourth or fifth grade, where I was old enough where it could have some impact on me.

During the year I attended first grade, the black school in Bay City went from grades one through twelve, so every day after school, I went out to watch my dad coach the high school football practice. When I was in second grade, they built a black elementary school, leaving the high school with grades seven through twelve. But my first grade year, I was at school with my dad. And that's the only place I wanted to be. After school was out, I made a beeline for the football field. I think he really enjoyed having me out there. He knew where I was.

As far as I was concerned, my dad was the greatest thing since sliced bread. Whatever he did, I tried to do. If he picked up a pencil a certain way, I picked it up the same. I would throw a football the exact same way. When he was showing those kids out there how to do certain things, I was out there watching. That's why I got run over on the field so many times, always in the way. I was following him, trying to be like him. Walking around with my arms folded.

I emulated what the players on the field were doing. I kicked the football and threw the football every day. A couple of those players were heroes to me; I was really crazy about them. Later on, one of them coached on my dad's staff and was one of my high school coaches. He also coached my little brother, not only in high school but in college, at North Texas State.

SN: *Did your father at any point encourage you to take football seriously?*
JW: No. He never forced or pushed us into any athletics. Maybe he suggested that we play Little League ball.

SN: *What were the athletic facilities like in the high school in Bay City where your father coached?*
JW: When you look back at them, Steve, oh man, they were terrible! He eventually got a field house built out away from the gymnasium. There was no whirlpool until my fourth grade. There was a heat lamp and a taping table, and my dad had a little office at the gymnasium. They had showers over there. There was no weight room. The only weights I ever saw at the time were on television. One of my dad's players would put cement into some little tin coffee cans, and he used those as weights. He made his own. So, as far as facilities, all they had were the balls, the equipment, and dummies—the basics.

The stadium was small, and in later years they ended up playing in the white high school stadium, when they allowed that. We had track meets at the white high school stadium. When I was in fifth grade, my dad let me run in one of the practice meets. I ran the hurdles. I came in last, but I finished.

My father always encouraged my brother and me to do different things, but he never forced us into athletics. But we were always in that particular atmosphere. When the track season came around, we ran track. The high hurdles were too large for me and my brother to really practice on correctly, so he would have the guy in the woodshop cut them down to fit us, so we could make sure we had the correct form. He always did whatever it took for us to be able to do things well. But he never pushed us.

SN: *What contacts did blacks in Bay City have with whites and with white institutions during your childhood?*
JW: At that time, blacks were basically isolated from the white neighborhoods. You were aware of a lot of things taking place around you, but you weren't aware of the reason. For instance, the whites in Bay City had a baseball league, and a team came to town that had a black guy on it. This black guy stayed with us. I had no idea why he was staying with us. I later learned that it was because they didn't allow blacks in the hotels in Bay City. All I knew at the time was that we had this baseball player, who was good, staying with us, and we were lucky enough to have him.

There was a little cafe we used to go to, where my dad would always buy us burgers on Friday and Saturday nights, and I never knew why we had to go around to the side or the back to get served. I always thought we did that because we were special, and they were giving us a good deal—giving us a little extra, you know, and treating us right. Come to find out, one of my dad's players did work there. And he'd always give us an extra burger or two. But the reason we went around to the side or the back was because we were black. Blacks weren't allowed to come through the front.

Growing up, you had your black neighborhoods, your black cafes, your black restaurants. Everything was basically black. You went to black universities. And that's all I ever knew.

SN: *There was a lot of civil rights activity in the South during the early 1960s. How much news about it filtered into Bay City, and what impact did it have on you?*
JW: As elementary school kids, we didn't know much about it. I vaguely remember some talk about voting, in 1963 or 1964. I think they had some kind of poll tax that my folks were having to pay in order to vote.

SN: *Did your parents vote in that period?*
JW: I want to say yes. I think I recall them voting.

SN: *Did you hear them talking about politics or any civil rights issues?*
JW: I think my folks basically shielded us from anything like that. For instance, in Houston there was this place where they had pony rides where blacks couldn't go, but I didn't know that until ten years ago. We'd go by this place, and we kids would always want to stop there. And for some reason, our folks never would stop. Maybe we did stop, but I know we never rode those horses. That place is still there to this day, and I have since gone there—not to ride, but to just stop and walk freely on the grounds. That was weird to me then, because

for the most part, my parents would always try to give us what we wanted, no matter what it was. But in this particular case, for some reason, they never entertained the thought of stopping there. Never did. I didn't find out until a few years ago that blacks weren't allowed there. So in order to protect us from rejection, and to make sure we had good feelings about ourselves, my parents didn't make that big a deal about riding the scraggly little ponies. They wanted us to feel that we were as good as anybody and could do anything we wanted.

SN: *How did your schoolteachers handle civil rights issues?*
JW: The subject may have been brought up, but I can't ever recall being told that "You can't do this, you can't do that." The books were for blacks, maybe by blacks. The curriculum was mapped out for blacks.

SN: *Just to interject one observation I've had in teaching. I taught at Memphis State University for three years before I taught at the University of Oklahoma. And the black students there who remembered the Jim Crow era were aware of the fact that the textbooks they had used in the black schools were the ones that had been discarded by the white system, after being used for six or seven years.*
JW: Yeah, but you don't realize anything like that until you're actually in a system where you're getting new books. As long as you've been getting those books year after year, you just figure, "Gee, they had them a couple years, the class before you."

At Bay City, we participated in a segregated Punt, Pass, and Kick competition sponsored by Ford. The whites held their competition one place, and we held ours another place, and eventually the results came in. And we always felt that because the competition was held separately, we were getting shafted. Your results were taken elsewhere, and the whites made the ultimate decision. So, you never knew what was happening. I was beginning, even at that age, to see that things between black and white weren't equal, but it just wasn't that big of a deal to us. One year, I got beat by two inches, and I was thinking that something wasn't right.

SN: *They have to pick someone in the region to represent it. This all ends up at some NFL stadium.*
JW: Exactly. I never went.

SN: *The whites took the figures from everybody, and made the ultimate decision about who won?*
JW: Yeah. Your figures were taken elsewhere. So, you didn't really know what's what. One year I finished first in the competition, one year I was second, and one year I was third.

SN: *What happened when you were first?*
JW: Nothing happened. I never went anywhere. You were supposed to move up to a higher level, from the city to the region, and so on. All I know is that when I finished first, that was it. I went to the Ford place and got a jacket, and that was it. There was nothing more. No fanfare. But I loved that jacket.

SN: *Was football at the high school where your father coached a major focus of black community life?*
JW: Oh, yes. Friday and Saturday nights. This was big. Yes, Sir-ree. Really big. Everybody turned out to see the Hilliard High Panthers. We had great rivalries. A lot of the towns were within seventy-five miles of each other, so you had a whole convoy of people coming in to root for the visiting team. I knew Mosley, my backfield coach at Oklahoma, while I was in first grade. His high school team in Wharton, Texas, twenty miles away, played my dad's. Everything shut down those nights when there was a football game.

SN: *This would be the number-one focus of interest in the town?*
JW: That was it. Yes, Sir-ree.

SN: *Did the white press in Bay City ever cover the black high school games?*
JW: Yes, they did, because they were always winning. How much they covered them, I can't recall. But I do recall us winning the state championship in 1959 and listening to it on the radio. Several of the games were broadcast over the radio.

SN: *Did your father ever have any aspirations for his own athletes to go into big-time college football? Were the black high school football players being channeled to the black colleges, many of which were outstanding in football, like Grambling? What was the outlook for a particularly talented black athlete that your father coached?*
JW: Oh, to go to a black college, definitely. The particularly talented players that my father coached would be recruited by the black colleges.

SN: *Did any of the big-time white college football programs show interest in recruiting his players?*
JW: The white colleges didn't show any interest until the late 1960s.

SN: *White colleges were not sending any recruiters down until the late 1960s?*
JW: Right. Just from the black schools. The black high school coaches had real strong ties with each other and with the black colleges in the region. So, players would go on to schools like Prairie View and Texas Southern.

SN: *Did your father ever talk about so-and-so, a player he had coached, that it's really a shame, he could have been as good as some of the All-Americans that you read about?*
JW: Yeah, we've talked about kids he had who could have made it either way. He definitely had some. One was a guy named Sam Clark—excellent running back. He probably could have played anywhere. And Carl Jackson, the guy who later coached for my dad. A great athlete—he was long jumping twenty-four feet in the 1960s.

SN: *What happened to Sam Clark?*
JW: I don't know. I think he went to one of the black colleges. That was basically it.

SN: *You moved from Bay City to Port Arthur, Texas. Was this because of the desegregation process, where they were closing down the black schools?*
JW: Yes. In 1965 or 1966 we moved to Port Arthur because they were closing down the black high school in Bay City, making it a junior high, as a result of desegregation. There had been two high schools in Bay City: Hilliard, which was black, and Bay City High School, which was white. Their team was called the Black Cats, which is ironic. I think Hilliard stayed open two years after we left, before they consolidated the two schools. So, with desegregation, my dad, being the football coach and athletic director, would lose his job and be dispersed to another job within the system, at a desegregated high school, where he probably wouldn't be the head football coach. As a result, he moved to a larger, all-black high school in Port Arthur to become their head football coach. That school played in the 4A division, whereas the one in Bay City was 2A. My dad had an offer to go to this same school in Port Arthur earlier and had turned it down. They'd been trying to get him there.

We came to Port Arthur when I was in sixth grade, and most everything was segregated there, too. My dad was coaching at a black high school, and my mom was teaching at a predominantly black elementary school. She was teaching fourth grade, and my future wife was attending sixth grade there. I hadn't met her yet. Her father coached the football team at the black junior high school that supplied my dad's high school with players. I played Little League baseball, and that was still segregated.

We lived out a way, rather than in the inner city, and so I attended a desegregated school in the sixth grade. This was my first encounter with white kids on a regular basis. My old neighborhood in Bay City consisted of blacks and Mexicans. Out of a class of thirty, we had about eight blacks. I hadn't wanted to leave Bay City, where I'd left all my friends. All I knew was that I was in a new school. Whether the kids were white, black, green, or polka dot, I was going into a new situation with a little anxiety.

But one thing I noticed right off the bat was that being a good athlete, you have a tendency to assimilate and fit in. They look at you differently and accept you more. That was evident right away. When it came to sports, I was going to compete. I didn't care who was out there, because I played with larger kids when I was little. And these were kids my own age, so, no big deal. I was ready to get in, and participate, and knock heads, and show my wares.

My sixth grade teacher, Miss Henry, didn't seem to care too much whether you were black or white; she treated everybody creepy. I just thought she was a mean SOB, period. Which was good, because a lot of kids probably went into a situation like that and did get treated differently. Plus, I was always treated pretty well anyway, whether because my dad was a coach, or I was a good athlete, or because my mother was a schoolteacher.

The next year, I went to the white junior high, Stephen F. Austin, which was connected to one of the white high schools.

SN: *Had the black community in Port Arthur been agitating for desegregation in the Port Arthur area?*
JW: I don't remember Port Arthur. I do remember Bay City. You know, we want to be able to go here and there. The one discussion I remember is why would we want to go do this, when we can have what we have, separate but equal. We can still keep our schools—especially when they started closing them down and consolidating them. They started thinking, "Hmmm, we're losing a lot of jobs, so let's keep ours. Just make sure we have all the facilities the white school has."

SN: *So, there was some division in the black community in Bay City.*
JW: Oh, yeah. You're hearing "Desegregate! We want to be able to go here." And I think later, you started to hear more about separate and equal.

SN: *Did your parents have any views on that?*
JW: If they did, I never heard it. I wasn't really aware. But I know when I arrived in Port Arthur, I got my first glimpse of racial disturbances. Fights

after school. Fights in school. Oh, man, it was unreal! You had certain blacks, they didn't want to be there. They didn't like whites, and they were carrying a chip on their shoulders. And vice versa. But again, I was an athlete, and I didn't have any problem.

SN: *Did they have a football team in junior high?*
JW: Yeah, they had organized football. I played seventh and eighth grade basketball, football, and ran track. I did real well at all of them. I was a top athlete. So, I never really had any problems with anything.

SN: *Were you aware of professional sports on the national scene at this time at all?*
JW: As a kid, I followed professional sports pretty closely. In baseball, I watched Roger Maris, Willie Mays, Juan Marichal, Sandy Koufax, Don Drysdale. Those were my heroes. They were the guys I grew up with. In football, it was Lenny Moore and Johnny Unitas. Oh, man, I loved Lenny Moore and Johnny Unitas. Living in Bay City, Texas, I was close to Houston. That was the old American Football League. So, I was a little bit closer to the AFL, the George Blandas, the Billy Cannons, Abner Haynes, Dickie Post, Paul Lowe, Ernie Ladd, Lance Alworth, Charley Tolar—the human bowling ball.

I guess I emulated all of them. I thought I'd be another Billy Cannon. I didn't realize at the time that Billy Cannon was six foot three, 230 pounds. I had no earthly idea he was that big. I never had anything close to the same kind of running style, but I just liked Billy Cannon.

SN: *Now that you're aware of all this out there on the national scene, this is a shift from your father's generation. He wasn't able to really conceive of playing on the national scene or big-time college football. Billy Cannon was from LSU, and a big-time college program like that would be closed off to blacks. But now already, you're telling me that in junior high you can start seeing this . . .*
JW: I didn't think of any of that. Never really thought about college. I thought about the Olympics. I'm thinking, I can do all these sports, I figured I'd be able to participate in the Olympics, in track and field. And then professionally, I'd be able to play baseball, football—not so much basketball. I had certain heroes, and whether they were black or white didn't make any difference to me. I was brought up that people were people, and my folks never did differentiate. So I was in junior high now, just waiting until the ninth grade so I can go to my dad's school. I was just biding my time. I wanted to go with my dad, and I

wanted to play football for my dad. That was one of the dreams I always had. As a kid I had two: play football for my dad and my little brother and I to be on the same team. I was two years ahead of him in school.

SN: *Had your father taught you anything specifically about football? Had you learned what you knew up to this point by watching the games? Had your father coached you in any way?*
JW: No, he had never really coached me. But he was always throwing the football to me and my brother together. He had good techniques. And when he was showing his players out there how to do certain things, I was out there watching.

For ninth grade, I enrolled at my dad's high school, Lincoln, and was going to play freshman football. During the second scrimmage though, my dad called me over and asked if I thought I could run against these guys. We were scrimmaging against Aldine Carver High School. All the black coaches were close-knit, so I'd known all these coaches since being a little kid. My dad's backs weren't running well, so he asked me if I could run against these guys. I said, "Sure, no big deal." I always felt that I was good enough to do anything. Even though I was a little freshman, 140 pounds, I was not in awe. I ran well. And everybody was saying, "Who is that? Who is that guy?" "That's the coach's son. That's Little Joe."

SN: *Your father's name is Joe, too. So, that's why you were known as "Little Joe"? He's "Big Joe"?*
JW: Yes. All those black coaches had seen me grow through the ranks, running around. I was always the little water boy for my dad's teams, carrying the towels out on the field. They couldn't believe it was actually me out there.

There had to have been some pressure on my dad in considering to have his son play varsity, so I ended up playing freshman ball the first game of the season. I was a little upset about it, because I thought I'd shown that I could run against these big guys. I never really confronted my dad about it. But he knew that I was itching to play. Eventually, he called me up from the freshman team.

SN: *Were you a running back in high school?*
JW: In high school, I played running back and wide receiver, but very little defense. I liked to hit, but guys were getting a little larger than I was. After my

sophomore year, my dad moved me to quarterback. I hated that. I didn't want to play quarterback.

SN: *Why not?*
JW: I knew I wasn't a quarterback. My little brother was a quarterback, and I didn't want to play his position. I wasn't a passer. I could throw. I had all the components and all the skills to do that. But I wanted to be a running back. My dad eventually moved me back to the running back position.

SN: *You had also participated in track. Did that contribute to developing some running back skills?*
JW: That's the one thing my father insisted on, that I run track to help my speed. He made me a hurdler. He wanted all his football players to run track.

Playing for my dad, at a time when our school had begun to play white schools, I got a chance to see the racial bias in officiating. Things being called back. Whistles being blown. I saw officials throwing flags, and how we couldn't get a break. Even when they had mixed officiating staffs, the black officials would make sure they weren't showing any favoritism to us by going the opposite way.

My senior year, my brother and I played in the same backfield; he was the quarterback, and I was the running back. There was always John Q. Public saying, "They're playing just because they're the coach's sons." But my dad was the kind of guy who would play a gorilla if he were eligible and could play.

My dad was tougher on us than on other players. He expected the little things out of us, and he expected us to do them automatically. He worked us hard. And I think we expected a great deal out of ourselves, too.

SN: *What kind of pressure was there at this level to win, for the sake of winning? There was a book,* Friday Night Lights, *that raised the issue of the people in that Texas community being obsessed with winning, to the exclusion of anything else. . . .*
JW: I read that.

SN: *It just struck me that there are different requirements at different levels. What works in the NFL isn't necessarily the kind of approach to use in high school.*
JW: I think basically coaching is really coaching. I think at all levels, there is a certain part that should be consistent on every level. As far as the emphasis on

winning in Texas high school football, hey, it's big. Coaches are fired for losing, everywhere.

SN: *Was there pressure on your father? Did he feel insecure in any way, if he didn't have the record in any particular year, that he might lose his job?*
JW: My dad's been under pressure in Port Arthur for the last twenty years, by the mere fact that he's been a newcomer, plus the fact that he played his sons. And with the notoriety he's gotten and the notoriety we've gotten, they've expected him to win all the time, until this day. Every year, they're asking for his job if he doesn't have a winning season.

SN: *The obsession with winning at the high school level may work against the long-term interests of the players, if they're just seen as material to be used for the won-lost record the fans want to see, without them realizing that some of the methods used to achieve that might be detrimental to the players.*
JW: The only time that the fans ever take that under consideration is if you're losing. If you're losing, then they are concerned about the methods, and what is detrimental to a kid's well-being. That is really the only time. Every now and then, you get a small percentage who are really concerned about the methods when you're winning, but he is the hard-core true fan. He's probably the guy who's just enjoying the participation and effort of the kids. He doesn't care himself whether you win or lose.

SN: *What about the stereotyping of black youth as athletes, and once they get injured, they can be just cast on the scrap heap, and nobody's interested in them, and there goes their future?*
JW: That wasn't the case when you had your black coach with his black athletes. Integration set up a totally different environment. Before that, the coach was really more involved in the community. He lived in that area. He knew the players' moms and dads on a first-name basis. These kids babysat for the coach. And it was the same in the white community. It wasn't as distant as it is now. It was more of a community-type situation. Now that is gone. The relationship is gone. Everything now is based on winning and losing and what can be achieved at the next level. Can this guy get a scholarship? After he gets a scholarship, will he be able to play pro? And you've lost your relationship that you once had when everything was segregated.

SN: *Your father was the coach, and I assume he was not going to make you play when you were hurt. But you do hear of some coaches getting so obsessed with winning that they would put a young player's future at risk just for the short-term goal of winning a game.*

JW: First of all, I don't think a coach really has to put direct pressure on a kid for him to try to play in a situation where he probably shouldn't play. I don't think a coach has to come up to you and say, "You gotta play. We need you. You oughta do this. I think you can go." Prime example. This happened to me in the pros. My first year with the Washington Redskins, I got injured the second game, the second play. I was out the next three and a half weeks. I started practicing that week for the game against the 49ers. Right before I went to practice on a Wednesday, my wife asked me how I felt. I said, "I know I'm not going to be able to go. My ankle is killing me. It really hurts." I told her I'd more than likely suit up, but I didn't think I'd be able to play.

Well, there was pressure on me to play, because we were losing backs, and we had started off the season 0-5. I was taped up on the sidelines, hobbling around, not going to play. The backfield coach asked me, "Joe, what do you think? How do you feel?" I replied, "Coach, I'd love to go, but shoot, I know I can't do it. I don't want to be a detriment to the team." Well, before I knew it, it was getting close to the half. I had my helmet close to me, because I was standing up there close, getting into the action. I wanted to have my helmet with me, so that when the whistle blew for halftime, I didn't have to go looking for it. Well, now I had my helmet on. We were driving. And the coach said to me, "Joe, what do you think?" I said, "Oh, I don't know." He told me, "Okay—go ahead!" And before I knew it, I was out on the field, and playing like a banshee.

It isn't so much the direct pressure from the coach, then. It's the pressure of being in a situation and competing. I don't care what level you're on. You're in a situation where everybody is involved, and as a player you really want to play no matter what. If you feel that there is the slightest way you can participate, all he has to say is "What do you think?"

SN: *What I'm saying is a more mature coach, a more responsible coach, might understand, as you understand, what the disposition of the player is going to be, in the overall environment of excitement and wanting to contribute, and might caution the player, whereas, say, a coach who is interested only in his own record, rather than the player's future, might give some indication—even saying it's up to you might not be the way a coach should handle it with a sixteen-year-old player.*

JW: I'm sure they do that. I think every coach is going to say, "It's tough, and we really need you, but it's up to you. If you feel you can go, you can go." And hey, that's pressure, no matter how you look at it.

SN: *Did you ever get hurt playing high school football?*
JW: Yep. My senior year in high school I broke my leg—my ankle, and a bone above it. I missed the rest of the season and possibly cost us the chance to win the state championship. Depressing, man. My little brother, our quarterback, had broken his left wrist the week before. They put a plaster cast on, and he continued to play. We still ended up winning the district. We lost the second or third playoff game. If I'd have played, we probably would have won the state. Just to show the kind of respect they had for us, even though we didn't play in the state finals or in the game before that, they still rated us the number-two team in the state.

That was probably our last true chance to win the state championship, because we had everything that year. Nonetheless, two years after that, they won the district because of my brother. He really made the difference in our football team. For three years, my dad didn't have to worry about a quarterback. He had a coach on the field. My brother was a great athlete, a guy with the right type of temperament. He ended up going to North Texas State, and he started there as a freshman. We were national college co-backs of the week, the only time that had ever happened. I really enjoyed playing in the same backfield with him in high school, because as kids, playing in the neighborhood, we were very seldom on the same team. Kids felt we had an advantage being the coach's sons and good athletes. So, we'd always end up going against each other.

SN: *What were the facilities like by this point? You commented that earlier they had struck you as very poor. Had they improved?*
JW: The facilities had improved considerably. When I got to ninth grade, they actually had free weights. By my senior year, we had a Universal machine. They were just coming out. The uniforms were great. My little brother and I designed them.

SN: *What accounts for this change? Was more money being contributed?*
JW: Yeah. Football is a big budget item in all institutions, whether it's college or high school or junior high. And in Texas there's more emphasis on it than in other places. You don't buy your own equipment. They supply it for you. So, you have two pairs of shoes . . .

SN: *In* Friday Night Lights, *the author talks about this high school team flying across the state in a chartered plane.*
JW: We didn't do that. You're talking there about a school in the oil patches, when the boom was big. That was an area where there was nothing much to

do but play and watch football. I think that made the community a little closer. They were a tight-knit community because of that. What was wrong with them having the type of interest in football and their kids and community that they do? I would think that the crime rate in that community is less than most other places, especially during football season.

What ticks me off about *Friday Night Lights* is the fact that the author came into that town and presented himself as an ally to them and a member of the community and then wrote about them in the manner he did. Granted, a lot of the things he said were exactly true. But he focused on football being an obsession, out of which nothing good could possibly come. I really resented that, especially with my dad being a coach.

SN: *But the author displays some sympathy for the coach. I remember one part where he said these people would put "For Sale" signs on the coach's lawn if he was losing.*
JW: Oh, yeah. Well, I know they did that once to Barry [Switzer]. They sent a moving van up to Barry's when we [Oklahoma] lost to Kansas.

SN: *You raise a point that's quite valid. There's nothing else to do in that town anyway. The concern I would have is that it seemed like they were trying to impose an NFL model in a high school. Very few people are ever going to make the NFL. You have to prepare them to do something else in life.*
JW: You can talk about them putting a professional emphasis on high school football, but it's hard for me to relate to not having that emphasis put on it. This is something special. It's something most people would love to do for life. A lot of these kids, after they take off their pad after that last game, will never play again. So, when you talk about putting a professional emphasis at the high school level, that's really what it is anyway.

I don't think a kid should go to high school today and not participate in some extracurricular activity. With all the single parents you have now, a kid should be at school as much as possible. You think back to the days when you were in school, and you walked to your neighborhood school, and you knew everybody. Kids weren't on the street as much because, first of all, they were in school. They were in the band, in the glee club, participating in some sport. So, when they went home, all they had time to do was eat, and do their homework, and then go to sleep, because they were tired. The fact that they are deemphasizing extracurricular activities, especially the arts, is killing institutions of learning.

SN: *Why don't we move on to the college level now. First, let's look at how you experienced the recruiting process. You had already established yourself as a high school player and had been in the All-Star games. . . .*

JW: At that time, I hadn't thought that much about college. I wanted to play pro, it seemed fun and all that, but no big deal. Being a Texan, I wanted to go to the University of Texas. I used to watch the Darrell Royal show on television, and when they played "The Eyes of Texas," I stood up at attention and put my hand over my chest. At that time, that was the gospel. I wasn't thinking white as opposed to black. I wasn't thinking in terms of color at this time. This was Texas, and I lived in Texas. They're playing "The Eyes of Texas are upon you."

I followed the Texas games closely and was familiar with the players, yes, Sir-ree. I loved their uniforms, until I got to high school. Then I hated the all-white. I needed something with color.

I was heavily recruited. In high school, I was All-Conference my sophomore year and All-American my junior year. I started receiving letters from colleges my sophomore year in high school. I guess I got a recruiting letter from every major college in the country.

SN: *Your father was very experienced with the recruiting process. Could you describe his role in this?*

JW: I was lucky that the recruiters had to go through my dad. I didn't have any direct contact with them until my senior year. My dad made sure that they were okay, and that there weren't any illegal offers. If I were to pick a school, I was going strictly on the merit of the university, not because I was induced. He made sure that if I got a car, he was going to buy a car for me. So, I never had any illegal offers made to me by any university. None whatsoever.

My father had had players who had gone on to colleges, including white universities. But this was probably a first for him, to have this kind of onslaught. But he felt he knew what was best for his son.

At that time, you could take as many visits as you wanted to, which I think is a good way to do it. I think you're limited to a certain number now. I took probably thirty-four or thirty-five visits. All weekends were gone, because I was gone all the time. Oklahoma was probably my thirtieth visit. If I had been limited to six choices, Oklahoma wouldn't have been one.

I had no idea where I wanted to go. I felt that I could compete no matter where I went. We always call it "athletic arrogance." As a kid, I loved the University of Texas. But as I grew older, I understood the reality of things. Not many blacks had gone there.

SN: *Well, Barry Switzer talks about you in his book,* Bootlegger's Boy *(William Morrow, 1990), as choosing the University of Oklahoma in great part because they had recruited black players.*
JW: That had a lot to do with it.

SN: *The University of Texas had not been doing that.*
JW: Right, but that really didn't bother me. I felt I could compete there.

SN: *But just from the social standpoint, I would think that would be a factor.*
JW: Not that directly. That became more evident to me after I had chosen the University of Oklahoma. Then it became clear that it was totally different from the University of Texas.

SN: *So Texas tried to recruit you?*
JW: Oh, yes. They didn't want to lose me to out-of-state.

SN: *Who would come down to talk to you? Did the head coach?*
JW: Texas had a guy named Fred Akers assigned to scout my area, southern Texas. At the time, he didn't know that I loved Texas. Of course, I was concerned that they didn't have a real good history of black players. But as a seventeen-year-old kid, thinking he's the greatest thing since sliced bread, I don't think I left with the impression that they thought that.

SN: *I take it you went to the University of Texas campus?*
JW: Yeah, I did. Texas did have me come out to the campus, but I just didn't get the right vibes from them.

SN: *How did they try to sell the Texas program to you?*
JW: When you go on these visits, they show you the facilities, where the players stay, the dining hall, and so on. At most of the places I visited, the facilities were pretty good. Texas Christian University's facilities weren't that great, when I visited there. But, Texas, my God! At Texas, it was more of a feeling that you were lucky to be there, rather than that they were lucky to have you. I did have a meeting with Darrell Royal. He's been one of my biggest supporters ever since I attended the University of Oklahoma. But I just didn't get real good vibes from him that day. He was cordial.

SN: *What else do they do on a recruiting visit?*
JW: They introduce you to the players, and the players take you around. They usually try to set you up with a date for a movie or dinner. I already had a girlfriend. I was real shy anyway. So, I really didn't want to have too much of that. Plus, you always hear these rumors about what happens on them. I wouldn't tell anybody, but I was always afraid of these rumors about what might happen. To be put in a situation to have to make a decision.

I went to Texas on a weekday, and went back home for a track meet that evening. So, I really didn't get the weekend flavor of the University of Texas.

SN: *Did they mention anything about academics?*
JW: All of the universities stressed the academic part of things on the recruiting visits, which I think you've got to do. They let you know what type of academic programs they had and the tutoring that you could get. At that time, I wanted to be a dentist. But I truly believe, for a kid to really choose where he's going to school, he's definitely got to put the athletics first when he's choosing. If you're satisfied with that, the academics will come a lot easier.

SN: *What were your top five places on your list of colleges you were considering?*
JW: I didn't have a top five. The way it was, I visited a school, and I liked it until I visited another school. The first school I visited was Texas Tech. The one thing I remember about being up there in the Panhandle was that it was extremely cold. I went to a movie and had a real good time. But I just wasn't interested in Texas Tech—maybe because they weren't as rich in tradition as what I was looking for. Even though I wasn't fully aware of this as a high school kid.

I knew I didn't want to go anywhere where the weather was cold. I visited Michigan State, and they had twenty-three inches of snow on the ground. I didn't want a place like that. So, I cancelled all my other trips at cold-weather schools, with Notre Dame and other schools in the Northeast.

When I visited LSU, I really thought I'd like to go there. First of all, they played on grass, and I kind of wanted to play on grass. Their colors were purple and gold, which were my high school colors. They played at night. Excellent, unbelievable facilities. The guy who ran the local sporting goods store, who had strong ties, was really interested in my attending LSU.

I was really impressed with LSU until that night when I attended the LSU–Notre Dame game. Notre Dame was also recruiting me. When the game ended, I was going to try to walk across the field and meet Ara Parseghian, Notre Dame's coach. LSU won the game, and the stadium went wild. Everybody was on the field. The guy who was showing me around was from my high school; he was at LSU on a track scholarship. There were too many people out there, and we couldn't make it across the field. So, we decided to turn around and head back to the dressing room.

All of a sudden, I heard this shot, "Pow!" I immediately felt this sharp pain in my shoulder. I was scared to look and see the blood. I was telling this guy, "Rob, I'm shot! I'm shot!" He stuttered, "Uh, uh, uh, uh." I told him, "Go get somebody, I'm shot!" He went to get a stretcher, but I was too proud to get on one. They eventually got me on it. But I wasn't shot. What had happened was the people had torn down the goalposts, and in swinging them across the field, they had hit me in the shoulder. I was the only one among all those people who had gotten hit. I decided then not to go to LSU. The reason I didn't go to LSU was because I got hit by a goalpost. I figured that was an omen.

One of the schools I had wanted to go to was the University of Houston, because Bill Yeoman, the backfield coach, had coached at my mom's high school in Lufkin, Texas, where my grandfather had been the principal. I had known him since I was a kid. I loved Bill Yeoman; he was a fine gentleman. But when I visited the University of Houston, everything was scattered out. You lived here, and the practice field was a mile away. It just wasn't the type of environment I wanted. But it broke my heart to tell Bill Yeoman I was going to Oklahoma. He told me he understood.

As far as my reasons for going to Oklahoma, when I visited there, it was a beautiful day. The campus was beautiful in the spring. There was a nice breeze blowing. The guy who was recruiting me for Oklahoma was Wendell Mosley, who had been Greg Pruitt's coach at B. C. Elmore High School in Houston. Before that, he had coached at Wharton, against my dad's team. I'd known him since I was a kid. My folks flew up there after I did. They showed me all the athletic facilities and the university dental facility in Oklahoma City. They introduced me to a Dr. Cox, who was a black dentist. I spent a little time with his family.

Another thing I liked about Oklahoma was that they were fancy. They wore white shoes before everybody else. And believe me, the uniforms had a lot to do with where I was going to school. I really liked Ole Miss, just because of Archie Manning and the uniforms.

SN: *But was it the uniform itself, or what the uniform suggests about individualism?*
JW: No, it was just the uniform itself. I liked Ole Miss because of the different colors—the gray, the red, the white, and the blue—even though it was the

gray and red of the Confederate flag. I didn't care. I just liked the color and the color design.

All these things were involved in my decision: what kind of helmet I would wear, the shoes they wore, and whether I would get to wear my high school number of 24. I knew the guy at Oklahoma who wore 24 would be graduating. So, everything clicked with the University of Oklahoma.

SN: *When did you start wearing silver shoes?*
JW: I didn't wear silver shoes until after my senior year in high school. I did it for the first time in the Texas High School All-Star game, where the North played the South, and I was with the South. It was August 1972, and I had already signed to go to Oklahoma. I liked the fact that they wore white shoes. If you wore white shoes, you were real flashy. Here was this white school, and they had their whole team, including linemen, wearing white shoes. I said, "Hmmm. I've got to do something to be a little different." My little brother suggested that I wear silver shoes with red shoestrings. That goes well with the red and white of Oklahoma. So, I decided to do it in the All-Star game. I wore them, and I kept slipping down. But I refused to change those shoes, because they looked great. After I'd fallen down so many times when I had chances to make a touchdown, I finally changed them. But I decided to wear the silver shoes again when I came to Oklahoma.

SN: *What I'm getting from this is a certain desire to be recognized as an individual and a kind of standing out. At some colleges, it's going to be very regimented. Everyone has a crew cut, like Vince Lombardi's style of coaching. It sounds like you wanted to play football, but not be repressed.*
JW: Exactly. Well, my running style basically summed up what I really was.

SN: *When did the Oklahoma coaches first see you play?*
JW: They had never really seen me play until the All-Star game, where I was the most valuable player. They got a glimpse of me there, and they thought, "Okay, he's all right."

SN: *Oklahoma had been recruiting pretty heavily in Texas.*
JW: Oh, yeah. Before that they had Mike Thomas, who later went to the Washington Redskins, and Greg Pruitt. You had backs coming out of everywhere—Kerry Jackson out of Galveston.

I know Wendell Mosley liked me. He told me, "Joe, you'll start as a fresh-man. All-Conference, All-American, you'll win the Heisman Trophy, and you'll be on a national champion and go to a bowl game." It did come true, too. National championship teams in 1974 and 1975. I went to a bowl game my sen-ior year and freshman year, and I probably would have gone the other years if we hadn't been on probation. We were on television my first and second years and should have been on those other years. And I probably would have won the Heisman if people had had a chance to see us play those years.

SN: *You started as a freshman at Oklahoma. Where were you on the depth chart when you came in?*
JW: I was about number thirteen on the depth chart when I came in. But it didn't bother me, because we hadn't had any scrimmages.

Barry Switzer always talks about how when I came in, I had my silver shoes on, but I didn't have any silver shoes. But that makes good copy. The first time I carried the ball, it was a play I love to run. I remember cutting and dodging and dodging and everything. After that I knew I had made an impression. I knew I was going to move up on the depth chart. I didn't think too many peo-ple could do some of the things I could do.

I knew I wouldn't get Greg Pruitt's position, though. He was a senior when I was a freshman. We roomed together on the road. And he'd tell me, "Joe, don't you ever say or think anybody is any better than you are." Greg had that certain type of confidence that rubbed off on me.

In the wishbone, running backs had to block for each other. One thing I noticed about Greg, at 178 pounds—that sucker blocked. I mean, he attacked people with a vengeance. He had a certain attitude about him. He wanted to block. And I blocked aggressively.

SN: *How much did you weigh as a freshman?*
JW: I only weighed 162 or 163 pounds as a freshman.

SN: *They didn't try to get you to gain weight? That's a little light.*
JW: It was light. I cheated when it came time to get weighed. I used to have little ankle weights that had little bars that you slide in. And I'd always take the bars out and put them in my hands, so I'd always weigh a little bit more. The Oklahoma coaching staff always thought I weighed 174. But I was never more than 163 in college.

When my first head coach at Oklahoma, Chuck Fairbanks, would come back to visit after he became head coach of the New England Patriots, he'd always tell me to put on a little weight, and that'd really tic me off. I figured if I put on weight, I'd have to start running over people. Then I'd have to put on another fifty pounds.

SN: *You didn't feel it was any disadvantage in terms of going up against 280 pound defensive tackles?*
JW: No. They always used to tell Greg Pruitt that he was too short to play. He used to say, "Hey, they don't make holes vertically. I don't need to be six foot five. They make them horizontally."

SN: *You see a lot of guys built that way in the NFL today.*
JW: Well, there are a lot of guys in the NFL today who are five foot seven, five foot eight, but these rascals weigh 195, 205. Barry Sanders is 205. Emmitt Smith is 207.

SN: *I remember back in the 1950s, the quarterback Eddie LeBaron was five foot seven, 165 pounds.*
JW: But there were not many like that and not many running backs at 170 pounds.

SN: *Your weight was never a problem for you, in any type of collision?*
JW: I always tried to avoid most of them.

SN: *Two guys can crash into you simultaneously, no matter how elusive you are.*
JW: Most of the time, running backs get hurt when they are being tackled. With running backs, you're going to get fractures, broken legs, torn up knees. I never worried about that. You figured if you played a game, you were going to get beat up anyway. It was just one of the badges of the profession. And you didn't mind showing your war wounds.

SN: *And it wasn't a problem with blocking?*
JW: With blocking, I had to make certain compensations. I couldn't take all these guys head on all the time.

SN: *So you were moving up the depth chart pretty fast freshman year?*
JW: Yes, to the point that by the fifth game of the season my freshman year, I was starting. We played Kansas State, with Greg Pruitt at right halfback and me at left halfback.

SN: *From that point on, you were in the starting lineup?*
JW: Right. Freshman year, I ended up being the second leading rusher on the team.

SN: *Your first year was 1972. What was Oklahoma's record that year?*
JW: We only lost one game that year, finishing 10-1; 11-1, since we won the Sugar Bowl, against Penn State.

SN: *Do you remember that Sugar Bowl game?*
JW: I didn't play much in that game. They played the senior, Joe Wylie. I was a little upset about that. They figured that I was a freshman and had three more years to play. But then we were placed on probation, and I wouldn't be back to a bowl game for another two years.

SN: *How about adjustment to college life generally? Any difficulties?*
JW: No, not really. I had a chance to go home on holidays. My folks came up for most of the games. So, it all worked out pretty well. You did get a little homesick. But my roommate was a high school teammate of mine. And the telephone was the next best thing to being there. That helped a great deal.

SN: *Was there anything going on in the larger community that the players got involved in—in social work, for example? Did they have any contacts in the black community? Did the black athletes have any contact with other black students on campus, or were the athletes kind of a separate world?*
JW: There weren't many black students at Oklahoma at that time, and the ones we athletes came into contact with were mostly in the black fraternities—the Omegas, the Kappas, and the Alphas. A lot of the black players were in those fraternities, so they meshed pretty well with the other black students. You knew them, you saw them, and you played pickup basketball with a lot of them. I ran into a lot of the other black students in classes, but you didn't really hang out with them. There were a lot of parties, but that was about it. But I didn't go to very many parties. I didn't just hang out much anyway. I didn't go to a lot of places. There were a few places I'd go by myself. But on weekends I'd go to Denton, Texas, to see my girlfriend.

SN: *What kind of physical training was there in the football program besides the practice sessions? Was there much weight lifting?*
JW: Of course, I spent a lot of time at football practice. Oklahoma emphasized running and physical conditioning. We did have a small weight room, and I'd

lift, but it wasn't something that I concentrated on in the same vein as my agility. I had real good natural strength, and I lifted just to tone and keep it. But I spent more time running than anything else, to keep my quickness and maneuverability. I stretched a great deal. Oklahoma had a great stretching program. They believed in that. They gave us a book, to make sure that we followed certain stretching rules. We also had something called Fourth Quarter in the spring that was a monster. It consisted mostly of a lot of running and agility drills. I must say I really liked it and never missed a day.

Under Chuck Fairbanks, the scrimmages would involve some contact. And there was one time when he made a player run a drill continuously because he didn't like the way the player was performing, and it cost us the player. The incident involved a black running back, Mike Thomas. Chuck didn't like the way he was blocking on one play in a goal line drill. So, he said, "Run it again for Mike Thomas!" We ran it again, and he still didn't like the way Mike blocked. "Run it again for Mike Thomas!" So we ran it again, and he still wasn't satisfied, and had us do it still again. By this time, Mike Thomas was on the ground, with his shoulder hurt. And Mike was never the same after that. It was always a question of whether his shoulder was well. He eventually ended up leaving Oklahoma and going to the University of Nevada–Las Vegas. There was a lot of grumbling among the players about what had happened to Mike. But I never saw anything racial in it. That's just how Chuck was.

The Oklahoma football program when I was there made sure that the players paid attention to their academic work. Port Robertson was in charge of that, and he made sure that you followed the right academic line. We had study hall for two hours a day. I think that should be mandatory—two hours at least.

SN: *What kind of student had you been in high school?*
JW: Good student.

SN: *Did you think you were pretty well prepared for college?*
JW: Oh, yeah. At that age, the mold is pretty well set.

SN: *How were your study habits?*
JW: My study habits could have been better. My mom and dad were always on me if I had a few Cs, because they knew I could do better.

Because of the structure football provided, I had my better grades during the football season. The times I made the dean's list were during the football season. Maybe once I made it in the spring semester. The reason for that was that I was on a schedule during football season: classes, practice, dinner, study hall, go to your room, retire. And when you have two hours of mandatory study hall, you're going to get something done. During the spring, my grades were not as good because I wasn't on a schedule. If I studied, fine. If not, I'd just go on whatever brain juices I could get going.

I think that the only reason that I did as well as I did academically was that I wanted to make sure that people understood that just because you were an athlete, it didn't mean that you were a dumb jock. I would just go ahead and make the dean's list, just to show them that I could do it.

SN: *How about the next season, your sophomore year? You were a starter from the beginning. Joe Wylie and Greg Pruitt had graduated, and you were the number-one running back.*
JW: We got put on probation that year.

SN: *What kind of impact did that have?*
JW: That meant our games didn't get televised, and we couldn't go to a bowl game. That was about the only impact of the probation. We still drew crowds. It was something, coming down that ramp and seeing all those people. So, it was pretty much the same as the year before.

SN: *Do any games stick out in your memory from that year?*
JW: The Southern Cal game.

SN: *That you tied 7-7?*
JW: Yes. We had a great year, finishing 10-0-1. Only Southern California, ranked number one in the nation at the time, managed to tie us. They had some great players, like Tony Davis and Lynn Swann, but they were lucky to tie us that game. They were *lucky* to get a 7-7 tie. They tied *us*. Remember that.

SN: *How would you compare the coaching styles of Barry Switzer, who took over as Oklahoma's head coach your sophomore year, and Chuck Fairbanks, who had been head coach your freshman year?*
JW: Chuck didn't interact with players very well. He was more aloof. Barry was a people person. He interacted readily, easily, without hesitation. Chuck would sit up in the tower, pretty stoic, unless something was going wrong. Barry would sit up in the tower and get excited and come down. If things were going real well, Barry was exuberant and excited about it. Barry loved it when we'd be

Barry Switzer. Courtesy of the Western History
Collections, University of Oklahoma.

practicing the option, and the runner would be slashing up there, and running forty, fifty, sixty yards down the field. That got him excited. Chuck thought it was good, but he wouldn't really get that excited about it.

SN: *Would Switzer be more willing to give an individual credit for a good performance?*
JW: Oh, yeah! That had a positive effect on you as a player. One thing that you want to know is if the coach is pleased with what you're doing. And if Barry saw something on the film that he liked, hey, you knew it right then.

SN: *In Jerry Kramer's book* Instant Replay: The Green Bay Diary of Jerry Kramer *(New American Library, 1968), he talks about Vince Lombardi rarely giving individual credit, downgrading, telling players they "need improvement." I would think at the college level particularly, when you're coaching people eighteen, nineteen, twenty years old, it might be more effective to give credit where it's deserved.*

JW: I don't know if I could have played for him. With young kids, you need to know you're doing something positive. Barry was the kind of guy that did that.

SN: *I could see from reading Barry Switzer's book that he was fairly tolerant, fairly relaxed, due in part to his own background.*

JW: Barry honored a certain type of individualism, but there were a lot of things that he was a stickler about. Practice. He believed in practice. Practice and go to class. If you practiced and went to class, he could be relaxed about some other things.

That's the problem he had with Marcus Dupree. See, Marcus came out of high school as this great hotshot athlete. When you're a hotshot athlete in high school, everybody will cater to you. Coaches will cater to you. It was different in my case, with my old man. He didn't cater to anyone. Much less his son, who thinks he's some hotshot halfback, the greatest thing since sliced bread. My dad believed in practicing, and Barry was the same way. But Marcus felt he didn't have to practice that much in high school. He came to the game and ran for 500 yards and 900 touchdowns. Okay. So, he comes to Oklahoma, and he feels he doesn't have to practice that much. And some days he gets away with it. And then what does he do? He goes out and runs for three jillion yards and 500 touchdowns. So, he's seeing himself perform in the same way he did in high school. Go to practice, play, do whatever I want. He thought he could go to Oklahoma, practice a little bit, and run all over people. He could usually do that, because he was that kind of athlete.

But Barry didn't believe in that. He didn't care who you were. Marcus Dupree, Joe Washington, you practiced. Lee Roy Selmon, you practiced. They butted heads on that. Barry wouldn't tolerate it. And with Barry having the type of defiance he had and being as honest as he is, he's going to tell you what he thinks. "You're big, you're fat, you're slouchy, you're up to 280 pounds. I don't care if you can run a 9.7, if you're down to 235, when you're in great condition, you can probably run a 9.3 and gain more yards."

SN: *How did sophomore year begin?*

JW: Well, we started off on probation. Barry Switzer became head coach at that time. He had been assistant coach under Chuck Fairbanks, and Fairbanks left to become head coach of the New England Patriots. I remember when Barry announced that the Oklahoma football program had been put on probation, which occurred shortly after he became head coach. I remember Barry saying he was a fighter, and they can take the bowl games away from us and the television, but they can't keep us from competing for the Big Eight and the national championship. They can't keep us from beating people. Him getting emotional up there—that sticks out. I knew even as a young sophomore that there was something pretty special about Barry Switzer.

SN: *Did Switzer have anything to do with building a positive racial atmosphere at Oklahoma? He gets credit, even from his detractors, for having good rapport with black players. There are a fair number of coaches who don't have that rapport. They were a conservative lot, generally.*

JW: Barry had good rapport with black players, but I don't think it was something he was consciously trying to do. It was just Barry, period. He just related. There was something pretty compassionate about Barry as a coach. I think it came from his growing up in a place where people looked at him as an outcast from the wrong side of the tracks.

Of course, we didn't know about Barry's background at that time. To us, he seemed to be the Establishment. The conservative Establishment. We saw him that way because, first of all, he was white, and second, he was coaching at a university that was predominantly white. But he was totally different from what we perceived him to be. Because of his background, he could relate to black players, and he recruited a lot of blacks to play at Oklahoma. He even had a black quarterback, Kerry Jackson, at one time.

SN: *That in itself is unusual.*

JW: Unheard of. I'm talking about 1972, a freshman quarterback.

SN: *Looking at your sophomore year, were there any areas you wanted to improve in then? Or were you generally satisfied?*

JW: One thing, as a little hotshot running back, I thought I should be carrying the ball more. I sort of took my running for granted. I didn't think there was anything I could improve on. As far as my skills as a running back, you could have taken me in high school and put me right in the pros. As far as maturity and being able to handle every situation, that's another story.

I enjoyed blocking and wanted to show our coaches that I could do it. That was the way we impressed them. They expected you to be able to run. But you wanted to show them that you could do everything, especially block. You wanted them to see that you were going in attacking, blocking.

From my sophomore year on, Barry kept me out of physical contact during scrimmages. That was sort of unheard of. He didn't allow certain players to engage in contact if he thought that their getting injured would hurt the team. He did this only with players he thought could handle it. He knew I was a hard worker. I wasn't the type of prima donna who felt he didn't need to practice. Barry knew that I had been brought up as a kid knowing that, to play well on Saturdays, you had to practice during the week. He just felt it wouldn't do any good for me to risk major injuries in contact, when participating wouldn't really make any difference. He did that with the Selmons and some of the other players, too. We went through everything else. We just didn't participate in the scrimmages.

SN: *On the Oklahoma schedule, Nebraska is usually the big game. What are your impressions of your Oklahoma-Nebraska games?*
JW: At Oklahoma, Nebraska was always *the* game. It took place around Thanksgiving, and it was usually for the Big Eight championship. You knew it was going to be tough. It was always cold. My freshman year, I had never been so cold in my life. Pruitt was hurt, and I started that game. They had a linebacker named Willie Harper, with great hands, who was impossible to block. I don't think I ever did block him in the NFL, when he played for the 49ers. They had a nose guard named Glover, a tough college player. I'd seen him whip many a center. That sucker was tough. He covered sideline to sideline.

There was always a certain kind of respect for Nebraska. It wasn't a dueling of words, like you had between Texas and Oklahoma. There was always animosity with Texas, because they felt Oklahoma was stealing players from Texas.

SN: *With Oklahoma fans, there's a lot of emphasis on spectacle. A lot of people are more there for spectacle—the Oklahoma-Texas game comes to mind. The students go down to Dallas more for what surrounds that game. These are not people interested in football, necessarily. Whereas the Oklahoma-Nebraska confrontation seems to me more the pure football kind of thing.*
JW: The students get Monday off for the Texas game. (Laughs) The Nebraska game was just pure football. There was nothing else to it. It came at the end of the season, and it was now down to brass tacks. It decided who was going to a certain bowl game, who was going to represent the Big Eight.

There was nothing flamboyant about Nebraska. Bob Devaney and Tom Osborne were pretty straight-laced guys. Nebraska players wore these dead suits—two-color uniforms. There wasn't any extra hoopla about that game. I kind of like that, though.

Nebraska was always a well-coached team, and they'd come at you and take their shots. I used to be a sore rascal after that game. I can't ever remember them jawing or talking that much. Just going about business. Whether they were winning or losing, it was always basically the same thing. You enjoyed playing guys like that. They'd take their shots. They'd try to kill you. But there was nothing cheap or dirty about it.

Other teams weren't like that. My junior year, we were playing Oklahoma State in Norman, and when I ran out of bounds, one of the coaches gave me a forearm to the cheek. I asked him what was wrong, and he said he was just trying to slow me down. But he actually threw a forearm shiver at me that caught me right on the cheek.

SN: *When were you beginning to think about the Heisman Trophy? When were you selected All-American?*
JW: The first All-American team I was ever placed on was the one selected by *Playboy* magazine, my sophomore year. I went up to the Playboy mansion in Chicago for that, and it was great. Right before that, some of the guys at Oklahoma, including me, shaved their heads. So, I was pictured in *Playboy* with a shaved head.

SN: *Was that just a frivolous act, not a political statement, a symbol of militancy?*
JW: There wasn't anything militant about us. I was having a very good year statistically my junior year, and at that time I started thinking about the Heisman Trophy. How many yards did I have? I knew I was going to be at a disadvantage here, because you didn't carry the ball a lot in the wishbone. And in the wishbone, the opposing defense could take out of the offense whomever they wanted to. If they didn't want you to carry the ball much, you didn't. I also knew that my chances would be slim because our games weren't on television.

SN: *You did get to a bowl game your senior year.*
JW: Orange Bowl. Played Michigan.

SN: *After beating Nebraska 35-10. Can you describe the experience of being in a bowl game? What were Oklahoma's and Michigan's rankings then?*
JW: We went in ranked number two in the nation. Ohio State, which had been ranked number one, lost earlier in the day in the Rose Bowl, giving us a shot at the national championship. Michigan was ranked somewhere in the

top five; their only loss had been to Ohio State. We won the game and the national championship.

The week going in to the Orange Bowl, I was really concerned about what shoe to wear. We had played in Miami earlier in the season, and the footing there was terrible. I always traveled with ten or fifteen pairs of shoes, for different surfaces. I knew how important that was. I had a shoe that was great, which I had designed. It looked good, too. Red shoestrings, and I was ready to roll.

SN: *What was the NFL drafting process like?*

JW: I hated it. Everybody wanted to come by and weigh you and see how fast you were. They knew how big I was, and how fast I was. They could look at me and see I wasn't that big. Everybody always talked about "his size, his size." That bothered me more than anything else. That's all I ever heard, "Well, he won't be able to play college, he's a little too little. He won't play pro, because he's too little, and he's not the world class sprinter everybody else is."

I was first-team All-American both junior and senior years. I had a lot of yards my junior year—1300 yards gained rushing, an average of 6.8 yards per carry. My sophomore year, I had 1189 yards gained rushing, for 6.7 yards per carry. Senior year, my stats weren't as high, 871 yards, and an average of 5.1. That isn't bad, but I was really disappointed about it. I was a little banged up that year, with a heel and foot injury. For someone like me, that was bad. I cut on my heel. I changed directions on my heel. And my toe and the instep of my foot was hurt as well. I was in terrible shape.

SN: *NFL teams were concerned about your size. Was that about it?*

JW: NFL teams were definitely concerned about my size. I don't think about my speed much. I only weighed about 171 pounds, maybe, and stood a little under five foot ten. When they weighed you, they stripped you down to socks and shorts. From reading *Street and Smith's Football Magazine*, I found out about these little wedges that you put in your shoes, which made you two inches taller. I got me some of those. So, I cheated on height. I took the little metal bars from my ankle weights, rolled them up, wrapped them in tape, and got on the scales with them in my hands. My weight would be up to 176 or 177 that way. I was so conscious of my size, that that's what I felt I had to do to get drafted high or even have the NFL teams interested in me.

SN: *Did you figure you would be drafted in the first round?*

JW: I was told that I was going as one of the first five players in the first round of the draft. There were two expansion teams—Tampa and Seattle, which got the first picks. The drafting order was going to be Tampa, Seattle,

New Orleans, San Diego. Up until draft day, I wasn't very much concerned; I just wanted to play. I couldn't wait, just to get my hands on the ball.

SN: *How did the draft process unfold?*
JW: When draft day came, it was assumed that I would be the third player selected. That meant that Lee Roy Selmon was going to Tampa, Chuck Muncie was going to Seattle, and I was going to New Orleans. I was on the phone with the guy from New Orleans. We were talking, and the draft had just started. He was telling me about how great it was going to be for me in New Orleans, because Hank Stram was the coach, and he loved backs like me. New Orleans was near Texas, and my folks would be able to see me play there. I would create all kinds of excitement in New Orleans. And I was thinking, "Yeah, yeah!" The New Orleans guy told me, "Joe, things are going fine. Tampa just got Lee Roy. Seattle should take Chuck, and then you'll be a New Orleans Saint."

I was just sitting there grinning and listening. He said, "Seattle's getting ready to select." Then he said, "Joe, hold it! Seattle just took Niehaus. I'll call you back." The funny thing about it was, that I didn't think anything of it. New Orleans ended up taking Muncie. That was good, because I went to San Diego. San Diego played on grass, and it was a team I had loved since I was a kid. They used to have Dickie Post, Lance Alworth, Ernie Ladd, and John Hadl. I used to love the AFC. I later found out that the Saints had still tried to go ahead and buy me for $500,000, but the Chargers wouldn't take it. That made me feel pretty good.

Looking back, you can say my ego was in pretty good shape. I just laughed. I was pretty honest with myself. I'd seen Chuck Muncie. Awesome. He's one of the best I've ever seen. I played with him in the Japan Bowl. He was 230 pounds, had great hands, and could run over people and around people. Nice guy, too. He had drug problems, but he was a nice guy.

Barry Switzer said I was probably the smallest player ever taken as high as I was in the history of the NFL draft. At the time, I weighed maybe 170, cheated up to 177. And I kept cheating in the pros, to where I always showed 185, when I actually weighed 175.

SN: *What were the contract negotiations like?*
JW: I didn't participate in the contract negotiations with the Chargers; my agent handled them. I wasn't satisfied, and thought I could have gotten more with another agent. And I think I could have gotten more if I hadn't been set on playing in the College All-Star game. You had to be basically signed by that time, if you were going to play in it.

SN: *Could you describe playing in the College All-Star game?*
JW: I played in the very last College All-Star game, and I was its most valuable player. We played the NFL champions, the Pittsburgh Steelers, in the rain. And I knew then that I could play in this league.

SN: *Did the Steelers approach it as a serious game?*
JW: Yes! Everybody was hitting. They were determined not to lose to a bunch of college guys. New, young guys that were supposed to be making all this money.

SN: *There must have been resentment about that. Big salaries and bonuses started to come in around the mid-1960s, with some rookies being signed for much more money than long-established veteran stars, like Donny Anderson at Green Bay.*
JW: Yes. It's always tough for an NFL veteran to negotiate up. When you're a rookie, this is the time you're supposed to get your money.

SN: *So, you have two things going on in this game. The world-champion Steelers want to show the college boys what the NFL is going to be like, and there's also some resentment about developments concerning salaries.*
JW: Yeah, and you probably had some guys on the college team who were going to the Steelers. I was just as excited as a pig in manure to be in this game. I was in the jersey with the stripes and the stars on the shoulders, and everything. We had Archie Griffin, Tony Davis, and Chuck Muncie as running backs on our team. And I started.

SN: *So, how did the game turn out?*
JW: One particular incident sticks in my mind. It was pouring, and we were playing on artificial turf. We were in the huddle, and all of a sudden a kid came sliding in and said, "What's the play?" I'll never forget that. He came sliding into the huddle and was looking up at us, drenched. People were all over the place, sliding.

The Steelers won the game. All I remember is that they stopped it at halftime, because the conditions were so bad.

SN: *How difficult was it for you to adjust as a running back to the NFL?*
JW: My running skills were such that I was definitely ready for the pros. Like I said, they never changed from high school to the NFL. I took my running for granted. But it was somewhat hard to adjust, because in the NFL they were

always trying to change everything. I remember a coach told Mercury Morris, who had been All-Pro for ten years when he came to the Chargers, that in order for him to play, he was going to have to change his stance. That shows in a nutshell the mentality of some of the professional coaches.

Some of the stuff they wanted you to run in I found restrictive. At Oklahoma, they were wearing these red, snap-in hip pads. I hated them. I couldn't move in them. You had to wear hip pads, knee pads, thigh guards, shoulder pads, and a mouthpiece. I didn't wear any elbow pads. I didn't wear any arm pads. At that time, you could wear a little tape on there, just to kind of prevent the turf burns. But after a while, that got too cumbersome. I figured that the less weight I carried, the better off I was. You wore either a long or a short T-shirt for the snaps on your shoulder pads. I would always wear a short T-shirt. If it got cold, I'd put on a longer T-shirt, but with short sleeves. And if it got really cold, you'd wear a long-sleeved T-shirt. I didn't like to do that. I didn't want to do anything that would keep me from holding onto the football. So, I wouldn't wear a long sleeve on my right arm, the arm I used to carry the ball.

I'd also wear a wristband, to keep the sweat off my hand. I really wore it more as a result of a childhood superstition. There was a cartoon I watched called "Space Ghost." The hero had these power bands. And every time he'd press these power bands, they'd energize them. From ninth and tenth grade on up, my sweatbands were my power bands.

My uniform had to always be a certain way. It had to fit right. My pants had to be 28 shorts. I always took my helmet home with me during the summer. I felt that if they refurbished it, they'd move the facemask on it. I needed my facemask loose, where I could pull it down, so I could see. I had a lot of face exposed. But I did wear two mouthpieces, so it didn't make any difference.

Most of what you need to know as a running back you should know by high school. As far as what made me Joe Washington, that had been mostly developed by high school. There isn't too much more that you're going to learn to improve your game, no matter how long you play. As far as things like cutting and changing directions, that's etched in stone.

I had already developed the running back's skills by the time I came to Oklahoma, and that's what allowed me to start as a freshman. I was already a complete football player, because my dad was my coach. I did get a little bigger in college, and maybe a little tougher, because I blocked a lot at Oklahoma.

SN: *I was watching Monday Night Football the other night, and the color man was criticizing this rookie that Dallas is playing now in place of Emmitt Smith for moving laterally, when he should be moving forward. He attributed this to his being a rookie.*

JW: It was a lineman, Dan Dierdorf, who made that statement. For as long as I was in the pros, it was always upfield, upfield. Yeah, upfield. I'll get upfield when there's a chance for me to get upfield. I never believed that if you run up in there, and there's nothing there, you just lower your head and run on in there. You should consider your other alternatives. Go this way or that way. I had tussles with coaches now and then about running north and south.

Here you are, you're running a sweep, and you've been coached to get to a certain point before you start looking upfield, and they say, "He's running laterally too much!" Well, the play is designed to go outside the wide receiver. Then you start looking for a place to get upfield. Now, there are certain plays that are designed to just run up in there, no matter what. But still, I was the type of back who could run those plays and turn them into lateral plays that ended up somewhere else. Once you've had that free reign from high school up to college, you expect that everywhere else.

SN: *One thing that comes to mind in terms of a running back's development is fumbling. Is that something that a more experienced running back is less likely to do? How do you learn how not to fumble?*

JW: I had learned how to hold the ball while running, so as not to fumble, by high school. I always carried the ball in my right hand. I might switch it every now and then. I had big enough hands where I could grab the ball with two hands if I got into a pile, and bring it closer to me. Fumbling occurs when a back feels more comfortable carrying the ball in a certain hand, and then changes from one hand to the other, back and forth. I very, very rarely fumbled the ball held in my right hand.

Of course, the method coaches recommended to you in carrying the ball didn't always work for your own style of running. They'd tell you to hold the ball with one finger over the point and to put the other point in the crook. Well, yeah, that's good if you're a big back, and you aren't going to run in the open field, and try to stiff-arm or finesse anybody. But if you're going to duck people and move, you've got to be able to hold the ball in a way where you can run naturally with it. So, I think a guy should hold a football in his most comfortable hand and position. If you're running along the left sideline and nobody's near you, I think it is really dumb to switch the ball into your left hand. That's the stupidest thing in the world to do.

If you're running on the left side, close to the sideline, and someone's getting ready to hit you, you need to go ahead and brace yourself to get hit and not worry about moving the football. There are just going to be some instances where you're going to fumble if you get hit right. I don't care how well you have the ball in your hand.

SN: *Whose fault is it usually if a fumble occurs on a handoff: the running back's or the quarterback's?*
JW: If a running back misses a handoff, it's usually the quarterback's fault. You're supposed to just make a pocket, and run where you're supposed to run, and he's supposed to look the ball into your pocket. It's the quarterback's job. If he's handing off, he doesn't have anything else to do but put the ball in your pocket. Now if you run too wide sometimes, okay. Even then, he's supposed to make sure he either can put the ball in your pocket or not handoff if you're too wide.

SN: *What do you do when you're playing in the rain?*
JW: I always held the ball the same way, no matter what the weather. They kept the footballs dry enough, so that you could hold them almost as well in a wet game as you would in a dry game. Rain wasn't much different from snow, because they were both wet. There are times in a dry game, because of your perspiration beading up, and where the grass is mixed in, when it's easier to fumble a ball.

SN: *What observations can you make generally about running in different weather conditions, like rain and snow? What adjustments do you make?*
JW: The biggest difference is between running on dry artificial turf and wet grass. The former is unreal. Dry artificial turf sticks, and you've got to be able to pick your feet up. You're worrying about making a cut, and before you make it, your foot grabs the turf, and then you're stumbling. I always got hurt making different cuts on that artificial turf and my feet not giving. And then you go to wet grass, where you've got a lot of give, and it's slick. Usually, the guys who have the biggest problems on wet grass are the fast, track-type sprinters. Football players have a tendency to run with a wider base. Track stars run with a very narrow base. They're more concerned with elongating their stride—one foot way in front of the other. With football, you want to have a wide base and keep both feet on the ground.

I never had much of a problem running on either dry artificial turf or wet grass. I had a wide base and my feet on the ground, and I was always able to cut at the drop of a hat, because I always had something on the ground that I could cut off of. I loved to get guys on wet grass. I was going to run just as fast and cut just as sharp as I would on turf, because of the way I run. Guys like Dickerson would have more of a problem on wet grass, because he had a long stride. It wasn't as elongated as a sprinter's, but he wasn't nearly as effective on wet grass. But, in reality, most backs aren't. Gale Sayers could cut on butter.

Wet artificial turf, if you've got the right shoe, is like playing on grass. When you make a cut, it gives just a little, which is what you want. You want a little give in your cut. So, I always wore a shoe on dry artificial turf that had a bottom that didn't grab as tight. When you planted your foot, it just gave a little bit, which is a little safer.

Artificial turf makes football a lethal game, because everybody is able to run fast. You have a little bit more spring in your stride. They say injuries are a little bit more severe on turf. I think they are. And one thing that you've got to take note of is the burns you get. Oh, man, that's terrible! I'm talking about taking off layers of skin, on your butt, shin, elbow—whatever skin that hits the ground, you can count on having a strawberry there the next day.

I got tackled at Oklahoma State my senior year, and fell on my calf in the end zone, and when I got up, I saw nothing but brown skin on the yard marker. A long, six-by-six-inch burn. Oh, it was horrendous! It was ugly. You don't get that on grass. If for no other reason, they should get rid of artificial turf for that. Plus, I think games are more exciting when it's muddy.

When I played at Oklahoma, everybody in the Big Eight used artificial turf except Missouri and Iowa State. I looked forward to those two games. I think it's slowly going back to grass now, which is the way it should be. If a cow can't eat it, you don't need to play on it.

SN: *What about running in very cold weather?*
JW: Playing in cold weather, even in severe cold, doesn't make much difference in how you play as a running back. We didn't play too much in cold weather in Texas. But when I got to Oklahoma and we went up to Nebraska, I'd never been so cold before in my life. And playing in Pittsburgh in the NFL—oh, my God! And I was the type of guy who couldn't wear all the thermals and the extra stuff underneath, because it cut down on my maneuverability. The best I could do was wear maybe a long T-shirt. I tried to wear a sweatshirt once against Nebraska, but I couldn't play in it because it was too bulky. You try to put gloves on, and that doesn't work. So, as a running back, you're playing in what you're normally wearing all the time.

Where cold affects you is when you're standing on the sideline. If you've got a long drive going, there's no such thing as cold. You don't feel anything at all. So, there's really no difference. The only problem is when you're waiting to catch a pass or a punt, then you can feel the cold. But as long as you're involved in the action, you just forget it. Of course, if it's cold and wet and you're standing in the huddle after a play, you know it's cold. You get in your stance, and your pants are wet, and all you have on underneath is a jock, and the wind is blowing. You're going to feel the draft.

SN: *How does the quality of your offensive line affect how you run?*
JW: I never, ever thought about how good or bad my line was, as long as I can remember. The only thing that really concerned me was the size. That's the only thing that really worried me.

SN: *Is size more important for pass blocking or drive blocking?*
JW: Drive blocking. A small line can get by better on pass blocking than on running plays. On pass blocking, they can finesse their way a little bit. They can use their quickness, and maneuver with their hands, and use a little technique. But drive blocking is different. When you're firing out on somebody, going bang, bang, weight has a tendency to come into play a great deal, especially late in the game.

SN: *You returned punts and kickoffs at Oklahoma and in high school. Punt returning strikes me as requiring a lot of nerve.*
JW: Returning kickoffs I think is more dangerous than returning punts, because on kickoffs everybody's going full speed and you're going full speed. With punts, they've got to let you catch it. Returning kickoffs is like being a kamikaze pilot.

SN: *Did you volunteer to do kickoff returns?*
JW: I've always returned kickoffs, but I never volunteered for it. No, Sir-ree! I didn't do it too much in high school. My last two years, my dad put other guys in to return kickoffs. I always returned punts because I had good hands. I would never volunteer for kickoff returns. I could do it, and I think I was good at it. But it isn't anything anybody in his right mind volunteers for.
   You have a better chance to make a movement if you're returning punts. They've got to give you a chance to catch the ball, so they have to brake down and gather themselves. Your first movement could be lateral, and they're coming at you vertically.

SN: *Is the blocking more organized on a punt return or on a kickoff return?*
JW: Your blocking is less organized on a kickoff return than on a punt return. The guys in the wedge in front of the kickoff returner are assigned

just to block anybody coming through the wedge. Everybody is supposed to have a certain man to block. But with guys running down the field at 500 miles per hour, and the blockers at a standstill, and then trying to catch up with the guys they're supposed to block, things can get disorganized. It's probably safer to be returning the ball than blocking on a kickoff, because you can't cut these big guys down running down the field at 500 miles per hour.

Now on punt returns, it's different. I had one guy assigned to protect me on punts when I was at Oklahoma. His job was to stand in front of me and make sure that I caught the ball. Everybody else is supposed to rush, make sure they kick the ball, then come around down the sideline and form a wall, whether it's on the right side or the left side. A lot of people got sophisticated enough to where they could have a center return. As a punt returner, you're on your own, once you catch the ball, to make sure you get to the wall. The guy whose job it was to protect me on punt returns at Oklahoma was Tony Peters. And believe me, when you get a guy as tough as Tony, and as ready to hit you as he is, you feel pretty good.

So I would much rather return punts than kickoffs, because all I had to do was catch the ball. I knew I had somebody in front of me to protect me. I could do what I do naturally, which was try to get to the wall.

The year I led the NFL in kickoff returns, I did it by trying to find a vacant place to fall. And if there's no spot to fall here, then you go a little further, until you can find a place to fall without it looking too bad.

SN: *Can any good running back return punts and kickoffs, or does it require any particular qualities you can identify?*
JW: One thing I can tell you right off the bat. You can tell a lot about a running back when you put him on kickoff returns. Not just his exterior physical makeup, but his interior, intestinal makeup. If he's tough enough. If he's a slashing type of runner. If he's the kind of runner who makes a decision and sticks with it. If he's a finesse-type runner. If this guy's a coward. Believe me, that will tell it all.

You don't have much time to make decisions on kickoff returns. You catch the ball, you head upfield, you make a decision, and you go with it. There's none of that having to make two or three decisions at a time, like on punts.

For punt returns, you need a guy with good hands, who's cool under pressure and has enough finesse where he can make decisions, change directions, and make people miss him. I don't think Earl Campbell would have been a good punt returner, because on punt returns, you need a guy who can run laterally fairly well, even though Earl was a great pitch sweep runner. He would have been an unbelievable kickoff returner, because he made a decision and was off.

SN: *What kind of role does superstition play in people's routines in football? You think in baseball of some guys who won't change a pair of socks when they're on a hitting streak. I guess it's because of the uncertainty, particularly with hitters, where even a .300 hitter fails seven times out of ten. So, you feel you need something else. Does this ever enter into playing or coaching football in any significant way?*

JW: I always put on my uniform the same way. I'd put on my socks, jock, T-shirt, and then just lounge around a little bit. Then I'd put on my girdle right before I put on my pants. I never put on my shoulder pads and jersey, my whole uniform, just to walk around. I would never wear my silver shoes out to warm up in. Never do that, never. That just wasn't done, not in America. I always warmed up in some regular white shoes and saved the game shoes for game time. I always carried my shoes separately. I never packed them with the rest of my gear. I didn't want anything to happen, because if I didn't have those, I wasn't playing. It was just as simple as that.

SN: *If your silver shoes got lost, say, on a road trip?*

JW: I never would have played. That never happened, because I carried them myself.

SN: *How about in a team sense? Did the team as a whole develop any common superstitions?*

JW: As far as the team went, at Oklahoma we were so good we didn't need any common superstitions. They had a sign "Play like Champions," and we'd always hit like that. Maybe some of the players and coaches had some superstitions that they performed as rituals that we didn't know about. Everybody probably had their own—little ones that probably made us as good as we were.

SN: *What was it like being in training camp with the San Diego Chargers?*

JW: Unfortunately, I got seriously hurt in my second preseason game with the San Diego Chargers. I had gone out to San Diego and played in the first preseason game. The second one was in Norman, Oklahoma, against the New England Patriots, coached by Chuck Fairbanks. I guess he arranged that game, because with me a number-one draft choice and him having several former Oklahoma players on his team, it would be a good draw.

I was having a great game when I got injured. I had already scored two or three touchdowns, and at that point I knew I could surely play in this league. I was doing everything I wanted to do. I was running and jumping over people, doing everything I had done at Oklahoma. I was getting ready to score again on a kickoff return. I broke through, and it was just me and the kicker. He was the only guy between me and the goal line. And you could hear the fans, because at Oklahoma, when I returned a punt, you could always feel people anticipating something when I touched the ball. I could feel it then. I was thinking, "Now it's show time." I was going into 300,000 different moves, and my foot got stuck, and I tore up my right knee.

I felt that pain. And a hush just fell over that stadium. It was like everything was in a time warp. I'd never been hurt on that field, never missed a game on that field. And I came back and ripped up my knee. You could hear it pop forty rows up.

After that game, we were scheduled to play in Japan, where I was fairly well known. I had played at the end of my senior year in the first Japan Bowl, an East-West Collegiate All-Star game. When I was at Oklahoma, we had also had a gentleman from Japan come and spend the whole season with our football team, learning American football. I think they broadcast one of our games back to Japan.

San Diego's general manager or head coach told me to make sure not to tell anybody that I wasn't playing due to the injury, because I was definitely a big draw in Japan. But I didn't really know then whether I was going to play or not, because at that time it wasn't really stated whether I would need surgery, or be out for the year, or what. At least nobody stated anything to me.

So we went over to Japan. And as it turned out, I didn't play. I didn't practice. I just jogged a little bit, and my knee swelled on me a great deal. It was sore, very uncomfortable. I ended up doing the color commentary for the game in Japan.

SN: *This was broadcast back to the United States?*
JW: Yeah. After that, we flew to Hawaii, where we played our last preseason game. I didn't play there also.

When we arrived at the San Diego airport on our return from Hawaii, I was met by an onslaught of reporters, asking me what I thought about the surgery I was supposed to have, and about missing the first part of the season. I said, "What surgery?" They had failed to tell me that I was going to have surgery. I was really upset about that. I was upset to the point that I couldn't see straight. Plus, I'd never had any type of operation. So, initially it scared me.

SN: *They had made the decision without consulting you?*
JW: Oh, yeah.

SN: *What doctor had you seen up to that point?*
JW: The team doctor.

SN: *So, what did you do when you learned this from the press?*
JW: The first thing I did was get a hold of the trainer, and ask, "What's going on?"

I did eventually have surgery, and I was back in four weeks. I worked hard to get back in shape. I ran the beaches. You name it, I did it. I ran the stadium steps and lifted weights.

SN: *Did they say that the surgery would take care of the problem completely?*
JW: They just said I had torn the cartilage, basically. They took out the inside cartilage in the knee. In the short period between the injury and the time I got my splint off, you wouldn't believe the atrophy. When I got that splint off, my arm was bigger than my right leg. It was the most depressing time I can ever think of.

I noticed during this time that something was wrong. The knee didn't feel right. I originally thought it was just the surgery. My little brother had had surgery when he was in the seventh grade, so I was calling him every night. I said, "Ken, did it feel like this, did it feel like that? Can you do this?" I must have run him crazy. But he was very supportive and patient with me and very understanding.

I finally got to the point where I was back working out with the team. But something just wasn't right. I was complaining that something was still wrong with my knee. They didn't take me off the roster, expecting me to be able to come back during the season. I was expecting to also. Well, I kept complaining. Then I started really getting ripped in the papers. They said I wanted to collect my money, but I didn't want to play. They said my best move was a limp to the sideline, that sort of thing. The press was actually calling the problem psychosomatic.

The main guy ripping me was a writer named Jerry or John Magee, whom I had had a slight discussion with the day I signed with the Chargers. He had asked me, "Well, Joe, they've got all these backs. What do you think?" I asked him, "What do you mean, what do I think? What do you think? They're obviously qualified players, or they wouldn't be here. What does that have to do with me? I'm the number-one draft choice. They expect me to come here and help, and that's what I'm here to do."

So, of course, when I responded like that, in the way an intelligent person would, rather than in the manner of some shy, inexperienced rookie, it upset him. So, he blasted me in the paper. It was horrible.

I started asking the Chargers to let me see my own doctor, Dr. O'Donoghue, in Oklahoma, who was world renowned. They kept telling me that I didn't need to see him, that it was all in my head. One day at practice, one of the coaches told me, "Washington, you can run faster than that!" I replied, "Coach, I can't. Something's wrong with my knee." That was it, and I just walked off the field.

That was very uncharacteristic of me. I loved practice; I loved the game. My dad was a coach, and I thought coaches walked on water. You didn't challenge them. But I went into the dressing room, and said, "That's it. I don't know what I'm going to do, but I can't handle this. Something's wrong with my knee."

SN: *What is the role of the players' representative here? There had been a players' strike in 1975 [this was 1976], and I would think this was the kind of issue . . .*
JW: The next year I was a players' representative. But this wasn't the kind of issue that I, as a rookie, would even think of. I wanted to play. My concern was being able to see another doctor. They were telling me it was all in my head.

That day, Coach Prothro came in and said, "Washington, if you need a security blanket, I'll let you go see your other doctor." It's funny, but I can still see him saying this. I left to go see Dr. O'Donoghue in Oklahoma. After a few seconds examining me, Dr. O'Donoghue said, "Joe, I wouldn't hesitate to operate on you again." But then, we always used to say he was kind of quick to cut. I went back to San Diego, and the surgeon who had performed the first operation went in again and took care of the outside cartilage.

SN: *This is about midway through the season?*
JW: The season was four or five weeks old at that point. Because of the second operation, I ended up missing the whole year.

The surgeon claimed that the problem had been caused by an old injury, something that had happened in college. Well, if that was the case, why hadn't he found that out when he went in the first time? That's what I was upset about, because if they had done it right the first time, I'd have been back playing already.

SN: *Had you ever been seriously injured in college?*
JW: Just ribs, foot, toe, heel. My senior year I had my toe, instep, and heel, elbows, and shoulder every now and then. But nothing that would really keep me out. So, this was really the first injury, other than in high school when I broke my leg, that kept me out. So, that was really, really tough.

SN: *What was the doctor's view of this injury after doing the second operation? Did he figure you could come back and start the next season?*
JW: I guess he felt that I'd have a complete recovery after the second operation, but I don't remember that ever being stated. The Chargers didn't have the type of equipment I wanted to work out on during the off-season, so I ended up looking for different places to work out myself. I used to drive down to Santa Ana or Tuston, to a health club, especially on weekends, to work out with their up-to-date equipment. I worked out real hard.

Unconsciously, at least, the Chargers were upset with me for being injured the whole year. They seemed to want to write me off as a bust. They had put billboards up, with my picture on it, around San Diego. Me, Charlie Joiner, Bill Walsh, and Ernie Zampese were going to be the new wave for San Diego in 1976. And hey, the main ingredient, the guy who was going to put the lightning back into the belt of the Chargers, wasn't there.

The next year, 1977, the Chargers wanted me to come to camp early, and that was fine with me. My backfield coach, who was black, told me Prothro wanted me in early so I could get my timing back. He told me that there wouldn't be any contact. Well, I said that was fine, because I was eager. And the first day I get to practice, they're going through a live drill. Hey, this was my first day back. I was a little nervous taking the ball, because this was a live drill, and they told me I wouldn't have to go through contact if I came in early. So, the first play I ran, the guys on defense just grabbed me, but they didn't tackle me. They knew I had just come off surgery. As I was walking back to the huddle with the ball in my hand, Prothro blew the whistle, and said, "Tackle him! Tackle him! This is live!"

I looked up, and everybody was chasing me. So, I was ducking, dodging, and weaving. I even grabbed the team owner, Eugene Klein, and pushed him in front of me. I was desperate now. They finally got me, a little tackle, no big deal. But that really set the stage of how things were. I was really upset about that.

SN: *What kind of record did the Chargers have the year you were out?*
JW: 6-10 or 7-9. I didn't get on a .500 team until my first year in Washington. They started me in a couple of preseason games, but I didn't play well. I made

some bad decisions. It was just a matter of confidence. I didn't play a lot, and I was upset about that.

I felt that being the type of runner I was, if Prothro could relate to me in any way, he would have had me run through situations where I wouldn't get hit, where I could run and actually get my movement down. Getting hit on my knee—what good was that going to do? My confidence was going to come when I was in a situation where I could take this foot and cut at a ninety-degree angle, without it collapsing on me. That was where the mystery lay, whether I would be able to do that.

I was never really with it during the first part of the season, but as the season progressed, I started getting a little more confidence, and they started playing me more. I won some games for them. Now, I was a little upset that I wasn't playing more. I was upset that they had thrown me to the wolves in training camp, and hadn't been allowed the chance to build up any type of confidence. Now Prothro was shuffling me in and out. What is this? I was really fed up. That season ended pretty uneventfully.

I had become the Chargers' player representative that year.

SN: *Why did they pick you as player representative? Are there certain qualities your teammates saw in you? Or was it that they weren't interested?*

JW: I hadn't really been interested, but the players asked me to do it. I had spoken up about a lot of things, because I was disgusted with everything. I was probably the most vociferous player on the team.

My third year, the coach wanted everybody to come to camp early again, but I refused. I was doing a United Way promotion in Utah, and I wasn't going to come in. I told the coach that reporting to camp early was not required by the Players' Association. So, I and some of the other veterans came into camp later, when you were supposed to report.

I had a pretty good preseason, and I went to the coach and asked him to trade me. He said, "Nope." So I asked him again, and he said, "You start playing football, and then I'll start thinking about trading you." In preseason, I probably made some bad decisions on some runs and some blocks. But hey, it wouldn't be the first time, and it wouldn't be the last time. At that point, he told me again that he wouldn't trade me and to start playing some football.

I ended up having to have another operation, this time on my eye. I got poked in the eye in practice, and that caused a detached retina. I had to have laser surgery on the eye. If you don't repair a detached retina, you can eventually go blind. I couldn't practice for about ten days. I was really disgusted about things.

SN: *Is it because they're not playing you enough, or are there other reasons you were disgruntled? Was it the personality of the coach, the nature of the team itself, how the players on it interacted, were there cliques?*
JW: Cliques and personalities on the team—that never concerned me. It was more the interaction between me and the coaches. My head coach and my backfield coach. I didn't really care about other guys in the backfield.

SN: *You thought they weren't giving you enough playing time. Were they critical in film sessions?*
JW: It all went back to the preseason, the year I finally played, the way I was treated with that. They even had me blocking punts. I don't block punts.

SN: *Why did he do that?*
JW: I don't know. I'd been returning punts all my life. Then they shifted me into the line to block punts.

We had gotten to my third year with the Chargers, and I was totally disgusted. You can tell if a coach wants to keep you in his plan. By this time, I was sure that he had just written me off completely. He just figured he had wasted a draft choice. I was still thinking, though, that I could work through all of this.

SN: *What was Tommy Prothro's background?*
JW: He was a brilliant guy and supposedly a great judge of talent. I guess he was pretty good at one time, because he drafted me number four in the first round of the draft. He had been an offensive lineman, a heralded college coach at UCLA and Oregon, and had coached the Rams. But I think that football had basically passed him by. I don't think he'd ever had a running back like me. There was basically nothing that he could tell me to coach me. He might have had a problem with that.

I definitely had a problem with Prothro telling me to lower a shoulder, and run over the biggest man on the football team, Louie Kelcher, who weighed 325 pounds. I didn't think that made any sense. I'm an improviser. I'm going to lose a few yards and get fifteen some times. I could see then that he didn't get it.

A few games into that third year, I was getting a little more confidence. I was playing real well, returning punts all over the place. My legs felt good, and I could cut. The third week of the preseason, I returned a punt about eighty yards for a touchdown. I was getting a little better press. But right after that third game, I got poked in the eye again in practice, suffered another detached retina, and had to have another operation.

SN: *Is the possibility of a detached retina something you have to watch out for frequently in games?*
JW: Guys wear these cages and everything. I started wearing goggles after that. I wore a small facemask, where it was easy to get poked.

After the eye surgery, I was just sitting up in my room watching television, when Prothro came and told me that the Chargers had obliged me and traded me to the Baltimore Colts. And I just said, "Thank you, Coach."

SN: *How did you feel about going to the Colts?*
JW: I thought Baltimore was a great place for me to go. The Colts had been one of my favorite teams as a kid. One of the reasons I wore number 24 was for Lenny Moore. And my little brother wore number 19, for Johnny Unitas.

SN: *What was the adjustment process like, moving to a new team?*
JW: It was hard adjusting to Baltimore. I moved from the newness of San Diego to a team that was practicing in a vacant monastery on an old field. I said, "My God, what is this?" My wife and I stayed out in a little hotel in a remote place until we got an apartment. It was different.

Before I could even practice, I had to go through a battery of medical tests, because I had had the knee injury and the eye injuries. Baltimore figured that they were getting a blind cripple. They told me that the Colts' quarterback, Bert Jones, came out in practice after he found out they'd traded for me in a sling and wearing a patch over his eye.

One of Baltimore's defensive linemen, Fred Cook, told me, "Joe, you just jumped out of the frying pan into the oven when you came here." I had been traded for Lydell Mitchell, a guy who'd done everything in the world for Baltimore and then had gotten traded over a couple of thousand dollars in a salary dispute. But I didn't care. I just wanted to be out of San Diego and with a chance to play.

SN: *Does it take a lot of time to learn the playbook?*
JW: Oh, yeah, because everything was totally the opposite of what I had been accustomed to at San Diego. At San Diego, the numbering system was such that odd plays went normally to the left, and even plays went to the right. With Baltimore it was just the opposite. The terminology was also different. So, when we got up to the line of scrimmage and lined up in the I-formation,

Roosevelt Leaks, the fullback, patted himself on the hip to indicate to me which side the play was going to.

SN: *When they traded for you, was it to get a starting running back?*
JW: No, they had traded for me just as a third-down running back and to return punts and kickoffs. I didn't get much of a chance to play the first game of the season against Dallas. All I did was return kicks and maybe one punt. They finally gave me a chance to run the ball a little bit in the second game against Miami. I ran the ball real well. So, I guess they saw I could run the football.

SN: *You had a performance on Monday Night Football that was voted the best . . .*
JW: Yes, in the third game. I had a real big day and was voted all-this and all-that for the week. I gained about 300 total yards and got headlines. We played the New England Patriots, who were coached by Chuck Fairbanks, who had been Oklahoma's coach my freshman year. At San Diego, I had called Chuck numerous times about making a trade for me. But nothing ever happened. I thought a little about that before the game. But it wasn't that big a deal, because I didn't think I'd get to play much.

But lo and behold, Don McCauley hurt his shoulder early in the game, and they had to put me in. I knew it would be a sink-or-swim situation for me. They didn't have my regular helmet for me yet, so I had to wear a typical helmet with the other facemask on it. And there was so much rain that I had to take my goggles off.

The game started off a little slowly, but it got really exciting. I was leading the field, coming back. Lanes were opening up all over the place for me. There was a lot of scoring back and forth. It boiled down to the last minute of the game. They had just scored and kicked off to us. But instead of kicking the ball up, they squib kicked it to me. I returned it ninety-one yards for a touchdown to win the game. I threw a touchdown pass in that game, caught one, and ran one. It was really a chance for everybody to see what I was capable of doing. They could see that I wasn't just a broken-down running back, that I could do anything you needed done. That was big. And I had good games in Baltimore from that point on. I was an alternate All-Pro that year.

The following day, San Diego fired Tommy Prothro as head coach and replaced him with Don Coryell. If Coryell had been the coach when I was there, I'd never have asked to be traded. He was the type of coach who could relate to someone like me, because he had had Terry Metcalf in St. Louis. I did get a chance to play for him the next year, when I went to the Pro Bowl.

People in Baltimore were crazy about me, and the next year I was All-Pro. We weren't winning many games, but I didn't care. I was playing well, doing all I could to help the team win. It just wasn't happening. That second year in Baltimore I led the NFL in number of pass receptions by a running back.

SN: *What's the mood like on a team that's losing a lot of games?*
JW: Oh, it's tough. You're on pins and needles. When a team is losing, the coaches have a tendency to reevaluate players. They get rid of a lot of people.

Unfortunately, they fired our head coach, Ted Marchibroda, at the end of the season. I really liked Marchibroda. He gave me a lot of respect. He gave me a chance to play. We could relate to each other well. He was the one who called me and told me I was going to the Pro Bowl. I got a big kick out of him telling me that.

Then they hired Mike McCormack, who was six foot five and 240 pounds, and I said to myself, "Oh, God, here we go again." When the head coach is a big guy, he's not going to be able to relate again. And Baltimore drafted a running back named Curtis Dickey in the first round, a big, fast specimen, a world-class sprinter running back. So, I thought I'd probably be challenged for my position.

At this time, Baltimore asked to renegotiate my contract, which was fine. I was going to ask them anyway. I had had two All-Pro years. I was probably the lowest paid guy at the Pro Bowl. They figured I'd probably come in, so they beat me to the punch. Dickey held out for three games, and when he signed, we started sharing time. I wasn't too pleased with the way McCormack was handling it. He was being dictated to by the owner, who wanted to play Dickey because he was the new kid on the block. I was still going back and forth with the owner, Irsay, about my contract. It was really aggravating. He wouldn't remember that we had talked. He was inebriated by a certain time. He forgot every doggone thing.

SN: *What were they looking for in negotiating the new contract?*
JW: I guess to tie me up a little longer. They were going to redo the contract because I was probably the lowest-paid guy at the Pro Bowl.

SN: *Was this to benefit you then, to take into account your performance?*
JW: Oh, yeah, they figured they were being good guys, because I was going to approach them anyway. And they probably wanted to stop what had happened before with Lydell Mitchell, because he had left over a contract. I don't

know if I can give them that much credit for that. They figured I'd probably come in, so they beat me to the punch.

We went through the whole season, negotiating back and forth, and finally agreed to some numbers that were basically fine. They were going to triple my present salary. They agreed to the numbers, and said they'd be back to me. Well, when they finally got back to me, they presented me with a deferment plan where ten years after I retired, I would collect maybe $2000 of deferred money one year, but the next year I'd get $15,000. Then another year, I'd get $1000, then another year, I'd get something. I said, "How are you all doing this? This isn't what we agreed to." I told them, "You can forget this. I'm not signing this. Unless we can get it back to what we agreed upon, then I'm out of here. You can trade me."

During that season, I was upset, because I was dealing with all this, plus splitting time with Dickey. We ended up playing about equal time. I was going from two All-Pro years to not starting every time. I was upset with that, but that was something you could deal with if you were getting paid the way you should be. So, I told them that they could expect to trade me.

I moped around after I told them I wanted to be traded, and I didn't go to any of the camps. Then they knew I was really serious. I was sitting home in Port Arthur, depressed. I didn't even want to go back to Baltimore. I was hearing rumors that I'd be traded to Houston, and New Orleans, and all over the place. Then on draft day, I got a call. My mother-in-law answered the phone. She said, "Joe, it's Coach McCormack." So, I knew then that I'd been traded somewhere. My wife and I looked at each other. I walked up to answer the phone, and he told me I'd been traded to the Washington Redskins. I said, "Oh, I don't believe that. I don't even have to move!" Then Joe Gibbs, the Redskins' coach, called. He had been on the Chargers' staff, and had been one of the coaches when I played in the Pro Bowl. He had told me then he would love to have me. I felt that I had just gotten a new lease on life.

SN: *What was it like at the Redskins' training camp?*
JW: I reported there, and I figured I had to show myself right off the bat. So, that's what I did. I just gave them a taste of some of the things that I was capable of doing. I started the season real well. Dallas beat us in the first game, but I caught ten or thirteen passes.

But then the next game, I got tackled and hurt my ankle, and was out for three or four games. They thought it was my Achilles heel, but I knew that it wasn't. That's one thing about getting hurt. You hate for them to tell you what they think it is, when you know that it's something different. I'm not crazy about physicians. I hate orthopedists. They think they know every doggone

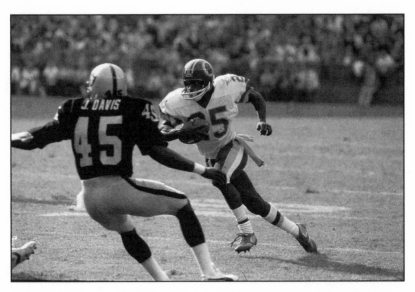

Joe Washington Jr. with the Washington Redskins. Courtesy of Jerry Wachter/
Sports Illustrated.

thing, and they don't. I can think of a lot of people I'd rather be friends with
than orthopedic surgeons.

Even missing those games, I still ended up with seventy-something pass
receptions that year and 900 yards rushing. I had a real good year. The team
only finished 8-8, because we started out 0-5. That was the first time in the
NFL when I hadn't been on a losing team. I wasn't on a winning team until
1982, when we went to the Super Bowl.

The next year, 1982, I got seriously hurt in a preseason game, and the
Redskins' team doctors told me to retire. I made a cut, and my left knee went
out on me. I not only tore cartilage, but I messed up my anterior cruciate ligament. It frayed like when you tear a piece of cotton, you see little strings. The
team doctors felt they couldn't perform reconstructive surgery, because a guy
like me relied on his quickness, and it just wouldn't work. After I had the surgery, though, I felt I could still play. I told them just to let me go rehabilitate it.

Then we went out on strike with the rest of the NFL players. I had been
going down to the Redskins' training facility every morning around five or
six o'clock for rehabilitation. But when we walked out on strike, they barred
us from using the training facility. So, I put the rehabilitating machine in my
apartment in Washington. The strike gave me a chance to rehabilitate my
knee and come back.

SN: *What was the experience of being on strike like? What was the feeling on the team?*

JW: Everybody on our team supported the strike. We knew we had a terrible deal. Washington was a pro-union team. Definitely pro-union. Our player rep, Mark Murphy, was a level-headed guy. He just wanted to be sure he had the support of the players. What we were striking for really wouldn't help guys like me, who was one of the higher-salaried players. We walked out more to help the younger players, to boost their pay to the level it should be.

I did feel that we didn't present our case in the right way. We presented it in a hard-nosed, hard-butting manner. Negotiating took place in the newspapers too doggone much. In addition, for the players to develop any kind of public sympathy, they can't go through the angle of trying to make more money. It's tough for the public to sympathize with a guy who's making six figures on up, playing a game.

I always felt that the players should have focused on injuries and benefits for care. They should have talked about guys needing knee operations ten years after they had finished playing and not being able to walk. Those are the things that you've got to bring to the forefront. People can relate to that. They can't relate to a guy complaining and bitching about making $100,000 and trying to make $300,000, when you've got homeless people in line and people out of jobs. I can't give anybody any type of sympathy in that type of situation, and you shouldn't expect it. If you want to appeal to a human's emotion, focus on the physical side of football. Look at guys getting paralyzed on the field every day. A guy gets hit, and you don't know if he's getting up.

SN: *How was the players' position arrived at? Were there meetings where the team would come up with a position? How did the different teams unite in the strike?*

JW: There's a player representative on every team.

SN: *They get the feedback from who's on their team.*

JW: Exactly. They take it to the executive committee, and you don't really know how that's received. Once things are in the executive committee's hands, it's basically how they feel they should proceed.

When you're a player, dealing with management, no matter who you are, you're on the short end of the stick. With management, you're talking about an entity that shares revenue, that doesn't need any one piece of the puzzle. There isn't any one player who can be a franchise player to bring more people into the stands. Joe Montana's gone, and San Francisco's still selling out. In that situation, you're going to lose, because you're dealing with an entity that can always replace one component. And that's all you are. Wear out one running back, bring in another running back who'll take less than what you're making anyway.

You have these strikes, they bring in replacement players. That can work, even with vastly inferior players, if the talent is at the same level. You will still see good football. You'll still see guys make good runs, good tackles, good catches, good throws.

Now, if you had one of the regular teams playing a replacement team, it would be different. Let's say you put replacement teams for Dallas and Washington on the field, and you put the numbers of the real players on the replacements. John Q. Fan couldn't tell. He'd still think he was getting real good football. He'd think that just so long as you had two teams playing each other that were comparable. People will watch, and think, "Hey, this is the NFL."

SN: *Nevertheless, this went on for fifty-seven days. And apparently there was strong solidarity among the players.*
JW: Oh, yeah. I was really impressed with that. What really helped was that the owners locked everybody out. If they hadn't done that, then guys would have eventually drifted back.

I hurt my knee a few more times because one of the cruciate ligaments wasn't stable. It went out on me in the NFC Championship game against Dallas. Going for a first down, I was jumping in from about eight yards out and missed it by about two inches. And then the next play I made a movement, and it just collapsed on me, and that was it.

We went out to the Super Bowl the next week, and I didn't know whether I could play, because I was in pain. The knee had collapsed on me three times since I came back to play. I was really concerned. I went to see a top orthopedic surgeon in Los Angeles, where the Super Bowl was being played. After my appointment, I went to see Bert Jones, the Colts' quarterback when I was there, who was now with the Rams. He had broken his neck in a game and was in the hospital. I was thoroughly depressed then, because the surgeon had told me that I should definitely quit. It wasn't one of my better days.

I didn't play in the Super Bowl against the Miami Dolphins, which we won. We practiced for it, and I suited up, and I was really thinking about playing. But there was no need for me to go in and be a detriment to the team. The worst thing I could have done was to have gone out there and not been able to protect myself. So, I didn't play. Then I had a couple of days off to see the doctor about my knee.

SN: *The Super Bowl is not a big up, because you were hurt and couldn't play in it.*
JW: We won the Super Bowl, and I was probably the only guy who wasn't as happy as he probably should have been. I was happy, but I was thinking about my knee. But I really would have been upset if we'd have lost.

Then I had surgery. I wanted them to operate on both knees at the same time. I had some type of growth on the outside of my right knee, for whatever reason, just from wear and tear. I wanted that cleaned out and the other knee done, too. That way, they could look and see how the two knees compared. They took the outside cartilage out of them, which I think cut down on some stability. I got out of the hospital on a Friday, and my daughter was born that Sunday.

After the surgery, the doctors said I shouldn't play again. But I was determined to come back for at least one year. There was no way I could just go out like that.

So I came back the next year, 1983, and had a real good year. I led the NFL in yards per carry, with a five-yard average. I think I had about 700 yards rushing. I was splitting time.

SN: *Would you say Joe Gibbs was attuned to your style of play, more than some of these other coaches?*
JW: I think he was, but he really wanted to play me more in third-down situations, because I was 174 pounds. Even though he saw that I could do all these things, it was just the mentality. He can do it, but he's only 170 pounds. So, I don't think he really wanted to play me that much. He mentioned to me that playing less would prolong my career, which I really didn't care about. I was always of the mind that "I'm a running back. Let me play, let me do it. If I get hurt, too bad; if I don't, good. Let me go out and do what I want to do." But Joe, whom I had a lot of respect for, felt that being the size that I was, I could do more and do it longer playing more in certain spots, which I probably could.

Like I said, I had a real good year in 1983, but my knee went out on me again in a regular season game against Dallas, and so I played sparingly in the playoffs. So, here I am again, doing everything to get them to the playoffs, and then I'm not able to show up again. And that really bothered me more than anything else. But I did play in the Super Bowl against the Raiders.

I came back again the next year, and was playing well. And then against New England I was trying to get out of bounds, and my foot got caught. The guy pulled me back, and it twisted my knee again. I was out a long time after that. I think that really made it tough on Washington. Because here I am—I run the ball on first down, on long situations, block, catch passes—I do some of everything. To replace me, they ended up having to put a tight end in my spot to block sometimes, and they needed another back for this, and another back for that.

SN: *What about the use of pain-killing drugs in the NFL? You read about mature, veteran NFL players sometimes using them so they can play hurt, and then going out on the field knowing that that can exacerbate the injury.*
JW: On no occasion during my career did I have a pain-killing drug injected to permit me to play while injured. I always felt that if I needed a shot to play, I didn't need to play. I'm scared of needles anyway.

But players do take injections. You have a certain amount of pressure on you when you're hurt, because football is your livelihood. There's always somebody on the bench, who's making less money than you're making who wants your job. So, you're going to do whatever you can.

That's why I can't put steroids in the same category as drugs like cocaine and marijuana. I may take a lot of flack for saying this, but I look at steroids in the same vein as a kid taking a class, and he's going to the library. There's this wealth of knowledge on the shelf at the library for him. Now, he has his own books and periodicals available to him. But here's a chance for him to increase his learning level, and his intellectual skills, by going to the library and gathering as much as he can. Using steroids is a guy's chance to increase his physical capability, to be as good as he can be. Not that I condone this. But I can understand why an athlete would do this, even though he knows that he shouldn't.

Of course, going to the library would have a better long-term, lasting effect on me than using steroids. But look at the length of an athlete's career, especially a football player's. As far as he's concerned, it's all for now. There's no tomorrow.

SN: *When did you first see steroids used?*
JW: I never did see steroids used. I always heard a little bit about them, though. I can think of two guys I played with at Oklahoma who were probably using steroids. But I never saw it. And as far as the majority of players are concerned, I can't say I know, because a lot of us were scared of needles. Why would you go and volunteer for a needle, when you don't even want to take a flu shot? I guess for the above-mentioned reasons.

SN: *How did you feel about getting traded to the Atlanta Falcons the next year, 1984?*
JW: The next year the Redskins traded for another running back, George Rogers, and traded me to the Atlanta Falcons. I was a little upset about that,

because I didn't know about it. I eventually understood that there weren't going to be enough balls around. You had Rogers, who was going to need it, and John Riggins was going to need it. Henning, the Falcons' head coach, had been offensive coordinator with the Redskins. He'd been trying to get me.

I think Henning, when he had been with the Redskins my first year, had pushed for me to be a full-time player. But he always told me Joe Gibbs kept saying, "Gee, Dan, he ain't but 170 pounds!" But Henning had wanted me to go full-time, carrying the ball twenty-five times a game, catching ten passes, and returning punts and kickoffs.

I really wasn't that pleased about going to Atlanta. I'd been through that already—playing with teams that weren't winning. You're at the bottom of the heap. Here I was at the end of my career, and I had to go through this crap again.

SN: *But you get more playing time, don't you?*
JW: Yeah, I did play a bunch. I went down to Atlanta and played well. I met the owner, who wasn't too pleased with having me there. He wasn't too pleased with Henning trading for all these ex-Redskins.

SN: *Owners seem to intervene a lot in player selection. I noticed, for example, that this punter for the Redskins shanked his first punt against Dallas—it went only twenty-seven yards—and the Redskins owner was already making comments that he'd have to get rid of the guy. I imagine owners are just amateurs when it comes to knowledge of football.*
JW: But it's their team. Owners look at things like spectators do. They watch games like spectators and comment like spectators. They'll see a player do something they don't like, and they'll say, "Oh, that's terrible. I'm getting rid of him."

SN: *Football is such a complex game that very few people can tell what's going on from the stands. Isn't that the thing with the owner?*
JW: Well, he feels he can tell. (Laughs)

SN: *How would a guy like Joe Gibbs react, who has such an impressive winning record in the NFL? What is the power relationship like when you have a Joe Gibbs getting communication from an owner about getting rid of a guy?*
JW: Let me give you a prime example of how an owner meddled with a team. When I was with Baltimore, we were playing in Miami. Irsay, the Colts' owner, called down to the coach, Mike McCormack, and said, "Look,

I want Bert Jones out at quarterback. I want you to play Greg Landry." And McCormack did it.

Once you do that, it's the kiss of death for a coach. First of all, you're going to lose the respect of your players. Nobody's going to respect you. His goose is cooked. How can you have any respect for a guy like that?

But owners order coaches to make changes, especially in the heat of battle when things aren't going right, and all these emotions are coming out. The owner thinks he can make key decisions, and he wants to get down there and get them done. It's his team, so he feels it should be done.

You've got to be able to have a strong coach, who can stand up to the owner. I can't see an owner telling a Joe Gibbs who to play and who not to play. If the coach succumbs to the owner, he can kill a team. I saw it happen. McCormack did it, and it was total chaos. He had no control afterward. None.

SN: *So, how did it go for you in Atlanta?*
JW: I played a year with Atlanta and came to the end of my contract. I had played real well for them. I was probably the second most productive player on the team, as far as the number of times I touched the ball. We were supposed to be renegotiating my contract. And all of a sudden, Atlanta told me they wanted to reduce my contract. They took a hard line. I said, "Reduce my contract? What is this? I'm the second most productive player on the team, and you want to reduce my contract?" They replied, "Well, we've got such and such a player, and you're making more than he does, and he's a star." I said, "Hold it. You've got to look at the fact that I've been in the league ten years. This is this guy's fourth year. I hope that when this guy reaches his tenth year he isn't making what I'm making now."

We went back and forth, and then the press called me. They said, "Joe, the reason they're doing this is because they want to release you, and then sign you back for less. Do you think this has anything to do with black-white?" I told them that I didn't know if it had anything to do with the black-white relationship. I knew that there were some instances where certain white players hadn't had as hard a time to get things done as some of the black players. I did know that. But as far as my case was concerned, I didn't know. I told them that I'd hate to think that that was the situation, because if it was, I wasn't going to stand for it.

We kept going back and forth, and finally, since I hadn't signed, they released me. They could then resign me. A reporter called me at that point, and I told him that if they released me to take a pay cut, then I'd just retire. I was at the stage then when I was thinking about retiring. I was getting tired of it. You know, getting up on those mornings, having to wear this little outside brace on my knee. I said, "If I'm going to have to wear a brace to play, I'm not play-ing." I didn't like the way it looked under the uniform. It stuck out, and I just hated it. The Falcons didn't seem to be too happy to have me anyway. The owner wasn't pleased about having me on the team. He couldn't understand the contribution I was making.

The reporter misconstrued everything I said to him, and said I had called them racist, which I hadn't. The things I said were definitely taken out of context. I just decided I didn't need this. I was tired. I thought it would be a good time to retire. So, I did. I had people actually call me to ask if I would consider coming back to play, even three years after that.

SN: *How did you feel, looking back on your NFL career?*
JW: I had played ten years in the NFL, which was long enough. It was longer than anybody ever thought I'd play. I'd played in this league for ten years at around 173 pounds, relying on my cutting ability. I was a unique type of run-ning back. I did things totally different from anybody else. I'd basically done everything possible that I could do. Never had a bad game.

When you retire when you can still play, you always think that maybe you left too early. It may be even better to stay too late than to leave too early. Because once you do, that's it. There's no turning back. That door is closed. So, occasionally, I think about that. But then, too, I think about the fact that I'm still able to do everything I want to do now. I can still play basketball.

SN: *So your knees are not giving you pain?*
JW: I do have a lot of pain. My shoulder's giving me a lot of pain. I wake up at night and I'm just in total pain. The shoulder constantly aches. Of course, I don't have much stability in my left knee. I was able to play three or four years after they told me to retire. I consider that being on borrowed time. I was lucky to have that. I look at it as having had a good career.

SN: *How many years were you All-Pro?*
JW: I was All-Pro two years, and I led the NFL one year in pass receiving, as a running back. I also led the league one year in yards per carry, and I led the conference in yards per kickoff return. And I was on two Super Bowl teams. I don't have any visions of making the Hall of Fame, because I don't have the stats. I never got 1000 yards rushing. I missed it quite a few times. That first year in Baltimore, I didn't play the first two games, didn't start until the sixth game, and still had 900-something yards. The next year with the Colts, I had 870 or 900 yards rushing, but I caught eighty-something passes, so I had another 800 yards pass receiving. I could easily have had a 1000-yard year, but it didn't

happen. I think it would be possible for me to go to the College Hall of Fame. That would probably be the highest one I'd be able to attain. But then again, you don't know what the criteria for that are, whether you have to be a Heisman Trophy winner or whatever.

SN: *Well, you made the Oklahoma Sports Hall of Fame. Oklahoma football history is such that that's quite an honor.*
JW: Oh, yeah, it really was. I couldn't have picked a better person than Barry Switzer to present me. It was very emotional for both of us. Barry was my kind of guy. He's always been one of my biggest supporters. Barry's kids, until they graduated from college, used to call me every year on my birthday. So, it doesn't really matter if I get into the College Hall of Fame, because that evening was really special.

SN: *What have you been doing since retiring from the NFL?*
JW: After retiring, I was in several different ventures, trying to find the right thing that I wanted to be in. I eventually found it in the consulting business, with my expertise in marketing products. I have several clients. And I play a lot of golf and tennis and read a great deal.

SN: *I notice on your wall that you have some plaques from charitable activities.*
JW: Yeah, I participate in a great deal of that. When I was a kid, I was fortunate enough to have two caring parents. I spent a lot of time with them. They took us to *everything*. What we had, we wanted. What we didn't have, we didn't know about. So, things worked out. Plus, my parents were professionals. They were in the school system. We were looked after real well.

So I always participate in any type of charity that involves kids. I'm on some charitable boards here in Baltimore and in Oklahoma. I just got back from Florida—the Children's Wish Foundation. They provide a wish for terminally ill kids. For instance, one kid wished to be a golfer, and meet Arnold Palmer, and take lessons from him. They got him a putter autographed by Arnold Palmer, a bag autographed by Arnold Palmer, and they're going to get him lessons at the Arnold Palmer Institute of Golf. And one day Arnold Palmer is going to be there.

I don't know if I look at it in terms of giving back. I just think this is the way it should be. This is the way it was when I grew up. Where would I be if I didn't have people who took an interest in me?

SN: *So how do you feel about having been a football player?*
JW: Playing football was what I was put here to do. I think I knew at an early age that I had a unique talent, and that I was a little different from everybody

else. I didn't do things in an orthodox manner. Just looking at that picture there, I'm jumping over him, changing directions. And I enjoyed every minute of it. I enjoyed waking up that next morning beat up, in pain, just to say, "I was in the pit yesterday. I had a good day, and I came out. I'm moving around a little slow this morning, but I'll live to fight another day."

I don't care how much money you make, you couldn't play the game with the passion, and the feeling, and the effort unless you enjoyed it. You can't, because how much money can they pay you to risk life and limb? And that's exactly what you're doing when you're out there.

You don't realize how violent this game is until you're actually away from it, and you watch it on television. Or what can be even worse, when you look at it close up on the field. When I went back to Oklahoma for Joe Washington Day, I watched the game from the sideline for a while, and the college kids were hitting the licks. Oh, man, it's scary! Every time I think of that, I'm glad I retired when I did. The longer you play, the more lives of the cat you lose. And you only get nine.

The game has changed a little bit. I don't think guys as a whole have as much passion as players once did. For the most part, the passion is only at game time now.

A lot of former players go out of their way not to talk about football. They say, "Well, it's over. I'm through with it." Hey, I'm sorry. It's in my blood. I don't have any problem with talking about something that I was good at. I don't mind talking to guys, hearing some of the stories they have to tell. They have stories to tell, just like I have stories to tell.

I truly feel football is the closest thing to life, as far as participating in different types of situations, interactions with people, responsibility, strife, stress. You can't get it any better than that.

From Oklahoma through the pros, I've kept contact with Tony Peters, Greg Pruitt, and my buddy Kerry Jackson, even though he didn't play pro. Tony and Greg have always been real good friends of mine. They'd do whatever they could for you. I know Greg did when he used to block for a little rookie running back. Yes, Sir-ree. Like I say, it was fun. I loved carrying that football.

STEVE ZABEL

TIGHT END, LINEBACKER

—Philadelphia Eagles, 1970–1974
—New England Patriots, 1975–1978
—Baltimore Colts, 1979

Steve Zabel played tight end and linebacker for University of Oklahoma teams coached by Chuck Fairbanks, one of which finished the 1967 season ranked number two in the nation, winning the Orange Bowl. He discusses how Fairbanks and his assistants, including offensive coordinator Barry Switzer, approached coaching, enforced discipline, and promoted physical conditioning and "mental toughness."

Zabel was the number-one draft choice of the Philadelphia Eagles, and played ten years in the NFL for the Eagles, the New England Patriots, and the Baltimore Colts, initially as a tight end, but mostly as a linebacker. He explains the very significant differences between the middle and outside linebacker positions and analyzes the personality contrast between offensive and defensive players.

A participant in the NFL players' strike of 1974, Zabel provides considerable insight into labor issues in pro football. He was introduced to the labor movement in football before his rookie year, when veteran players appealed to his College All-Star team to help them win a better contract by not playing their

Steve Zabel with the Philadelphia Eagles. Courtesy of Steve Zabel.

scheduled game against the defending NFL champions. Zabel carefully analyzes the roles of club owners, player representatives, and the rank-and-file player in NFL labor disputes. He was also a leader of a 1975 wildcat strike initiated by the New England Patriots, which several other NFL teams joined.

Zabel examines how owners, coaches, and team trainers react to player injury and the importance to players of overcoming pain. He saw teammate Darryl Stingley permanently paralyzed by a hit from Jack Tatum, an experience that profoundly affected him. Zabel examines the factors involved in a player's decision to retire and the adjustment to being away from the game. He also reflects on the inadequacies in the NFL Players Association leadership and outlook during the 1970s, which he believes place football retirees in a much less desirable situation than their major league baseball counterparts.

STEPHEN NORWOOD: *Why don't we begin by talking about your background, where you come from, the kind of community in which you lived during the early part of your life. From there, we'll look at how you got involved in sports.*

STEVE ZABEL: I was born in Minneapolis on March 20, 1948. My parents divorced when I was five. During those troubled times as a three-, four-, and five-year-old, I actually lived with my mom and my father's parents in St. Paul. In the year between my mom's divorce and remarriage, my mother and sister and I moved to the Winnebago Indian reservation in Nebraska, where my mother's mother lived. We kind of regrouped there.

SN: *What led your mother to move there?*
SZ: My mother and several of her brothers and sisters had been fostered out during the Depression. Their mother, my grandma, had made the decision after her husband died. He died from asphyxiation trying to fight a fire on the reservation. When he died, my grandmother had no choice but to foster out several of the kids. But my grandmother and quite a few of my mother's brothers and sisters stayed in Winnebago. For over thirty years, my Uncle Walt was the head custodian for the Indian school, and my Aunt Alice was the head cook.

SN: *You had no Native American ancestry?*
SZ: I don't know if I have any Indian blood. My mother tells me I don't. But her whole family grew up in the Winnebago-Walthill area, where there is the Omaha Indian reservation, and the Santee Sioux reservation, and the Winnebago reservation. I have lots of cousins through intermarriage who are half to one-quarter Indian.

My first schooling was at the Winnebago mission school. My mother recalls that she went up to the first parent-teachers' conference and asked how her son Steve was doing. And the teacher said, "I don't recall that we have a Steve in class. What does he look like?" And she said, "Well, he's real tall, and thin, and has husky eyebrows," and the teacher goes, "Oh, that's Tommy White Deer!" Apparently, because I was in a class full of Indians, I had taken on the name Tommy White Deer, maybe as some sort of escape mechanism. I'd really like to be able to say that I was Indian. I really identify with the Indian culture.

After nine or ten months in Winnebago, my mother remarried. Zabel is my stepfather's name. My father's name was Bill Barkacs. He was a strapping six-foot-three, 200-pound Bohemian. He's passed on now. He was an extremely handsome man. The women just flocked to him, and he didn't have the discipline to say no to them.

SN: *What was your father's occupation?*
SZ: He was a police officer, and my mother said he was so handsome in that policeman's uniform that women were really attracted. My parents were very young, and unfortunately they divorced.

My mother then married Glenn Zabel, who was a Minnesota native. He came from a very German household. They spoke German around the house. When my mother and stepfather married, they moved to Denver, Colorado.

The last thing I remember of Winnebago was my mother putting me on a bus and sending me to visit my dad in Salt Lake City. I didn't think much of it. Now, the thought of putting a six-year-old kid on a bus and sending him halfway across the country is really frightening. During that summer my mother and her new husband moved everything to Denver. And at the end of the summer I joined them there.

SN: *Can you describe what it was like growing up in Denver, and how you became involved in sports?*
SZ: I loved growing up in Denver. We lived about six blocks from a big park. We were only a mile or so from Mile High Stadium, where the Denver Broncos now play. Back then it was where the Denver Bears Triple-A minor league baseball team played.

What first got me involved in sport was my speed. In elementary school, I was very proud of the fact that I was never defeated in a foot race. The big thing was that the elementary school always had a field day in the spring or early summer. I always won the races and the high jump. And I remember as a third grader going to a city-area field day, where I competed with boys from all the Denver schools. It was bigger than life to me. In our entire school, I was the only one who did anything noteworthy. I came in second in the fifty-yard dash. As a third grader I set a softball throw record that stood for twenty years in Denver. I threw the ball so much farther than any of the other kids that everybody took note. I'll never forget being identified in a school awards assembly as a third grader as the top athlete in the school. But that one city-area field day as a third grader really got me excited about competing against kids I'd never seen before. That really kindled my desire to become an athlete.

SN: *When did you start playing football?*
SZ: In third grade I became involved in my first organized league sport, through Denver's Young America Football League. It provided several levels of competition, but they also had what they called the associate program, for boys who were too young or too little for the other levels. My first football experience was for an associate team, the Hawks.

SN: *Did you play with shoulder pads and helmets?*
SZ: We played full contact tackle football, with helmets and shoulder pads, though we didn't have facemasks.

SN: *What was your mother and stepfather's attitude toward sports and toward your getting involved, at this young age, in these activities? And how about football, which is a contact sport? Was there any concern that this was dangerous?*
SZ: My stepfather, Glenn Zabel, had been a very good high school athlete. My second year in the Young America Football League we lost our first game. The next morning, I got up, and here was my picture on the front page of the *Rocky Mountain News*, trying to tackle a kid. The caption was, "Hawks' Would-Be Tackler Steve Zabel is Thrown as Bobby Jones (or whatever his name was) Goes for a Touchdown." My stepfather was upset that I had missed the tackle. Immediately after the game, he took me out into our backyard, and said, "I'm going to throw a dollar bill down here. If you can tackle me within the next five minutes, it's yours." It started out as a game. I'd go into him and he'd knock me down. I'd get back up and he'd knock me down. I was crying because I wanted to get him down, and I almost got him, but I never could get him off the ground. My mother was upset. She was on the patio watching all this stuff. After it was over though, my dad made his point: "You've got pads on, kid. If you're going to be a football player, you have to be more aggressive. You can't play like a little sissy, like you did before."

To be honest, I didn't understand the real implications of that psychodrama. As years went by and I got better and better and more aggressive, I remembered that day when my dad kind of beat me around, to prove to me that you got the pads on, and you're really not going to get hurt. The more aggressive you are in football, the better.

I played football with the Hawks up through eighth grade. We won the Denver city championship that year.

SN: *What sport did you prefer playing in junior high school?*
SZ: At that age I preferred baseball to football. Football is so demanding and so tough that I honestly think few kids growing up could say that they really loved and enjoyed football, like they loved and enjoyed baseball, or basketball, or track.

SN: *In sports, even the best players are going to have moments when they make mistakes. It's inevitable. I would think it's probably good training to experience these moments when you're younger and develop some perspective.*
SZ: In the fourth or fifth grade we had a baseball coach named Dale Inegaki. He was a Hawaiian guy who had been an All-American football player at the University of Denver back in the early 1950s. I'll never forget, I was playing third base, and I let three balls roll through my legs. I innocently went up to the coach after we came off the field, and said, "I think you ought to put somebody else in my position. I'm hurting the team." The coach took me out. And I didn't think anything more of it. But after the game, the coach really berated me in front of the team and called me a quitter. That hadn't even entered my mind. But from that point on, after being berated so severely, it registered with me that an athlete is not supposed to quit. In life, I've learned that it's sometimes all right to quit. But it's hard to overcome an attitude instilled so young.

In 1978 when I was with the New England Patriots, we had won our division, and we were getting ready to play Houston in the playoffs. I had been hurt late in the season and had missed the last six games, with partially torn ligaments in my right knee. My knee still hurt, but I felt I was ready to play in the playoffs. The very first play of the game, Houston ran a quick toss to Earl Campbell. I was playing him along, waiting for Earl to make up his mind when he was going to turn up, when their tight end, Mike Barber, really went down on my knees, and he really reinjured my right knee. I looked up, and there was Earl Campbell upon me. I didn't have a chance to regroup and get into a striking mode. I was just able to thrust my body at him and bounced off him thinking what a wonderful lick I'd put on him, and surely I must have knocked him down. But he was running downfield with two safeties on his back.

At that moment I should have realized that I was really hurt, and I should have gone off the field and let somebody take my place. But it was so ingrained in me that if you're a quitter, you're a loser—that winners never quit, and quitters never win. My performance deteriorated badly during that game, and towards the end of the game I was getting handled pretty good. And I thought, "I want to go off, this is ridiculous. I'm embarrassing myself. I can't believe the coaches can't see how bad I'm playing. Why aren't they taking me out?" But I never did quit. There are things that are instilled in you as a young boy that carry over to your high school career, or college career, or pro career, and can hurt your performance rather than help it.

I know that in my mind and in my heart as a young boy growing up I always had a yearning for a 100 percent identity with my father, where I could just hug him and could know that he loved me as much as I loved him, and that he was my father. And basically because of the divorce, I really wasn't able to interact with my real father very much. It was a real frustrating, tough situation.

SN: *You saw him only infrequently?*
SZ: Yes. My father lived in Utah and then in Idaho and Minnesota.

SN: *How many children in the household in which you lived?*
SZ: My sister and I were stepchildren, and I had three brothers who were full blood.

SN: *And you perceived some favoritism on your stepfather's part toward his own children?*
SZ: Oh, yeah. There was no question my stepfather favored his own children.

I was always looking for approval, and I was always looking for love. And when I did great things on the athletic field, it seemed like my situation at home was much better than it was during the summertime, when I wasn't actively engaged in sports, other than baseball games. It seemed that my biggest problems came before I was playing football and basketball on a regular basis. Quite honestly, it's been difficult for me to overcome the attitude that if you do good things, you're going to be liked, and if you do bad things, you're not. I always longed for that unconditional love—I don't care whether you fail or you don't—a constant kind of situation. That perception that I had to do good things in order to be loved, which was emphasized at home, was further reinforced by my relationships with coaches. Consequently, my whole life has been a series of performances so coaches or friends would perceive me as a better person.

SN: *The team is like a family in a way.*
SZ: When I was growing up, the love that I really got that I needed was from my close friends and teammates. Through the first seven, eight, nine years of

my marriage, my wife always made the comment that she wished she was as good a friend to me as my friends were. That was very difficult to overcome. I've only been able to overcome it through the realization that I didn't need to be a people-pleaser, I needed to be myself and to be accepted for what I was.

Still, although my stepfather is not my blood father, he certainly was my father. He raised me from the time I was six. I'll be forever grateful for the times that we had playing catch with a baseball. We'd go down to the ballpark and he'd let me pitch to him. He always took an interest in my sporting career.

SN: *How about the larger sports culture at this time? Did you follow sports at the professional or college levels when you were growing up?*
SZ: Yes, I did, particularly major league baseball. That was my favorite sport. My favorite team was the Brooklyn Dodgers.

SN: *Any reason you were drawn to the Brooklyn Dodgers?*
SZ: I just liked those Brooklyn bums. They were kind of like the underdog. When World Series time came up, I just couldn't wait to get home from school to watch the Dodgers and the Yankees. For some reason, Roy Campanella was my hero. I'll never forget how tragic it was to me when he had the accident and was paralyzed. That really affected me. And then all of a sudden they moved to L.A., and I got off being a Dodger fan.

Every Saturday morning they had the "Game of the Week," with Pee Wee Reese and Dizzy Dean. I just couldn't wait to come home from a baseball game, or from practice to watch the "Game of the Week."

SN: *Did you also follow minor league baseball in Denver?*
SZ: Yes. Denver had a Triple-A ball club called the Denver Bears. The Bears were real active within the community. They did things like if you made straight As, you got tickets to go to the Bears games. When I was in elementary school, I got straight As all the way through, and so I got tickets to the Bears games.

SN: *Did you also follow pro football at that age?*
SZ: I watched pro football as a boy. I remember watching the L.A. Rams when they had Dick Bass, way back in the 1950s. I remember watching one game and he made a 100-yard kickoff return. I was intrigued by it, but honestly, even through high school, football was my least favorite sport. Baseball was always my favorite sport.

But in the ninth grade, when we moved to Thornton, Colorado, I totally abandoned baseball for track. Thornton High School included the ninth through twelfth grades, so I had an opportunity to make the high school track team and actually letter. The thought of getting a letter jacket and being in the in-crowd overrode any thought of continuing my baseball career. So, I went out for track as a ninth grader and lettered as a high jumper and high hurdler. In high school, I concentrated on running track, and playing basketball and football.

SN: *What impact did your high school football coach have on your development as a player?*
SZ: My high school football coach misjudged my talent and discouraged me from wanting to go on and play at a higher level. My senior year I was captain of the football team. We didn't have a very good team, but one night we rose to the occasion and beat the first-place team. I had a tremendous game. After the game, several of my friends and I went out and bought some beer. The coach found out about it. He questioned everybody about their participation, and everybody lied, except for me. I said, "Yeah, we were drinking beer." The coach really berated me, in the way I had been berated when I asked to be removed from that baseball game because I thought I was hurting the team, and he kicked me off the team. He had been a successful player at a lower division school, Pittsburg State Teachers' College. He thought I might have the ability to play at a small college, but certainly didn't have the ability to play at a major university. In fact, when the University of Colorado offered me a track scholarship and I told them I wanted to play football, I was told that the football staff there didn't want me. They thought I was an alley cat, a bad seed.

SN: *They got that view from your high school coach?*
SZ: I'm sure they got it from him.

SN: *Did you learn anything about football from your high school coach? Obviously, coaching is an important ingredient in a player's success.*
SZ: Right.

SN: *I imagine there are some players who are pure naturals, but they must be rare. You have to get some instruction in how to play.*
SZ: Well, I didn't have much coaching in high school. The things I did were inherent from my athletic ability.

SN: *What position did you play in high school?*
SZ: I was an end and played both ways, offense and defense, and punted, and kicked extra points, and ran back kickoffs and punts. By the time I was a senior in high school, I had played football for ten years and pretty much knew what I needed to do and how to do it.

SN: *What did you not like about high school football?*
SZ: High school football was tough and physically demanding, and I can remember days of not wanting to go to practice and not wanting to play football. They would work you in the practices until you just didn't think you could do one more thing. But again, I had developed this attitude that I wasn't going to quit, I wasn't going to quit, so I just kept on playing and playing.

SN: *Did you get hurt at all playing football in high school?*
SZ: I really didn't get hurt, other than some bumps and bruises.
   I was a much better basketball player and track athlete in high school than football player, and I was fairly highly recruited by colleges in basketball and track. My senior year I was state high jump champion in Colorado. I was the state pentathlon champion. The pentathlon was a series of five events—the 100-yard dash, the high hurdles, the high jump, the discus throw, and the mile run. My senior year I set a state record in the pentathlon that lasted almost twenty years.

SN: *Did you ever think about playing football in college?*
SZ: What I most wanted to do was to become a decathlon star. Growing up in the 1950s, the Olympics were really something big in my life. I remember the Americans competing against the Russians, and I remember particularly John Thomas battling Valery Brumel.

SN: *In the 1960 Olympics in Rome.*
SZ: Yes. They were Western rollers, and that's what I did. I was just infatuated with high jumping. I had won the school championship in pole-vaulting as a seventh grader, and vaulted just under thirteen feet when I was in high school. And I could broad jump and I could run, which was perfect for a decathlete.

SN: *What were your college plans as you were finishing high school?*
SZ: I had pretty much decided to go to Colorado State University in Fort Collins, even though I had an opportunity to go to the University of Colorado and play basketball or run track. Colorado State offered me a football-track

scholarship, and their coach wanted me to become a decathlete. I actually signed a letter of intent to go there.

But my plans changed the summer before I was supposed to go, when I got a job mowing and doing maintenance work at a basketball-baseball camp up in the mountains at Breckinridge, Colorado. They had the Colorado head basketball coach, Socks Walseth, and Bob Bowman from the Air Force Academy up there as coaches. Both of those guys just couldn't believe that I had such athletic ability. And Bob Bowman offered me an opportunity to go to the Air Force Academy. Somehow, the Air Force Academy was able to talk to Colorado State and get me released from my letter of intent. But, because of the timing, I had missed going into the academy with the class I would have gone in with. The academy talked me into going to New Mexico Military Institute in Roswell, New Mexico, prepping for a year in a junior college. When I got to the academy, I could pick the sport I wanted to concentrate on.

SN: *How did you get recruited by the University of Oklahoma football program?*
SZ: Oklahoma had been interested in my roommate at New Mexico Military, Rick Mason. In looking at the football game films, the Oklahoma coaching staff said, "Yeah, Rick's great, but what about this kid?" I was that kid, and they asked me to come to Oklahoma on a recruiting trip. Even though I didn't like the military aspect of what I was dealing with, I stoically wanted to go to the Air Force Academy and be another Doc Blanchard or Glenn Davis. I agreed to go to Oklahoma on a recruiting trip just because I thought it would be fun.

SN: *Did you know much about the University of Oklahoma program or about its reputation as a football powerhouse?*
SZ: I had no real knowledge of Oklahoma and didn't know what a great tradition they had. I just knew that Oklahoma was a state somewhere to the south and east of us. I'd never seen Oklahoma play in the 1950s and 1960s, when Bud Wilkinson was there.

SN: *So when you were being recruited, you were really not very aware of which schools had the major programs?*
SZ: Right.

SN: *And you didn't have strong feelings about playing here or there or with this coach or that coach?*
SZ: That's absolutely correct. But I'll never forget watching the Oklahoma players when I came down on the recruiting trip. There was something

intangible that they projected—a closeness, a real earnest desire to be better and to work hard. And there was a physical toughness that I saw in the players that really intrigued me. I wanted to be like that.

SN: *What was your impression of Oklahoma's coaches when you met them?*
SZ: I was taken into the coaches' locker room to meet the head coach, Jim Mackenzie. And then I was introduced to Barry Switzer. I didn't know Barry Switzer from Adam. But that first meeting I had with him was paramount in my decision to come to Oklahoma. When I shook his hand, he took me by the hand and he kind of pulled me close to him, and he said, "We really want you to come here. You'll be a star at Oklahoma. We really want you." Of all the coaches I had talked to, none had made an impact on me like he did. And that, along with the feelings I had about the players, made me say right then and there, that's where I wanted to go. I also wanted to go to Oklahoma to prove myself against Colorado.

SN: *What was moving to Oklahoma like?*
SZ: When I came to Oklahoma the summer before my first year, all I had was two pairs of jeans, a pair of desert boots, and six T-shirts. I didn't have a car. I had to take a bus from Minnesota to Oklahoma.

SN: *What do you remember about your first football practices at Oklahoma?*
SZ: At the end of that summer, I was probably in the best shape that I ever was in in my whole life. The first two days of fall practice we had a test on our physical conditioning, and I was winning everything. It really opened the door for me to have an opportunity to succeed. The first day of practice they put me on what they called a board drill. They put a two-by-twelve down on the grass and the offensive guy had to block the defensive guy off of the board. And the defensive guy had to knock the offensive guy off the board. The first blocking assignment I ever had was against Granville Liggins. I didn't know Granville from Adam. I came off the ball and did way better than anybody ever imagined I could do. And Granville got yelled at, and he was embarrassed. They immediately made us go again. Granville didn't underestimate me the second time, and defeated me soundly. But I was the first player, as far as I know, who ever came in from a junior college program and didn't go through spring football, who was able to start the next year. I started every game at Oklahoma from that point on.

SN: *What was the coaching like when you were starting out at Oklahoma? How much instruction did you get your first year in pass receiving and blocking?*

You're moving into a much higher level of competition now. Which coaches did you work with most closely?

SZ: It was at Oklahoma that I first experienced real coaching. My first year, my sophomore year, I played tight end exclusively. We had an offensive line coach named Buck Nystrom. We had a receivers' coach named Galen Hall. As a tight end I worked with the tight ends in pass drills and route running. I also had to go with the offensive line in blocking drills.

Back in those days at Oklahoma, you could have twice or three times the number of players per class than you can now. The number of scholarships wasn't restricted like it is today. It was typical for there to be seventy-five players from one class on the team. So, the coaches were determined to make it so tough in practice that they would weed out the players who would be likely to quit on them during a game. They felt that if the player quit in practice, he'd likely quit during a game. So, we had guys leaving at three o'clock in the morning. They were quitting the team every day. The coaches let everybody know that there was going to be a day or two that year when you would be tested to the limit. You could either put up with it or quit. It didn't matter whether you were the biggest star or just a guy trying to make it. Everybody was called upon to find out how much intestinal fortitude they had, how much they really wanted to play football, and whether they were tough enough to stick it out and be a part of a championship program. The coaching staff was so tough, that those guys who were borderline would quit. When I graduated as a senior, there were only six or seven guys left from the entire junior class, out of the original seventy-five.

SN: *These are just the regular practice sessions that were this grueling?*

SZ: Right. Buck Nystrom, who was the meanest, toughest coach I ever had at any stage of my football career, put me through sheer torture at one point during my junior year. I had suffered a stress fracture of my small toe on my left foot, which caused me to miss the two-a-day practices before the season.

I had played real well and had caught four touchdown passes going into the week before the Texas game. We always had an open week before we played Texas. During that open week, Buck Nystrom took it upon himself to make me pay for missing the preseason two-a-day practices and to catch up with the rest of the team on conditioning. There was one day when he made me do a blocking drill nineteen times in a row, while all of my teammates watched me being tortured. I remember making it to the eighth or ninth time and wanting to quit, and wanting to quit, and wanting to quit, but then thinking how bad I felt for those guys who had quit, and how much I didn't want to run or walk off the field and quit. There was a cottonwood tree on the south side of the practice field, and we kept getting closer and closer to that tree. And I thought, if I could only get close enough to that tree where I could run into it and knock myself out, if I could make it look legitimate, then I wouldn't have to go through any more repetitions. I would rather have done that than quit. Thank God, after the nineteenth time Buck stopped. Somehow, someway, I had persevered. Buck had taken me to the absolute limit of what I could do physically. And I didn't quit.

Coach Nystrom could get really impatient when he didn't think players were pushing themselves hard enough. He'd even physically involve himself in the drills. I remember once when he got real mad at the fourth and fifth team red-shirt guys, who were basically the starters' common fodder. They were called the "Scout Squad," but were commonly referred to as the "Turd Team." Buck felt they weren't going hard enough in this drill. So, he told them to all get out of the way, and he went one-on-one with everybody on the offensive line. He became the defensive lineman, and we were the offensive linemen, and he went up against us with no helmet, no shoulder pads, nothing. Quite a few of the senior offensive linemen viewed this as an opportunity to really put it on Buck. Some of the larger, more experienced guys really stuck Buck big time.

That evening, Ken Mendenhall, one of our starters who went on to play pro football for eleven years, and I went out to Braum's to get an ice cream. As we came out of Braum's we ran into Coach Nystrom. He was carrying his baby under one arm, and he had a T-shirt on. We could see that his arm was all black-and-blue. Buck said to us, "Wasn't that the greatest practice that you ever experienced!" And we went, "Yeah, Coach, kind of." And he said, "Look at this!" and he lifted up his T-shirt and he had a bruise in the middle of his chest the size of a helmet. He thought that was absolutely hilarious, that he had been beat up like that. That shows you the kind of coach he was.

Another time Buck even went too far for Coach Fairbanks. We were doing a blocking drill where we would have to fire off on the ball and stay low enough to go under a steel bar. The bar was set there to make sure that we stayed low when we made contact in our blocking drills. But even though we were all going under that bar, Buck didn't think we were staying low enough. So, he sent his assistant trainer, who was always by his side, into the locker room to get a baseball bat. We would have to fire off, and Buck would swing that baseball bat over the top of us. For the first two or three guys, everything was working out great. But then you could see it in his eyes that he wasn't happy with what was going on. And rather than swing the bat horizontal to the ground, he started going up a little more perpendicular, and started actually hitting some of the guys in the butt and in the back. Coach Fairbanks was in his tower watching, and he absolutely flipped out. He hit about five steps coming down that tower, and came over to us, and went, "Buck, what in the world are you doing?" And Buck just kind of went, "Uh, nothing, Coach. Here, take this bat. Okay, boys, let's go."

But that was Coach Nystrom. He was just hell bent for leather. He would take you to the limit, whether you liked it or not. His attitude was that those guys who stick around will be players for me, and those guys who quit are cowards and would have quit anyway. So, good riddance.

SN: *What was the Oklahoma coaching staff's approach toward maintaining discipline in the football program?*

SZ: The Oklahoma coaches enforced a very, very strict discipline. They imposed severe punishment for many infractions. My sophomore year, the night after we beat Colorado 23-0, a lot of us broke curfew and went out partying. We stayed out pretty much all night. Our head coach, Chuck Fairbanks, found out about it. On Monday morning, he came in and went through the athletic dorm, and I had never been so scared in my life. He just absolutely went berserk. He came in my room and told me he knew I'd been out partying. He gave me two options. I could either quit the team, or I could show up the next morning at five o'clock, and he would run me until I either quit or died. He went through the dorm and got in the faces of about fifteen of the players who had been out partying. They were all told to be out at the stadium at five o'clock the next morning.

We initially thought that this was a disciplinary problem that would be handled by Jerry Pettibone, who was a dorm counselor. We all knew that if Jerry was there alone, we could get some slack on the deal. But when Chuck Fairbanks drove up in his long yellow Oldsmobile, everybody knew that the jig was up, and that we were really going to pay. As his car approached us, it was real ominous. I can still see the smoke billowing out of the car as he pulled up. It was just pitch black dark, five o'clock in the morning on an early November day. Fairbanks got out of the car and ordered everybody to start running. The whole time we were running, he was honking his horn and yelling, "Run faster, run faster!" We ran in the stadium from five o'clock until eight o'clock. Of the fifteen guys who had started out, at eight o'clock there were only two of us left, myself and Bruce Stensrud. Everybody else was puking and crying and they'd quit. Coach Pettibone said, "Okay, you have 100 yards to go, and then you're through." And I'll never forget the joy and satisfaction of me winning that last 100-yard race, and running up the ramp, and looking at Coach Fairbanks, and smiling, as if to say, "I took it! I took it!" It was one of the most gratifying things that I ever remember doing in my life.

SN: *How would you compare being a student athlete at Oklahoma in the late 1960s with the situation twenty years later, when some players were out of control, involved in a gang rape, a shooting, and so on?*
SZ: Port Robertson, the academic advisor, enforced very strict discipline within the dorm. A lot of the guys left because of Port's discipline. Over the years I've talked with quite a few people who witnessed the decline in discipline in the University of Oklahoma football program. To me, it's pretty simple. Port Robertson retired from Oklahoma in the early 1980s, and they didn't hire anyone to fulfill his responsibilities.

Now Port Robertson was a bear of a man. If you got into trouble with Port, you had several options. You could go up to the wrestling room with Port and wrestle him for thirty minutes. Only a few guys took him up on that, and they were sorry they did. You could get up early every morning and wash dishes before classes, and wash dishes at lunch, and wash dishes at night. Or they would punish you through physical exercise. They'd start you at five o'clock in the morning running stadium steps, and wind sprints, and grass drills. Those coaches would push you until you'd pass out, or throw up, or quit. That was a huge deterrent for me wanting to get into trouble.

SN: *Looking back, how do you view the Oklahoma coaching staff's approach toward maintaining discipline when you were playing?*
SZ: I've got real positive views about the approach the coaches used to instill discipline and to promote physical conditioning and mental toughness. I wouldn't want to go through it again. But I'm glad that I did. It's made everything else in life substantially easier. It's helped me to be a taskmaster, to be a survivor, to understand the importance of finishing a task that you started. The one thing that I learned at Oklahoma that was more beneficial to me than anything was to do a job and don't make excuses, just do the job. That regardless of the physical, mental, or emotional impact, my job was to perform my task and not make excuses or look for shortcuts, to dot all the Is and cross all the Ts, and pay attention to detail. The University of Oklahoma's whole coaching philosophy while I was there was to pay attention to detail and to do the small things right. If you did that, the big things would all fall into place. We'd run one play eighteen to twenty times before we moved on to another play. The players would look at each other thinking, "Wasn't that perfect, wasn't that perfect, wasn't that perfect?" Yet, we still had to do it again.

I'll tell you this. In 1967 we were picked before the season to finish fourth in the Big Eight. Instead we won the Big Eight championship, going undefeated in conference games, and lost only one game the whole season and only by two points. We ended up number two in the nation and won the Orange Bowl. If you looked at the sizes and the strengths and the speed of the players that we had on our team and compared them to teams of other eras, I don't think we would have stacked up very well as far as sheer physical ability. But we were very, very mentally tough, we were very well conditioned, and we were very well coached. And the combination of all those factors allowed us to be successful.

SN: *What was your academic experience like as a football player at the University of Oklahoma?*
SZ: When I enrolled at the University of Oklahoma, I majored in business education. I had completed one year of junior college at New Mexico Military, where I had taken primarily arts and sciences courses in order to fulfill future requirements at the Air Force Academy. I had pretty close to a 3.4 grade point average coming out of junior college. After my four years of college I still had two more classes I needed to take, and I needed to student teach, in order to receive my degree. After my rookie year in the NFL, I came back and fulfilled those requirements and received my degree.

SN: *How did you stay in condition during the summer?*
SZ: Besides working a summer job, we were required to work out on our own. They would send you a workout card every week. You were responsible for running the activities on that card, and then filling in the card and sending it back to the coaching staff to show them that you were working out.

SN: *How did the coaches determine that you were really doing that?*
SZ: Well, you were on your honor. But each week the activities got harder. The first day of two-a-day preseason practice you had to run everything that was on that last card. Whether it was a hundred 100-yard dashes, and forty 40-yard dashes, and ten or twelve stadium steps, and three or four 440-yard runs, and a mile run under so much time, you had to fulfill that. So, the bottom line was, if you had lied and hadn't been working out like you said you had, it was very apparent to the coaches watching your performance that first day of two-a-days. One of the things that really helped me in my football career was that I really did work out.

SN: *How did Oklahoma do your first year with the team?*
SZ: The Oklahoma football team had a very successful season my first year, when I was a sophomore. We went 10-1, losing only to Texas by two points. I played tight end exclusively that year. I caught the fifty-two-yard pass against Missouri to get us down to the five-yard line and set up the winning touchdown. And I caught the game-winning touchdown pass against Kansas. We won the Big Eight title, and that victory got us into the Orange Bowl. We had heard before the game that every orange in Oklahoma had been sold. As we were walking into the stadium, we saw people selling bushels of oranges. It really didn't dawn on me what was going to happen with those oranges until after I caught that touchdown pass. And then, from everywhere in the stadium, the field was just bombarded with oranges. It developed into almost a frightening situation. The fans in their zeal were throwing them at the Kansas players and hitting them, and the players were picking them up and firing them back at the fans.

That one pass set the course for the rest of my life. If I had missed it, I'm sure I never would have played another down at Oklahoma. But because I was successful, we won the game. There's a real fine line between succeeding and failing. A lot of times guys fail because they don't have the moxie to just go ahead and win. They subconsciously don't really feel like they deserve to win or deserve to be catching that pass. And they think about it, "What if I miss it, what if I miss it?" And then they end up missing it. There weren't any thoughts like that that ever went through my mind at that point in my life. It was, I'm open, here's the pass, catch it, and the rest is history. Even today, if you talk to somebody about my football career, they'll always say, "Oh yeah, you're the guy who caught the pass against Kansas in 1967."

We had been picked to finish no better than fourth in the Big Eight, and yet through a tremendous work ethic and camaraderie and team spirit we won the conference, and we won the Orange Bowl. That's something that we players from the 1967 team can still look back to today.

SN: *You also played defense later at Oklahoma.*
SZ: My junior year, I played outside linebacker in addition to tight end. After losing three of our first four games, Chuck Fairbanks called me into his office and asked me to switch to defense. He felt we really needed help there. After I switched to linebacker, we won our last five games in a row, including a 47-0 victory over Nebraska on national television. I was named Sooner Outstanding Defensive Player that year.

My senior year I was one of the team's four cocaptains. I made All–Big Eight my junior and senior year and was named to some All-American teams those years as well. But that didn't prevent Coach Fairbanks from openly berating me in front of the whole team after we lost to Texas. Texas won the national championship that year. But if we hadn't fumbled two punts inside our five-yard line, we would have beaten them that day. When we gathered together to watch the game films, Coach Fairbanks' opening remarks to the team were: "Steve Zabel, you ought to turn in your uniform because you played absolutely the worst game that I ever saw anybody at Oklahoma ever play!" Of course, I was totally embarrassed to be belittled like that in front of my team-mates and friends, guys whom I loved and respected. After we finished look-ing at the films, Coach Fairbanks told everybody but me to go out and run. He ran the projector and made me go back through the game play by play by play by play. It was probably the longest hour of my life. The best thing I can remember him saying about my performance in any particular play in that game was "That was horseshit!" He used that word about nine million times.

SN: *You didn't fumble the punts, which were the most glaring mistakes made.*
SZ: No, I didn't fumble the punts. After we got through looking at the films, Coach Fairbanks asked me if I had anything to say, and I said, "Yeah, coach. I agree with you I didn't play very well. But I didn't play near as bad as you're telling me I played. And I think if you think about it, you're going to be embarrassed that you put me through this." And I left. The next day he came up to me and apologized for embarrassing me the way he had. And he said, "You're right. You didn't play as bad as I thought. There were a lot of other guys who played twice as bad as you did." And that was that.

SN: *How would you describe Chuck Fairbanks as a coach, looking back? You played with him in the pros, too, with the New England Patriots.*
SZ: I probably played under Chuck Fairbanks longer than anybody that he ever coached. He was a great, great disciplinarian. He was a good motivator. But his strong suit was that he could really delegate authority. Chuck had great assistant coaches who were great teachers. And he let those guys run their own programs. That was why he was so successful, whether it was at the University of Oklahoma or with the New England Patriots.

SN: *What did you think about Barry Switzer as a coach?*
SZ: Barry Switzer was the offensive coordinator the whole time I was at Oklahoma. He was a very smart play caller. He designed our whole offense to be deceptive. We would run off tackle with Steve Owens left and Steve Owens right. The safeties would commit too quickly, and we'd throw a play action pass. Barry's style was he did whatever it took to win a game. If you look at the

Chuck Fairbanks. Courtesy of the Western History Collections, University of Oklahoma.

offensive records of the teams during the time I played, you'd see that Steve Owens is still one of the leading rushers. He still holds the record for the most touchdowns. Eddie Hinton from our time period holds all of the pass-receiving records. And I'm still somewhere around the all-time top five or six receivers at Oklahoma. Bobby Warmack was a very gifted quarterback, who could run the option and pass the ball as well as any quarterback who ever played at Oklahoma.

Switzer had a great knack for forming an unbelievable relationship with the ballplayers, just through his genuineness and his sincerity and his zest for life. He was somehow able to extract more from the players. I think that his ability to relate to the players, particularly the black players, really allowed him to be as successful as he was. Coming from a small town in Arkansas, having grown up in the black culture there, he was able to relate to the black players.

SN: *What was the racial situation like at that time in the University of Oklahoma football program?*
SZ: Both Chuck Fairbanks and Barry Switzer recognized that segregation was on its way out, and that it was just a matter of time before all of the universities really opened up and accepted the black players. I think Oklahoma was definitely in the forefront of recognizing the importance of the black athlete in football. If you really wanted to pinpoint *the* reason for Switzer's success, it was because he was able to recruit superior black athletes. Because of Barry's ability to relate to the black players and to their families, he was very, very successful.

SN: *How many black players were at Oklahoma when you were there?*
SZ: I was at Oklahoma during a period of transition, from 1967 to 1969. My first year we only had three or four black players, and by the time I got to be a senior, we probably had fifteen to twenty. Granville Liggins was a great, great player for us. And Eddie Hinton was a great, great player for us. And before that we had Eugene Ross and Prentice Gautt. Those guys were the real pioneers of the black players at the University of Oklahoma.

SN: *How did the black players adjust to playing at Oklahoma? Was there any racial tension on the team?*
SZ: If there was anything that was going on that was controversial, or racial, I sure wasn't aware of it.

SN: *Who were some of the best players on the Oklahoma teams you were on? You've already mentioned some who went on to careers in the NFL.*
SZ: We had a lot of talent on those Oklahoma teams that I played on. In fact you'd have to go back and look real hard at any year that Oklahoma had three players drafted in the first round of the NFL draft like we did my senior year. I was the sixth player picked in the first round, Jimmy Files was the thirteenth player, and Steve Owens was the nineteenth player. Steve Owens won the Heisman Trophy that year. I was drafted by the Philadelphia Eagles, Files by the New York Giants, and Owens by the Detroit Lions. We also had Ken Mendenhall, who was drafted in the fifth round by Atlanta and went on to play eleven years with the Baltimore Colts as their starting center.

There were great players from other classes on our teams, too. Probably the best defensive player at Oklahoma when I was there was Granville Liggins. Granville was a nose tackle who made All-American two years in a row. He was undersized, about six foot one and 230 pounds, and really didn't fit the mold of NFL players. But he went up to Canada and had a very successful career. Eddie Hinton was a great wide receiver who was drafted in the first round by the Baltimore Colts and went on to play many years in the NFL. Bob Kalsu was an All-American tackle who was drafted in the second round by the Buffalo Bills and then was drafted into the army and killed in Vietnam.

In my senior year, when we went 6-4, we didn't play in a bowl game. But Steve Owens, Ken Mendenhall, and I all got invited to play in the East-West Shrine game, which was a postseason All-Star game, and in the Hula Bowl game, and Jimmy Files got to play in the Senior Bowl game. So, there were four of us on that team that went to a bowl game, even though the team didn't.

SN: *Why don't we look at the NFL drafting process now. When did you become aware that you were a good prospect for the NFL draft in a high round? Did the Oklahoma coaches indicate to you that you would be?*
SZ: My first real exposure to the possibilities of playing pro football came after my senior year when I was invited to play in the East-West Shrine game in San Francisco and in the Hula Bowl in Hawaii. It was while I was practicing in San Francisco that agents really started pursuing me, talking about being drafted and what that would mean for me financially. There was a lot of talk among them that I'd be a first- or second-round NFL draft choice. There were also scouts out there that wanted to time you. But it really wasn't anywhere near as sophisticated a system as they have today. Now, before the guys go into training camp or get drafted, they're physically tested, and mentally tested, and evaluated under specific circumstances, whereas the players from my era were basically drafted on raw ability. There might be a few times where a scout looked at some film and saw you play, but you were drafted by reputation primarily.

In the East-West Shrine game our team won, but I hurt my back. I was covering a kickoff and basically got wedged. And then I went to the Hula Bowl, and the first week I was in Hawaii my back was killing me. I could hardly practice. When you're hurt in football, you really feel ostracized from the team. It's an attitude of "If you're not useful or helpful, get out of the way."

Nevertheless, we had a great time at the East-West Shrine game, and we had a great time at the Hula Bowl. If anything, I helped my position in the draft. I had a real, real good game against the East All-Stars. I caught five or six passes and blocked real well, and we won the game.

When I got back from the Hula Bowl, the first thing I did was have microscopic surgery on my nose. I'd busted my nose up and had to get seventeen stitches from a plastic surgeon so I wouldn't have a bad scar.

Then my wife and I—we had just gotten married—went up to Minnesota where my parents were living and waited for the draft. The draft certainly wasn't anything like it is now, where it's all televised and they take the top possible choices up there for interviews. Back then it was you sit by a telephone, and you hope, and you wait and see what happens. I sat at the kitchen table with my mom and dad and my wife, having coffee and waiting.

SN: *Did you have any sense as to what round you would get drafted in?*
SZ: Based on what I heard, I could possibly get drafted in the first round or early in the second. Lo and behold, at eight thirty-eight that morning, I got a phone call from Jerry Williams, the head coach of the Philadelphia Eagles, and he said, "Congratulations! We've just selected you in the first round, as the sixth player taken." That totally shocked me. I was the first player picked in the Big Eight that year. I was the sixth player picked in the draft. I hung up the phone, and I just went, "Philadelphia. I never even heard of them." I had no idea that Philadelphia was going to draft me.

SN: *They had quite a tradition, that franchise. They had had Norm Van Brocklin, Pete Retzlaff, Tommy McDonald, who was from Oklahoma. . . .*
SZ: Yeah, as I learned more and more about the personalities and tradition at Philadelphia, I was happier and happier. They had had Chuck Bednarik, Timmy Brown—some great names. They had won the world championship in 1960. But I was kind of in shock. I had no idea what being drafted in the first round really meant.

SN: *They were selecting you as a tight end?*
SZ: They drafted me as a tight end. They told me they wanted a tight end like Ron Kramer used to be with the Packers. They wanted to run the football, they wanted to control the football. And having blocked for Steve Owens at Oklahoma and having gone through three years of the training I had had with Buck Nystrom, there was no question I could block. So, they told me to get as big as I could get. I proceeded to get up to 265 pounds, which is what I weighed when I reported for the Chicago College All-Star game.

SN: *Did they advise you how to do that? Did they say just gain the weight, or did they recommend a certain way to do it, a certain diet. . . .*
SZ: No, they didn't tell me anything. From the time I was drafted, almost two months went by before I heard from the Eagles again. Then Pete Retzlaff called, and he asked me to come to Philadelphia with my agent, Jack Mills, to talk about my contract.

We met with Retzlaff, and do you know what his first question to me was?

SN: *What?*
SZ: "How is your knee?" And I said, "How is my knee?" And he said, "Yeah, last year, as a junior, you had your knee operated on. How is your knee?" I replied, "My knee's fine. I played my whole senior year and never had a problem with it." That kind of set the tone for my exposure to negotiating contracts in the NFL. It totally caught me off guard.

SN: *How did you negotiate this first contract?*
SZ: Retzlaff first offered me a $15,000 signing bonus and salaries of $14,000, $16,000, and $18,000 for the first three years. After talking and arguing for several hours, I just politely excused myself and said, "Jack, this is why I brung yah. Do what you can. I'm out of here." So I went out and kind of putzed around for a couple of hours. Then Jack Mills came out of the meeting and asked me, "How does this sound?" It was exactly what we had been hoping to get. So, I said, "Fine, let's sign."

That year I was one of the first, if not the first, first-round draft picks to sign. Looking back on it, I'm sure I made a mistake. I should have thought more of myself and been a little more antagonistic and not been so humble. But back in those days humbleness was part of what they tried to teach you. But the guys that I look back on who really did the best with their careers were the guys who had a more cocky attitude, who were willing to step out and take risks, and who were willing to rock the boat for their own benefit. That really wasn't part of my psyche at that time. My psyche was, "Keep quiet. Be humble."

SN: *Well, there was only one team to deal with. You couldn't really go any-where else.*
SZ: Yeah. Of course there was the option of trying to drum up some interest in Canada, but everybody knew that wasn't very profitable. Canadian football wasn't a real threat to the NFL. I signed my contract and started working out. I had to get ready for the training camp coming up.

SN: *You did play in the College All-Star game first.*
SZ: Yes. My next stop was the Chicago College All-Star game, where the college All-Star team was to play the NFL's defending champions, the Kansas City Chiefs, who had defeated the Minnesota Vikings in Super Bowl IV.

SN: *What was it like preparing for that game?*
SZ: It was apparent from the early going that weighing 265 pounds was not the best thing for me to have done. I also still had some lingering problems with my back from the East-West Shrine game. On our team as tight ends we had Raymond Chester, who became a perennial All-Pro for the Oakland Raiders and the Baltimore Colts, and Rich Caster, who later played for the New York Jets and the Houston Oilers. Both of those guys were six foot four and 225 or 235 pounds, and they could both run ten-flat 100-yard dashes. At 265 pounds, I could barely run under eleven seconds in the 100-yard dash. So, things started out rather difficult for me at the Chicago All-Star game.

After I'd been up there for a couple weeks, the coaching staff came to me and said, "You're not going to get to play much as a tight end, because we're really going to throw the ball, but we really need help at linebacker. How about playing linebacker for us?" So they switched me to linebacker. I was prepared for that because I had played linebacker at Oklahoma.

Before the Chicago All-Star game four NFL players visited us at one of our team meetings in Evanston. One was Alex Karras. They came to us and basically said, "Gentlemen, after this game that you're playing against the Kansas City Chiefs, you are all going to be part of the fraternity of professional football players. And right now we players are at an impasse with the owners over a new collective bargaining agreement. If you guys would agree to walk out on strike and not play the Chicago All-Star game, it would benefit our cause. Please do this for us." Our reaction was pretty unanimous and spontaneous. Everybody said, "All right, we'll do it!"

SN: *What particularly appealed to you about the request from these veteran players? Was it just wanting to show solidarity with the veterans, or were there any specific issues, as they explained it to you, that got you interested?*
SZ: I don't recall any of the issues that were presented and even if there were issues presented. It was simply a matter that we were after this game going to be a part of this NFL players' fraternity, and they were asking for our help in achieving a satisfactory labor contract. We told Otto Graham that we weren't going to play in that game. They suspended practice, and we just kind of hung out.

After four or five days, the NFL players signed a contract with the owners, and we were told to go back and play. So, we did. And it was kind of beneficial for me, because my back had been acting up a little bit. Having that week off helped it tremendously. Still, playing in that game was a rude awakening for me. I broke my little finger. I should have had an interception that I dropped. And we ended up getting beat 23-7 or something like that.

SN: *What was it like adjusting to the NFL as a rookie? You were the number-one draft choice, so they obviously were expecting that you would become a starting player.*
SZ: My rookie year with the Philadelphia Eagles was very frustrating. The reason they had made me the number-one draft choice was to come there and be a blocking tight end. But because I had lost three weeks playing in the Chicago All-Star game, I was way behind the other rookies and the veterans when I came to training camp. Other organizations handled things better. For example, the Oakland Raiders had drafted Raymond Chester as a tight end. They immediately brought him out to Oakland and put him through a mini-camp. They taught him there how to get releases from a linebacker, and how to read pass coverages, and all kinds of things that would have been helpful for me to have been taught before I arrived. But Philadelphia didn't do that and Oakland did, and it was to Raymond Chester's benefit and to my detriment.

SN: *You were drafted as a tight end. Was there a veteran tight end that you were supposed to be competing with?*
SZ: There was some tension in that I competed for the tight end job with a veteran, Gary Ballman, who had played five years with the Pittsburgh Steelers, and then three years with the Eagles.

SN: *And he had friends on the team.*
SZ: And, of course, he had friends on the team. Gary was a very good athlete, about six foot two, 215 pounds. He was really an oversized slow wide receiver who could run pass routes. Gary helped orchestrate some of the kidding that went on about me being six foot four and 265 pounds, and about my agility versus his agility, and about my pass route running ability versus his. But that's all part of what goes on. You come in as a number-one draft choice and people are looking at you with certain expectations.

SN: *What was the coaching staff like at Philadelphia? Who was the head coach?*
SZ: We didn't have a very good coaching staff. In the five years that I spent at Philadelphia, we had three different head football coaches. I played my rookie year as a tight end, my second year as an outside linebacker, my third year as

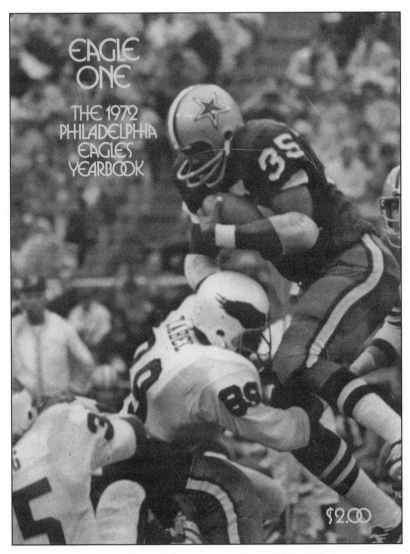

Steve Zabel tackling Dallas Cowboys running back Calvin Hill. Courtesy of Steve Zabel.

a middle linebacker, and my fourth and fifth years as an inside strong stack linebacker. So, I played four or five different positions for three different head coaches in Philadelphia.

The first coach I had was Jerry Williams, who was an extremely brilliant man and had a law degree. He was also a former Philadelphia Eagle. But he really had a problem relating to the players. It was almost like he was too intelligent and would talk above us. Hardly anybody would catch his gist when it came to jokes or sense of humor. His coaching staff was made up primarily of his old teammates and buddies.

SN: *How did the Eagles do your rookie year? How much did you start?*
SZ: My rookie year I played on a losing team that only won three games, lost ten, and tied one. I got to start about half the games, and we won three of those. We beat the Miami Dolphins, who that year went 10-4 and were on their way to future Super Bowls. But we generally had such a sorry team that we were behind after the first quarter 14-0 or 20-0.

SN: *How did you feel generally during that rookie year and about how it had turned out?*
SZ: Because we had such a bad team, I took it personally. My retaliatory nature was surfacing. The intensity and emotion that I had building up because of the frustration came out. I got kicked out of three games for fighting my rookie year. In the last game of the season we played the Pittsburgh Steelers. My wife had parked out in the stadium parking lot. Our car was packed. We were checked out of our apartment. I just wanted to get out of Philadelphia. I wanted to get away to the safe confines of Oklahoma. I wanted to forget about my rookie year.

My wife was listening to the game on the radio and with about two minutes left to go in the game Pittsburgh had kicked off to us and I was trying to block Mel Blount. He gave me a forearm shiver to the head, and that burned me up and I went after him. My wife tells me the announcer said, "There's a fight breaking out on the field and it looks like—yes, it is, it's Steve Zabel again, and he's being pummeled by five or six Pittsburgh Steelers." And that's about the truth of it. I got into something over my head. All I could do was hold on to my helmet, because they were trying to rip it off and work on me pretty good.

I got thrown out of the game and I went in and changed. I was out of the locker room and in my car as soon as the game was over. I was glad to say good riddance to that rookie year. I had to deal with the pressures of being a number-one draft choice and not fulfilling the expectations of the fans or my own.

SN: *How did your second year begin?*
SZ: My second year with the Eagles I was switched from tight end to outside linebacker. After my rookie season, the coaching staff had come to me and said, "You have an opportunity to become a great offensive tackle. Why don't you gain ten, fifteen, twenty more pounds and play that position?" I didn't want to do that. So, they said, "Well, we need some help at outside linebacker.

We really think you could become a big impact player for us as an outside linebacker rushing the passer, creating havoc."

SN: *What did you think about switching positions?*
SZ: That appealed to me, because as a junior at Oklahoma I had played both ways and made some real big plays on the defense, quarterback sacks. I welcomed that. So I came into training camp for my second season as a 225-pound linebacker, having lost 40 pounds in the off-season. I had my quickness and agility back.

We had a new coach that year, Eddie Khayat, who took over when Jerry Williams was fired after we lost our first three games.

SN: *What did you think about your new coach? How did he approach coaching?*
SZ: I really enjoyed playing for Eddie that year. Eddie was from Moss Point, Mississippi, and had been a defensive tackle for the Eagles. He brought a real fun approach to football. He could really relate to players, totally the opposite of Jerry Williams. Jerry Williams was an aloof statistician, a strategist. Eddie had a way of keeping the guys pretty loose and pretty focused. His whole approach was a maul 'em attitude. Just go out and knock the hell out of somebody. Don't worry about the outcome, just play as hard as you can.

SN: *How did you feel about your second season in the NFL?*
SZ: That whole season was really enjoyable. We finished the season at 6-7-1, after losing those first three games. We ended up on a real positive note. I had a very, very good year and got a lot of my confidence back. I started every down as an outside linebacker. Our defense for the last fourteen games gave up less than eleven points a game, which was a real good mark for that period. I also played tight end in short-yardage situations and caught two touchdown passes. And I played on every special team.

SN: *How did you feel about playing linebacker, as opposed to tight end?*
SZ: In pro football I really enjoyed playing linebacker a lot more than I ever did playing tight end. The reason was simple. As a tight end, the rules then allowed people to grab you, and hit you, and hold you, and run with you, and harass you. It seemed like as soon as you got rid of a linebacker, there'd be a safety in your face. Tight end was a real frustrating position for me, particularly when I weighed 265 and had lost some quickness and speed.

Linebacker allowed me to play football the way I needed to play it. It allowed me to play emotionally and to play reactively. Offense is more of an interaction than a reaction. On offense, everybody has an assignment, and your job is part of the teamwork that is necessary for the plays to be successful. Defense, on the other hand, is reacting to what you see. I was a lot better reactor than I was an interactor.

In addition, I had a retaliatory personality that was much more suitable to defense. I played with such emotion that when a guy stuck his finger in my facemask or gave me a cheap shot, I wanted to retaliate. And you can't play offense and be successful if you're a hothead. If you're a retaliatory type of person, it's counterproductive. Defense is more free spirited. It's a little less responsible than playing offense. So, I enjoyed playing defense a lot more in the NFL.

However, I much preferred playing outside linebacker to middle linebacker, which I played my third year in the NFL. The Eagles' management decided they didn't want to pay Tim Rossovich, our middle linebacker, what he was asking, and they traded him to San Diego for a first-round draft choice. Rather than trade for an established middle linebacker, they came to me and said, "Steve, you're a great athlete. You've got a knack for going to the ball, and you're our new middle linebacker."

What I should have told them was, "No, I'm staying where I am. I like the position I'm at. I know how to play this position. I've never played middle linebacker in my life. No thank you." But being humble and wanting to help the team, I agreed to make the shift.

SN: *What are the differences between playing middle linebacker and outside linebacker?*
SZ: Middle linebacker, for somebody who has never played it, is a very demanding position at the professional level. I was six foot four, six foot five and 230 or 240. If you look at the great middle linebackers, they're more compact than I ever was. The only way the middle linebacker and outside linebacker positions are similar is that they're both called "linebacking" positions. At outside linebacker, you're at the periphery of the defense. You have certain keys that allow you to react to certain things as they're happening on the field. You learn how to play off blocks and how to react. But at middle linebacker, instead of being on the periphery, you're right in the heart of the battle.

SN: *Do you do less pass coverage at middle linebacker?*
SZ: No, you do the same amount of pass coverage at each position. The difference is in who to key through to stop runs, in angles of pursuit, in running around blocks, in knowing whom to avoid and where you need to be.

SN: *What was your third year with the Eagles like?*
SZ: Nineteen seventy-two turned out to be a lot less pleasant than 1971. I had two operations that year, and we ended up with a 2-12 record. I played middle

linebacker during the exhibition season. I tore up my right knee during a full-tilt goal line scrimmage at Reading, Pennsylvania, that was held at nine o'clock the morning after we had played an evening game in Washington against the Redskins. We had returned to Reading by bus—a three-hour trip. We lost two other starters to injury in that one practice. I got helicoptered down to Philadelphia, and the doctor determined that I had a partial tear of my right medial colateral ligament. They put me in a cast for six weeks, and I missed the first five or six regular season games. Then I came back and played middle linebacker for another five or six games. I ended up in the hospital with my *left* medial colateral ligament torn. I had to have my right elbow operated on at the same time. By that time I was just beat up.

SN: *Why did the team decline that year?*
SZ: One of the main reasons why 1972 turned out to be such a disastrous year was that, for some strange reason, Eddie Khayat during the off-season let the pressure of the coming year really get to him. The first thing he did when we came to training camp for the 1972 season was make everybody go get a haircut. And everybody had to shave off mustaches and beards. We had guys on our team who were twenty-eight and thirty years old, who were grown men, who had had mustaches their whole adult life. That really started the slide of the Philadelphia Eagles. Not only did we have a bunch of injuries that year, but Eddie Khayat changed from Dr. Jekyll to Mr. Hyde.

SN: *It strikes me as odd, a coach ordering NFL players to shave. I could see that on a high school team, maybe.*
SZ: See, this was one of Eddie's problems. He couldn't tell you that you weren't playing this defense right, or that you were a lousy player, or whatever. Anytime that this anxiety would build up inside of him, he would always get on us about getting a haircut or getting a shave. It was too bad, because to this day Eddie is one of my favorite people ever in pro football. But Eddie went from being a happy-go-lucky guy that would give you just unbelievable pep talks and make you so comfortable, to becoming so absorbed with the pressures of the game that it caused him to change his coaching style to the extent that nobody ever knew where they were at.

SN: *There was a players' strike in the NFL in 1974. So, labor discontent was brewing among the players in the early 1970s. What issues were the players concerned about, and how did the 1974 strike develop?*
SZ: In 1974 we struck over "No freedom, no football." We were striking for free agency. We thought that was the way to go. Ed Garvey was our supreme commander. We weren't very mature. It was a macho type of thing.

Alan Page of the Minnesota Vikings (right) and Ed Garvey, executive director of the NFL Players Association, leading pickets in the 1974 NFL players' strike. Note the slogan on the t-shirt: "No Freedom, No Football." Courtesy of AP/Wide World Photos.

SN: *On management's side you have middle-aged guys who are wealthy businessmen. They have lots of money and a whole staff of attorneys. On the other side you have guys ranging in age from twenty-one into their thirties, a pretty young group. You haven't really done anything other than be a football player at this stage of life. You don't have very much work experience and no business experience. You haven't been in face-to-face labor negotiations.*

SZ: We were way overmatched and had no chance of success. My first recollection of the strike is being up at Roman Gabriel's football camp in northern Philadelphia with a bunch of the Eagles' players.

SN: *How did the Eagles' owner react to the strike?*
SZ: The Eagles' owner, Leonard Tose, got wind that there was going to be a players' strike. And he flew up to Roman Gabriel's camp to visit with us. After practice was over, we all kind of got around Leonard. And, I'll never forget, he basically said that what he wanted us to do was, whatever we did, to do it as a team.

So the strike was on. There was some picketing going on. The veterans hadn't agreed to come to camp. But there were rookies in camp, and they were starting to play exhibition games with rookies. And some of the higher salaried veterans were going in.

SN: *Was there complete solidarity among the Eagles players?*
SZ: On the Eagles there was complete solidarity. Mike McCormack, who was then the head coach of the Eagles, called a meeting at the Hilton by Veterans' Stadium, and we were all requested to attend. Leonard Tose wanted to speak to us. It was real shocking, because he had gone 180 degrees in the other direction. Apparently, the owners were putting pressure on him to stick together and follow one common course. So, Leonard went from appealing to us to stick together as a team to individually calling different players on the team, including myself, and trying to bring as much pressure to bear on us as possible to crack us and get us to go in. Tom Dempsey, our player rep, caught all kinds of hell. The mental anguish that he was subjected to by Leonard Tose and Mike McCormack was unbelievable.

Because so many players started to go in, the Players' Association thought it would be best just to save face and go in together. So, that's what happened in 1974.

SN: *What were the players' objectives in the 1974 strike?*
SZ: The strike centered around free agency, and the slogan was "No freedom, no football." The NFL Players' Association printed up T-shirts with a big arm and a flexed muscle, "No freedom, no football."

By that time Tom Dempsey had been traded and John Bunting was elected our player rep. The job was developing a stigma. All the players wanted to have a player rep, but nobody really wanted to be it. The election the Eagles players had was more "Who can we stick with this?" than "Who really wants it?" John Bunting got elected, and he agreed to take the heat. John was a real independent thinker from North Carolina. And John did a heck of a job.

During the strike we held voluntary practices. All the players on the team got together on their own, and we tried to practice, and run pass routes, and do agility drills and conditioning.

SN: *Looking back, what do you think about the strike's focus, on free agency?*
SZ: Instead of talking about "No freedom, no football," what we should have been talking about was "No Pensions, No Football." But for some strange reason, nobody really focused on the pension situation. When you're twenty-one, twenty-two, twenty-three years old, you're not thinking about being forty-five or fifty-five or sixty-five. But that's what we really should have been talking about.

I was kind of torn during the strike. We had gone a year without a labor agreement, and here we were out on strike. I didn't think the owners would ever give up on free agency. I felt like they'd seen what had happened in basketball and baseball, and they weren't going to fall into that trap unless they were forced to. I was coming back off a ruptured Achilles tendon. So, I decided that if we reached a certain day without an agreement, I was going to go in.

SN: *Did this lead to any friction with other teammates?*
SZ: There were a lot of guys, I'm sure, who felt less of me, because I told them up front, "Hey, I'm giving this thing forty-five days or whatever, and if it's not resolved, I'm going in." When that day came, I went in. It just so happened that the day I went in, they all decided to go back. I always regretted going in, even though I was proud of the mental process I went through to come to that decision. I did it independently of all the pressures that were there. Yet, I never felt afterwards that I was as close to a lot of the players as I had used to be, players who had looked up to me and respected me. I think they now looked more to John Bunting than they did to me. And that bothered me.

SN: *What led up to the Eagles trading you?*
SZ: After the 1974 season I had completed my fifth year with the Eagles, and my contract was up. I had played the whole year as a starting outside line-backer. I started negotiating a new contract in January 1975.

SN: *Did you do this yourself, or with an agent present?*
SZ: I had an agent with me, and I went in and said I wanted a raise, and they said they didn't want to give me one. For six months it got into a real

heated debate. And the real debate was not so much over whether I was going to get a raise, but whether or not Philadelphia thought I was a good enough player to even be on their team.

I had decided that before I did anything drastic, I wanted to have a meeting with the general manager and the head coach. I asked them to bring in all the tabulations for all the games. All the players are graded each game. Their playing is evaluated play by play and assignment by assignment. And you're given a grade for those games.

SN: *This is based on the coaches watching the game films?*
SZ: Yes.

SN: *This can be difficult to do, since football doesn't lend itself to statistical measurement the way baseball does.*
SZ: That's exactly right.

SN: *I would think that system would leave a lot of room for confusion. In a labor situation they could say what they wanted about the player's performance, and he'd have a hard time challenging management's assessment.*
SZ: Often there is a lot of room for argument. Management negotiated the same way they had in the first meeting with me after I was drafted. They invested a lot of time and money and drafted me as their first pick. And the first thing they asked was "How was my knee?" So that's where they're always going to be coming from when you negotiate. During the season, they pat you on the back when you play with a hurt knee, or broken fingers, or stitches in your nose. "You're wonderful, go get 'em boys." But when it comes time to negotiate a new contract, they just want to dwell on all the negatives that they can, to argue for not giving you more money.

During the negotiations, the head coach, Mike McCormack, told me that I had busted a defense, a specific pass coverage, fifty-six times during the year. And he told me that I had played bad in this game and bad in that game. I thought the games he said I had played bad in, I had actually played well in, based on the input that I had had during and after the game. There were games that I knew I hadn't played great in, but during the meeting they said that those were the games they had graded me the highest in. During the meeting I told Mike McCormack that if I had in fact busted a pass coverage fifty-six times during the year, if it was wrong fifty-six times, shouldn't a coach have told me about it, so I could have corrected it? Nobody would have let a player go fifty-six times without correcting them and making some adjustments. That led

Coach McCormack to talk to Coach Michaels, and Coach Michaels lied and said, "Well, I told Zabel about this."

After the meeting was over, I got up and told them that I wouldn't sign even if they offered me $100,000. As I walked out the door, I turned back and said, "Well, I probably would for $100,000," and I left. The next day I got a call, and I had been traded to the New England Patriots. Chuck Fairbanks, who had coached me at Oklahoma, was their head coach. I was sad to leave Philadelphia and to leave the friends and teammates that I had had for the previous five years....

When I joined the Patriots, they were a young, up-and-coming team. They had a lot of talent. When I got there, Chuck Fairbanks took me into his office, and said, "Okay, you negotiated for a contract for six months, how much were you asking for?" I had asked for $75,000 for that next year, and then $85,000, and then $95,000. Chuck said, "No problem." And we wrote a contract and I signed it that same day.

SN: *So, you got with the Patriots what you were going to ask with the Eagles?*
SZ: Yes, I sure did.

SN: *You mentioned to me that the New England Patriots staged a wildcat strike, in which you participated. How did that develop, and what issues were involved?*
SZ: We played five exhibition games and still had no collective bargaining agreement. The main issue was still free agency, although this time there was a little more emphasis on pension benefits. After about three exhibition games, the owners gave us a proposal for a new contract that was absolutely ridiculous. They were getting worse instead of better. We were getting ready to play the New York Giants at Yale, and we were out on the field at Schaeffer Stadium having a pregame practice before getting on the buses to drive down for the game. Out on the fifty-yard line we decided, independently of the Players' Association, that the New England Patriots were not going to play another football game until we signed a collective bargaining agreement. We did one of those Alamo scenes. We said, "All right. Everybody who wants to strike, step over the fifty-yard line, and everybody who doesn't, don't." Out of forty-six guys on the team, forty of us stepped over the line. We talked to the other guys, and said, "We're not going to do this unless we're all unanimous. Do you guys want to reconsider?" And those six guys hesitantly stepped across. We formed a real, real close bond when I was with the Patriots.

I was disgusted with the Players' Association. I was disgusted with the owners. There were a lot of guys on the Patriots who felt that way. We had a lot of very strong-willed, confident people on the team.

SN: *At that point it was just one team, the Patriots, that was going to go out?*
SZ: Yes. It was a wildcat, unauthorized strike. There was no forewarning. We never told the Players' Association. It was the Alamo all over.

SN: *How did the coach respond?*
SZ: We went into the locker room and told Coach Fairbanks that we were not going to the game. And at first it was the Leonard Tose response, "Well, whatever you guys want to do, stick together as a team." We thought, "All right, the coach is for us." Well, he went back upstairs, and he called the league office, and told them that there were problems, that the Patriots were not going to play the last exhibition game and that they were out on strike. He came back and told us if we didn't get on the bus and go right then, we would all be black-balled forever, and we would never play another down of football in the NFL. He really came down hard on us. And everybody to a man told Coach Fairbanks that we weren't going to play, regardless of any threats. We had made our decision, and we were going to stick it out.

Later that day and that night, we heard that the St. Louis Cardinals had agreed to go out on strike with us, and that the Washington Redskins had also agreed. Momentum was building. Five or six teams had decided to strike. We missed the last exhibition game, and we didn't practice on Monday or Tuesday. We had meetings every day. Of course, the national press was up there all the time, covering what was going on. Ed Garvey came up and just really applauded us for having the initiative to do something that really looked like it was going to work out.

William Usery was hired as a federal mediator to mediate this action. Usery and Ed Garvey came up to New England and called us together and applauded us for what we had done, but said that the owners had agreed to bargain in good faith. They said we needed to go back in and play the season, because anything that we did beyond this would be counterproductive. They claimed that the owners would work up a new proposal over the weekend.

So, we went back in and played the Houston Oilers on Sunday and got beat 7-0. We had missed out on a whole week's practice. I have no doubt that we would have won if we had prepared like we normally did. That loss catapulted the Patriots on a course where we ended up 3-11 in 1975.

Usery and Garvey invited everyone on the Patriots to the opening round of the collective bargaining agreements the following Monday night in Chicago. Fourteen or fifteen of us, including myself, went. But even though the owners had agreed to make us a better offer, what they presented was actually worse than anything we had ever seen. The owners had duped us, and they had duped Usery and Garvey. We were already back in, and once you lose momentum like that, you can't redo it.

If we had continued along the course of action that we had initiated and that was starting to take a foothold, we would have gotten everything that we wanted in 1975 from the owners. But the owners now understood how serious this thing could become, and they began to cover their bases. It was at this point that they started to set aside funds for strike contingency purposes. The World Football League was ultimately a protection for the NFL against player strikes. The NFL wanted to develop a league with also-ran players, where they might be able to develop one or two players off each team who could go on to the big league. But their real motive was to have an established athletic team available in the event that the players ever went out on strike again. I guarantee it.

SN: *They'd bring one of those teams into the NFL?*
SZ: If a strike occurred, they'd bring all of the WFL players in as strikebreakers. That was their player protection pool.

SN: *It was a conscious plan in your view.*
SZ: It was a very conscious plan. In 1975 the Patriots had the pro football world by the shorthairs. If we had had adequate leadership and continued our strike, even through a couple of regular season games, and established a final resolve and unity, it wouldn't have taken twenty more years to establish through the courts what they now have. Basically, after that strike, they moved towards resolving the issues in the courts. The owners proved to be totally devious. They had all the money, and they controlled the press. The public perceived the football players as a greedy bunch of spoiled brats. As we know today, all of the court actions stood up. And now we have true free agency in the pro football world. The sad thing is that the guys like me and the Steve Owenses of the world, who made $100,000 tops for a season, would today be making one or two million dollars.

I told Chuck Fairbanks that I wasn't fortunate enough to be around when they signed the Magna Carta or the Declaration of Independence, but I was really proud to have been a part of what we had done during that week of striking. It helped me reestablish my confidence in my ability to make decisions.

It overturned that hollow feeling I had from the 1974 season when, if I had gone with the crowd and waited a couple of more hours, I wouldn't have been branded a turncoat. I was fortunate to have been part of a real independent, courageous bunch of guys up at New England. For us guys, unauthorized by anybody in the world, to just go in and tell a multimillion dollar industry that we were diverting traffic for a while to see what was going to happen. Everybody to a man on the Patriots really stood up, and was more than a man under those circumstances. It was a great experience. But, because of the owners' deviousness, what could have been was lost.

SN: *I imagine the players today have never heard of this, the ones who make the one million dollar a year salaries?*
SZ: I don't think that the players of today really have any idea or understanding of the labor strife that went on for twenty years.

SN: *It took a long time to get to the point where the players are getting the kind of money, benefits, and pensions they get today.*
SZ: It took a long time because of the owners' deviousness. They basically had a monopoly and were allowed to do anything they wanted to under antitrust rules.

SN: *How would you compare the achievements of the NFL players with those of the major league baseball players?*
SZ: I have the utmost respect for the baseball players' union. Look at the afterlife benefits that the baseball players receive, and compare them with what we football players accomplished for ourselves. They did much better than we did.

SN: *How do you explain that?*
SZ: In part, because we never had adequate leadership. We had Ed Garvey, who wanted to use his executive position in the Players' Association as a springboard for his own political career. We never hired anybody of the caliber that the baseball players hired when they hired Marvin Miller to run their negotiations and to formulate their goals and objectives.

Because we didn't have the leadership, we focused, and groped, and struck for things that were not achievable. "No freedom, no football!" We were thinking, well, this is for future generations. That was all very altruistic. But we should have been thinking more about pensions, about protecting ourselves after retirement.

When I talk to my friend Bobby Murcer, who played major league baseball for many years, and I compare his physical well-being with mine, the differences are significant. "Bobby, how many knee injuries did you have?" "Well, not too many." "How are your neck and shoulders?" "Oh, they feel pretty good." And then I say, "What kind of pension benefits do you have?" The bottom line is, the baseball players are looking at age forty-five, for a ten- to fifteen-year career, at $30,000 to $35,000 a year. As a football player, I'm looking at $5000 a year. If you extend that out to age fifty-five versus age fifty for the baseball players, there's probably a three-to-one or four-to-one disparity, in their favor. You're looking at $18,000 a year for a football player versus $50,000 or $60,000 a year for a baseball player.

Those are things that were negotiated through their players' association, whereas the NFL Players' Association was kind of mired out in the nebulous field of ultimate goals and desires. We chased those rainbows. I don't ever remember any of the Players' Association meetings that we had that talked about issues, specific goals, and objectives. It was more like this is a power game, with an element of machismo. We're going to strike, we're not going to strike. But the owners knew exactly where they had us—and where they had us was that we had incompetent management and leadership in our union.

For a long time, the owners successfully played a waiting game. But they realized that sooner or later all of the court cases were going to catch up with them, and they were going to have to step up and pay the piper. Now football players are making more and more money, but the owners have also inserted a salary cap. If you get up into a position where you make a million dollars or more a year, you damn sure better be able to play, because if you can't, they'll be getting rid of you. If you get in three or four years at that high salary, you'll be fortunate.

SN: *Did you sense when you played that the public was more on the owners' side? You indicated that a lot of people felt you were getting pretty big salaries.*
SZ: The fans really didn't understand the players' situation. The average fan just wants to go to a football game. That's their purpose in life on that particular day. And they don't want to be inconvenienced. It's not so much that they think the owners are right or the players are right. The average fan didn't realize that when a player went out on that field, in most cases if a guy lost his courage on one play and looked like a coward, he could be cut the next day. They didn't realize that if you got hurt one year and weren't able to come back and play—like so many guys had happen to them—that you were out forever. And most of those guys are walking around with hips replaced, and

ankles replaced, and arthritis. They don't understand the sacrifices. They don't understand what Darryl Stingley is going through for the rest of his life.

SN: *You played with Darryl Stingley.*
SZ: I watched Darryl Stingley, who was one of our wide receivers, get his neck broken when Jack Tatum of the Oakland Raiders hit him. Stingley was paralyzed for life. I was on the sideline, not fifty feet away from where it happened. I saw it all the way. When you're in pro football, the fans cheer, and all the players cheer, when there's a big hit. It doesn't matter whether you're on the team where the guy got hit or you're on the team where the guy did the hitting, a big hit brings out a tremendous uproar. And it stays that way as long as the guy gets up. But Darryl didn't get up. And Darryl didn't move.

SN: *Exactly what happened when Stingley was hurt?*
SZ: Jack Tatum, the Raiders' defensive back, didn't have to do what he did. Darryl got hurt on a quick slant play. For that play to be effective, the quarterback has to take the three-step drop and deliver the ball. What happened was that, rather than throw the ball on timing, our quarterback, Steve Grogan, pumped once, because he thought Darryl was covered, and then he threw the ball. That gave Tatum a jump on the deal. But the ball was way overthrown, and Tatum had time to pull off the hit. He didn't have to do what he did. Darryl had enough time to see that he was coming, and he instinctively ducked his head. And when Tatum hit him, it just broke his neck. Now, whether he could have pulled off on that hit, I don't know. Football is a game of intimidation. If you get a legitimate chance to put a hit on somebody, any football player would do that.

SN: *How did the Patriots react?*
SZ: When Darryl got hit, we wanted to kill Tatum. There were guys who were going out of their way to try to get him if they could. I don't think Tatum is well liked or respected by many football players.

SN: *Tatum wrote a book called* They Call Me Assassin *(Everest House, 1979). It sounds like he was bragging about the hit.*
SZ: Tatum was bragging about the hit. To this day, I don't think he has ever apologized or acknowledged to Stingley that the event ever took place.

SN: *How did the Patriots do when you were with them?*
SZ: I played four years for the Patriots, from 1975 through 1978, and three of those years we had really strong teams. We finished 3-11 the first year, and

then went 11-3, 9-5, and 10-4. In 1976 we were in the playoffs. In 1977 we went down to the final game of the season, and we missed because of a mathematical deal, and in 1978 we won our division.

Probably the best coach I ever had from a position perspective was a guy named Rollie Dotsch, the outside linebacker coach for the Patriots. In 1976, I probably had the best year that I ever had in pro football and should have made the Pro Bowl and All-Pro, but didn't. Rollie really helped me play that year. He would suggest subtle things, like you need to lower your stance a little bit, you're playing too high. You need to widen out a little bit. Look here, this back's cheated over here. And this lineman's tightened down a little bit. Rollie helped me more than any coach I ever had. He had a lot of confidence in me.

In 1976, after going 3-11 the year before when we had walked out on strike, we finished 11-3 and went to the playoffs. We were the only team that year to beat Oakland, who went 13-1. We beat them 48-12. We played them in the opening round of the playoffs, in Oakland. To give themselves an advantage, Oakland had let their grass grow about six inches and they had watered down the field, and it was sloppy.

SN: *How would Oakland benefit from that?*
SZ: They were a bigger, slower team that liked to run inside. They really liked to run the ball to set up a play action pass. We had a lot better athletes. Our defensive team really thrived on quickness and speed. I think Al Davis just felt like it would be to their advantage to have longer grass. It was like whenever Oklahoma used to go down to play Missouri. Missouri would let that grass field grow up long, and they'd try to water it down if they could, to try to offset our superior athletic team.

We played in Oakland and were ahead by four points going into the last two minutes of the game. We had third down and one going in from about their thirty-five-yard line, and Pete Brock jumped offside. So, we had third down and six, and they called a play action pass to Russ Francis. Phil Villapiano, who was outside linebacker for the Raiders, jumped on him, tackled him, held on to him, and did everything he could, and never got called for pass interference. Our quarterback, Steve Grogan, ended up throwing the ball away. So, we had fourth down and six. Rather than punt the ball, Fairbanks elected to go for a long field goal. We missed it. So, they had sixty-five yards to go for a touchdown. A field goal wouldn't win it; they had to get a touchdown.

During that last drive, an official made the worst call I've ever seen in pro football. We had them third down and twenty-one, and Kenny Stabler threw an incomplete pass. Ray Hamilton was well into the air and on his way to hit Stabler. But he held his hands up, and didn't take any kind of extracurricular hit on Stabler. Amazingly, the official called a roughing-the-passer penalty. That allowed them to get a first down and gain yardage. Then there were another couple of penalties. The bottom line was, Kenny Stabler bootlegged the ball in on the last play of the game and beat us with no time left on the clock.

Oakland went on to beat Minnesota 45-14, a team we had beaten during the season big time. We knew we would've, and should've, won the Super Bowl. There's no question.

SN: *What happened the next year?*

SZ: We had another good year in 1977 and just missed going to the playoffs. We just kept getting stronger and stronger that year. I have no doubt that, if we had made the playoffs in 1977, we would have won the Super Bowl.

Nineteen seventy-eight also proved frustrating, although we made the play-offs that year. In the eighth or ninth game of the year, I hurt my knee against the Houston Oilers and had to sit out the rest of the year rehabilitating my knee. I was back to play against the Oilers in the second round of the playoffs. That's when I hurt my knee again on the first play of the game. . . .

All football players get hurt. Whether they have a knee operation, or an elbow operation, or a hip operation, or whatever, the physical beating that your body takes to perform at the level that you perform at has cumulative and ongoing effects. When you're forty-five, or fifty-five, or sixty-five, all of those bumps and bruises are still there, and arthritis is an inevitable result.

SN: *How do coaches view this? Jerry Kramer, in his book* Instant Replay, *talks a lot about injuries and being pushed to get back on your feet and get out there. Vince Lombardi's approach seems to have been to try to get the player back out there as soon as possible. Do coaches think more in the short run, "I need this guy two weeks from now, I'll just get him ready," rather than think, "Well, maybe next year he'll suffer if he's not allowed to recuperate properly"?*

SZ: In pro football, if there was any way in the world that you could play, you were supposed to play. It's part of the inbreeding that takes place when you become a football player. Everything in football is knowing the difference between having pain and being hurt. If you're hurt and can't perform, then you shouldn't be out there. But if it's a matter of overcoming pain, then you should never quit. I remembered my experience as a young boy, of quitting as a baseball player, and how I was berated, and how it made me never want to quit again. Against the Houston Oilers in the playoffs, even though I hurt my knee on the first play of the game, I couldn't quit. I couldn't go up to Coach Fairbanks and say, "Coach, I quit. I can't." That was a miserable experience for me.

Having to overcome pain is just something that's inbred. It's part of being a man. Football players, because of those years of overcoming pain, have extremely high pain thresholds. I remember at Oklahoma one year, the first day of two-a-day practices, I fractured my foot, and it hurt like the dickens. But I thought I had kicked myself, and I kept thinking what a sissy I was. I had no idea there was anything called a stress fracture. I couldn't imagine how something up here in my foot could be broken just from running. So, I toughed it out for the next two and a half hours of practice and never missed a beat, only to go in and have an X-ray taken, and they go, "You got a fracture, you're out of practice for a while." You learn to overcome the pain.

The worst I was ever hurt in a game was when I ruptured my Achilles tendon; I knew for sure that I'd been hurt bad then. But when I hurt my knee the worst, it didn't hurt all that bad. Other than my knee being unstable, I really didn't realize that I'd hurt it.

The coaches' attitude was, if you don't have a cast on, if you're not in the hospital, scheduled for surgery, you should be out there. And when you are hurt, with a muscle pull, or a sprained ankle, or a partially separated shoulder, or whatever, and you're not playing, you feel inadequate, and you feel ostracized from the team, whether that's real, or imagined, or implied. I guarantee you that every player will tell you that when you're hurt, even if you might have been the star player, you go from being a star to being a turd. You're just viewed as somebody that's there.

SN: *It's very different in the military. Football is often compared to combat, but the military awards the Purple Heart when you get wounded, and it's a medal to be proud of. If you're doing your job, you can get hurt. I would think it would be similar in football—if you're making the effort, giving 100 percent, you can get hurt.*

SZ: Well, the coaches feel they have a job to do and can't spend time worrying about you or trying to make sure that your feelings aren't hurt. They've got to motivate you either through positive or negative reinforcement, which is normally by ostracizing you or using some form of negative psychology to make you get back sooner.

SN: *What about the use of painkilling drugs to enable players to return to the field when injured? Pete Gent made a point of that in his book* North Dallas Forty *(Ballantine Books, 1973).*

SZ: When I was with the Eagles, I took injections, local, xylocane, cortisone-type injections, for injuries to be able to play. I never took anything in the knee that I can recall, other than whenever they would drain your knee, if you had fluid on it, they would normally shoot you with xylocane and cortisone. That seemed to help quiet things and make your knee not hurt quite so bad. I had injections in my foot, and in my ankle, and in my shoulders. I had lots of injections.

SN: *But if you sustain an injury, you don't feel it. Pain is a warning.*
SZ: That's very true. Fortunately, I never got hurt worse than I was already hurt when I got injected. But to show how ridiculous it could be, or was, two years before I ruptured my Achilles tendon, I started complaining that my tendon was hurting me. The doctors told me that I had tendonitis, and they started giving me some cortisone shots in the butt. Their theory was that the cortisone would migrate down into the tendon, and it would help things out. What I found out after my operation was that, during that two-year period, it was already starting to unravel. I got kicked in the tendon one time, and it pulled a couple of strands off. And then another time, and another time, and ultimately it just pulled apart. But I was getting cortisone shots in the butt for that.

There's no question that the owners were paying you money, and that team trainers were paid to help you get back out on the field. I don't recall too many instances where there were guys who were just forced to go out like the *North Dallas Forty* deal—come on, Bob Hayes, let's shoot it up, you'll be all right. I do know that most everybody that I played with would not take an injection in a muscle—if you had a pulled hamstring or something like that. At least I felt that I knew that that was taboo. Any time I got an injection, it usually had to do with a bone, or joint, or something like that. It was never into a muscle.

SN: *How did you feel about playing on artificial turf?*
SZ: The introduction of Astroturf, or tartan turf, in the NFL on a wide scale beginning about 1970 led to more injuries. I hated playing on artificial turf. It was so resilient that if you made a cut, it was just like cutting on sandpaper or on glue. There was no give to it. Besides that, it was hard. They'd clear off a field, and they'd put asphalt over it, and then they'd put bristles on it. On a hot day with no moisture, if you fell on that stuff, it would tear off two inches of your hide. Turf toe appeared soon after Astroturf. I needed operations on both my elbows from falling on artificial turf, and it ruptured my bursa sacs. You'd have scrapes on you that wouldn't heal until February or March.

Nobody had any consideration for the players and their health. Artificial turf was basically installed to save money on maintenance and to make sure that if a thunderstorm came, or a snowstorm, that they'd have a surface that they could play on. Now there's a big swing back to regular turf. They realize how tough that turf really is on players. It's ridiculous, it's so hard.

SN: *To what extent was it possible to put concern of injury out of your mind?*
SZ: Football players in general are not normal people. They don't do normal things. They walk a very fine line between reality and nonreality. If a football player really sat down and tried to introspectively examine what he was about to do, it would frighten the hell out of him. I mean, nobody in his right mind would do something, where the consequences of getting hit in the wrong position might be that you'd be crippled forever or that you might die. There's something that draws people like me to it, whether it's machismo or simply the lure of gratification.

SN: *So, then why do you think you became involved in football?*
SZ: I got involved in football because I was searching for acceptance from my father. I continued to be involved because I was searching for acceptance from my coaches. You want the guys to talk about you as the guy who made the big hit or the big touchdown. You want to be the star of the locker room. I think that people who have been successful in pro football are all overachievers. But in my case, I was looking especially for my father's acceptance. And then it just kind of graduated to the coaches, and the players, and the fans.

I was always struck by the amount of attention I received from my wife's family, which is made up of successful, well-educated professionals. She has a brother with a Ph.D. from Princeton and another brother who is a surgeon. Both her sisters graduated from Baylor University. Her mother has a fine arts degree; her father is an attorney. But whenever I went to their household for Christmas or Thanksgiving, I was the one who got fawned over. I was always the one who got the accolades. And I can honestly remember, back in 1970, 1971, 1972, thinking, "This is ridiculous. I'm playing a kid's sport."

I can say, though, that playing pro football took 100 percent emotional commitment, 100 percent mental commitment, and 100 percent physical commitment. In the locker room before a big game, all the guys are sitting around, and it's final preparation. The adrenalin is pumping, and you're getting ready to play in front of millions of people. You're ready to go out and spill your guts and do whatever it takes, and you have total disregard for anything but winning that game. You wanted to make sure you didn't quit and were never a coward.

Football was the most honest activity I ever took part in; it was impossible to conceal mistakes. Pro football players are always under intense scrutiny. We used to film pass rushing drills, or pass coverage drills, or defensive or offensive game plan preparations. And then there were always the dreaded film sessions after the games. You were accountable for your actions on a play-by-play basis. They used to say, "The eye in the sky doesn't lie." If you were a coward on a particular play, you were revealed as a coward. If you were looking for a place to hide, if you were trying to miss a tackle and not take on the full force of a tackle, all these things showed up. But I liked that, because in order to be successful, it took a total commitment. If I prepared myself mentally so I was aware of all circumstances as they unfolded, and I made a commitment to be aggressive, to believe in my instincts, and go 100 percent on a particular play, I felt a tremendous sense of accomplishment. To perform at a championship level, and continue to start, and be a team leader and a team captain was tremendously gratifying.

SN: *When, and why, did you decide to retire?*
SZ: I had decided that I would retire after my tenth year in the NFL. There were four reasons behind that decision. First, ten years in the NFL had a real ring to it, even though if I had played eight or nine years, that would have been a significant accomplishment. Then, at the start of my eighth year, I saw Darryl Stingley break his neck. Here was this great physical specimen, an unbelievably gifted athlete, a guy that you would think could never get hurt. And to see him paralyzed. Even though I had had a ruptured Achilles tendon, and three knee operations, and an elbow operation, and broke five or six fingers, and had all sorts of bumps and bruises and aches and pains, I'd never seen anybody break his neck before. And from that point on, I was literally terrified to step on the football field. My efficiency as a player declined. I did a lot of bargaining with God for the rest of my career. The next two years, it was always, "Oh, take my arm, take my leg, poke my eyes out, break my knee, but not my neck." That's too serious a price to pay to play football. So, that was another determining factor.

Third, in the preseason of my last year, I was missing some tackles that I normally would have eaten up. I could tell that I was just *this* much off. A step in football is everything. When you're a linebacker, you have to know that you're really into it. If you're out there, and you're dreading it, and you're thinking, "Oh, I hope I don't catch him, because I might have to hit him," it's time to get on and get out.

And finally, I had a job in the off-season in Oklahoma in 1979 selling drilling mud in the oil business, and with my bonuses, and my salary, and my benefits,

I was making more selling drilling mud than I was playing football. Some of my oil buddies were eccentric, nouveau riche kind of guys who made millions of dollars and couldn't wait to buy an airplane and buy a boat. They'd tell me, "Zabel, do you remember last year when you guys played in Pittsburgh, and it was thirty below zero in the mud, in the rain? I was sitting in the Bahamas, and I won $20,000 on that game. That's more than you made!"

After Fairbanks resigned as our head coach, I felt that I owed enough to the Patriots that I would tell the new head coach that my intention for my tenth year was to retire after the season. I had always had a real honest relationship with Fairbanks, even though my honesty had gotten me in some trouble when I was with the Eagles. So, when Ron Erhardt was appointed the new head coach, I told him before training camp that that was it, that I was just going to play that last year. The minute I told him, I knew I had made a mistake. Because from that minute on, I was just phased out. I was making $115,000 a year, and they had a young draft choice who was making about $25,000 a year. They penciled him into my spot and developed him during training camp. During the exhibition season, I maybe got to play in only two games, for a couple of quarters. I felt like I had leprosy. And then they cut me. . . .

I got claimed off the waiver wires by the Baltimore Colts, who knew me pretty well, since New England, and Miami, and Baltimore were always playing for the AFC championship in that period.

SN: *How did you feel about going to the Colts?*
SZ: I had enjoyed playing against the Colts. They ran the kind of offense I did well against. Raymond Chester and I had battled on the line. Bert Jones was their quarterback, and I had always admired him as a fierce competitor. Ken Mendenhall, who had been my teammate at Oklahoma, was their center. So, I was pleased when the Colts picked me up. I thought that I had played well enough against them that they wanted me.

Of course, I was rusty, since I'd been in only a handful of plays during the exhibition season. There is a tremendous difference between exhibition football and regular season football. The level of intensity and competitiveness cannot be compared.

The first play of the season was embarrassing. We were playing the Chiefs in Kansas City, and I was on the kickoff return team. I was standing on the sidelines with Bert Jones, and Mike Barnes, and a couple of other Colts, and they were going, "Okay, Zabel, we'll be watching you real close on this kickoff return, and we want you to just knock somebody out." And of course I went,

Steve Zabel with the Baltimore Colts. Courtesy of Sunstaff, The Baltimore Sun.

"No problem." This was the first year that you couldn't block below the waist on the kickoff or punt returns. So, I went out there, and tried to block a six foot five, 250-pound backup tight end running full speed. He just put me in the nickel bleachers. When I walked off the field, after gathering myself from being knocked back twenty yards, those guys were shaking their heads in disgust. But later when we scored a touchdown and kicked off, I made the tackle for the kickoff team, and redeemed myself.

But here I was in my tenth year playing on special teams. I had hoped to cruise out without having to do that.

SN: *Who generally plays on the special teams?*
SZ: The special teams are always something for the younger players, and front-line players normally didn't play on them. When you line up next to the kicker, and you know your job is to run down there, and fire into the wedge that's running back at you with several large bodies, you wonder why you decided to play your last year. I played special teams for the first five or six games. I also played in some short-yardage situations, where I came in on what they call the "nickel package."

Then, with five games to go, they moved me in to the weak-side linebacker position. The Colts had drafted as their number-one pick Barry Krauss, who had played strong-side linebacker in a 5-2 defense in college. But the Colts had started the season with a four-man line and three linebackers and planned to use him as a middle linebacker. But he didn't know how to play that. So, with five games to go, they scrapped the 4-3 defense and went to a 5-2. They made Krauss the strong-side linebacker and moved me to weak-side linebacker.

SN: *How did you feel about playing weak-side linebacker?*
SZ: It's a lot more fun than playing strong-side linebacker. You weren't always the center of the attack. You had a chance to run by and around people that you couldn't hide from on the strong side.

I also helped formulate the game plan we used to beat the Patriots in Baltimore.

SN: *So, they valued you particularly then since you knew the Patriots.*
SZ: Oh, I had the inside knowledge and so was able to work out a plan that proved very effective. On a certain down and distance, we were able to do certain things to force them into what we wanted. I also knew who signaled in their defenses, and I was able to steal their signals. The Colts gave me the game ball, because I had helped formulate that winning game plan.

Unfortunately, the second time around, when we went up to New England to play them, the Patriots beat the tar out of me. They figured out that I had stolen their signals, and for the second game they used two or three different sets of signals. But it still turned out to be a good year and a good way to go out.

SN: *In football, when you make mistakes, can you just shake them off, or do they stick with you?*
SZ: One of the brutal things about playing professional football is that your mistakes stay with you a long time.

SN: *What's unusual about this line of work is that your mistakes are in full public view, and highly publicized. You see them all in the film sessions.*
SZ: You have to answer for all your mistakes. Part of the terror and price of being a pro football player is that it's so competitive that you're always being scrutinized. And when you make mistakes, everyone sees them. They stick in your mind, and you can get real depressed.

I'll never forget a game in 1975 between the Patriots and the Jets, when Coach Fairbanks bawled me out for missing a tackle, which cost us the game. I was playing right outside linebacker, and John Riggins ran a play right up the gut. I should have realized that the play was going nowhere on the inside, where it was jammed up, and that my responsibility was to protect the flank. Instead, I took the tight end and tried to wad him down inside, and I got involved in a tackle that I had no business getting involved in. The next thing I knew, Riggins decided to bounce the play outside. All of a sudden, I was eyeball to eyeball with him. The next thing I knew, I was chasing him. The cornerback and I hit Riggins at the same time, he going in one direction, and me going the other. But Riggins just shed us both off like a bug hitting a windshield, and ran for a forty-five-yard touchdown. I'll never forget the coach going, "God, Zabel, I can't believe you couldn't make that tackle!" Later on, I had a roughing-the-passer penalty, which gave them fifteen yards and kept a drive alive. Then I got a holding penalty on the goal line. We lost 35-31, and I knew I had cost us the game.

SN: *I was talking to a guy at a card show in Texas last summer who was complaining about Jackie Smith getting selected for the Hall of Fame. Smith was a great player, an excellent pass receiver, but this guy was upset because he had missed one pass in the Super Bowl.*
SZ: Reality is that Jackie Smith, even though he's in the Hall of Fame and was a perennial All-Pro, will be remembered for floundering in the end zone, after missing a pass that I know from playing pro football was a brutal pass. He was kind of on his knees, and the pass was straight in on him. He took a shot straight on, into the pads. It just hit his pads and bounced out. Probably nine out of ten pass receivers would have missed that pass.

SN: *Does that stick in a football player's mind that on any given Sunday something could happen that would make you into a goat?*

SZ: The fear of playing a bad game and looking bad in the films is very motivational. Most of the guys who played in the NFL gave forth so much effort because they knew that if you didn't, you'll be gone. In practice, in seven-on-seven drills, in fact, everything we did, practice and games, was all filmed. And if you ran up on a kickoff return, and you had an opportunity to put a guy in the nickel bleachers and didn't take it, you're gone, man. That fear of being caught loafing or in the act of cowardice forced you always to play your best.

SN: *Of course, football is such a complex game that it's often difficult to determine who is really responsible for a mistake. I'm sure the fans much of the time can't tell.*

SZ: There's no question. In my job as a linebacker, I made most of my plays taking on fullbacks, taking on guards, closing down holes, and shutting holes so that the back couldn't run through the hole as he was supposed to. You would try to make him bounce it outside, so that a safety or somebody else could make the tackle. Well, the average person would look at the film and go, "Oh, he's supposed to keep the ball from going outside, if the tackle's not made." Well, no, defenses are designed to work where every contingency is covered.

In the defenses I played in, everybody had primary responsibilities but also secondary ones. They might tell me as an outside linebacker, "Okay, you rush the passer, but you have to maintain an outside contain position. If you have a chance to duck underneath to make a tackle, you better get the tackle, because if you screw up, and duck under, and he rolls outside for twenty yards, like a Fran Tarkenton, or a Roger Staubach, or a Terry Bradshaw would do in a heartbeat, that's your responsibility.

My last five years I learned to play more conservatively. I decided after I had that bad game against the Jets that I was going to study and do everything I could to recognize what I needed to do on each play to protect my own area. I concentrated on doing my own job first, and didn't worry about anything beyond that or more spectacular than that. So, I studied a lot. I learned tendencies. I knew formations.

SN: *Did you do this on your own? When you were a younger player in the NFL, did older veterans take you aside to offer instruction?*

SZ: I learned to do this on my own. There was never any veteran who took me aside and really tried to help me do anything. And most of the coaching that I had in pro football was really inadequate.

SN: *Why do you think NFL coaching was inadequate?*
SZ: The inadequacy of the coaching was due in part to the fact that you had a fraternity of guys in the NFL who stayed together and just moved around the league. Those guys weren't real great coaches. They would just move from team to team, as assistant coach, or defensive coordinator, or offensive coordinator.

I did have some great coaches working under Fairbanks. He always had an ability to get coaches who were really teachers. And Jimmy Carr, the defensive coordinator for part of my time with the Eagles, was one of the best. He was a real student of the game, and we always had defensive game plans that gave you some real statistical information—the probability of a certain play coming in a certain position on the field, in a certain formation. Rollie Dotsch, however, was my favorite coach. He really helped me advance to another level as a player. He helped me to play more consistently, to pay careful attention to how I played as an athlete, as far as, you're stretching out too much, your center of gravity is off, you need to play lower, break down more, be more conscious of how your feet are positioned, or the angle that you're going away from the ball or towards the ball. Be conscious of your shade on the tight end when you line up over him. If you've got a certain defense, you've got to be sure he can't hook you. Don't put yourself in a position where that can happen.

SN: *What was adjusting to retirement like?*
SZ: I've had to make tremendous adjustments. When you're playing football, you're around your best friends, day in and day out. Even though there are so many adversities, there was always the tremendous camaraderie and the tremendous cause. Each week was its own focus and its own goal. If you participated in a championship season, and made the playoffs, and performed well, those next six months, you're living on a cloud.

But in the business world, you're isolated. Everybody has a job, and your friends and acquaintances move on. Guys have wives, and children, and jobs. So, that closeness that you had with those forty-five guys diminishes over the years. There's only a handful of former players that I keep up with on a regular basis, the guys that I was the very closest with. I was always closest to defensive players, especially to linebackers.

When you play pro football, you live in a real closed environment, where there isn't any room for liars. It was never enough to say that you could do something. You had to prove you could. So, if John Hannah told me something, I took it to the bank. If Steve Nelson told me something, I took it to the bank. If Chuck Fairbanks asked me to run through that brick wall, I trusted and believed that there was a reason for me to do that, and I did it.

When I left that closed environment and moved into the business world, I experienced real problems. After retiring, I came back to Oklahoma with more money than I've ever had since and met a lot of new people. But unlike in football, I hadn't been with these people when they were tested under fire. I was real gullible, way too trusting, and way too honest. And I got taken advantage of big time.

SN: *What kind of work did you get involved in?*
SZ: In 1978 I had moved back to Oklahoma in the off-season and taken a job in sales with a drilling mud company in the oil business, which was really starting to boom. I was making more money selling drilling mud than playing pro football. That got me to thinking that I didn't need pro football anymore. So, I played through 1979 and retired.

After two years in the mud business, I got involved in the oil business first hand. I became partners with Steve Casteel, an ex-linebacker and former teammate at Oklahoma, in buying leases to drill some shallow wells. I set up a company to raise funds to invest in other wells and invested a lot of my own money in the oil and gas business as well. I decided to invest as much money as I could, in as many wells as I could, to take advantage of the tax incentives.

But I was duped into getting involved with some people who really took advantage of me. And then the oil business itself collapsed, and I went bankrupt. That's kind of like wearing the Scarlet Letter. But I faced up to it. I didn't cheat anybody, and I sold off all the assets that I could. It wasn't me voluntarily filing bankruptcy. It was the lender saying, "Hey, we're selling your house next week, unless you do something about it."

The oil business is definitely not for conservative money, and when I got out of pro football, I was anything but conservative. Rick Mason, my roommate at New Mexico Military Institute, who later became my business partner in the oil business, pointed out to me years later that I had played linebacker and tight end, and asked me, "Do you think anybody who's conservative would play those positions for twenty-five years like you did?" And that was the bottom line of why I was a risk taker. The oil business was real exciting, hands on, out in the wilds.

I wish I had had what most of the successful men my age had, a conservative mother and father, able to instill that attitude in me. But because of my upbringing, I've been fairly independent since I was twelve years old. I never had anybody slap me in the face and say, "Hey, kid, when you get some money, put it in the bank."

SN: *What did you do after the setback in the oil business?*

SZ: When the oil business went bad, I decided that I would take the necessary courses and tests to set up my own brokerage house. Rick Mason and I became partners and set up a company. Later, I went into the telecommunications business. I was very successful with that.

It's really kind of neat to look back at where I started, and where I am, and the ups and downs, the good times and the bad. But I learned from playing football all those years to get up off the ground. I had a coach at New Mexico Military Institute who used to yell at me, "Get off the ground, Zabel! The ground is your enemy!" Going through football for so many years, you learn survival instincts.

TONY PETERS

SAFETY, CORNERBACK

—Cleveland Browns, 1975–1977
—Washington Redskins, 1978–1985

Tony Peters was an All-Pro defensive back who played eleven years in the NFL, with the Cleveland Browns and the Washington Redskins, and participated in the 1983 Super Bowl. As a junior college transfer to the University of Oklahoma, he first attracted significant attention shortly after joining the Sooners, when he shut down Lynn Swann, star receiver of number-one-ranked Southern California, preventing him from catching a single pass in the game. He played on two national championship teams at Oklahoma, in 1973 and 1974. Oklahoma did not lose a game during Peters' two years there.

Peters discusses sport and African-American community life during early childhood in the small Oklahoma agricultural town of Pauls Valley, as well as the transition during junior high school to the northeast Oklahoma City ghetto, including his exposure to gang violence. He describes his experience in Pauls Valley's desegregated high school, which he later attended, and playing junior college football at an institution that set out to eliminate players with a brutal drill called "The Hamburger."

Peters comments on the disciplinary procedures, training regimen, and academic experience in the University of Oklahoma's top-flight college football

Tony Peters, defensive back with the Cleveland Browns. Courtesy of Tony Peters.

program and on players' relations with boosters. He compares the approach to coaching of Chuck Fairbanks and Barry Switzer at Oklahoma and assesses the coaching in the NFL of Forrest Gregg at Cleveland and Joe Gibbs at Washington. He analyzes the physical and mental aspects of playing the cornerback, strong safety, and free safety positions, including the use of hands and forearm blows. He explains how defensive backs and receivers verbally and physically intimidate each other.

Peters discusses his participation in the 1982 NFL players' strike with the Redskins and his experience negotiating contracts, being traded, and adjusting to a new team. He also talks about injuries and playing with pain.

After retiring from the NFL, Peters returned to the University of Oklahoma to complete his degree, where he spent some time monitoring the study hall for the athletic department. He offers some shrewd observations about contemporary athletes in a big-time college athletic program. He then made a successful transition to coaching high school football.

STEPHEN NORWOOD: *You were born in 1953. Tell me about your parents' background and the town you came from.*
TONY PETERS: I grew up in Pauls Valley, Oklahoma, a small, predominantly agricultural town of about 30,000 people. I was born in Oklahoma City, even though my family lived in Pauls Valley, probably because there was medical treatment available there for African-Americans.

My parents were both very uneducated. My mother went as far as the ninth grade; my father only went as far as the third.

SN: *Were they from Oklahoma, or had they migrated from elsewhere?*
TP: My mother migrated from Arkansas, but her family originally came from Mississippi. My dad came out of Texas.

SN: *What kind of work did they do?*
TP: When I was in school and they asked for my father's occupation, it was somewhat embarrassing. My father was an alcoholic for most of his life. I always asked my mom, "What kind of work does he do?" He did various jobs. In school, we put down "common laborer." He did handle large construction equipment on some of the jobs. As I got older, prior to going to college, we often worked together in building homes. My mother basically did domestic work, one of the main opportunities for work for black women.

I was one of eleven children—the middle child, basically. Three of us ended up going to the University of Oklahoma to play football. My brother Terry played a couple of years in the NFL and in Canada. My brother Carl also played at Oklahoma, but hurt his ankle there, and that ended his career. Another brother played at Southern University and then ended up at Southwestern Oklahoma.

SN: *When did you get involved in sports? At what level in school? Was sports in Pauls Valley an important part of community life?*
TP: Sports was a big part of African-American community life in Pauls Valley. All the small towns in the area had baseball and softball teams, which would play each other every weekend—Pauls Valley, Ada, Chickasha, Wynnewood. They'd have girls' teams and guys' teams. They'd play the girls' teams first, then

the guys' teams. As a kid, I watched my mom play fast-pitch softball. She was quite an athlete, even though she was very small.

SN: *Was this just African-American teams playing each other?*
TP: Yes.

SN: *Pauls Valley was a small town. Was it residentially segregated, with blacks living in one section of town and going to their own school?*
TP: Oh, sure. We went to our own all-black school, Dunbar Elementary, which went up through the sixth grade. Prior to the early 1960s—I wasn't part of this—they'd actually bus the black kids after they finished sixth grade to Wynnewood to go to high school. They had a black high school down there. But that changed around 1964, when the schools were desegregated.

SN: *Was there any kind of civil rights activity in Pauls Valley?*
TP: No, I can't remember any strikes or protests in the town.

SN: *Did your parents talk to you much about their lives in the past, their experiences?*
TP: Very, very little. My mom worked a couple of jobs, so I didn't see her much until late in the day. My dad was around, but he never lived with us. We pretty much had to be independent as children.

SN: *Did any of your older brothers or sisters look after you?*
TP: It was difficult for me, because I had the biggest gap in age separating me from my older siblings. The sister older than me was three years older, and the next brother was five years older. So, by the time I was twelve, my sister was fifteen and going through puberty, and my older brother was getting ready to go into the military. So, a lot of the burden fell on me to have to tend to the last four or five kids.

SN: *Did you have any uncles or aunts who were involved with your immediate family?*
TP: No, not really. My family was more or less the black sheep of the entire family, as far as my paternal grandmother was concerned, anyway. She was my only grandparent who was alive when I was a child, and she didn't get along with my mother.

S N : *When did you first begin participating in organized sports?*
T P : In fifth and sixth grade, through Pee Wee teams sponsored by the Pauls Valley Kiwanis and Optimists' Clubs. We played tackle football, with helmets and shoulder pads.

Working as the water boy for the high school football team also contributed to my interest in football. One of my older brothers played on the team and some of my older cousins. I remember sitting on the bench, and these guys would come off the field with all this blood, and split lips, and sweat pouring off them. They told me, "Go get me some ice, or take this towel and put it in ice water, and bring it to me." I remember those looks, and the blood, and guys that had no teeth.

I played a couple years of Pee Wee football, but then, unfortunately, in 1965 my mother moved our family to Oklahoma City, where I went to junior high school.

S N : *You had been born in Oklahoma City, but had you ever been back there?*
T P : No, so this was quite a big change for me.

S N : *From the standpoint of Pauls Valley, this is a big city.*
T P : Absolutely. It was really a big, big culture shock. We lived in northeast Oklahoma City, which was pretty much the ghetto. I was exposed to a lot of issues for the first time. In Pauls Valley, a lot of the real issues never touched you. People mostly read the local newspaper, which didn't cover real issues. And when you got a single mom trying to raise eight or nine kids, your access to real issues is going to be somewhat limited. She's spending most of her time working, trying to make sure there's food on the table. By 1965, when we moved to Oklahoma City, the civil rights movement was pretty much over, but there were a lot of things starting to develop, with Malcolm X, the Black Panther Party, and so on.

In Oklahoma City, I remember surviving, more than anything. Unlike in Pauls Valley, I didn't play sports there, and I became involved in youth gangs.

S N : *You're coming from a small town, where there weren't gangs, I assume. When did you encounter gangs, and how did that affect your life?*
T P : My exposure to gangs came at lunch period on my first day at Moon Junior High. I was with a friend. Some guys jumped him to take his lunch money. So, I stepped in to help him. The attackers were members of a gang. The next thing I know, I got people coming at me, so I had to quickly associate myself with another group of kids, associated with a gang called the "Soul Brothers," an older group at Douglass High School. These gangs weren't as strong as today's street gangs, but they would pick on weaker individuals, and beat them up, and steal their lunch money. It was a pretty scary environment.

SN: *Did the gang members carry weapons, knives or guns?*
TP: They didn't necessarily carry guns. Knives were normally as far as they would go, clubs on occasion. Back then, if you had a problem with an individual, he was man enough to deal with you one on one. But you always had your backup, in case something went down. For instance, if two guys agreed to hash out a difference, and one picked up a weapon, then he would be converged on by a group of ten or fifteen people, who would manhandle him, and then possibly stomp on him—what they called "stomp on his chest."

SN: *Did this go on in the school, or on the school grounds?*
TP: There was a tradition that kids from one black school, Kennedy, came to Moon the last couple days of the school year to "tear it out"—that was the term. For years and years, Kennedy had supposedly the strongest group of kids and dominated Moon. It would be a miniriot. They would just come through the school and beat up whomever they saw. The teachers would be running and the security people. It lasted five or ten minutes. They'd come in quickly and go out, like on a raid. Similar raids were staged by groups from Central High School, who'd pick the largest guys at Moon Junior High School to beat up. What the reason was, I don't know.

There would be fights at our school nearly every day, but the problem was not as serious as it is now. Most of the fights were one on one. Only once or twice a year would fifteen or twenty guys from each gang clash within the school vicinity. The gangs possessed a lot of influence, but it hadn't reached the point where they thought they could rule over authority.

SN: *Do you remember any adults intervening to try to stop the gang violence in the school?*
TP: The adults would try to intervene, and they dealt with whomever they caught, through a paddling or a suspension. I would get my hands dirty, just like the rest of the kids at the school. But whenever adults came around, hey, you would just run, and you'd meet up with your friends later. I did get suspended a couple of times for fighting at school. But you had to stand up and protect yourself, or you were picked on from then on. I developed a certain sense of confidence in myself from that experience.

SN: *What about the academic side of the school?*
TP: From an academic standpoint, I think we were getting the best that was available, and better than most. I remember some great teachers.

SN: *So there was learning going on in the school.*
TP: Oh, absolutely.

SN: *Today you think of certain schools as just processing people through with nothing being learned.*
TP: It was just between the classes that you had to worry about. (Laughs) Even the guys in the gangs went to class, although they weren't really learning. Years later, when I went back there to visit, I found that most of those guys were either in prison or dead. I think if I had stayed in that environment and had not moved away after three years, I probably wouldn't be here today.

SN: *I take it there was much less emphasis on sports in the school in Oklahoma City than in Pauls Valley.*
TP: There was no emphasis in Oklahoma City. The school system did offer after-school football, but you had to go over to Douglass High School to play, which was too far for me. I also had a paper route at that time, which prevented me from participating.

SN: *People didn't play basketball in Oklahoma City? It's an urban sport.*
TP: No, in our free time we went to rob things—stores, whatever—generally in groups. You had to associate.

SN: *Did you become involved in sports again when you moved back to Pauls Valley?*
TP: Yes. We moved back to Pauls Valley when I was in ninth grade. Everyone was involved in sports there, and if I didn't get involved, then I'd kind of be the last guy out.

SN: *You weren't aware yet that you had unusual talent in sports?*
TP: No, because I was still pretty small. In eighth grade I was four foot seven. I'm now six foot two. I grew about three inches between my sophomore and junior years in high school.

SN: *Was high school football regarded as a major event in the social life of Pauls Valley? You mentioned earlier that you were introduced to the sport at a young age.*
TP: Sports in Pauls Valley was just entertainment for families and for people on Friday nights. It was not the situation described in the book *Friday Night Lights*. There was really no special treatment for the athletes. There was no fanatic focus on winning. It was just good, plain, competitive fun.

I played basketball and ran track in the ninth grade in Pauls Valley. Our track coach instilled a real work attitude. That was the beginning of realizing what it took to be the best at your particular job.

SN: *You went to a desegregated high school in Pauls Valley? Were there any black teachers or coaches?*

TP: It was a desegregated school. They had closed down the black high school in 1964 or 1965. The high school was small, with only about 350 students; my graduating class had 104. Blacks made up only about ten percent of the student body. There were only eight or nine blacks in my graduating class. We only had one black teacher. He had been the principal at the black high school and was hired on at the white high school after it desegregated.

SN: *He just became a teacher, not an administrator? Not even an assistant principal?*

TP: He became less than a teacher; he was hired as a shop teacher. He had been a principal and had the credentials to be more than a shop teacher. After years and years, within the last four or five years, they finally made him principal of a junior high school. Anyway, he was the only black that we had as a role model. There were no black coaches at the high school.

SN: *When did you start playing high school football?*

TP: As an eleventh grader.

SN: *What position did you play? Did you play both ways, offense and defense?*

TP: I was mostly a linebacker and also played running back a little. I played mostly defense, very little offense. I had great success as an inside linebacker. I wasn't very big, but I was tough. I was one of the best players on the team.

SN: *Did practice require a lot of time after school?*

TP: I'd practice with the team after school from three o'clock until about five fifty, when I had to go to my after school job, cleaning out a drugstore. I mopped and dusted. They wouldn't let me get near the cash register. The next year I got another job, from six o'clock until nine thirty or ten at night, that paid fifteen dollars a week.

SN: *Would you hand your earnings over to your mother?*

TP: For the most part, I handed the money I earned over to my mother, who used it for meals or for games for the kids. Christmas, we might get a good pair of pants and a couple shirts. Toys were out of the question.

SN: *You say there were eleven children in your family. What was your house like?*

TP: Our house was pretty jammed, even though by my high school days, my older brothers had all left home. Every room was a sleeping room, except the rest room and the kitchen.

SN: *How would you do your homework in those surroundings?*
TP: I didn't take my schoolwork very seriously then, and I never did any homework. The only homework I remember doing was in seventh grade, when I practiced the clarinet.

SN: *Did you ever skip school?*
TP: I never played hooky; I always went to school. I was about an average student. I didn't really perform unless I had to. In other words, if I made a bad grade on a test, I felt embarrassed.

SN: *Neither of your parents made it to high school, and here you were now in high school. Any sense of what you would be doing in the future?*
TP: I had no sense of where I was headed.

SN: *There was no one helping you?*
TP: Right. The only real goal I remember was to join the air force and become a pilot. But I never did the things necessary to prepare myself for that. That was more due to ignorance and not knowing where to look, than anything.

   After I got to college, I was rather bitter about Pauls Valley, because I didn't think the advisors and teachers took enough interest and put enough thought into helping the students who needed assistance.

SN: *You made All-State in football your senior year. Was this at linebacker or running back?*
TP: Wide receiver. (Laughs) I had moved over senior year to wide receiver and running back.

SN: *How often did the team pass a game?*
TP: About ten times a game, which was a lot for a high school team.

SN: *Were you a sprinter on the track team?*
TP: I was a hurdler and could run the 100-yard dash in under ten seconds. My junior year, I was the top hurdler in the state for the 2A high schools. [4A is the highest classification; B is the lowest].

SN: *Who taught you how to run pass patterns? Did you get any formal instruction from coaches?*
TP: No one really taught me how to be a pass receiver. Today football is a year-round thing for the kids, and they get more instruction. Back then, we played

football, we played basketball, we ran track. So, there wasn't a whole lot of time to learn technique.

SN: *Had you thought about going to college at all?*
TP: I had really planned to join the air force and not go to college. But my senior year East Central University, in nearby Ada, Oklahoma, offered me a scholarship to play football and basketball. I met with their coach in Ada and signed with him after one visit. That's how naive I was about the recruiting process.

SN: *Did you know of other athletes from Pauls Valley who had been recruited?*
TP: I hadn't been aware of anyone else getting recruited before me. I was the only guy from our team who really got recruited that year. I went up to play in the All-State football game in Edmond.

SN: *What position did you play there?*
TP: For that game, they made me a defensive back, the first time that I had played that position. They had plenty of talent there, and they had to find a spot for each player. But I knew how to tackle from having been a linebacker, and I had the speed. I had a great week in practice, and I really shook up some guys from the big, 4A schools.

My performance at the All-State camp attracted the attention of the recruiters there from the University of Oklahoma, Leon Cross and Larry Lacewell. They asked me if I had signed with anyone, and I told them I had, with East Central. Then they asked me if I would consider going to a junior college, Northeastern Oklahoma A&M (NEO) in Miami, Oklahoma, for a year, after which they could offer me a football scholarship to the University of Oklahoma.

SN: *What was the purpose of that exactly? To see how good you were as an athlete, to get additional academic preparation?*
TP: They wanted me to put on some weight, since I was almost six foot two but weighed only 162 pounds. From the academic standpoint, I needed more preparation as well. My ACT score wasn't high enough to be accepted at Oklahoma. It was only fourteen, and you needed about a sixteen. And my high school record wasn't all that great either. I had about a 2.5 grade point average. Three or four other guys from the All-State game had signed to go to NEO. I decided to go up there as well, instead of taking the offer from East Central. If I made good, I had a good chance to go on to play football at the University of Oklahoma.

I wanted to play football a lot more than basketball. There'd be more positions available to me in football. At six foot two, I knew that I'd have to move from forward to guard in basketball. And point guard was out of the question, unless I put a lot of work into it. Football provided a better opportunity. . . .

I went to NEO for three semesters, before transferring to Oklahoma, and played football and ran track.

SN: *How large was the school?*
TP: It was a very small institution, with 1600 or 2000 students. Even then, it had a reputation for athletic success, particularly in football. It was the only junior college in Oklahoma that had a football program. Quite a few of the football players moved on to play at four-year colleges and universities.

SN: *Did you live in a separate athletic dorm there?*
TP: All the athletes there lived in a separate dorm.

SN: *Did the University of Oklahoma have an arrangement with NEO then, because of the quality of NEO's football program?*
TP: The recruiting relationship that the University of Oklahoma established with NEO developed in part from the fact that NEO's football coach, Chuck Bowman, had played center at Oklahoma. The football program was considered to be very strong, and NEO played the top junior colleges from around the country, as well as teams like the University of Georgia freshmen.

SN: *What was the ratio of blacks to whites in Miami, where NEO was located, and at NEO?*
TP: The town of Miami was all white, although about ten or fifteen percent of NEO's students were black. There weren't many black women compared to men, because most of the black men had come to NEO as athletes. The football team was at least fifty percent black, although there were no black coaches. Nine of the eleven starters on defense were black.

SN: *Was there pressure on you at NEO to take certain courses?*
TP: I was able to choose my own classes at NEO and decided to major in sociology. Of course, you took the normal freshman requirements. NEO was an agricultural and mechanical college, and I was somewhat interested in mechanical science and took some motor repair. But growing up in the 1960s, with the Civil Rights Act and Voting Rights Act major issues during my adolescence, sociology was a hot topic.

I was somewhat introverted then, coming from a small town environment, and threw myself into academics. I left NEO with between a 3.6 and 3.8 grade point average, which obviously qualified me for the university.

SN: *Did the other athletes consider it unusual for you to have such a high GPA? There have been Ph.D.s playing quarterback in the NFL and so on, but at the same time a lot of athletes don't seem to take academic work very seriously.*
TP: There was no peer pressure not to do well in academics. As I started to get these good grades, my two roommates would come to me for assistance with their schoolwork.

SN: *Was the incentive to do well academically the ability to transfer to a major college football program?*
TP: No. It was more that I was a little afraid of getting into the mainstream of college life.

SN: *How many hours would football practice consume?*
TP: Football practice took up two or two and a half hours, Monday through Friday, with film sessions and just a light workout on Sunday, the day after the game. But I always found time for my studies.

SN: *How would you compare junior college football to high school football?*
TP: The major difference was the emphasis on winning. At NEO, the emphasis was on being the best, separating yourself from the mediocre. Our coach, Chuck Bowman, knew what it took to get to the next level. There was no question that NEO was a football factory, where winning was the focus. It's not that they'd do anything illegal to win, but the work ethic certainly increased.

SN: *Did NEO recruit anyone you thought was academically unqualified?*
TP: The requirements are somewhat different in junior colleges. You could play football in junior college and be academically ineligible in a lot of places.

SN: *Do you feel playing in junior college made it easier for you to make the transition to the University of Oklahoma?*
TP: Well, I almost didn't make it. We had 160 people coming out for the NEO football team, and the way they eliminated people was through a brutal drill called "The Hamburger." They would line up two linemen on each side, offensive and defensive, with a linebacker behind the defensive lineman. A quarterback would hand off the ball to a running back. No passing was

permitted. The drill was conducted in an area only five yards wide, with cones set up to mark the limits. You were not allowed to move outside those cones. The drill almost always resulted in a head-on collision between the running back and the linebacker.

They tested everybody with The Hamburger. Everybody would have to get in line, and we would run this drill for two hours, three times a day, for a week. They had two or three groups out there doing this at one time. There was a lot of hitting and collisions, and you'd get many migraine headaches. It was called a running drill, but I called it a tackling drill.

SN: *How would the coaches react? Did they berate people loudly and publicly?*
TP: Oh, sure. You would get a lot of verbal abuse from the coaches if you went about it in a cowardly manner. The guys who couldn't withstand it were eliminated from the program. It was just a game to eliminate the weak. It was the old Roman view of gladiators—they place you in a cage, and the strong survive.

SN: *Looking back, having been an All-Pro NFL player, was this something you think was necessary to prepare you for what you're going to see in a game?*
TP: Having played in the NFL for eleven years, I don't think that drill improved your ability to function in a game. It doesn't take a whole lot of intelligence to run and stick your head through a wall. It was just their way of eliminating about eighty people from the squad. Every night, you'd hear cars starting up and doors slamming. Guys were going home.

After a couple of days, The Hamburger was just too much for me to bear. I called up my father and asked him to get someone out there to pick me up. I was ready to quit. And he told me he knew that I would be calling. He said he thought I was going to quit, that he knew I wouldn't make it.

SN: *Why do you think he said that?*
TP: I never asked him why he said that—maybe he was hoping to hit a nerve that would make me not want to quit. But at the end of the conversation, he said, "Go ahead and stick it out another couple of days, and you'll be okay." And I did that. I knew he was very proud of me and talked about my successes with relatives and other people. He was only able to live long enough to see me get drafted in the NFL. He never saw me play there. But he knew I'd gotten drafted, and he saw me play at Oklahoma.

SN: *You complained to your father, but did you complain to the coaches?*
TP: After that conversation with my father, I went and talked to my defensive back coach, Robert Maxwell, and I told him I couldn't go on with those drills.

I'd developed migraine headaches. I felt that I had shown my abilities through those drills, and I had not backed down during them. Maxwell explained to the head coach that I had developed migraine headaches, and I got out of the last couple days of the drill.

From that point I started to develop an attitude that I maintained for the rest of my career. My attitude toward the game was, hey, I'm going to work hard, but if it got to the point where the return was going to be negative, then I would just shut down. And I would tell them "Hey, look. That's just as far as I can go."

SN: *What kind of verbal abuse did the coaches hurl at the players during these drills at NEO?*
TP: Well, I had another bad experience playing there with one of the coaches who was both verbally and physically abusive. I'd been a star my freshman year, and we'd gone 8-2, ending up number three or four in the national junior college rankings. The next year, they were short at linebacker, and they asked me to move there, knowing I'd played that position in high school. We'd gotten a new head coach that year, who later went on to coach in the Canadian Football League. He was a fiery guy and was hoping that coaching at NEO would open opportunities for him to coach at the major college or professional levels. He wasn't really concerned about our welfare. That attitude is typical of most coaches that I've observed. They're ego driven, looking to use whatever situation they're in as a platform to get to bigger and better things.

This coach was very verbally abusive. And in one scrimmage, he was cursing me to stop this play, get up in there, stick your nose up in there. He called me all these names, "coward" or whatever. He was walking behind us, and he was really upset that the offense had been getting the better of us. I was lined up at my linebacker position, and all of a sudden, he kicked me in the ass, and said, "Get up in the line of scrimmage." Instead of putting his hand on me and moving me up to where he wanted me to be, he kicked me. I brought it up to him later on, and he apologized, saying he did it in the heat of the moment. But I don't think he would have apologized if I hadn't brought it up. It was something that stayed with me, and I can even feel it today. If he called me to ask me for a favor, I'm sure I wouldn't give it to him.

SN: *Do you think he would have treated a white player that way?*
TP: I'm sure he would have done the same thing to a white player. It was more of a consuming attitude on his part—ignorance and insensitivity towards people, period, and to their development. Besides, he was probably Italian or something. He wasn't pure white or anything like that.

SN: *So how did your junior college football career turn out?*
TP: It was successful, and I was selected junior college All-American as a defensive back. I played cornerback my first year and safety my second. After that incident where that coach kicked me, I said I wasn't going to play linebacker for him. The defensive secondary coach I played for was Coach Maxwell, who was a genuine, genuine individual. We still confer periodically today.

SN: *What were the facilities like at NEO?*
TP: The athletic facilities and equipment at NEO were pretty good. We stayed in motels on the road and ate pretty well. We had diehard fans in Miami. It's a town of only about 12,000 or 15,000 people, so the junior college was pretty much all they had, besides the high school. The community really adopted the football program. There were booster clubs, business people who would supply a pregame meal or even a postgame meal, which was quite a treat. We traveled to our away games by bus, which often meant long hours on the road. The bus frequently broke down. They'd start it up at the beginning of fall practice, and a big cloud of smoke would come out. Then they'd run down the road and try to get it tuned up.

We had an outstanding season my second year, ending up 10-0-1, and were rated number two in the national junior college rankings. We played in the Mid-America Bowl game at Tallequah, Oklahoma, which was a national bowl game—as national as junior colleges can get.

SN: *How much did you develop your football skills at NEO?*
TP: One of the things that benefited me most at NEO was that during the summers they'd bring back guys who had played there previously, and then had moved up to big-time college programs or to the NFL, and they'd help us work out. I learned a lot about playing defensive back from Ralph McGill, a black guy who played that position with the San Francisco 49ers and the New Orleans Saints. He was All-Pro a couple of times in the NFL and had played quarterback for NEO and the University of Tulsa.

SN: *What did you learn specifically about playing defensive back?*
TP: It's not that I mastered any technique at NEO, because I really didn't, but my physical ability really came to the fore when I played defensive back. My first year I played cornerback, which was a great experience, because it puts you out on an island, pretty much by yourself. You had to rise to the occasion, "Hey, can I take this guy?" My footwork certainly improved. I was always able to run backwards well, at a high rate of speed, which you have to do as a defensive

back. For me that was pretty much a natural thing. My sophomore year I
played free safety, which was different, since I wasn't responsible for covering
anyone. I led the team in interceptions both years. That gave me the confidence
that I could play several positions. I began to develop the attitude that it didn't
matter where I played, so long as I made a contribution.

SN: *Did you start getting recruiting letters from other college football programs
besides Oklahoma's while you were at NEO?*
TP: When I finished the fall semester of my second year of NEO, I received
letters of interest from several major programs besides Oklahoma—Nebraska,
Duke, San Diego State, Tulane, University of Tulsa, and Oklahoma State. I had
pretty much made up my mind to go to Oklahoma, largely because it was close
to home. I wanted my parents—my mom, really—to have a chance to see me
play. I wanted to be close to her and still felt responsible for my younger brother
and sisters. Oklahoma also had had that great battle in 1971 with Nebraska in a
nationally televised Thanksgiving Day game. During that game, a sportscaster
made the comment that Oklahoma was really the University of Texas, because
they had no players from Oklahoma, just from Texas. So, I wanted to show people that Oklahoma really did have Oklahoma players.

But I did go on two other recruiting trips, to Oklahoma State and Tulane.
I also visited the University of Tulsa, which was right nearby.

SN: *Could you describe what happened on these trips? What did the coaches
say to you?*
TP: There were three of us at NEO who were highly recruited, Donny
Vincent, Larry Hutchinson, and me. They brought the three of us down to
Oklahoma State in a private plane. We toured the university and met with
players. Then we went to coach Jim Stanley's office. He was sitting in a big
leather chair in a huge office, smoking a cigar. He looked at Donny and Larry
and told them he'd give them a scholarship that day. He looked at me and told
me he couldn't offer me a scholarship, that he needed more film. And I said
to myself, "Well, thanks very much. I just came on the visit because Donny
and Larry wanted me to come." He didn't know that they weren't going anywhere unless I went. That had a lot to do with the fact that I had done very
well academically, and guys would come to my suite and ask me about how
to study. I had become quite a leader in that respect. I like telling Oklahoma
State fans that story, since I was the only guy out of that group to make it.

I went on a one-day recruiting visit to the University of Tulsa, which was
pretty informal. The coach told me he had gotten Ralph McGill drafted by

the San Francisco 49ers. That's what coaches generally do on recruiting visits, they tell you about guys who went on to play in the NFL. And they show you the campus and the athletic dorm and introduce you to some of the players.

SN: *Tulsa, as I recall, in the 1960s emphasized the passing game much more than other college teams. It was more like a pro-type offense.*
TP: And that was one of the things they tried to sell me on.

SN: *Did the coaches tell you anything about the academic programs?*
TP: I don't remember any of them getting into academics. They never showed me a school course catalogue or asked about what I was interested in studying.

I also went down to Tulane, in New Orleans, for a weekend. They used the standard approach of telling me that they had some great players, that they were building a dynasty, and that I could be part of that. They also took me down to the nightspots in the French Quarter. The school was pretty nice, but I figured I'd do too much partying there. One of the problems there was that they turned you over to a player, whose responsibility was to entertain you. They think you'll be more comfortable going around with a player, who's roughly your age and has the same kind of outlook socially. The university should be aware of the fact that most of them will just get drunk.

I think the whole recruiting process is wrong. If the schools are going to offer scholarships, they have a responsibility to make sure that a kid has proper goals. They could do this through an interview with an academic advisor. They try to sell a kid on the athletic program, without selling him on other things. As a result, they're losing kids left and right. Of course, the vast majority of players in even big-time college football programs never make it to the professional ranks. And obviously, athletics is not the type of thing you can do forever. I don't think that's taken into consideration enough in the recruiting process.

SN: *Were the football scholarship offers basically the same at all the schools? They're not competing with each other to top the other's scholarship offer?*
TP: No, the offers are all pretty much the same.

I had already pretty much determined to go to the University of Oklahoma, and I signed with them soon after I returned from Tulane. The NCAA had just changed the rule that prohibited junior college players from transferring to four-year colleges until they had completed four semesters. You were now allowed to transfer after three. Leon Cross called me from Oklahoma to notify me of that change. He said that Coach Lacewell would be down to sign me the next day. I signed with him, and then a day or two later I drove down to Norman and enrolled.

SN: *What was it like adjusting to the football program at the University of Oklahoma?*

TP: I started off rather slowly. During spring practice, I twisted my ankle severely playing basketball during one of the weekends I went home. It was placed in a plaster cast. So, I didn't get to participate much in full live practice. I wasn't having any contact, so they didn't know how much I could do.

SN: *Where were you on the depth chart when you started practicing?*

TP: When I first got to Oklahoma, I was way down on the depth chart, number nine at my position, one of the corners. That was the first day. It was somewhat of a shock that they had so many people. But I was aware that this was the big time.

After a couple days, I knew I was competing for the starting position against Kenith Pope, who had been an All-American the year before. He was a senior, and I was a junior. I finally displaced him that fall, in the second game of the season against Southern Cal.

I hurt my shoulder during preseason practice that fall and didn't start in our first game against Baylor. But I played a little over half the game. Coach Switzer started Kenith Pope again in the second game. But he started out slowly, and Switzer pulled him and put me in during the first quarter. They knew I was the best covering guy anyway. And from then on, it was my job.

SN: *Your first big test in a game was against Southern California, which was a real powerhouse. Barry Switzer talks about this game in his book,* Bootlegger's Boy, *and about your performance in it, shutting down Lynn Swann.*

TP: The game against Southern Cal was a really big one, since they were ranked number one in the country. By contrast, we had been picked to finish in the middle of the pack in the Big Eight. The game was played out in California. We flew out there in a small plane. They had some great players, like Anthony Davis and Lynn Swann, whom I had to cover. He had quite a reputation, so I knew this was going to be a real test. If I could play him, then I felt I had pretty much arrived. I wasn't nervous at all. I accepted the challenge of trying to see if I could play at that level, with the type of player Lynn Swann was considered to be. I just lined up and played. He ran patterns, and I ran with him, and that was it. They threw at him, and I deflected them or was in a position to prevent him from catching them.

We dominated the game for four quarters. We outrushed them—we had 380 or 390 yards rushing to their 100-odd yards. They really did nothing. The game ended up in a 7-7 tie. We had a great team, even though we had to play that year on probation.

SN: *Why was the Oklahoma football program placed on probation?*
TP: Because one of the coaches had committed a recruiting violation. I can't remember who it was. He resigned after that. Kerry Jackson was projected as our starting quarterback, and his high school coach had altered his high school transcript. That allowed Oklahoma to recruit a player who was academically ineligible. An Oklahoma coach knew about it. He might have suggested it to the high school coach; I have no idea. So, the NCAA imposed sanctions. Oklahoma was placed on probation for two years, 1973 and 1974. In 1973 Oklahoma could not win a United Press national championship, and none of its games could be televised in 1974. It was not permitted to play bowl games during those years. And there was also a reduction in scholarships.

SN: *How does the college academic program get set up for a football player? How do you choose your courses?*
TP: The academic advisors for the athletic department want you to work towards your degree, but they also want you to maintain your eligibility. They see a lot of these kids taking all these classes and then not making it. So, they'll steer you to things they know you can make an A in, to keep your grade point average up. Say you're taking a five-course load. The academic advisor will make sure that two of your classes are real easy ones, like "Theory of Basketball," or "Theory of Golf."

SN: *What is a "Theory of Basketball"—type class like?*
TP: Courses like that are pretty basic, and involve reading just one book. I took "Theory of Golf," and we read *Ben Hogan's Five Steps to the Game*. Tests were just multiple choice. It's not like it should be in a college class. To be sure, there's the genuine concern that you won't be able to handle too much, since football practice is going to consume a lot of your time. During the spring, it's not so bad. But during the fall, you have to put in a lot of time practicing from three o'clock to five thirty or six, and you might have a meeting afterwards to watch film.

SN: *I notice they send very few athletes into my "History of Sport in America" course.*
TP: It's not just the athletic department that warns students away from taking academically rigorous courses. As a returning student, I was told by my regular

college academic advisor not to take your sport history course, because it was too hard and required too much reading.

SN: *When you were with the Washington Redskins, you played with Dexter Manley, who went through Oklahoma State without learning how to read. Did that situation ever develop at Oklahoma when you were there?*
TP: The athletic program did monitor how well you were doing in your courses and would get two- or three-week progress reports from the instructors. If your grades dropped below a certain level, you were required to attend study hall every night. Our athletic department academic advisor, Port Robertson, would break your plate if you didn't go to class, and then you couldn't eat in the athletic dormitory.

SN: *So, you're saying the situation was totally different from what it became in the late 1980s, when there was a real breakdown of discipline.*
TP: We never had the problems with discipline that developed later on in the program. We had a good, solid group of guys. Obviously, you're going to have a percentage of people who are just hell raisers. But the percentage wasn't high enough to swallow the entire barrel. The athletic dorm was supervised in a very professional manner. What happened later on was that they started to recruit people who probably didn't deserve to be on scholarship.

In the recruiting process, the kids are told how great they are and how much difference they're going to make when they get into the program. And they actually begin to believe that stuff. The next thing you know, they're way in the outer limits somewhere, just completely lost.

I also think that Brian Bosworth had something to do with the decline of discipline in the program. Brian got away with a lot. And, of course, everybody else was saying that they were as good as he was, so they could do the same thing.

SN: *Many people felt the coaching staff had abdicated its responsibility to impose discipline. These are the adults who have to lead and set a standard of conduct.*
TP: Of course, Coach Switzer wasn't the most glorious role model himself. He genuinely enjoyed college ball and genuinely enjoyed people. He was satisfied where he was and didn't have any aspirations to move on to the pros. But he absolutely enjoyed females. That was probably part of his problem. At that time, Coach Switzer was married and had a couple of kids. But you heard rumors. And as time went on, given the type of things that happened to him, you realized that the rumors were probably true.

I played under two head coaches at Oklahoma, Barry Switzer and Chuck Fairbanks, although I didn't get a chance to know Fairbanks well. I only spent a couple of months with him.

SN: *How would you compare Chuck Fairbanks and Barry Switzer as coaches?*
TP: Fairbanks was a distant, untouchable type of coach. He reminded me a lot of Jim Stanley. I went in and talked to him. I don't even remember him getting up out of his chair. He was sitting behind a big, huge desk in a dark office, smoking a cigar. The desk is separating him from you. He seemed to be a power, a guy who was interested in having power. He and his huge office exuded power, rather than exuding care and concern.

Barry Switzer was much more personable. He would sit and chat with you. Fairbanks would sit in the tower. Switzer was more active. He'd be out on the field, standing and talking to you. He would challenge you from a physical standpoint. He'd say, "You're going against a guy this week who'll kick your butt." Whereas Chuck Fairbanks was the power. I would compare Chuck Fairbanks to Douglas MacArthur. He'd put the shades on, the hat, and the jeep.

SN: *Did any cliques develop on the team, or did people pretty much function as a unit? Were there racial divisions on the team?*
TP: We had no real cliques on the team, and we never experienced any racial problems. There might have been a couple of players from California, but most of the team came from Oklahoma and Texas. Blacks pretty much ran with each other, but we were all on speaking terms. If you needed a dictionary, you could go into any room in the dorm and get one. If you needed help in a class, you had no problems getting that. I roomed with Randy Hughes, who was white, for two years on our away games. We had no problems. We both played together in the secondary.

If I needed a couple hundred bucks, I could get it. I took it for family support. Where it came from, I don't know. I'm sure it was a violation. When we went to the pros, guys would always ask us if we had taken a pay cut when we went from Oklahoma to the NFL.

We also sold season tickets to boosters, who were supposed to buy them. That was a way to supplement our fifteen dollars a month spending money— laundry money, they called it, which is what our scholarship called for. That's ridiculous. We'd get ten or twelve Texas tickets, and we could sell them for a couple of hundred dollars each. We scalped them, basically. You just had to give the tickets to a player who knew the right person to contact, and they'd sell your tickets for you. And the next thing you know, you got your money and played poker.

You had opportunities with a lot of those boosters. I think they've outlawed that stuff now. It used to be that you could go to one of the local car dealerships and buy a new car. The car might cost you $12,000. By selling your season tickets, you might come up with $5000 or $6000. You might pay the dealer $3000 for the car, leaving $9000 to pay it off. The athletic department would get us these summer jobs to help you pay the car off.

SN: *The athletic program could get you jobs?*
TP: Well, they'd tell you where the jobs were. We'd get paid ten dollars an hour on these jobs, which back then was a lot of money.

SN: *What kind of jobs were these?*
TP: Most of the guys worked out in the oil fields, on oil rigs, or for trucking companies. If you worked forty hours a week, you made some pretty good money, and that would help pay your car off. I never took that route, because I didn't want to be making those payments. I couldn't afford it. I was still contributing to the support of my family in Pauls Valley.

Now that I think about it, I'm sure the white players got better jobs than the black players. I only worked for one summer, since I came to Oklahoma as a junior. I worked that summer on the assembly line at Westinghouse. I had a choice of oil field or Westinghouse, and I chose the latter, because I didn't want to go out there and work on the rigs. But when I look back on it, it's clear that while there were whites who worked on the oil rigs, there were some who worked at the stockbroker's office or at the bank. If I got a job at Westinghouse, I'm sure one of the white guys was able to get a job with Merrill Lynch somewhere, just going out and participating in various functions and getting paid for it. Some of the wealthy donors may have set them up like that. Had I been at Oklahoma for four years, I'm sure I would have found out what was going on and raised some hell about it.

SN: *How were the Oklahoma football practices conducted?*
TP: When we were practicing, we were permitted to drink water only during breaks. Later on, as public awareness developed, when you had kids from all over the country dying of heat exhaustion and heart attacks, water became more of an issue. Then they let you have water at any time. But we weren't allowed to do that.

SN: *Was there any sense that the team trainer had the authority to step in at any point and say the coaches were pushing it too far?*
TP: Oh, no. Anytime that you complained about things going too far, the response was that they were trying to test you and that you could go a little farther. They'd tell you that you could push your body farther than you really think you can. That's probably true. But why should you, when you've got three weeks or a month before your first game, and this is the first day back? Even to this day, I've never been a supporter of all this running after practice. By the time you get to college, you should be mature enough to know whether you need to get in better physical condition. I don't need somebody to tell me I can go farther.

SN: *Isn't the coaches' argument that in a game you'll need to push your body to the limit?*
TP: You can push yourself to the limit, but whose limit is it? I think you have to understand what *your* limit is. The way it's done now, it's not based on your limit. It's based on what they think your limit is.

My first year at Oklahoma, I told Coach Farrington during practice that I was tired and needed to stop. He responded, "Come on, you got to go, you got to push yourself." The older players, like Ken Pope and Clyde Powers, told me that you can't tell the coach what to do. My response was that I wasn't telling him what to do. I was tired and needed a break. That was it. They looked at me like I didn't have a right to say that.

My senior year I did the same thing. We practiced, and then we had the gut check, which involves running miles and miles. After practice, I made it to about three quarters of the mile, and then just stopped and started walking and kept on walking to the dressing room. The response was, "Hey, you're a leader, you're a senior." And I'm saying, "Hey look, I'm tired. We'll get back at it again tomorrow. But this is as far as I can go." That was just my body telling me to stop.

SN: *Did any other player ever do that?*
TP: Not to my knowledge.

SN: *It was like an act of rebellion.*
TP: It wasn't rebellion. It was just what I needed to do at that time. I was a pretty straightforward and honest person. Who knows, if I had gone ahead and pushed myself to the brink, I might not be here today to say anything.

SN: *Were painkillers used to get players on the field?*
TP: No. My junior year I separated my shoulder the first couple weeks of fall practice. It was a slight separation, but enough to keep me out of five or six

games. The decision was mine whether to play or not. We went through different tests to determine how much strength I had in the shoulder. If I didn't have the strength, the consensus was to hold me out. So, I ended up missing five or six games. And I had really wanted to play my junior year. I'm pretty sure everybody else was dealt with the same way.

Of course, you do get some players who don't respond very well to pain and don't do the things necessary for rehabilitation. So, there is some disgust expressed by the coaches in those cases.

SN: *The Oklahoma football program is in many ways the major focus of people's attention in the state. How far did this extend? Was it of interest in the black community, in the northeast Oklahoma City neighborhood where you had lived, among blacks in Pauls Valley? The University of Oklahoma had been an overwhelmingly white institution for many, many years. Norman had been a "sundown community" where there were signs posted telling blacks to leave at sundown.*
TP: As a kid growing up, the black community hadn't shown very much interest in University of Oklahoma football, simply because they had no one to identify with. The student body itself was overwhelmingly white. But the black community was becoming more interested at the time I was at Oklahoma. I was the first black ever from Pauls Valley to come to Oklahoma on an athletic scholarship. A couple of white players had come, but that had been about twenty years before. After I came to the university, the black community's interest rose considerably.

Now, if you go down through there, Oklahoma football is one of the main topics of interest. In Oklahoma's urban centers, the interest was always higher, because the black community had greater access to the mass media that covered the football program. In Pauls Valley, you're not going to read the *Daily Oklahoman* [the Oklahoma City newspaper]. You're going to read basically what the local paper puts out, which is a lot less. There also had been black players from Oklahoma City playing at the University of Oklahoma, like Prentice Gautt, who was the first black in the program, back in the 1950s, and Ben Hart, both of whom came from Douglass High School there.

SN: *How many black students were at the University of Oklahoma when you were there? Do you recall any racial tensions on the campus?*
TP: We probably made up less than three percent of the student body. But it was a fairly closely knit group of people. We did a lot of things together, athletes and nonathletes. A lot of the guys were in fraternities and the girls in sororities. So, we did associate a lot together. We brought in a few speakers. Nikki Giovanni was the most militant. I think our success on the athletic

field did a lot to reduce racial tensions on the campus. I never saw any evidence of racial problems when I was a student. I just don't recall any incidents.

But again, the athletes are going to shy away from thinking about racism, because you're pretty much in a different class. You're pretty much gods. As far as your family goes, if they're suffering from discrimination, you're often able to take care of them. If something needs to be done, you can push the right button. That's really a fallacy, however. You're not dealing with society as it really is. The reality is that the color barrier is very much present.

SN: *How did you do academically at the University of Oklahoma?*
TP: I was a good student until the end of my junior year, and then I kind of lost track of where I was headed. I got some bad grades and had to really scramble to stay eligible for the next couple years. It wasn't because I couldn't do the work, but that I got caught up in the fun times at college. We liked to go out and party, and drink beer, and basically chase girls.

SN: *How close to finishing your college degree were you when you went into the NFL?*
TP: I needed about fifteen hours, plus student teaching, which was eight hours.

SN: *How many football players generally graduated at Oklahoma in that period?*
TP: The number of players was fairly small—I would think less than fifty percent. Most NFL teams, when they draft you, suggest that you move to their city. That interferes in your coming back to school the next year to finish your degree.

SN: *After your junior year, how were you regarded at your position?*
TP: As one of the top defensive backs in the country. I began to think about the NFL draft. But it never became an obsession with me. I was a cornerback but was projected to play safety. There apparently was some concern on the part of NFL teams about my size. At that time I was six foot two and 180 pounds. And to play on the inside, I obviously needed to pick up a few pounds.

For scouting purposes, most NFL teams at that time used combines. A combine was a group that sent out scouts to evaluate college players. NFL teams paid the combine to do the scouting and supply the information. As part of the scouting process, the combine would give the player a personality test. It was like an SAT test. I guess they did it to see whether you could read or write or were insane or not. Around 1977, the NFL Players' Association had it written into the collective bargaining agreement that you couldn't use them.

SN: *In what round did you expect to be drafted?*
TP: I was projected to go somewhere between the first and the fourth rounds in the NFL draft, and ended up getting picked by the Cleveland Browns in the fourth round. I was the seventh or eighth defensive back selected. I wasn't disappointed. I was the 103rd player selected overall in the draft, so I was in the top 125 people taken. That's pretty high.

SN: *How did you negotiate a contract with Cleveland? What salary did you sign for?*
TP: I signed a three-year contract. I had an agent representing me. The total package without incentives was a little over $100,000. You signed three one-year contracts, with a fourth option year. To me that was a lot of money. There were incentive clauses, providing a bonus for playing in fifty-five percent of the plays on defense, for making all-rookie, and for being in the top three on the team in tackles and in interceptions.

The day I went to Cleveland to sign the contract, there were still some differences to be worked out. Cleveland management and my agent asked me to sit in one room, while they went into another room to hammer out the differences.

SN: *How did you feel about being excluded from these direct talks?*
TP: That upset me. I felt that I had flown all this way to be a part of the negotiating process. As a youngster, you heard things about collusion between agents and team management, at the player's expense. I'm not saying it happened in my case, but I can't say that it didn't, because I wasn't there.

SN: *Did you get any advice from the Oklahoma coaching staff about what to expect in these talks?*
TP: You never got any pointers about what to expect in contract negotiations after you got drafted from the Oklahoma football program. That was kind of strange, and I think that situation continues today.

My father had died the month after I got drafted, so I never had that fatherly figure to direct and guide me. Obviously, he never spent a lot of time with us. But he might have served as a wall for me to bounce thoughts off of. The contract negotiations with Cleveland made me aware that this was a business thing and that you had to be careful.

That summer I went to Chicago to play in the College All-Star game against the defending Super Bowl champions, the Pittsburgh Steelers. Those of us selected for the College All-Star team missed the first two weeks of training camp with our NFL teams. I think the NFL owners abolished the game after 1976 because they didn't want their rookies out of camp for two weeks.

SN: *What was it like reporting to the Cleveland Browns training camp as a rookie?*
TP: I attended my first minicamp with the Cleveland Browns in May 1975. The whole team was there, not just the rookies. The Browns concentrated on charting the physical abilities of the players. We did a lot of pass drills, seven-on-seven drills, linebackers and secondary mostly, against wide receivers, tight ends, and running backs. We didn't wear pads, just helmets. They had you run little shuffles and timed you to test your agility. You ran five yards and came back to the line, then ten yards, then fifteen yards. They wanted to see how quick you were and how much balance you had. They had you do vertical jumps to see how high you could jump from a standing start. You ran three or four forty-yard dashes for time.

The biggest problem with the Cleveland Browns was Forrest Gregg.

SN: *Was this his first year as a head coach?*
TP: Yes. He brought in a mentality that just wasn't acceptable to that day's new breed of player. He had played under Vince Lombardi at Green Bay, and he brought that mentality to Cleveland. He was a strict disciplinarian. His approach was based on the notion that, to be successful, you had to be better conditioned than anybody else. Physical conditioning was the key to success.

SN: *What approach did he use to achieve that?*
TP: You had to be on the practice field a long time, doing different drills. We would do an average of seventy up-downs before practice. You run in place, jump down, push up, jump up, run in place, and repeat the process, on and on and on. And this was twice a day. It backfired on him. The players' attitude was, if we can get through these up-downs, then we've got it made through practice.

My first week at training camp, after getting there from the College All-Star game, I told our assistant coach, Richie McKay, that I felt I needed a break, because he had run us so hard. Those were the days when there weren't any mandatory water breaks. You only got water when the coach wanted you to.

SN: *It seems like it was viewed as some kind of reward extended by the coach.*
TP: Yes. It was like you were supposed to kiss his hand if he brought out Popsicles. I loved Richie. He gave me my opportunity and was the one guy who believed in me there. But when I asked him for a break, he started literally

Tony Peters with Cleveland Browns. Courtesy of the Cleveland State University Library.

foaming at the mouth. Clarence Scott and some of the older veterans came over to me and said, "Don't do that. You can't do that. This is the NFL, and you can't tell the coach what's going on." It was the same kind of response I'd gotten from Ken Pope and Clyde Powers and those guys at Oklahoma when I said I thought the coaches were overdoing it at practice. But I think I also gained a lot of respect from the older veterans, because I would at least stand up and state my feelings.

SN: *The NFL had been through a players' strike the year before, and the players still didn't have the right to get water? Was there a players' representative on the Browns who could intervene with the coaches on an issue like this?*

TP: The NFL Players' Association at that time didn't have much pull. The battle for players' rights had not even really begun. The player representatives were totally ineffective. We called those guys the "Nod Squad." They'd go in and present our views to Coach Gregg, and he would turn around and tell them the way it was going to be. And they'd just nod their heads okay.

The thing that set me apart and that allowed me to take a stand was that, while I enjoyed playing the game, I could take it or leave it. I enjoyed playing, I enjoyed the camaraderie, and I enjoyed the competition. But my ego never needed to be fed through sports. So, I wouldn't let myself get pushed beyond certain limits. Rather than blindly accept something that I didn't think made any sense, I would say, "Let's sit down and talk about this for a minute."

Later on in my rookie year, I got into a real altercation with Forrest Gregg after he insulted me during a game. Forrest had a real penchant for cursing and calling you yellow, and less of a man, and all of that stuff. We were going through a pretty dismal year; we finished with a record of 1-13. Forrest was really frustrated. In a game against the Houston Oilers, I thought I had made an exceptional play. I had been covering a receiver named Billy Parks, man to man, bump and run. We had been pushed inside our five- or ten-yard line, and Houston was trying to score. If I had wanted to take the easy way out, I would have just covered Parks man to man and not worried about the run. You've got to be concerned that if they throw a quick pass, they can get a touchdown. My job above and beyond the call of duty would have been to cover him, realize the play was a run, and come back in on the play. That's not easy to do, when you've got your back to the action. On this play, the receiver's action off the ball, or lack thereof, and my ability to sense that it was a run allowed me to fall back in and make a pretty good play, which stopped the running back for a one- or two-yard gain. I was ten yards outside the play and fell back in to make the tackle. They eventually did score, a couple of plays later.

But as I got up after bringing the runner down, and looked over at the sideline, I saw that Forrest was in his usual tirade. His face was red, and he was frowning. I couldn't hear what he was saying, but he was yelling, screaming at somebody.

SN: *Why was he doing that?*
TP: I don't know. I had made the tackle, and he had no reason to be bitching. When I came off the field, after Houston had scored, I asked him, "Hey, were you talking to me?" And he said, "Yes. You're all a bunch of yellow sons of bitches." That was one of his favorite words. So, I told him to just fuck off. It was at the end of a long season, and he was frustrated and upset with the whole defense.

SN: *So you're going to be the lightning rod for his emotions.*
TP: Yeah. I told Forrest, if he thought he could do a better job, to take my uniform and put it on and then go out there and do it. And he said, "Well, I will!" We argued on the sideline, and Clarence Scott came up and pulled me away. He said, "Tony, Tony, man, it's okay, man. Forget him. He's crazy, he's crazy. Don't ever get into an argument with him."

It's true everybody scored on us that year. Of course, when you're doing seventy up-downs before practice every day, you tend to let down during the game.

SN: *How did the team respond to Gregg's approach?*
TP: The team's response was very bad. Everybody just hated him. He was the main topic of conversation whenever we got together to play our weekly poker games.

Forrest also had some strange ways of spying on players he suspected of breaking curfew. This was a professional team that did not live in dormitory during the regular season. We lived at home, in houses and apartments. From Wednesday to Saturday, Forrest imposed an at-home curfew. We had to be home by eleven o'clock. Now, these are grown men. One day Steve Holden, a veteran, and Mack Mitchell, our number-one draft choice, walked into a team meeting. Forrest asked Mack what time he had come home the night before. And then he asked Steve the same thing. Steve replied, "Well, I was home all night, Coach." And then Mack said, "I was home by eleven, Coach." Forrest called him a "lying motherfucker." He said, "You were out at such and such a time, coming out of Steve's apartment." And he fined Mack $1000. Forrest said, "If you think I'm lying, you can ask my wife, Barbara, because she's the one who saw you." He was having his wife check the street at night to see who was out after eleven.

Another method Forrest used for determining whether you broke curfew and deserved a fine was looking at the redness of your eyes. If your eyes had any hint of redness in them, then you were doing something wrong. He didn't let you wear shades. Steve Holden would wear them on the plane, and Forrest would come by and tell him to take them off. "I need to see your eyes," he'd say. Things like that would constantly keep players on edge.

Forrest also hated guys who were not married. He thought if you weren't married, you weren't mature. Guys who were single always seemed to receive the brunt of his anger.

SN: *Would he check into other aspects of players' lives, like political affiliations or activism or beards or hair length?*
TP: No. His thing was conditioning and discipline, but he didn't object to individuality.

SN: *So even the shades and the watching when you went to bed were related to the physical conditioning issue?*
TP: It was related to the discipline side. Above all, Coach Gregg wanted to strike fear into you. He would come to our meetings and flash his Super Bowl rings. He wore probably two or three at the same time. He'd go into what it took to get those. Then he'd tell us that if you didn't do that, you'd be out selling insurance. He made it out like selling insurance was the lower dregs of society. It was like, if we didn't win this game, if we didn't do this and do that, then we wouldn't be here next year. His approach was to try to achieve a mental and a physical breakdown of the player. He wanted to completely control your every thought and your every physical response.

SN: *It sounds like he used the same approach with every player.*
TP: Coaches have to know who you've got to push and who you don't have to push. I didn't need the pep talks every day. Forrest just dogged everybody.

Forrest Gregg was our coach for three years, and he became increasingly paranoid about people in the Cleveland organization being out to get him. My third year we were at a team meeting, toward the end of the season. He was giving us a speech about somebody in the organization reporting back to the owner, Art Modell, everything that he said. He said, "Well, I know that I'm going to get fired." He was very bitter. Then he slowly walked over to a door, and opened it. As he did so, Bob Nussbaumer, our director of player personnel, fell through the door! He had been listening. So, Forrest said, "You see! I knew there was someone out here going back to tell Art everything I've been saying." He started to handle Bob like a rag doll—picked him up by his collar, shook him around a little bit, and then literally slammed him into a chair. Then he picked him off the floor. Forrest Gregg was about six foot four, 270 pounds. Nussbaumer was probably about five foot nine, 160. But you could see this body flying through the air. It was the most unreal sight I've ever seen. I was just dying. Everybody was trying to keep from laughing. But I was saying, "This guy's out of here." Clarence Scott was sitting next to me, and he was hitting me and saying, "Stop it, stop it!" But I couldn't stop laughing.

SN: *Did this incident contribute to Gregg getting fired?*
TP: Yes. Fortunately, Forrest didn't hurt Nussbaumer, but that was his last week with the Browns. He got fired. Throwing a guy through the air like that showed he had lost control. It had gotten to the point that I would always sit miles away at team meetings, just in case chairs started to fly. Forrest was into throwing chairs at the wall.

Coach Gregg was a great individual and obviously was a great player. But his coaching philosophy wasn't the proper one to take at that time. Another day and time, he might have been another Vince Lombardi. But not then.

SN: *Was it hard making the adjustment to playing defensive back in the NFL? Obviously you see a lot more passing in the NFL than in college.*
TP: I learned a considerable amount about playing defensive back during the three All-Star games in which I played after my senior year at Oklahoma. In 1974, Oklahoma was on probation, so we didn't get to go to a bowl game. When teams don't go to bowl games, a lot of their senior players will go to All-Star games. So, I was able to participate in three of them: the Senior Bowl, the East-West Shrine game, and the College All-Star game. At those games, I was able to get together with all the top-notch defensive backs. We would have skull sessions together. I learned considerably more from them than I had at Oklahoma, as far as man-to-man coverage. I was aware that that was an area in which I needed to improve.

SN: *Aren't NFL quarterbacks much more expert in picking apart a defense?*
TP: You'd be surprised. There were a few who were very exceptional, but only a few. The people who come to mind quickly are Roger Staubach, Fran Tarkenton, and Sonny Jurgensen. But there were very, very few quarterbacks like that. Most of the time, we were facing average quarterbacks.

I wasn't in awe of the talent in the NFL, although I respected it. But I felt that I was on the same level. It all depended on who was capable of making quick decisions, in two or three seconds, or getting the proper read. You might have a quarterback who was very good at reading a defense or a defensive back who was very good at disguising a defense. The mental approach was critically important.

SN: *What are the requirements of playing the defensive back positions? What physical attributes do you need, and what kind of thinking is involved?*
TP: The defensive backs are probably the best athletes on the field. They are required to run, and jump, and catch, and intercept, and tackle. But their biggest attribute is the ability to forget. If you constantly dwell on the fact that you got beaten, then that becomes a handicap to you. I don't care who you are, you're going to get beaten.

Defense involves reacting. I've got to react and beat you at what you're trying to do. So, for the most part, I'm going to be a step behind. I'm at a disadvantage from day one when the other guy lines up, because he knows exactly what he wants to try to do. It takes a lot of determination and a lot of desire to overcome that. It's like running a 400-meter dash, and you're ten yards behind from the start.

Not many receivers or running backs could switch over and play defensive back.

SN: *Why is that? A receiver has to be fast, or quick, and be able to jump for balls.*
TP: Very few receivers could run into a 200- or 300-pound guy to make a tackle. It's just not natural to stick your face into a mass of humanity going three times the speed of sound. It takes a special, unique person to play defensive back.

If you look at all of the qualifications for a defensive back and the things they're called upon to do, you can take most of them, and they can play almost any other sport. I've always felt it was the most demanding position on the field.

SN: *What are the specific requirements of playing the cornerback position?*
TP: Cornerback is probably the most demanding position of all, in pro football especially. You've got a little more speed out there, and your reaction time is cut down to hardly anything. You've got to be able to respond very quickly to whatever is happening in front of you. Anytime you're faced with forcing a

run, you've got a lot more distance to cover, and the collisions are probably going to be a lot more severe. If you're a smaller guy, you've got to be very imaginative about how you attack a sweep. Imagine four or five blockers weighing 270, 280, coming out in front of the running back. It was the most scary position that I played. But it's a challenging position. I had some advantage, because I was a little bigger than most cornerbacks, at six foot two, 195. I could get in close with the receiver and bump and run.

SN: *I imagine you really have to study receivers and their moves, along with a team's general offensive pattern, the way baseball pitchers keep books on hitters.*
TP: I studied my opponents, the pass receivers, very carefully. I kept a film projector at home, and at night I would sit and watch film and study a guy's moves. He may have some tendencies, the way he comes off the ball. He might bob his head when he wants to make you think he's going long. I would preread the offensive tackle before the snap. Most of them are big guys, and they would normally show you run or pass. Their posture would be a little bit different. If you watched them, you'd have a step up on what was going on. Now, everybody didn't study film at home. Most guys, once they got their job done during the day, that was it. But studying film was the type of thing you had to do to get an edge.

Early in my career in the NFL, you were allowed to bump and run. You could engage a guy up to fifteen yards, as long as the ball was not in the air. Most NFL routes are going to happen in a twelve- to fifteen-yard area. When the receiver took off, there'd be a six- or seven-yard cushion between us. I would stay in my backpedal and stay close to him. They'll weave as they come off the line of scrimmage, so you've got to weave, too. I would keep a distance from him that's as far as I can stick out my arm, about two feet. When he was in that two-foot area, my shot would come, my jam would come, and most of the time that would throw them off balance. We would be back there together, scrambling to get back for the ball. That was the technique I used. It allowed me to cover closely and not worry about a guy going by me. As soon as he decides he wants to go long, you extend your arm, jam him, and get into a footrace. That rule was changed in 1978 or 1979, to where you could only bump him in a five-yard area. Then you had to come off.

SN: *You were an NFL All-Pro at strong safety. What are the requirements of playing that position?*
TP: When I moved over to strong safety, I had an advantage in that I had good speed. I could isolate quite quickly on the tight end. Traditionally, the strong

safety was like a fourth linebacker. He had to be capable of making strong tackles. If he could cover, it was a definite plus, because in a lot of offensive schemes the tight end was a big weapon. John Mackey revolutionized the tight end position.

SN: *What did he introduce that was different?*
TP: He had the ability to run deep, catch a ball, and then break tackles. It's a lot easier to pass to the tight end than it is to a wide receiver. With most tight end passes, you've got a straight line shot from the quarterback because of his alignment position. If you've got a tight end who can get off the ball with speed and catch the ball, you've got a very dangerous weapon, particularly because most strong safeties can't cover.

I was always able to cover the tight end one on one. For most of my career at strong safety, which was mostly with Washington, I was isolated. I was very successful at shutting the tight end out of the game. It didn't matter who it was.

It's a different cover at strong safety than it is at cornerback. With a tight end, you have to slow yourself down just a little bit more and be a little bit more patient. You can back out of there too far, and guys can eat you up all day long in front of you, with eight- and ten-yard passes. So, I just pretty much stayed in his face, and I was strong enough to withstand the pushing and shoving that occurred. Tight ends are notorious for pushing and shoving. They're big, strong guys.

In playing strong safety, the guy you need to key on is the tight end. You can't be caught looking at the backfield or looking at the quarterback, because the guy who's going to tell you what's going on is the tight end. If he blocks down, the play is outside. If he turns out, the play is inside. If he releases off the ball, ninety percent of the time, it's a pass.

SN: *So, the strong safety focuses on the tight end himself. What do you do at cornerback?*
TP: As a cornerback, it's a little different. There you first preread the tackle. He'll tell you whether it's going to be a pass or a run.

At the same time, quarterbacks are keying on certain players on the defense. If you're a quarterback, and you look out while you're preparing to get up underneath the center, and you see the cornerback locking in on this receiver out there, you're going to be thinking, "Why, he's got man-to-man coverage!" It depends on the offensive scheme. Some quarterbacks will look at the free safety to determine whether he's going to the center of the field, to see whether it's a zone defense or man to man. He may look at other things.

As a defensive back, you try to give the quarterback false reads. A cornerback might be standing straight up before the ball is snapped to make the quarterback think, "Hey, he's playing zone!" Then he needs to figure out what kind of zone it is. There's a lot of thinking involved, and there were only a few quarterbacks who were great at being able to make those decisions.

Whether I was playing man or zone at strong safety, I would line up in the same position, the same way, every time. So, the quarterback could not get a preread on me. If I was playing man to man, that would make it difficult, because I would be lining up outside. I then had to move after the snap from one to two yards outside to one yard inside.

SN: *What are the requirements of playing the free safety position?*
TP: Free safety, which I also played, is a very demanding position. You've got to have a tough guy who has tremendous range across the field. He needs to be tough, because you get a lot of serious collisions at that position. He has to have the ability to read the quarterback's eyes. You also have to be able to tackle. In most defensive schemes, the free safety is the leading tackler on the team. He'll outtackle the middle linebacker. Like the middle linebacker, he's in the center of the field. He has a perfect picture of what's going on, with no obstructions. So, a lot of times, he should be able to make a play all over the field. He's got to have good speed to cover the ground. If you're a little bit taller, it helps, because you can see over everything.

In most of the defensive schemes I played in, with the Cleveland Browns and later with the Washington Redskins, I was always the signal caller, whether I was at cornerback or safety. We'd have to make adjustments, depending upon the offensive formation that was presented before us. In Cleveland, even as a rookie and a second-year man, I found myself making a lot of those play calls for the secondary and the linebackers.

SN: *How come you became the signal caller? It's interesting that they'd entrust that to a rookie.*
TP: I ended up doing that largely because I had more confidence than the others. Nothing against the guys I played with, but a lot of times it came down to confidence.

When I was a rookie and second-year man at Cleveland, we'd have to do take-home tests, and guys would always be looking to see what I put down. They'd give us a five- or six-page formation sheet and ask us what adjustments should be made. We'd have to turn them in at practice the next day.

Every morning as I walked in, there would be five or six guys around my locker trying to see what I had put down.

One of the things I always enjoyed being able to do was knowing what everybody on a particular defense had to do on a particular play. I tried to know what everybody did—the linebackers, the secondary positions, the linemen—what their responsibilities were. That gave me an overall picture of what was going on. It's pretty easy when you get a playbook two and a half inches thick to just go through it and know exactly what you have to do. But it's not as easy to know what everybody does, because then you have to study every position. That's a lot of work. But I felt more comfortable knowing where my help was and where the weaknesses were.

SN: *When you joined the Washington Redskins, a much better team that went to the Super Bowl, I assume you weren't looking at the secondary and seeing those blank looks.*
TP: Well, you did, but not from the safety position. When I moved to the Redskins, I got some help in making the calls from Mark Murphy, the free safety. He had gone to Colgate and was a very, very intelligent guy. He and I were the safeties, and it worked out real well, because we knew what we were doing. In Washington, with Murph and myself, I can't ever remember blowing a call. But even at Washington, you'd always see that undecided look in the corners, because they were saying, "What'll I do?"

SN: *How did you make the signals?*
TP: We always signaled our calls out loud, by yelling them. We had code names, like Wheatstick, Zorro, Key, that were all names for a defense.

SN: *Don't you have to change the signals during a game, because the offense gets wise? In baseball, there's a long tradition of stealing signs.*
TP: No, because the offense is not listening. They had other things to worry about. First of all, they're worrying about the snap count. They were looking to see where you were lined up at and listening to the quarterback, because he could change the play on them.

SN: *Which pass receiver was the toughest to cover?*
TP: I'd have to name Paul Warfield. There were some great players in the league. But if I had to put together a guy who had size, strength, speed, the ability to run exceptional routes, basically the total package as a wide receiver, it would be Warfield.

SN: *How do NFL teams evaluate player performance?*
TP: NFL players get graded for each game. During the game, assistant coaches mark down the play call and the adjustment made. On Monday, after the game, you come in to watch the game films. It used to be Tuesday, but they changed it to Monday. That way, if players had been injured, they can get it reported and you can get treatment. The coaches would probably stay up the night before evaluating the game film. And then the players came in and listen to the coaches' comments. If you received too many negative comments about your play, they'd set up a conference with you to find out why you were making so many mistakes.

The whole team would watch the films of the special teams. Special teams is a job that requires quite a bit of sacrifice. During practice all week, they're a skeleton team, a scout team. They're the guys the starters beat up. During most of the game, those guys just sit on the bench. It's kamikaze, basically. So, they try to build those guys up.

In Washington, there were bonuses offered to the guys on the special teams for big hits that they made during the game. They would get $100 or $200, just some extra pocket money. Local merchants would donate items like television sets and golf clubs. The film session was the time to distribute the goodies. A "KO" called for a bonus. A KO was when you hit a guy during a game, and really KOed him. "Pancake him," they called it. Send him down on his back. They hit him and throw him on his back.

There were also bonuses that were given to the starting players. If you made an interception, you might get $100. If a wide receiver got 100 yards, he'd get $100 or a Western belt buckle or cowboy boots. It was always something arranged through the community to keep morale high.

SN: *So the whole team would first look at the special teams films. Then you break down into what, offense and defense?*
TP: Even more individual units—defensive backs, linebackers, and so forth. We'd look at the entire game. We'd look at each play we ran and rerun it. You'd evaluate yourself and see whether or not you'd given up any tendencies that would give an opponent an edge. After that, the game's pretty much history. You may watch it again if you play a team in your conference twice a year. Then we'd take the three or four most recent games of an upcoming opponent and break them down.

To prepare for an opponent, the entire defense would meet. And you'd get a sheet listing all their players at the different positions, giving their names and weights. From there, we'd go through our game plan. We'd look at the ten or fifteen defenses that we were considering using against particular formations. If we had somebody who had played on the opposing team recently, then he might give a quick scouting report on what to expect. Then we'd break up into our individual units. The defensive backs would break down our opponent's wide receivers and tight ends. At the same time, the defensive linemen would be watching end zone films, and watching line formations, and talking about the various moves or techniques they were going to use on the offensive linemen they'd be facing.

SN: *What did a week's schedule for a player look like?*
TP: When I was at Washington, my schedule for the rest of the week began with weight lifting in the morning. It was mandatory there that you lift, although it wasn't at Cleveland. I usually came in at eight thirty in the morning and did that, and then at nine or nine thirty practiced on special teams. Then the regular team meeting started at about ten o'clock. Coach Gibbs would say a couple things, and then we'd break up and meet with our individual groups until eleven or eleven fifteen, have lunch, meet for an hour or so after that, and then go on to the practice field until three thirty or four o'clock. Six or seven hours constituted a day, with a six-day week. We got one day off.

SN: *How much dirty play went on in the NFL?*
TP: I've never been part of a program that intentionally set out to go beyond the rules on the playing field, poking opponents in the eyes or deliberately trying to injure them. Sometimes when there's a tense rivalry involved, like the Dallas Cowboys and the Washington Redskins, there may be people who have been constantly a thorn in your side—like Roger Staubach or Tony Dorsett, whom you'd like to disable, so that they don't have the opportunity to make the big play at the end of the game. In cases like that, you might put extra energy into trying to deliver a blow. But I never intentionally set out to do anything that would be considered beyond the rules.

SN: *How much verbal exchange, or insult, goes on between pass receivers and defensive backs?*
TP: I played the game according to my opponent. If he decided to be verbally abusive, then I would be verbally abusive.

Verbal abuse is used to intimidate, and there are certain guys who do it more than others. Guys like Lynn Swann wouldn't talk much. But Kellen Winslow would just want to talk about anything and everything under the sun. He'd talk about your mother and your father, to throw you off emotionally. It's like, "You sorry son of a bitch, I'm going to kick your ass."

Playing defensive back, especially cornerback, is a very delicate thing. If you find yourself having doubts at that position, then you can be in for a very long day. It's a position where you can't afford to let people intimidate you. If a wide receiver is able to do that, then they're going to have a great time.

SN: *How about use of hands by receivers?*
TP: Wide receivers are not supposed to use their hands to gain an advantage by pushing, shoving, or grabbing. But they do it all the time. As a defensive back, if you're frustrated by that, then you're going to get beaten. You can complain to the referee, and it's not going to get taken care of.

SN: *So how do you compensate?*
TP: Well, when they push, you grab. You maintain your ground. You don't give up your position, your space on the field. You have to be as clever as they are clever. You can't survive without that. It's not peaches and cream on the field.

You can't be so naive as to think that people are going to play by all the rules. If you are that naive, you won't last long. If you play strictly by the rules, you're going to get beat most of the time.

If you wanted to play where you grabbed facemasks, then we grabbed facemasks. Or we talked about each other's mother or origin of birth.

I was once covering Lynn Swann during the time the Pittsburgh Steelers were headed for Super Bowls and were known as a pretty physical team. I don't think they were a dirty team. They just did whatever it took to win games. Maybe they went a little beyond the rules. I was covering Swann on a deep run-in. Pittsburgh used to do a lot of deep run-ins, fifteen yards and then inside, across the field. We played a lot of man to man. On this particular play, I had him covered pretty well. As we moved inside, he realized I had him covered. His only way of defeating me was to make something happen. So, he reached out and grabbed me by the facemask, and pulled it down, and broke to the inside and made the catch.

Any time when Stallworth or Swann were inside your twenty-yard line, as a defensive back you'd have to be ready for them to use their hands to push off. Now, the defensive player is supposed to be the only guy who can use his hands and then only to avoid a guy. They've extended the rule somewhat to allow offensive linemen and receivers to extend their hands to block, but they're not supposed to get outside their shoulder pads. Of course, that rule is broken all the time. The hands are always outside the shoulder pads, and they're always grabbing. The referees never see that. On pass plays, the receivers tend to extend their arms and push off in order to gain an advantage, and they're not supposed to do that. A defensive back is not allowed to put his hands on the receiver after he's covered five yards, and the same goes for him. But it's usually the wide receiver who initiates the contact, if the defensive back has very close coverage on him. If you watch a game very closely, you'll see it's done all the time. It does a defensive back no good to push a receiver off when he's getting ready to make a break, because it causes separation, and separation is not what you want. It's to a defensive back's advantage to be as close as possible to a receiver before he makes his break.

So in the NFL, it's basically like the survival of the fittest. You've got to adjust your game according to your opponent as you play. I remember some serious battles between our offensive linemen at Cleveland and Dwight White and Greenwood and Joe Greene of the Steelers during their heyday. Greene and those guys would literally stomp or kick or step on our offensive linemen's hands. But I'm not sure if that wasn't retaliation against some of the tactics that were being used by our offensive linemen.

SN: *Like what?*
TP: Forrest Gregg was a competitor, and he didn't care what it took for you to beat up another guy. He came out of the older school with Lombardi, and they did a lot of weird stuff. Forrest didn't teach leg-whipping, I don't believe, but he didn't care how you got it done.

SN: *Could you define "leg-whipping"?*
TP: If you're beat as an offensive lineman, then your last resort is to swing your leg around to trip a guy or hit a guy in the kneecap, and that's some brutal stuff. That's what they call "leg-whipping." I'm sure our guys did a lot of that, and did a lot of holding, and did a lot of trash talking. I'm sure they'd rather do it for two hours against Mean Joe Greene than face Forrest Gregg for the next week.

SN: *What happens when a penalty flag gets thrown on an offensive lineman for leg-whipping? Is the head coach going to take the blame for it?*
TP: Of course not. (Laughs). It's the stupid player's fault.

I know our offensive linemen used to have some silicone spray they put on their jerseys, so that when the defensive linemen tried to make their moves to rush the passer, they would be more difficult to grab. The jerseys would be slick. You'd see them all the time spraying down before the game. That was a little beyond the rules.

You can only depend upon yourself to correct wrongs done to you on the field. If you're violated, it does no good to complain to the referee, because then they call you a crybaby. The referees are out there on a macho trip, too. They're on an ego trip about what they're doing, as opposed to looking out for things that may lead to injuries.

SN: *How would you compare the roughness of play in the NFL with college football?*
TP: Things are rougher in the NFL because the players are better. At Oklahoma, when we won the national championship and went undefeated for a couple years, we were a very physical team. We knocked a lot of players out. You don't go into it to knock people out, at least I never did. But if I had an opportunity to deliver a blow, then I delivered a blow. My philosophy was, if I had an opportunity to hit a guy, I wanted to hit him as hard as possible, because I wanted to discourage him from coming into an area again. That makes my job easier. I've hit guys right in the head. In junior college, I broke a guy's jaw in three places with a forearm blow. I wasn't trying to hit him in the jaw.

SN: *How much did you use the forearm as a defensive back?*
TP: I always came with my forearm when I had an open shot. Sometimes I'd just lead in with my shoulder pads, but whenever I had the opportunity to deliver a good hit, most of the time the forearm would come. It was like a sixth sense jab to me. I tried to use the principles of boxing and karate in my approach to the game. I would try to delay the hit until I was six to eight inches away from the individual. That way I would get the entire coil effect. The vibration is at its maximum. It's like as a boxer, you try to move in and maneuver and dodge a blow, until you can get to the point where you can deliver the blow with your arm slightly flexed. As it extends, it's like that fist is going through that object, so it's going through and out the other side. As a boxer, if you're totally extended on your blow, there's nothing there. You have to make the contact at, say, a forty-five-degree angle, and then you get the maximum results. I never would come at a guy's head. But his head might get in the way sometimes. I remember a playoff game against the Minnesota Vikings in 1982 where we pretty much decapitated a couple of receivers.

SN: *Decapitated?*
TP: They were high-flying acts where you catch a guy going up for a ball, and you would hit him with a forearm.

SN: *What happened when Jack Tatum paralyzed Darryl Stingley?*
TP: I think it was an accident. I don't think Tatum set out to be disrespectful of Darryl or wide receivers.

SN: *Was Tatum considered a dirty player before he hit Stingley and disabled him?*
TP: No, I don't think so.

SN: *What about calling his book* They Call Me Assassin *and not showing remorse?*
TP: I think he just saw an opportunity to cash in on some notoriety. As a defensive back, you can't afford to be intimidated. If you worry about what's going to happen when you hit somebody and have that remorse that people are looking for, then you may as well give it up. You can't afford to do that. I know it sounds callous. But if you dwell on those things, you're distracted. And as a player, you can't afford to get distracted.

SN: *You were injured more than once when you played at Cleveland. How did the team handle that situation? Were painkillers prescribed?*
TP: My first introduction to cortisone came in my rookie year with the Browns. I had fallen on practice Astroturf at Baldwin-Wallace College, in Berea, Ohio, where we trained, and had slightly separated my shoulder. The Cleveland Browns played their regular season home games on grass, but we practiced on artificial turf, because management didn't want to tear up the grass on the regular field early in the year. When I hurt the shoulder, I was in serious, serious pain; I couldn't even shift my car. At Cleveland Clinic, they injected me with cortisone. If you hit the right spot with cortisone, it completely eliminates the pain. In a matter of thirty seconds, there was no more pain. I could do almost anything I wanted to with my shoulder and arm. And that completely scared me. I had never seen anything respond so quickly. I knew that that was the last injection I would ever take. I made a conscious decision not to go through the shot process anymore. But everything was fine with the shoulder from then on.

My second year with Cleveland, I hurt my wrist in the second or third game of the season and ended up playing the rest of the season with the injury. I was on the kickoff team, and Henry Lawrence, a big offensive tackle with the Raiders, pushed me after I got by him, and my foot got caught in the turf, and I stumbled and fell on my wrist. I ruptured some ligaments. Usually they X-ray these things after the game, but I don't think they did that time. At halftime, they diagnosed it as a sprain, and they just taped it up. I played the rest of the season with it taped up.

SN: *It bothered you the whole season?*
TP: Oh, absolutely! It was the most excruciating pain I've ever experienced. You have five metatarsal bones that encompass your hand. They're held together by ligaments. I learned later that the ligament was totally ruptured. So, what happens when you're a defensive back jamming somebody on the line of scrimmage, and these bones start to move around, which they do all the time? It's pretty painful!

The team physician had diagnosed it as a severe sprain, even though it continued to hurt all season. Today they'd be more likely to send a player to a specialist. But a lot of these team physicians are so caught up in working for an NFL team, with all that prestige, that they don't look as deeply into things as they should.

SN: *How was the injury treated, besides wrapping it up?*
TP: Icing was the main treatment he prescribed, to get the swelling down, and then ultrasound, which was supposed to increase your blood circulation. You have to be careful, because ultrasound and heat increase the blood flow, and then you can get swelling.

When I got back home to Oklahoma that year, I went to Dr. O'Donoghue, the University of Oklahoma football team physician, and he sent me to a hand specialist, who diagnosed it in five minutes.

SN: *At the end of the season it gets diagnosed in five minutes, and the Browns' physician couldn't do that?*
TP: Right. He said it was an injury that was often misdiagnosed. It turned out to be a ruptured navicular ligament. They had to go in and open it up.

So I had surgery, and they drilled holes in the bones, and tied them together with a tendon. Basically the ligaments were repaired, and a pin was placed in the bones to keep them immobile for six or seven weeks. I wore a cast for eight weeks. From that point, it was just a matter of trying to get the strength back in it. I was able to play the next year.

SN: *How did Cleveland management respond to the specialist's diagnosis?*
TP: Cleveland management wanted me to have the surgery done at the Cleveland Clinic, where our team physician worked. But I said, "You guys couldn't find the problem from the start, so I wouldn't feel comfortable. I'll get it done here, in Oklahoma City." They said, "Fine, just send us the bill," which I did. The surgery was successful, and now I just have the scar.

My fourth year with Cleveland, I suffered another painful injury, turf toe, during a preseason game with the Buffalo Bills.

SN: *What is "turf toe"? Is it called that because it was associated with artificial turf?*
TP: Turf toe is like a dislocated finger, except that it's in the toe. It occurred because of the advent of artificial turf. A guy fell on the back of my foot and dislodged three toes—the big toe, and the second and third toes. An injury like that, on something so vital as the feet, can be the kiss of death.

SN: *Did it hurt all the time?*
TP: Yeah, all the time, pretty much twenty-four hours a day. But I played through the pain, limping the entire year. The turf toe affected my ability to maneuver at close quarters. The team trainer inserted a plastic plate in the bottom of my shoe, so that I wouldn't bend my foot. That way I would run straight-footedly, not on the injured toes. We didn't use any pain-killing drugs on it, just ultrasonic treatments every day.

SN: *The Browns traded you to the Redskins after four years. Did you insist on the trade?*
TP: I ended up leaving Cleveland in large part because of conflicts that were building up between me and team management. The way the wrist injury was handled was just one of several conflicts. After my third year, Forrest Gregg was fired as head coach and replaced by Sam Rutigliano.

I had personality conflicts with the last two defensive backs coaches. I'd always been the type of player who was somewhat introverted. I prepared myself for the game mentally more than most guys. I wasn't a rah-rah type person. I tried to lead on the field. A lot of coaches wanted to see some outward emotion expressed, and I was never that type of person. We had discussions about that.

Two years in a row, I had played with excruciating pain. I felt that I had proven my toughness. But Chuck Weber, the defensive backs coach, called me over the summer and told me they were going to move Clarence Scott over from cornerback to strong safety, and that I was going to have to compete with him for the job. That was the position that I had been playing. Clarence and I were very good friends. He was getting up in age, and I felt that, based on what I had done for the Browns, it should have been my job for Clarence to take. But Weber said that we were going to start off even in training camp and that the best man would take the job.

I had also been dissatisfied with the last contract I had signed with Cleveland. I felt I had been forced into signing it because I had turf toe. I knew that was a pretty serious injury. So, I felt that I had to go ahead and sign. Whenever you're injured and go in to negotiate a contract, team management always emphasizes the negative. "Well, you were hurt. Where's the guarantee that you're not going to be hurt again?" So, I signed a contract I wasn't happy with.

I worked out very hard that summer. And when I got to training camp I practiced the first day as hard as I ever had in my life, just to show them that I was completely healthy. And that evening I went and told them that I was leaving. I wasn't interested in playing for Cleveland any longer. I felt the lack of respect that Cleveland gave to its players. There was no communication there. I didn't want to be part of an organization that was so alienated from the players. There was a lot of selfishness in the organization, and it trickled down from the top. I had played the four years required to qualify for an NFL pension, and I thought that was sufficient.

SN: *Did you know what you would do if you left football?*
TP: Luckily, I ran across some people in Oklahoma who offered me a position working with New York Life Insurance, working in marketing, with a salary equivalent to what I had been making in the NFL. I was very close to accepting that offer.

During the three or four weeks after I left training camp, I received phone calls from my agent and from the Browns' general manager. My business relationship with my agent had by that time pretty much died out, and I only had contact with him because I still had some investments through his law firm in Houston. But in desperation to get me to return to Cleveland, the general manager had called him, and he called me. He asked me what was going on, and I told him I wasn't interested in going back to Cleveland. He replied that, "Well, careers aren't that long, and you should take advantage of their offer." I responded that I just wasn't interested in doing that. That was it, and he hung up.

The next phone call I got was from the general manager, who told me that if I didn't want to come back to the Browns, I would never play in the NFL again. And I said, "Well, if it works out that way, then so be it." He threatened that I would be blackballed from the league.

Another week or so passed, and I received calls from several NFL teams, including Atlanta, Dallas, Washington, and Minnesota.

SN: *Had they heard you were disenchanted? Had Cleveland contacted them?*
TP: I'm not sure. I talked to a guy from Minnesota on the phone and told him that I wasn't tired of playing, I was just fed up with the Cleveland situation. But when I told him that I would not play under the same contractual agreement I had with Cleveland, he said Minnesota wasn't interested.

The policy in the NFL was that teams did not renegotiate contracts. If you were under contract with one team, and that team traded you, then that contract moved with you. In no other business in the world did it happen that way. That was the effect of the NFL's monopoly position. Of course, rules could be bent. There was, for example, another unwritten rule in the NFL that veterans didn't get signing bonuses. But I got a signing bonus when I signed my last contract with Cleveland, as a veteran. So, I knew that it was possible to get a contract renegotiated.

I talked to Mike Ullman of the Washington Redskins and told him that I would be interested in coming back to play, but only if my contract were renegotiated. Teams like Washington, Dallas, and Minnesota always impressed me, as far as their organization, their ability to win, and always being in the playoffs. Having come from an institution like the University of Oklahoma, where we didn't lose a game during my two years there, those things impressed me. So, it was exciting to have those teams show interest in me. But I had to feel comfortable about the kind of money I would get.

I came to a basic understanding with Mike Ullman about what I would sign for, before he consummated a trade with Cleveland. I wanted six figures, which I had never gotten. I felt I was one of the top defensive backs in the NFL throughout my career. But I was only making $63,000 a year at Cleveland. Within a couple of days, they made the trade, and I flew to Atlanta to meet the Redskins. Then I went on to Washington.

SN: *What was it like adjusting to a new NFL team, the Washington Redskins?*
TP: I joined the Redskins at Redskin Park after they had broken training camp at Carlisle, Pennsylvania, and Richie Petitbon, the defensive coordinator, welcomed me to the team. He gave me a playbook, and told me to look through it, and that at the next day's practice he would give me a couple of plays to do, and that would be it. Richie was a great coach to work for, but for me preparation was always the key. I was always that way. I studied the book the entire night.

Incredibly, the next day, Richie sent me through every defense they had. It wasn't so much a problem of the defenses being different. It was terminology and associating the terminology with the defense. Everybody plays basically the same defense. But the terminology is different. We went through every play in that playbook, thirteen, fifteen defenses. But I didn't blow a play. I did not blow a play the next day in practice. I felt good that I had studied that stuff and felt confident and comfortable after that first day.

But I was bothered that no one mentioned the contract. So, I went to see Bobby Beathard, the general manager. I told him what was on my mind, and what I had discussed with his representative on the phone. And he said, "Well, whom did you speak with?" I said Mike Ullman. Beathard said that Mike had been wrong, because the Redskins didn't renegotiate contracts. I replied, "Well, you guys ought to communicate a little better than that, because had I known all this, you could have saved your time and my time and not brought me here." And I told him to get his secretary, and have her make reservations for me, because I was going home and forgetting about the Redskins. But Bobby said, "Well, that's like putting a gun to my head, if you're not going to practice until I can get you some answers." It was like he could not make the final decision. It's possible that he needed to confer with Edward Bennett Williams and Jack Kent Cooke, the owners.

We ended up signing a two-year contract extension, which, with some bonus money, put me up to the numbers I wanted. They basically maintained the Cleveland contract, adding some bonus money. That allowed them to save face.

SN: *How did your first year with the Redskins turn out?*
TP: I had a great experience there. We had tremendous success, finishing at 10-6. I didn't start a lot, playing behind Kenny Houston at strong safety, but I ended up the leading tackler in the secondary that year. I played four different positions, both corners and linebacker in our nickel-and-dime packages. I ended up logging more time in games than Kenny, who made All-Pro that year.

SN: *Was there any tension between you and Kenny Houston, in that you also played his position? He was fairly well along in his career at that time. He was headed to the Hall of Fame, of course.*
TP: No, certainly no tension on my part. I learned a tremendous amount from Kenny and from Joe Lavender and Art Harris. I was always that way, absorbing knowledge from watching guys and trying to incorporate their game into my game. The competition was strong between us. But I thought it was good for him, and it was good for me. Kenny at that stage of his career didn't do a great, exceptional job. He'd lost some speed, he'd lost some quickness. He was getting to the point where he was having a little difficulty getting where he was supposed to be. But he still did a very credible job. He was still very consistent. And that was fine. You can get by with being consistent. You don't have to be great, great all the time. He was accorded a lot of respect

around the league. Maybe it would have been better to bring him in periodically, but, hey, they owed it to him. The guy had played *great* for years.

SN: *How would you compare the mood and atmosphere on the Redskins with the Browns?*
TP: It was totally different. One thing that really surprised me when I joined the Redskins my first day of practice, Joe Theismann [the quarterback] walked up to me, introduced himself, and asked, "Do you have a car?" I didn't because I had just arrived there. And he gave me the key to a Mustang, a dealer car he had. He was working for a car dealership there. And he said, "Drive this for a couple days." It was like, "Wow, I don't know this guy, I never met this guy, and he's doing this for me!" Joe and I got along great throughout our careers. My kids went to his kids' birthday parties later on. The difference in mood and atmosphere between Washington and Cleveland was like night and day.

SN: *How were defensive signals called in the secondary on the Redskins?*
TP: Mark Murphy and I would make the calls from the safety positions. Lemar Parrish, who played cornerback, was always funny. He was a very hyper guy, and he'd get nervous. You'd tell him the call, and he'd go, "What? What? What? What?" Lemar was one of the greatest cornerbacks ever, and he played thirteen years in the NFL. He never lost his speed. But he was not a big guy at knowing everything. Mark Murphy and I were a little more into that part of the game. We'd have to calm Lemar down and tell him the defense or where to go.

You can play at cornerback without knowing what's happening all around you, especially since we played a lot of man to man. It was just a matter of whether the cornerback would take away the inside or take away the outside. If a certain flow of the defense frees the safety up, he may tell the cornerback that he may be getting some help. We had special signals, like a "cut" call, where we'd just yell, "Cut, cut, cut." That meant that I was telling the cornerback that I was inside and that he could move outside at that point. That would happen on the run.

The defensive backs at Washington forged a very close bond. For three or four years, we were the best secondary in the league. What was neat for me was to be surrounded by a Kenny Houston, a Lemar Parrish, a Joe Lavender. Those guys had been in the league seven, eight, nine years and were all All-Pros. So, I could learn a lot. We taught each other. That's how a team gets better and better.

SN: *The Washington Redskins went to the Super Bowl in January 1983 against the Miami Dolphins. This was also a year when the Players' Association went on strike and the season was shortened somewhat. What was it like going out on strike that year? How was the strike conducted?*

T P: The strike came after the second game of the season, when we were 2-0. All the teams had meetings, and communicated with each other, and discussed the possibility of striking. Mark Murphy was our player representative, and he would inform us of what the other teams were doing. The player representatives from all the teams met once or twice a week, through conference calls or whatever, and then let us know what management's position was and what they thought we needed to do. Each team was to vote as a team on whether to strike, and then we would send our vote to the headquarters of the NFL Players' Association in Washington, D.C.

S N: *What issues did the players strike over?*

T P: We were concerned about pensions and free agency—whether or not a team had to be compensated for a player who became a free agent, and the number of players on a team. There was controversy over what the owners' contribution to the player pension plan would be. The owners had been holding back funds on their contribution. We were also interested in getting severance pay.

S N: *Did the Redskins team remain united during the strike, or were there divisions?*

T P: Salaries were pretty far apart, and some of the guys with the higher salaries didn't particularly care for striking. I had a slight encounter with Dave Butz, who wasn't interested in striking. He was making a lot of money, so he wasn't interested in a lot of the guys who were making less. I was making good money at the time, but I knew there were a lot of guys who weren't. And there were guys, like Joe Theismann, who were making a lot of money but still favored a strike.

Our team's vote to strike was nearly unanimous. After we decided to walk out, we tried to keep the guys together by holding our own workouts, at a high school in Reston, Virginia. That way we could stay focused for any resumption of play.

S N: *How did the Redskins coaches react to the strike?*

T P: Our coaches didn't get into any heated exchanges with us, but they tried to discourage us from taking the position we did. The coaches are part of management. Coach Gibbs wanted to continue on with the season. But the decision was up to us. We told the coaches that we were going to stage some informal practices, and they were pleased about that.

SN: *Were the informal practices that the players set up as rigorous as regular practices?*
TP: Oh, obviously not, because you're in control of it. (Laughs) But we worked pretty hard. We had some guys who were real workaholics, like Art Monk, who was a real leader as far as working out. Joe Theismann was a hard worker. He's a very competitive individual. We kept the practices going, and a lot of guys worked real hard to stay in top condition.

In the meantime, we asked the NFL Players' Association to conduct some games between the striking teams to raise money for the strike fund.

SN: *What kind of strike fund did you have?*
TP: We didn't have any strike fund at all.

SN: *So you live on your savings, plus what you can earn from exhibition games?*
TP: Right. A lot of guys were upset because they weren't making any money. We arranged one against the Giants in Washington, which didn't go off all that great. About 20,000 people showed up. We set up another game in Toronto two weeks later, but the agreement was signed and we canceled it.

SN: *Did the team meet regularly to discuss how the strike was going?*
TP: We had team meetings once or twice a week during the strike, maybe more than that. There was never anyone even contemplating breaking the strike.

The Redskins were one of the strongest union teams when I was there, in part because of our close proximity to the Players' Association headquarters. We had some very outspoken individuals on the team. Since George Allen was head coach, the Redskins had been a veteran team. Those guys had been through the wars, and they had learned to prepare themselves for life after football. It was important to them to have a strong pension.

SN: *I take it it's a lot different today on the Redskins.*
TP: Yes. They've lost that understanding. It's pretty much a selfish thing for them now, just looking out for yourself as opposed to the group.

SN: *Did the owners consider bringing in strikebreakers to replace you?*
TP: The owners were not in a position to bring in strikebreakers, because we caught them by surprise in the way we staged the strike. Had we struck during

the preseason, then they would have time to recruit replacements. But we waited until we were a couple games into the season. Even if they had tried it, I don't think they would have been very successful. The fans come to see good, professional entertainment. They don't want to see scabs out there fumbling and bumbling around.

The strike was settled after six or seven weeks, and the agreement increased the owners' contribution to our retirement benefits and arranged for severance pay for retirement.

SN: *The Redskins went to the Super Bowl that year. What was that experience like?*
TP: We went 8-1 that season, losing only to the Dallas Cowboys, and went into the playoffs. We had the best record, so we got the home field advantage throughout the playoffs. That's a significant advantage, especially at RFK Stadium. There was a mystique that went with RFK. It's a pretty small stadium, seating about 55,000 people, and the spectators are real close to the field. They've got a section of the stands there that seems to rock, or jump up and down, or move when people get excited. It can be pretty intimidating for a visiting team. We played the Detroit Lions first, with Billy Sims and some other outstanding players, and beat them. And then we beat Bud Grant's Minnesota Vikings. We had an advantage, because we played on grass, and both of them played in domes on Astroturf.

We had some things that really pulled the team together. We had the "Fun Bunch." They were the guys who started the first celebrations in the end zone. That began in 1982. The Fun Bunch included Rick Walker, Charlie Brown, Alvin Garrett, and a couple of other guys. It was four or five guys who would get together in the end zone when one of them scored. They would all run out and do the bugaloo and high-five each other. It was pretty wild.

SN: *Did the Fun Bunch consist of all black players?*
TP: Yes.

SN: *Why do you think blacks were more drawn to that style?*
TP: As a black person, you go through life constantly faced with insurmountable odds, so that any type of victory brings great emotion and elation. For a group that has been oppressed for so long, any victory seems like it's cause for celebration. I remember having some outbursts of jubilation, but nothing that was planned or would have me stand out. I didn't need that for my ego.

Our team really started to form some singular identities. We had the Hogs, our offensive linemen, and we had "The Diesel," John Riggins. John played great all year. Whenever we needed that first down, some kind of way the Hogs and John Riggins would get it. The Hogs were real close. They were friends off the field. Joe Theismann, Curtis Jordan, Russ Grimm, Jeff Bostic, and myself all got together every week to play poker at each other's houses.

SN: *What was it like playing the Dallas Cowboys for the NFC championship?*
TP: They were the only team that had defeated us that season. They were our traditional rival, and they had a great team, with Danny White at quarterback, Tony Dorsett, Tony Hill, and Randy White. We had only played them once during the season, because of the strike. I'm sure that they came in with a lot of confidence. But we were looking for revenge.

Our rivalry with Dallas was somewhat exaggerated by the press. There had been conflict when George Allen had coached Washington. Allen was very paranoid, and he always felt that Dallas had spies at his practices and helicopters flying overhead taking infrared shots. And you had Diron Talbert in those days, creating controversy by calling Tony Dorsett "bug eyes." But the rivalry didn't get to the point that the players hated each other, like the fans did. The players had mutual respect for one another.

SN: *Do you get more nervous playing in a big game like that?*
TP: No, I tried to make every game the same and didn't prepare any differently. I always played a little better against Dallas. Being from Oklahoma and having grown up with Dallas fans, there was always some extra incentive for me. I knew my family would be watching.

SN: *How about the Redskins coaches? Were they nervous?*
TP: Of course, the coaches were nervous. Coaches are always nervous.

It turned out to be a good game. We played 'em hard, we hit 'em hard, and we ended up winning 31-17. We beat them pretty bad.

SN: *How did the Redskins prepare for the Super Bowl against the Miami Dolphins? Does it differ from other games in how you prepare for it?*
TP: We tried to prepare in the same way that we had for our previous games. Most athletes and coaches have some degree of superstition. You feel that if you change something, it puts you off balance. The one thing that was different about that year was that the strike had shortened the season, and then the playoffs had run over beyond the usual time, into January. So, they shortened

the time between the conference championships and the Super Bowl to one week. Normally, you had two weeks to prepare for the Super Bowl. We felt it was an advantage for us, because we had been rolling along pretty well.

SN: *What kind of team did the Dolphins have? How would you compare them with Dallas?*
TP: The Dolphins at that time were playing pretty well. They had the Killer Bees and the Blues Brothers, the Blackwood brothers, in the secondary. Their weakest position was probably quarterback, with David Woodley. They had a good tight end, and two capable wide receivers, and some good running backs. We thought that they were pretty much on a par with Dallas, except maybe at quarterback. Danny White was maybe a little better quarterback than David Woodley.

SN: *The Dolphins were favored to win, weren't they? Did that upset you?*
TP: They were, but that didn't upset us. That was the position that we wanted to be in. We were underdogs most of the year in most of the games. We reveled in being underdogs.

SN: *Can you describe the game itself?*
TP: We fell behind early in the Super Bowl. We had a special teams break-down, and they scored on a long kickoff return. And they hit us with a seventy-six-yard touchdown pass.

SN: *How did the team respond to being behind at halftime?*
TP: We were behind 17-10, but we went right to work on the things that had happened in the first half. There was no degree of panic.

SN: *How does the team divide up at halftime?*
TP: The defense goes to one room, the offense to another. The coaches go and meet other coaches who are upstairs in the press box. We tried to figure out how to counteract the plays that they had been successful with. If a team has success with certain plays, then they're going to come back with those plays. Then we pulled the offense and defense together, and Coach Gibbs said, "Hey, we're down 17-10, but we've been there before. Let's go out and do the things we know we're capable of doing." That was pretty much it. He was not upset. I think he was challenged. And we, as a defense, were challenged.

Tony Peters (23), Joe Theismann (7), Charlie Brown (86), Tom Landry, Mark Moseley (3), and Mike Nelms (25) in a publicity photo at the NFL Pro Bowl in Hawaii. Courtesy of Tony Peters.

SN: *What happened during the second half?*

TP: We went out and shut them down. They were zero for eleven in their pass attempts in the second half. They didn't complete a pass. We came out and we did our job. And, of course, John Riggins made the big run, and we ended up winning 27-17. We shut them out in the second half. It was quite a feeling to be able to do that. Riggins' touchdown went down in history as one of the greatest runs of all time.

SN: *So how does winning the Super Bowl feel?*

TP: As a player, you set as your goal reaching the position where you're considered the number-one team in the world. It's even more satisfying when you're selected All-Pro, and you go to the Pro Bowl in Hawaii, because all the players there look at you like, "Wow, I wish I could have gotten there and experienced that." They've been at home for a couple weeks watching you on television. So, it's like, "Wow, I gotta touch you. How does it feel?" You realize that you're at the top of your profession, and no one can take that away from you. It's a fantastic accomplishment and one that will forever live in your memory.

SN: *What happened that led to the NFL suspending you for the next year?*
TP: In 1983 I was arrested and charged with conspiracy to distribute a controlled substance, cocaine. I was suspended by the NFL for the 1983 season. It's a complicated story, which began during the 1982 strike, when I went up to Toronto to play in an exhibition game set up by the Players' Association to raise money for our strike fund. I had a half-brother who lived up there, who had played ten or eleven years for the Toronto Argonauts in the Canadian Football League. His name was Charles, and he was the child of my father and another woman. Charles was probably fifteen or twenty years older than me. He had grown up for the most part in a different household. I'd seen him only two or three times.

SN: *In your whole life, you'd only seen him two or three times?*
TP: Yeah, as a kid. Once he went to Canada, he very seldom came back. When I was sixteen, he came back once.

Earlier in 1982, Charles and his wife had come through Virginia, and he had spent a couple of days with me there. At that time, he mentioned to me that he was looking to get some cocaine. My response was, "Look, I'm not into that. I really have no idea if any could be had." I dropped it at that. He did, too. He never called me about it.

I thought it would be neat when I went to Toronto to play in the exhibition game to see Charles. The game was canceled after I arrived there, because the strike was settled. I stayed in Toronto one night, and Charles and I went to dinner. We went to a club and messed around. Charles' wife lived in Pittsburgh, and he was living with some guy named Nick, who was supposedly his friend. That night, Charles mentioned this cocaine thing to me again. And again, I said I didn't know anything about it.

We played the rest of the 1982 season, went on to win the Super Bowl, and I went on to Hawaii to play in the Pro Bowl game. Then in June 1983, before training camp began, I got a phone call from this guy Nick, who identified himself as Charles' friend. He asked me, "What's up, man? Is it snowing there?" It was June, so I said, "Hey, man, it's not snowing." But what he was really doing was asking whether there was any coke around. But I wasn't into that crap. It was at least four or five years since I'd had any involvement with taking drugs. It was so far away from my mind that you never put two and two together.

I later found out that Nick was a Royal Canadian Mounted Policeman and that he was taping the call with me. He went by the name Nick Cola. Nick Cola, cocaine, okay. That's how stupid they were. Had I been a criminal, I would have been aware of all this. Nothing really transpired.

When I got back from Hawaii, an old friend called me. When you get into a situation where you're making a lot of money, you get people from all over the place who want a portion of it. I really like this guy, Ron; he's still a good friend. But he wanted a loan to start up a business, a dance school. He and his girlfriend, who was a former roommate of Debby Allen at Howard, wanted me to put up all the money, and they'd run the school. That didn't sound too smart. So, I told them I couldn't do it.

Then Nick called again, and he was with a guy named Mike, whom I later found out worked for the Drug Enforcement Agency, the DEA. Mike was working on this side of the border. Nick asked me to go out to dinner, and he brought this guy Mike along, whom he introduced as his buddy from here. They said they had just come back from Florida and had made these really big drug deals. They wanted some more drug connections. I told them, "Hey, I'm not into that."

So, I was getting pressure from two sides: from an old friend who wanted to borrow money and from these two guys who wanted to deal drugs. I really couldn't help either of them. But I had a bright idea, which was to put these two groups in touch with each other, so that they'd leave me alone.

SN: *Why were the Royal Canadian Mounted Police trying to set you up in this sting-type operation? Where did they get your name from?*

TP: They had gotten my name from my brother Charles. Charles said that he was upstairs one night, and he came down and found Nick looking through his phone book. That's how Nick got my number. He stole it out of the phone book. The Royal Canadian Mounted Police had been determined to put a dent in the drug market, and to do that they decided to knock down some high-profile athletes.

The sum total of my involvement in the drug dealing that I was accused of was putting an old friend who wanted to borrow money from me in touch with Nick, who said he wanted to buy drugs. It was just two people who were bugging the hell out of me, and I thought that that was the way to get rid of them. I told my friend Ron, who wanted to set up the dance school, "I know you're not into it [cocaine] now, but I know it was something you used to do, and would you still have any contacts in that area?" And he said he did. To me, that was the perfect union, because these were two people willing to do business.

Nick called me within a week and said that he was coming through. I said, "Great. I've got a friend of mine I'd like you to meet." I thought that that would solve my problems.

What I didn't know was that this was really the beginning of my problems. Had I been into drugs, I would have checked out this guy Nick, whom I'd never met. I'd just talked to him on the phone. I never called my half-brother to check him out. So, I met Nick and my friend Ron in D.C., and introduced them, and we went to lunch in Georgetown. They sat in one booth; I sat on the other side. Nick brought in two other people, whom he claimed were friends of his who lived in the area. It turned out later that they were from DEA. I talked with the guy from DEA about everything under the sun, except drugs. We never talked about drugs, and I never discussed any financial gains from the arrangement, because it was not my intention to profit from it. My intention was simply to get two people off my back and satisfy their desires. What they talked about at that meeting was their own business. I never heard their conversation.

After the meeting, I took them back to the hotel in my car. They were staying at the Key Bridge Marriott in Arlington, Virginia, right across Key Bridge from Georgetown. Ron's car was at the Marriott, so I dropped him off immediately. He got out of the car, and said, "We're going to get something going in a couple days." And that was it.

A week or so later, I got a call from Nick's friend Mike, the DEA guy. Once this thing started to develop in the United States, the Canadian police were out of it. Nick had gone back to Canada. The DEA took over, under this guy Mike Pavlovich. He became the main guy dealing with my friend Ron. Mike told me, "Yeah, we got together with Ron, and everything went great. We did some things. We're going to meet with him in a week or so. We'd like you to come by and have dinner." I wasn't aware of it at the time, but they were trying to get me to meet them at Key Bridge during their transaction. But I told him on the phone, "Look, there's really no need for me to be there, and there's things I need to do." I was pretty busy. We'd just come off the Super Bowl, and your time is being demanded by everybody under the sun.

Mike called me again after I went to training camp in July. Apparently, he had done two or three deals with Ron. He left a message for me, and I called him back. I asked him, "What's up, man?" He replied, "Oh, nothing. We were thinking about coming down this weekend." I didn't understand, so he said he wanted to come down to the Redskins' training camp at Carlisle. He said he just wanted to thank me for introducing him to Ron: "We've really done some things, and we really want to do something for you for all this." I said, "You don't need to do anything for me. I'm just glad you guys worked things out." I said there was no need for him to come up to Carlisle. I told him that I was coming home that weekend and that we could get together at a club and have a drink.

And that was that. That was the conversation. It turned out that that phone call I made to him was the phone count. They charged me with eighteen felony counts. The phone count was for allegedly trying to set up a drug deal over the phone. That count alone carried a ten-year prison sentence.

SN: *Based on what you say the phone call consisted of, how could they interpret it that way?*
TP: You tell me. (Laughs)

SN: *What was their argument in court? How did they explain it?*
TP: There was no argument in court because I ended up plea-bargaining.

I went home that weekend and met Mike at a club called Bogart's, which was a normal hangout for a lot of the players. My wife came with me. The music was extremely loud. I assumed this was just a case of a guy calling me up, and saying, "Hey, man, let's go have a drink." "Hey, no problem," because I was always that type of guy. I didn't feel like I was on this pedestal. I didn't feel like I was above anybody. That was part of the problem, because you have to separate yourself in order to protect yourself.

Anyway, Mike hands me $3000, which at the time I didn't know was $3000. He just said, "Hey, look, this is for helping us out." I replied, "Look, like I told you before, I'm not interested in any money." But he said, "No, no, take it, take it." So I said, "Well, if that's what you want to do, that's fine." And I took the money. I sent the entire $3000 to my mom. It turned out that they were using that money to build their case.

The judge threw that out. They never presented any evidence that I had arranged for any pecuniary gains. So, that was null and void. They had been hoping that during this conversation, I would commit to some arrangement, which would implicate me.

SN: *Were they bugging the conversation?*
TP: Yeah, but the problem with the bugs was that, at the two restaurants where I met them, the music was too loud. So, the bugs were useless.

SN: *If they were bugging you, why did they go to a club with loud music? Was it their choice?*
TP: Well, it was my choice. They used that to try to build their case against me. They claimed that I was the mastermind of this drug ring, and that I never got my hands dirty. Each time we met, it was at a noisy location, so that I could muffle any wiretap. And they claimed that my phone conversations

were so smart, that I avoided ever talking about the issues at hand. Any time they brought the subject of drugs up, I would go on to another subject. But, of course, it wasn't that. It was simply that I wasn't interested in drugs.

SN: *So they made these substantial charges beyond that you were involved in just that one deal?*
TP: The DEA's claim was that I was in charge of a drug ring that extended from Miami to New York, from Oklahoma through the South. They said Miami, because one of Ron's buddies was in Miami. They claimed that I never got my hands dirty. Of course, if I was that guy, I was a hell of a guy. But it wasn't me.

On August 3, 1983, I was at training camp in Carlisle, and I got a knock on my door about six thirty in the morning. It was Richie Petitbon, and he said, "Tony, there are some people here to see you." I thought, "People here to see me? What's going on?" So I walked out, and it was the DEA. They had come there earlier that morning and explained to him what the deal was. Now, they wanted to talk to me.

We went downstairs to the coaches' lounge. There they read me my rights and explained to me what the charges were. And I looked at Richie, because I still wasn't clicking. They wanted to put handcuffs on me. I asked them if that was necessary, and they said that it was. So, they handcuffed me and took me downstairs to drive me to Harrisburg. It was a federal charge, and that was the nearest federal court.

In Harrisburg, we met a magistrate, who set the bond and read the preliminary report. It charged that I had met this guy, and I met this guy, and I met this guy, and met this guy. The judge asked me whether there was anything that I wanted to say on my behalf, before he set bond. And I said, "Well, I met this guy." He replied, "I don't want to know whether you met anybody or not." I was trying to be honest. I said I had lived in the area for a number of years and owned a home in northern Virginia, so it's not like I'm going anyplace. So, he released me on my own recognizance.

From that point, I had to go from Harrisburg to Alexandria, Virginia, to be arraigned. Once the United States set bail, I could be released. Charlie Casserly was with me, who at the time was basically an errand boy at Redskins Park. He wasn't anywhere near being a general manager. But he was a good guy. He basically watched film and ran errands for the coaches. He and I drove to Alexandria for the arraignment. As we drove, I told him the entire story. I said, "I don't know what these guys are talking about. This is unbelievable that this has happened." We got to Alexandria, and the Redskins arranged to provide my attorney, Greg Murphy, who later was Lorena Bobbitt's husband's attorney.

I had been charged with interstate conspiracy, from the District of Columbia to Virginia. They claimed that I needed attorneys from both places. I finally got the D.C. stuff dropped, because there was no basis for it. But I ended up keeping the attorneys, Williams & Connolly. Larry Lucchino, the former president of the Baltimore Orioles, was one of my attorneys, and Greg Murphy. The Redskins found the attorneys and told me that they had everything arranged.

SN: *Who paid for the attorneys?*
TP: I did.

SN: *What was the Redskins management's reaction to the news?*
TP: The Redskins stood behind me. Obviously, I had been a very valuable member of the team and a very solid citizen and had never given them any indication that I was trouble, or had a drug problem, or anything like that. They told me from day one, "Hey, we're going to be with you throughout this ordeal."

Williams & Connolly was basically the Redskins law firm. Edward Bennett Williams still owned about twenty-five percent of the team; Jack Kent Cooke had taken over majority ownership. Greg Murphy was just a guy whom the attorneys for Williams & Connolly knew, who was really successful, and knew the ins-and-outs of the eastern district area in northern Virginia.

The DEA had spent a lot of time and money on these transactions, and they had nailed a couple people. My friend Ron had gotten five years in prison, on two or three transactions. They had also arrested one of his friends in Miami. They had been doing a deal at National Airport in Washington. They had made two or three other arrests, and then they had come and got me.

But when these two DEA guys walked through and saw me, they didn't look like they were very happy about all this. I don't know if they felt, "Well, we don't really have enough on this guy." Because when I had met them at the club and they'd given me the money, they hadn't been able to get a commitment out of me to get involved in the drug deals. They never really had anything solid on me. But they felt that maybe they could get something out of it because of the notoriety. So, they hit me with eighteen felony counts. If found guilty on all counts, I could get a maximum sentence of 110 years.

SN: *What were the charges?*
TP: The major charges were conspiracy to distribute cocaine, illegal use of a phone to conduct illicit activity, some other type of conspiracy, conspiracy to commit interstate crime, all this crap. There were a lot of duplicate type charges. Illegal use of a car to commit a felony.

Then the news hit the fan. And having been All-Pro that year, it was big news all over the country. I had friends in Germany call me and tell me that it was on TV over there. There I was, being flashed around the world, over something that should never have gone beyond the tenth page. The whole thing was quite upsetting to me. It had not been my intention to do anything illegal.

As this thing had developed in Washington, as I had introduced my friend Ron to Mike, for the purposes of doing a drug deal, I hadn't felt that I had been doing anything wrong. To understand that, you have to look at my upbringing as a child and adolescent. When you're raised in an environment where crime is common, as I was, and drugs are there, and everything is out in the open, it becomes nothing to you. You don't see it as a big thing. You look at it, and you say, boy, that's life.

For example, if a person from an upper middle-class background and a kid from South-central L.A. both witnessed someone being shot, their reactions are going to be very different. The former is going to be shocked; he's more likely to be a witness for you. But the kid from South-central L.A. won't think as much of it; he's seen it many times.

SN: *Had you seen people get shot?*
TP: From when I was a kid, I'd seen people shot and killed. I had a cousin get shot and killed, when I was standing right there. And I saw a guy shoot his father.

SN: *Was this in Pauls Valley?*
TP: Both of those incidents occurred in Pauls Valley. I saw a couple of stabbings in Oklahoma City, and I saw a guy get stomped pretty good by about twenty guys. These things happened between the time I was twelve and fifteen.

When the guy shot his dad, I was running an errand for my mom. I was in the seventh grade. She was down at the beauty parlor, and she sent me to the store to get her a bottle of Coca-Cola. As I was walking down to see her, I saw a guy, his name was James, who was about three or four years older than me. He and I were pretty good friends. And I said to him, "Hey, James, how's it going?" He replied, "Not much, what's happening?" And he just walked right by. I went to get the Coca-Cola and came back, and here's James again, walking a lot faster and looking down. I'd heard a pop, but I didn't think much about it. So, I walked around the corner, and there was his dad lying there.

SN: *Bleeding to death? Or dead?*
TP: Bleeding to death. He'd shot his dad with a shotgun. His dad died en route to the hospital.

SN: *This must have been quite a shock to you, as a seventh grader.*
TP: No, it wasn't that big a shock to me.

SN: *Why had James killed his father?*
TP: James' dad, who was a part-time minister, was abusive, in a way. I suppose that was why James did it. James ended up doing about twenty or twenty-five years. He got out about four or five years ago.

When I was sixteen, my mom thought that it was necessary for me to have a handgun. She knew me. I had run-ins with people, and I normally didn't back down from them. My mom said that she feared for my life. She told me to go down and pick a handgun out, and she'd pay for it.

When this thing developed in Washington, I didn't feel that I had done anything wrong, because it was something that I had seen most of my life. Drug deals were not such a big thing then. The first time I saw marijuana, I was in ninth grade, about 1967. But what I saw on an everyday basis was alcohol—wine and things like that. My father was an alcoholic. Even in a small town like Pauls Valley, you had five or six people you saw everyday who were drunk on their tail. Just staggering, slobbery drunk. They would be on the corner, or at the two bars they had in town, or sitting on the bench drinking. Someone in an upper-class environment wouldn't see that. They'd be in the house drinking.

SN: *How did the experience of the drug conviction affect you?*
TP: The arrest and the drug conviction was a very positive experience for me, because it allowed me to grow a little more. I had to raise my moral standards to a higher level, because from a moral standpoint, I was definitely wrong. Although I may not have committed a serious crime, I was condoning one.

At the time, of course, I was concerned about just trying to defend myself. I sat down with my three attorneys, and we discussed all the things that had happened leading up to the arrest. Greg Murphy told me that they tell you in law school not to believe everything your client says. I can understand that. But I told them that I didn't think it was a black-and-white thing.

SN: *How did your attorneys want to handle your defense?*
TP: Their response was that the best procedure for us would be to plea-bargain. I couldn't see myself plea-bargaining for something I didn't do.

SN: *Did your attorneys think you were guilty of some of the charges?*
TP: Oh, absolutely. They didn't think I was a big drug kingpin, but they thought I was doing some kind of lower-level dealing. And they never

checked out the entire story. The problem was that it was only my word against
the DEA and the Royal Canadian Mounted Police. No one else had been present, except Ron, who was the guy who had made the transaction. Even at that
time, no one asked me to take a urinalysis, which you'd think they'd do if they
wanted to solidify their case. Maybe I should have suggested it. I didn't take one
until we had to do our presentencing report.

I told the attorneys that I'd like to speak to each of them alone, and I asked
each what he thought. They all thought we should plea-bargain. We were able to
reduce one of the conspiracy charges to a reduced conspiracy charge. Then I
plea-bargained to two felony counts out of eighteen.

SN: *What was the sentence?*
TP: I ended up getting sentenced to 500 hours of community service, and got
fined $10,000. That was on top of losing my salary for that year, because the
NFL suspended me for two years. They let me back in after one year, however.
They had said I could appeal after one year.

SN: *What did you think about the NFL suspension?*
TP: NFL commissioner Pete Rozelle was extremely harsh in the punishment
he inflicted. The judge in the case, Judge Bryant, who was a powerful guy in
the eastern district of Virginia, said it was a garden-variety case. He said had
it not been for the fact that Mr. Peters was a well-known sports figure, this case
would never have come before him. It was like a misdemeanor. But Rozelle took
a different position. He hit me with the maximum suspension, even though
there was no drug use involved, and there was no solid evidence that I had done
what I had been accused of doing. I had committed a moral crime. As far as
the NFL was concerned, the crime I had committed was a plea-bargain. Once I
pleaded guilty on those two felony counts, they felt, boy, that was it.

SN: *What did your legal fees come to?*
TP: The case probably cost me $600,000, with salary and everything.

SN: *What was your impression of Pete Rozelle?*
TP: I only met Pete a couple of times. I spoke to him in Hawaii at a social
gathering, and he was feeling pretty good. I think he liked to have a good
time and seemed to love the spirits. It would have been interesting to have
given him a urinalysis. It might have revealed a high level of alcohol. Not that
alcohol is illegal. But they don't want players out drinking.

I just think that the two-year suspension was a big suspension, although they allowed me back in after a year. I wasn't allowed to work out at Redskins Park during that time. I think the NFL was trying to set an example with this drug thing, and I just happened to be the person who was readily available. And they exercised the maximum suspension, two years.

I completed the community service and then applied for reinstatement.

SN: *What did the community service involve?*
TP: I was assigned to Community Action, a placement service for people who wanted to volunteer for different things. Any organization that needed a volunteer would send us all the information, and we would go about placing qualified people. I also worked at juvenile detention centers in northern Virginia. I went there every day and just sat and talked with kids who had committed major crimes, like murder and robbery.

SN: *Was drug use by NFL players very common when you were playing?*
TP: No, it was not a very serious problem. Yeah, people did it. But it wasn't an abuse thing. On a team—and I'm guessing—say, on our team, there were three or four guys that I knew of, out of forty-five or fifty, who used cocaine and maybe one or two guys who abused it. But their performance never showed it. They always did their job, and they were always at their job. They never showed up late. So, it wasn't a major problem, as far as *I* knew. Those were the guys that I hung out with.

Of course, amphetamines have always been part of the game. When I first came into the league, a lot of the old-time players used them. They took them before games to increase their alertness. I took a couple of amphetamines in one game during my rookie year, because of the influence of the older players. It was a fast-paced game, and I decided that was not the way I wanted to go. Of course, your alertness is up, you're keen. But I felt I was maybe a little too keen.

SN: *Did the coaches know about players' use of amphetamines?*
TP: I doubt if the coaches knew, and I doubt if they cared. You have to understand, when I first came into the league, a lot of those older players were as old as some of the coaches. And I'm sure the coaches probably used all those amphetamines and painkillers as players. As long as your performance was there, you wouldn't get much of a second look.

SN: *What was the 1983 season like for you, not being able to play?*
TP: The low point of my career was sitting out the 1983 season under suspension, when the Redskins went to the Super Bowl again and lost to the Raiders 38-9.

SN: *That year the Redskins, as defending Super Bowl champions, were the favorite.*

TP: Yeah, and guys were shooting for them. Other teams play that much harder against you when you're the defending champion, because they're measuring themselves against you. If they have success against you, that gives them confidence.

It was frustrating watching that Super Bowl and not being able to participate, especially when Marcus Allen broke the long run on our strong safety, Ken Coffey, who was playing the position I played. He had an excellent opportunity to stop Allen behind the line of scrimmage. I mean, he had the guy wrapped in his arms for a two- or three-yard loss and failed to execute the tackle. The guy ended up running seventy or eighty yards, for another Super Bowl record. And we had the infamous screen pass to Joe Washington that was intercepted.

SN: *How long did you play in the NFL after that?*

TP: I returned for another two years after the suspension was lifted. The Redskins didn't have as much success during those years. And I had a couple of injuries. I pulled a hamstring that slowed me down somewhat. I played decently; I didn't play great. And then in 1985, Joe Theismann got his leg broken.

SN: *How did the year's layoff affect you as a player?*

TP: Coming back in 1984 didn't affect me from a physical standpoint, but it did mentally. There was mental drain from having to deal with 500 hours of community service in a two- or three-month period. That's a lot of hours in a short span of time, but I had to do it to be eligible to be reinstated in April, which is when we held our first minicamp.

SN: *You came back and started?*

TP: I did, but football didn't seem as important to me.

SN: *What happened to the guy they had been playing in your position?*

TP: Ken Coffey, who had replaced me the year before, got hurt early in training camp.

My problem after coming back was that I couldn't really concentrate fully. Many times, I found myself drifting off at meetings, thinking about something else. In any sport, you've got to have a high degree of focus when you're on the field and be able to visualize what you would do in a given situation.

When I went through the case and the plea-bargaining, football had to take a back seat, because I was basically fighting for my life. After that I had to put myself into performing community service. And I didn't want to perform it just to do it. I wanted to make it meaningful. So, I spent a lot of time at youth detention centers, doing stuff for handicapped people, doing community work in a sincere way, trying to make up for the mistake I had made.

It was a really important period in my life. Everything I did was a sincere effort to gain a better understanding of myself and of what was expected of me by society. I don't regret what happened, in a sense, because we all learn differently. It could be our destiny to experience certain things in order to allow others to benefit. Had I not been suspended, then it's quite possible I could have played another four or five years. But who knows, because you never know about injuries. I went through my first eight years in the NFL, and never missed a game. So, I had already beat the odds in a sense.

I came back too soon from the hamstring pull. The minimum down time with a severe pull is two or three weeks. But because I came back too soon, it nagged at me for most of the rest of the year.

When you injure something, you put stress or pressure on some other area of your body. I ended up pulling a stomach muscle lifting weights on a new weight machine working on the abdominal muscles. It was something that really required two or three weeks off, but I never took any time off for it.

SN: *Was that your decision?*
TP: The decision was a combination of two, the way it always is in sports. They have a way of leaving the decision up to you. But they also have a way of implying that you need to get out there.

I ended up getting placed on injured reserve the last four or five games of the season, because the stomach muscle never really came around, although the hamstring eventually did. It was pretty frustrating, because I had missed a year and was trying to readjust my mental processes, and then suffered two muscle pulls, and tried to come back too quickly. Had I taken the time to heal, maybe I could have added more years to my career.

So 1984 was a disappointing year, and in 1985 there were similar problems and disappointments. I made it through training camp, but then strained a hamstring the last day. It was not as severe as the previous year, but other things happened as well. I hyperextended my knee, and then pulled a groin muscle against Dallas and came back too soon. We were playing San Francisco, and an offensive lineman missed his block. And I happened to be running by, and he dove out and hit me on the ankle and messed up some tendons. At that point, about midway through the season, I knew it would be my last year. I had been very fortunate over the years to be fairly injury-free, and when you start to get hurt and you're already struggling with your mental preparation, then it's time to do something else.

I could have tried to play more, but we had had two mediocre years, and I was ready to retire and get out of the game. It was not a pleasant way to go out. But it was one I had decided to make my own, about midway through 1985.

SN: *What did being retired from football feel like?*
TP: Retirement slapped me back into reality quickly. When you're a player, and have success on a professional team, you're treated like an icon throughout the community. You get special favors. You go to a bar or a restaurant, and the owner knows you, and there's no charge. As a player, you lose sight of reality.

SN: *Had you thought about what you would do when you retired from the NFL?*
TP: I had decided to go into commercial real estate and had gotten my real estate license back in 1976. I thought I would be as successful in that, as I had been as an athlete. But it did not quite work out. I soon found out that there were obstacles that I would have to deal with as a black individual.

SN: *This was in the Washington, D.C., area? What exactly did you do?*
TP: I had been looking forward to retirement after a pretty long career and to new challenges. I looked for opportunities with big commercial real estate companies. I wanted to work in the District of Columbia. I went to a couple of places, and it was a rude awakening. The response was that because I was black, it would be very difficult to succeed in this business.

SN: *This was said openly, to your face?*
TP: Oh, yes. I think they told me that, in trying to be quite honest about the situation.

SN: *In a city that's overwhelmingly black?*
TP: The mainstream businesses in the District are all controlled by whites. I was told that I could not succeed, because a lot of the business deals would be with white America. I was told that unless I were white and had graduated from the University of Virginia, then I should seek some other employer.

Eventually I did get hired by a firm and went to work in commercial real estate in Virginia. And this prediction became true, because in a lot of cases it was very difficult to get in the front door.

SN: *Does the NFL do anything to assist players when they retire?*
TP: It's interesting that the NFL, with its ability to avoid antitrust regulations and to make the kind of money it makes, is not concerned about helping its players make the transition to retirement.

SN: *You're saying that Redskins management has no policy of assisting retiring players to establish contacts in the business community and secure employment and get training?*
TP: To my knowledge, no NFL team does that.

SN: *There's no network of ex-players you can rely on?*
TP: No. You're on your own entirely.

Retiring is also difficult because you've been part of a group for years, and it's hard to break away from that. When you ask players what they like about playing, they always say, "Well, the camaraderie, the association." There was a program on ESPN last night on some of the successful Green Bay Packers teams. And the guy commented, "We were all like brothers." So, when you all of a sudden lose about forty-three brothers, it's like forty-three deaths all at one time. The emotional strain from that is severe, unless you've prepared yourself mentally to make that transition. You're faced with the fact that as a black, it's going to be difficult, and as an athlete, people think you made an astronomical salary and don't need a job.

I worked for the commercial real estate firm in Virginia for a couple years, and then I went into the restaurant business with a couple partners. We opened two restaurants in northern Virginia, one in Manassas and one in Centerville. I invested my money in that and became a big loser.

SN: *You returned to the University of Oklahoma to complete your training in education.*
TP: Yes, with the objective of moving into coaching and teaching.

SN: *At what level?*
TP: Right now, I'm interested in secondary education. If I went to the collegiate level, then it would be strictly coaching. If there's a genuine interest and the situation suits me, then I would consider it.

But Oklahoma is where I wanted to settle. I have two boys who are growing up, and I wanted to raise them in this environment. I enjoyed it as a kid.

I think it would be beneficial to them to be in a little slower-paced environment, in Norman.

SN: *Could you describe the work you did for the University of Oklahoma athletic program?*
TP: While I finished up my degree at the University of Oklahoma, I worked for the university's athletic program in the student life section. This is a model program involving academic advising of athletes. It was here when I was playing at Oklahoma back in the mid-1970s, and I'm sure prior to that. But they've really improved it over the years. They've got full-time academic advisors and thirty or forty computer stations.

They help the players plan out an academic program, so they know where they're going, and they try to keep them on track. They've transformed two whole floors into a state-of-the-art study facility, with cubicles and a library, and three or four large study halls, with huge tables and soft chairs. And there are several tutors there on a full-time basis. They've incorporated a math study lab, with a full-time tutor.

If you're an athlete at the University of Oklahoma, you have to maintain a certain grade point average, and if it drops below, say, a 2.0, then you're required to come to the study hall five nights a week, two hours a night. They have tutors to help you.

SN: *What did you do exactly?*
TP: My job was to monitor the study hall activities during the evenings and to make sure that everybody shows up on time and gets to the station that they're supposed to be at if they have an appointment with a tutor or in the math lab. In addition, we check classes to make sure that kids are attending class.

SN: *You walk by the classroom, look in, see if the athlete is there, and make a note of it?*
TP: Yes. If a student isn't in there, we'll report it to the athletic director and the student's coach. Each coach gets a daily report about class attendance.

SN: *Now you come to the study hall, and stay there supervising it?*
TP: Right. Those in study hall have to study for two hours. There is not supposed to be any talking. Of course, we run into problems with students coming not being prepared to study.

SN: *How do you handle those situations?*
TP: We give them a warning. If they refuse to behave, I dismiss them from the facility and report that to the coaches. The football coaches will then make them run laps at six o'clock in the morning.

SN: *Does that work? Do they then stop their disruption, or do you see people having to constantly repeat running laps?*
TP: Personally, I'm not sure whether that's the answer. Maybe a psychologist would be a better solution. Of course, when a kid is in great physical shape, then running a few miles is no big thing. Some of the kids have a history of disruption. Some just don't respect authority, period.

SN: *How would you compare the situation today with what it was like when you were a University of Oklahoma football player?*
TP: When I was in study hall here, we only had one or two guys who were really disruptive, and I was never one of them. We didn't have these facilities when I was a student. We met in the old business building, sitting on hard-back chairs, in uncomfortable surroundings, for two hours. Whereas they've got nice, huge rocking chairs, four- or five-inch cushioned seats, and huge tables where you can spread out to do your work.

The athletes get a lot of privileges now. They never have to go to the school bookstore, because we have our own bookstore right in the athletic department. Their course books are brought over by truck, carried up the stairs, and set up for them right where they are. So, they don't have to wait in any lines. It's the best of all worlds. And to constantly show insubordination is beyond my imagination.

Being monitor is not a fun job. Once, I had to take over the other study hall, because the guy running it had lost control over it. He had, I admit, the rough lot of kids. Basically, they were the football players.

SN: *He lost control of the study hall? How did that happen?*
TP: It's a tough job having to fight kids every night. They test you to see how far they can go. If you allow them to get to a certain point, then you pretty much lose control.

SN: *When disruption occurs, aren't there players mature enough to help out the monitor?*
TP: (Laughs) No, I doubt it.

SN: *Did the athletes in the study hall ever threaten you?*
TP: Oh, sure. They'd say, "I'll kick your butt," or "You don't have any authority to do this or that," or "I'll get you fired." They didn't just say it to me, but
to the person who runs the whole program. When a player told me that I
couldn't force him to leave and that he would kick my ass, I said, "Well, you'd
feel pretty embarrassed if, at my age, I whipped your ass. You would also feel
embarrassed if you whipped my ass at your age." Obviously, you try to avoid
physical contact as much as possible. But I wouldn't be afraid to defend myself
if it got to that point.

Most of these kids have been heavily recruited, and they assume that as a
high school superstar, their wish is always granted.

SN: *Maybe because Oklahoma is such a top-flight program, they fear they
won't be up to the challenge, even if they were a great high school player?*
TP: I'm sure there's also some frustration involved, because a lot of times,
when things don't work out as you'd hoped, then you've got to rebel against
something. It seems to me that in the recruiting process, you should try to
make the person understand that while it might not work out for him on the
athletic side, that if you work on the academic side, it will work out for you. I
think that maybe we're selling the wrong commodity here.

We've got a lot of kids in the night class that the professors are having a
heck of a time with. We've got ten or fifteen athletes in one class. Kids are
getting up and walking out in the middle of the lectures. It got to the point
where we put a monitor in the class each night to make sure that there's no
disruption.

SN: *I imagine the Oklahoma football program is recruiting a lot of players from
economically deprived backgrounds, from father-absent households, whose problems adjusting to university life are different from those of most students.*
TP: It is different from your normal student environment, where a lot of the
kids come from middle-class families and they have a better idea of what they're
trying to do. A lot of these athletes are from the lower-income brackets and
don't have a grasp of what's happening around them. Their experience is of
neighborhood fights and standing up for their manhood. Some grew up in the
Fifth Ward of Houston, and they're used to fighting their way all the way back
to the house.

I was only involved in one meeting with the coaches about disciplining a
player in study hall. The player denied that my report about his behavior was
accurate. And he complained that I told him, "Get your ass out of here!"

SN: *That's not legitimate to say in disciplining a player?*
TP: Not according to him. He said that even his mother doesn't curse at him. I think that his manliness was hurt, when I told him to get his ass out in front of the entire group.

I don't just throw kids out. I talk to them. Even the guys I've thrown out, I did just about anything I could do to assist them. When I first became a monitor, I explained where I came from, and why I was back. And I tried to tie it all together and emphasize the education side of it, and then go from there. I've seen some attitudes change—some who've stepped forward to discuss academics or explore why they've done certain things.

SN: *You don't see many blacks being considered for NFL head coaching jobs. I noticed that the Redskins fired Charley Taylor, a Hall of Famer who had been in their organization for many, many years. He never got a head coaching opportunity, nor did Willie Wood. . . .*
TP: Charley was in the organization for many, many years. He started out as a scout after he finished his playing career with the Redskins. He's done the dirty work. He's gone out on the road. He's done pretty much whatever they've asked him. He was selected for the Hall of Fame on the first chance he had. Charley spent thirty-odd years of his life giving to that organization, and all of a sudden they have a down year—three years after winning the Super Bowl—and he's one of the people they release.

They never gave Charley the responsibility he deserved. He would be capable of being a head coach or offensive coordinator. It would have been interesting to allow him to implement some of his ideas, and the things that he had learned as a player, and later as a coach. He did work with and talk to individual players. But you could tell that he didn't have any authority. And consequently, what happens is that you don't get respect from the players.

SN: *Well, what was his exact title?*
TP: No one knew, not even Charley. He walked around without a title.

Other guys are getting head coaching positions who don't have Charley's credentials. Charley is in the Hall of Fame, and guys in the hall study a lot harder than the guys who don't quite make it to that level. And, with his experiences coaching with Joe Gibbs and those guys for fifteen years, he's picked up a lot of things in addition to what he learned as a player. I would want to tap his knowledge.

SN: *It's interesting that the Redskins decided to go into the Dallas organization to get a head coach. You don't even get the sense that the Redskins considered Charley Taylor at all.*

TP: He wasn't even considered for assistant coach or even for the scouting department. I just can't see why guys like Charley Taylor and Willie Wood aren't getting the opportunity to show their wares. It's quite upsetting that people that qualified are still being overlooked.

SN: *What was Bobby Mitchell's role with the Redskins? He was another Hall of Famer.*

TP: Bobby's title, I think, was assistant general manager. But that was definitely a figurehead title, because he didn't have general manager responsibilities. I think his actual title was community liaison. If things came up that required a Redskins office person to attend, then Bobby was chosen—insignificant things.

SN: *Are there any blacks at all in positions of responsibility in the Redskins front office?*

TP: No, not really.

SN: *The Redskins team is about sixty percent black, so you wonder why the front office positions are still closed.*

TP: You really begin to wonder. Charlie Casserly came in as a college senior and volunteered to work in public relations. In training camp, he was an errand boy who ran film over here and over there. That was it, he had no other responsibilities. The next thing you know, Bobby Beathard leaves to go to San Diego, and Charlie Casserly is his new general manager. Jesus, you've got people who've spent their lives playing this game, and studying this game, and becoming Hall of Famers, and considered the best at what they did.

SN: *Do you think the issue of coaching opportunities for blacks is being discussed?*

TP: The hiring of coaches in the NFL is a real buddy-buddy system. A lot of times, it's not based on abilities but on who you know. A lot of these guys get fired from one position and end up at another. It's a big fraternity. You got a guy like Chuck Knox—and I'm not taking anything away from Chuck Knox— but he's had twenty-five, thirty years in the NFL and could have won five, six, seven, eight championships. I don't know if he's won any! Give someone else an opportunity, someone who's played the game, who's put their lives on the line for an organization, especially when they've put in the time with an organization like Taylor put in for the Redskins. They should show a little appreciation. You have to feel sad about some of his comments. It was like, "I was willing to do almost anything."

Look at Paul Warfield, the best receiver I ever faced. When I was playing with the Cleveland Browns, there was a guy named Chip, who was our ball boy. He did some work with computers and eventually became a player personnel director. And Cleveland hired Paul Warfield as a figurehead, and Chip was his boss! How can you justify this? I'm sure that Warfield has forgotten more things about players and how to play the game than this person could ever, ever learn. I think Warfield would make a great head coach.

KEN MENDENHALL

CENTER

—Baltimore Colts, 1971–1980

Ken Mendenhall was an All-American offensive lineman at the University of Oklahoma, who also played center for ten years in the NFL for the Baltimore Colts. He describes playing in a top-flight high school football program in Enid, Oklahoma, in the 1960s, arguably the state's top high school football program. Games there, attended by a uniformed pep club of 400, attracted crowds of about 10,000.

Mendenhall examines the differences in personality between offensive and defensive linemen and analyzes the requirements of offensive line play at the center, guard, and tackle positions. He compares contemporary NFL offensive linemen with those of the 1970s and describes the nature of injuries most often sustained by offensive linemen. Mendenhall also explains why offensive linemen generally have an easier time retiring than other players.

Experiencing a difficult transition to pro football, Mendenhall played for four different NFL teams in a single year. He discusses the experience of being cut and of joining two different taxi squads before winning a permanent position with the Colts. Mendenhall describes witnessing Johnny Unitas's farewell in Baltimore and later playing center for several years with one of the NFL's premier quarterbacks, Bert Jones.

STEPHEN NORWOOD: *Let's start with when and where you were born,*
and who your parents were, and then move on to your first exposure to sports.
KEN MENDENHALL: I was drawn to football early and had a real passion
for it almost immediately. I grew up in a small town in northeastern Oklahoma
called Pawhuska. I was born on August 11, 1948, in Stillwater, Oklahoma, the
summer after my father had graduated from Oklahoma A&M, which is now
Oklahoma State University. He had come back to Oklahoma after the war.

I began to watch sports on television from an early age and remember watching the St. Louis Cardinals, because the Dallas Cowboys were not even in exis-
tence. There were no organized sports for grade school kids in Pawhuska, but
we always got out in the yard and played touch, and sometimes tackle, football and basketball. We always got gear for Christmas—a football helmet or
even shoulder pads. We just had a constant football game going on all the
time in our front yard and in neighbors' yards, probably to their irritation.

SN: *Whom were you playing with?*
KM: I would play with my brothers and with neighborhood kids. I have three
younger brothers, but one was able to keep up with me. When there wasn't
anybody to play with, I would play games by myself. I would throw the ball,
and catch it, and run, and simulate being tackled.

SN: *How would you describe Pawhuska then?*
KM: Pawhuska was an oil town, which was sliding during the 1950s, and there
was a lot of cattle in that area as well. It was losing population. It was located in
Osage County, and there was a significant number of Osage Indians living there.

SN: *Did your father have any interest in sports? Had he played any sports? Or*
did you just pick up sports from television and the peer group?
KM: My dad had played high school sports, and I went to quite a few high
school football and basketball games with him. He loved basketball, which
had been his best sport. He didn't like baseball. He said the only thing that
baseball taught you was to chew tobacco. Consequently, I was never interested in baseball.

SN: *What kind of work did your father do?*
KM: My father worked at a local bank, but he bought some land outside of
town and tried to do some farming. So, part of the time we were in Pawhuska,
we lived on a farm. We had four boys in our family, and my father thought it
would be good training for us.

My main link to sports came from a high school student whom my dad had hired to work on our farm. He was the quarterback on the high school team, and he started on the basketball team as well. We always went to his games and watched him play. It was cool to be his younger buddy. He was not only a great athlete but a wonderful human being, an excellent student, and a great role model.

SN: *Was the main sports activity in Pawhuska in the high school? Were there any oil company teams?*
KM: No, it was centered around the high school, where they had some excellent basketball teams. They won a state championship while I was in junior high, and they had good football teams as well. So, we had a very strong exposure to high school athletics.

I started playing organized football in the seventh grade, which is when you started in Pawhuska. I was a halfback that first year and also played defense. But in the eighth grade, I moved to the offensive line, where I remained for the rest of my career. I also played linebacker on defense.

SN: *Did you choose to be an offensive lineman?*
KM: Nobody chooses to be an offensive lineman. I just wasn't fast enough to be a halfback. I was fairly strong, although I still wasn't very big in junior high. If I wanted to play, that's where I was going to play.

SN: *How seriously was football taken in junior high school?*
KM: It was taken seriously. We worked out hard, and we had plays that we ran and executed. We played an eight-game schedule and traveled good distances to away games. When I was in ninth grade we traveled to Miami, Oklahoma, a 100-mile bus trip. Miami had Steve Owens, and he was their best player.

SN: *Were you getting good instruction from the coaches? Do you think it's important at that level to get good instruction?*
KM: I had a good junior high coach. The most important thing at that stage is that you're not taught any bad techniques, like making false steps.

The thing about junior high football is that there is a wide disparity in size and strength. Some kids in ninth grade are very mature and are about as good as they'll be when they're high school seniors. But others are undeveloped; they haven't gone through puberty.

SN: *Did you ever think then that you wanted to become an athlete?*
KM: Even at that age, I wanted to play college football. Since my father and all of my relatives had gone to Oklahoma State, that was my team. I hated the University of Oklahoma, their rival. When I was in grade school, we went to some games at Oklahoma State and sat in the end zone for a dollar.

SN: *Did you have a sense in junior high school that you might make the NFL?*
KM: No. I wasn't a standout player in junior high. I was probably one of the better players, but there are millions of junior high football players. But probably none liked the game more than I did. You've really got to love it if you're a lineman.

SN: *When did you leave Pawhuska?*
KM: Prior to my sophomore year in high school, my family moved to Enid, Oklahoma, which had a large high school, with probably the strongest football program in the state. It was sending as many as three or four players a year to major college football programs.

SN: *Were you a starting player your first year at Enid High School?*
KM: No. So many guys went out for football at Enid High School that the starting lineup consisted almost entirely of seniors. About 120 guys went out for the team, whereas in Pawhuska I would have started as a sophomore. At Enid I just played on the sophomore team and didn't even suit up for Friday nights.

SN: *Who did Enid play? How many people turned out for the games in Enid?*
KM: Enid was in the Mid-State Conference, which consisted mostly of Oklahoma City schools. We had a tremendous following and often had more people in the stands when we would come to Oklahoma City to play than the Oklahoma City schools. Enid High School Stadium seats 9000 or 10,000, and it was *packed*. Every Friday night, they had a pep club of 400 out there in uniform.

After we won the state high school football championship my junior year, the town went crazy. We came back home, and the bus went around the town square in Enid at midnight. Fans were lined on both sides of the street, cheering. Then the town paid for us to go to the Bluebonnet Bowl. We spent four or five days there. The year before, the coaches were given brand new cars. There were people willing to open their pockets to support the program.

SN: *Did Enid High School's football success result in academics being short-changed?*
KM: No. Academics weren't short-changed. Some of our best players were excellent students.

SN: *What was the pressure on winning?*
KM: I can't say. Since we didn't lose, we never found out. We lost one game my junior year and won the state championship, and we lost one game my senior year and won the state championship. The year after I graduated, they lost one game and won the state championship.

SN: *Were you starting as a junior?*
KM: To show how much depth Enid High School had, I was the only junior who started on offense. There was one other junior who started on defense. So, coming back my senior year, we had two returning starters, and we won the state championship. My senior year, I was the only starter who played both ways. That's extraordinary for a high school team to have such depth.

I had a fabulous line coach at Enid, named Rex Martin, who moved me to center. Looking back over all the coaches I had over the twenty-odd years that I played organized football, he was as good a coach as I had. He was a great teacher, and the techniques he taught didn't change. He had an extensive off-season weight program, which he had initiated in the early 1960s. In fact, he had a far more sophisticated weight program than they had at the University of Oklahoma. He was really ahead of his time. We didn't necessarily have big teams, but we had strong teams. He turned that weight program into an advantage for us.

My senior year, I was named Lineman of the Year in the state, as a center. At Enid High School, we would generally have either the Back of the Year or the Lineman of the Year.

SN: *Being All-State, did you think about getting a scholarship to play in a major college program?*
KM: I was definitely interested in playing college football, and I started receiving letters from major colleges that were interested in me after my junior year. We had guys coming out of our program playing all over the place, so it wasn't that big a deal, the way it would have been in Pawhuska. Enid had players going on football scholarships to Oklahoma every year, to Oklahoma State, Arkansas, to Kansas, all over.

SN: *What was your parents' view of your playing football in high school and college?*

KM: My parents were incredibly supportive of me. They never missed a ball game. My motivation was never that of trying to prove something to my parents. I never felt pressure from my dad—pressure that I saw a lot of other dads put on their sons. I didn't get singled out by my parents because I had some athletic success. They were just as supportive of my brothers, who didn't have as much athletic success.

Initially, my mother hated for me to play football. Part of the negotiation with her was that I had to take piano or dancing to be able to play. So, I took dancing. But over time my mother became resigned to the fact that I was going to play and that I really enjoyed it.

SN: *What was the college recruiting process like?*

KM: I wasn't highly recruited. I had offers from Oklahoma and Oklahoma State, and Texas Tech, and from Arkansas, and maybe Kansas and Kansas State.

SN: *Did the Enid High School coaches advise you in any way about the recruiting process?*

KM: No, they didn't do that. Part of the reason for that was that we had so many kids going to the major colleges.

SN: *Because I would think they would have all kinds of contacts, since Enid High School was one of the big powerhouse programs.*

KM: They did, but the films were available to the colleges. We were in playoff games every year, and the college coaches were there watching us. When Enid played the big high schools, there'd be maybe two or three college assistant coaches at the game. There was a lot of exposure.

SN: *Your family had gone to Oklahoma State, so did you want to go there?*

KM: Although all my family had gone to Oklahoma State and we'd been big OSU fans, I got soured on them because of how their coach, Phil Cutchin, treated his players. Cutchin was a Bear Bryant disciple. He came in to Oklahoma State and did a lot of abusive things—behavior that a college coach couldn't get away with for ten minutes today without a lawsuit. He ran a lot of kids off.

One of Cutchin's casualties was this high school hero of mine, the young man who had worked on our farm in Pawhuska. My dad was somewhat of a father figure to him. His father died when he was very young, and he was raised by his mom. So, when things started happening over in Stillwater, he would come and tell my dad what was happening on the football field and about the coaches' antics. He was not a quitter. But he couldn't stomach a lot of the things they were doing there, so he left the team. As a result, I wouldn't consider Oklahoma State.

SN: *So it comes down to Oklahoma, Arkansas . . .*
KM: I leaned to the University of Arkansas, which was coming off a couple of Southwestern Conference championships, rather than the University of Oklahoma, which had finished 3-7. Arkansas had a great player named Harry Jones, who was from Enid. He ended up being the number-one draft choice of the Philadelphia Eagles. I went out to Fayetteville for a visit and had a great time there.

But that year Jim Mackenzie, who had been at Arkansas, was named head coach at Oklahoma after Gomer Jones left. Mackenzie said he really wanted me. As soon as he got in place at Oklahoma, he called me after school one day and asked me whether my mother had already started supper. I checked with my mother, and she said, "No." So Mackenzie told me, "I'm going to get my car now, and I'm coming to Enid, and I want to take your family out to dinner." He arrived, and we all went out to a local restaurant—my parents, my three younger brothers, and me. Mackenzie communicated to me and my parents how much he wanted me to come to Oklahoma. One comment really made an impression on me. My dad asked him if he would red-shirt me as a freshman. Mackenzie looked at my dad, and said, "We don't red-shirt players that good." It was really important to me that he said that.

SN: *The other schools wouldn't get with the family like that?*
KM: I never had another head coach in my home, other than Jim Mackenzie.

SN: *Could you describe what it was like when the recruiters had you visit a campus?*
KM: Generally, when you went on a campus visit, they'd have the players show you around. There wasn't a lot of structure on those visits, which were held on weekends. They might have a date for you on Saturday night. At Texas Tech, we went and listened to Bill Cosby. On Sunday morning, you'd meet with the coach, and then you'd fly back. Arkansas was pretty neat, because Harry Jones showed me around, and he'd just made the cover of *Sports Illustrated*.

SN: *Did recruiters tell you anything about the academic program in the effort to get you to come to their school?*
KM: I wanted to be a pro football player, so the academic reputation of a school wasn't a big issue with me. My dad was a banker, and I thought afterwards I'd just head into business. What they were selling was the football program, and that was what I was most interested in.

When Oklahoma was recruiting me, I did get stacks of letters from businessmen, people of distinction from all over the state, encouraging me to go to the University of Oklahoma. Jim Mackenzie obviously asked them to write to me.

SN: *What did the letters say?*
KM: They all said they were alumni and that Oklahoma had a great, rich football tradition, and that they were convinced the program was going to turn around under Jim Mackenzie's leadership. A lot of them said, "If there is anything I can ever do for you. . . ." No promises though.

But the most impressive thing about Oklahoma was Jim Mackenzie.

SN: *How would you describe Jim Mackenzie?*
KM: He was a fireball. I say this in a positive way. He wasn't an overly sophisticated guy; he was a shirttail-out type of guy, enthusiastic. Oklahoma should have been anticipating some real trouble recruiting, since they were coming off a 3-7 record and they had lost to Oklahoma State. Arkansas had had a perfect 11-0 record the year before. Arkansas thought they had a really good chance to recruit Steve Owens, who was from Miami, Oklahoma, a stone's throw from Fayetteville. He was highly recruited around the country. But with his enthusiasm, Jim Mackenzie was able to get Owens to come to Oklahoma, and a kid named Rick Baldridge from Lawton, who was coback of the year with Owens, and another highly recruited player from Tulsa named Joey Grayson. Mackenzie pulled off a pretty phenomenal thing in recruiting a lot of key players.

Jim Mackenzie would have been a great coach, but he died after that first year of a heart attack. Still, he turned the team around, from 3-7 to 6-4, which nobody had anticipated.

SN: *What was it like adjusting to the Oklahoma football program as a freshman?*
KM: I arrived at the University of Oklahoma at the start of Coach Jim Mackenzie's reign, when a lot of changes were being implemented. Mackenzie thought the varsity was fat and out of shape, and he had introduced an off-season fitness program that was just supposed to be horrendous. I don't

know how many hundreds of pounds the team was supposed to lose, but they were really running them to get them in shape.

My freshman coaches were Larry Lacewell and Billy Gray. At one point, Lacewell told us that we didn't have any players who would amount to anything. He put it in pretty graphic terms. Interestingly, we had two players on that freshman team, Jim Files and Steve Owens, who later were first-round draft choices in the NFL. And I was a fifth-round choice and played in the NFL for ten years, and another guy named Jack Porter was drafted and played for the New York Jets for a while. So, we had four NFL players off that freshman team.

SN: *Did Lacewell make that comment early in the season?*
KM: Yeah. He might have been aggravated about having to be the freshman coach, plus the fact we lost to Kansas State. He, of course, later distinguished himself by becoming one of the best defensive coaches in college football.

SN: *Barry Switzer was on the coaching staff. Can you describe your impressions of him?*
KM: I learned what a great motivator Barry Switzer was my freshman year. Jim Mackenzie had hired him as the varsity offensive line coach. As freshmen, we didn't ever practice with the varsity, but the varsity coaches would come and watch us on Friday afternoons, when they had a short varsity practice. The freshman team was scrimmaging, and the varsity coaches were all around, yelling encouragement or chastising. Football practice is controlled mayhem. The coaches wouldn't hit you and slug you, like they did at Oklahoma State. But they'd scream at you. During a scrimmage, I fired off the ball and got a good block driving the defender down the field. As I lay in the pileup after the play, I heard someone yelling my name, screaming. Then as the players got up off one another, somebody grabbed me from the back, where my shoulder pads were, and pulled me up. It was Switzer. He grabbed my facemask, and spun me around. And nose to nose, he said, "Kenny Mendenhall, you're going to be a great football player!" Then he shoved me back towards the huddle. That's how Switzer motivated. There was just an electricity about him. That incident is etched in my memory.

SN: *The coaches tried you briefly on defense. How did that go?*
KM: In spring ball my sophomore year, the coaches put me on defense, but that experiment didn't last long. I had been the starting center in all the freshman games. But I'd increased my speed during the off-season, and they put me at what they called a defensive end. In pro ball, it was basically an outside

linebacker position. I made it through the first week of practice in that position. Then in the first scrimmage, the quarterback, Bobby Warmack, ran an option toward me. Bobby was a real elusive guy, equally adept at running and passing. He was a good player who was the most valuable player in the Orange Bowl his junior year. My assignment as the defensive end was to take the quarterback. He came down the line on an option towards me, and I was all set to tackle him, but he faked a pitch and I tackled the halfback, and Warmack cut upfield and went sixty yards for a touchdown. The next Monday, I was on offense, at guard.

I was an offensive lineman from that time on, and that's when Buck Nystrom got a hold of me. He was the line coach, and I've never done anything hard since playing for Buck Nystrom. He was hard-nosed, and he'd get carried away—really carried away. It wasn't the abusive stuff that was personally degrading. But he got more out of you than you thought possible. He pushed us beyond our limit. We didn't have as much talent as players today, but I don't think very many players today could survive Buck Nystrom.

One time in spring practice my junior year, Buck decided that the offensive linemen needed to practice on off-days. You were limited to twenty practices in the spring and Buck felt we weren't progressing rapidly enough; we needed more work. He had the offensive line practice all by ourselves. We were incensed. Eddie Lancaster and I got together and called the Norman *Transcript*. It was the middle of the afternoon, and we had to go out and practice in an hour. We asked them, "Is Oklahoma practicing today?" And they said, "No, this is one of their off-days." And we told them, "You better check." Whatever happened, it got shut down. Chuck Fairbanks, the head coach, probably didn't know Buck was doing that.

Buck was a work of art. We'd do these board drills. The board was one foot wide and maybe ten feet long. It was between your feet and it made you keep a wide base when you blocked. At the end of the board was a dummy. And when we would hit the dummy, Buck would say, "Be a red-blooded American! Don't be a Communist!"

Buck could never have been a head coach. He wasn't tactful enough. You couldn't have done an interview with him. You'd have to bleep everything.

Buck kept talking about an All-American he'd coached named Joe Romick from Colorado, who'd had a blocking sled or a blocking dummy in his dorm room. He used to study for a while, and then he'd hit the blocking dummy. They recently released the all-time All-Big Eight team, and there was Joe Romick on it. He had been a guard at Colorado in the early '60s. I couldn't believe it. None of us had ever heard of him. We thought Buck made him up.

Buck was tough, but fair. He treated all of us equally bad. And we were in great shape.

Buck knew a lot about run blocking. Hit, hit, drive a guy, scramble. We had real small offensive linemen. The center, Bob Craig, a senior, weighed 205 pounds. One guard, Eddie Lancaster, weighed 198, and I, the other, weighed 195. Bill Elfstrom, another guard who played when I moved to center, weighed 195. The two tackles were slightly bigger, but both were under 220. Bob Kalsu was one of them, who was later drafted by the Buffalo Bills and then was killed in Vietnam. We would play teams much larger than we were. But coming off the ball, we were like lightning. We hit guys when they were just getting out of their stance.

We did a lot of scramble blocking, which Buck taught very well. You'd come out and hit a guy. As long as you could maintain a contact with him, you stayed with him. When you began to lose him, you'd get down on all fours and you'd scramble. You'd stay in his legs and you'd tie him up. You would never quit. For smaller linemen like us, it was a very effective technique.

But Buck couldn't teach pass blocking. He was too aggressive. Pass blocking is passive. You counteract. It's like counterpunching in boxing. We didn't throw much—mostly play action passes. In a play action, you make it look like a run, so you never drop back. Buck couldn't teach the traditional pass blocking. But he could impart aggressiveness, and speed, and tenacity.

SN: *What were your impressions of Chuck Fairbanks, who took over as head coach your sophomore year, after Jim Mackenzie died? Could you assess his approach to coaching, how he related to players?*
KM: Chuck had had a reputation as a really hard-nosed guy as an assistant coach. He was kind of scary. He had a volatile temper and a low flash point. He was extremely organized, and he seemed like a good manager. Practices were very organized. He kind of moved around the field. He knew both offense and defense, having coached both. I don't necessarily view him as a great motivator—locker room speeches and that type of stuff. He was a bit of a stoic. But he had you well prepared. And there was fear of not pleasing him.

SN: *What would he do when players committed mistakes?*
KM: He would get mad at individuals, but it seemed like it was more directed toward the team, if it didn't perform in a certain way. Of course, with Buck Nystrom, we had enough to be afraid of. Nothing Chuck would do to us would be something Buck hadn't already done.

SN: *Can you describe how your sophomore year went, as you joined the varsity?*
KM: My sophomore year was a magical season. My father wrote me a letter
prior to my first varsity game, talking about how proud he would be when he
saw me coming down that ramp. It was really a meaningful letter. We went on
to the Orange Bowl that year and beat a fabulous Tennessee team. They had
more talent than we did. We got them down 19-0, but they came back. At the
end they missed a field goal, which would have won it. We had been picked
to finish fifth in the Big Eight. But the only game we lost that season was to
Texas, at the Cotton Bowl. We beat Kansas, when Steve Zabel made a big catch
with 1:02 left on the clock, and we beat Nebraska in Lincoln. We came within
a whisker of winning the national championship and ended up number two.

SN: *You had played guard that season and later played center. Did you have
any preference between the two positions?*
KM: My junior year, I shifted back to center from guard, because Bob Craig
had graduated. I was a better center than a guard. I had played center in high
school and so the quarterback snap was second nature. They played a five-man
defensive line in college, so the center always had a man lined up against him.

I had a successful year at center my junior year, and United Press
International named me a second team All-American. But my senior year
Fairbanks shifted me to offensive tackle after the second or third game. We
were having trouble at that position. I played tackle the rest of that year.

SN: *How much did you weigh then?*
KM: By that time my weight was up to about 220. But I just wasn't a tackle. I
didn't have any experience there. It was my third position in three years, and
I found it frustrating.

SN: *How did the next two years go?*
KM: We'd had a successful year my junior year, winning the Big Eight championship again. But the next year we finished only 6-4, despite having three
number-one NFL draft choices on the team. A lot of our junior class had
quit, and Fairbanks benched a lot of seniors who had been two-year starters
on two Big Eight championship teams in favor of an untested group of sopho-
mores. Those moves led to a lot of disharmony, and he nearly lost his job
during the next couple of years.

SN: *You played in the East-West Shrine game in San Francisco and then in the
Hula Bowl in Hawaii. How are those games viewed by the players in comparison to, say, the Orange Bowl?*

KM: Those games were like a vacation. You can't put too many plays in those games; they keep it pretty simple. We practiced a lot harder for the East-West Shrine game than for the Hula Bowl. It was definitely more fun to have participated in those games than in the Orange Bowl. If you're competing for a national championship, bowl games are not fun. Miami's a nice place, but it was hard workouts for the Orange Bowl.

SN: *The NFL draft took place after these games?*
KM: Yes. There were NFL scouts swarming all over the East-West game and the Hula Bowl, using the tape measure and the stop watch, timing guys and checking their height and weight, in preparation for the draft. If I have any complaint about scouts, it is that they are too concerned with the types of things they can measure. Of course, you can't measure a guy's heart. That's why drafting is not an exact science. Lots of times guys who are first-round draft choices wash out. They may keep them around two or three years, just to save face. They miss almost as much as they're right. Physically, you can have it all but just aren't a player. And the guys who are good never plateau, they continue to progress.

SN: *Stamina is hard to measure, desire, the ability to withstand pain.*
KM: Yeah. A lot of being a football player is instincts. It's not so simple as the scouts would like it to be.

There were three things that possibly could have hurt me in the NFL draft. Being an offensive lineman from Oklahoma, the scouts had no clue whether I could pass block, because we never had drop back passing. We were always in a four-point stance, which you never were in in pro football. You were always in a three-point stance in the NFL.

SN: *Which is harder to learn, run blocking or pass blocking?*
KM: Pass blocking is much harder to learn.

SN: *Can any offensive lineman good at run blocking learn pass blocking?*
KM: Not necessarily. An offensive lineman has to have quick feet. You have to have size, but if you can move your feet, you can usually learn to pass block. It takes time to learn pass blocking, a couple years.

Secondly, my senior year, I played tackle instead of center, my best position.

Finally, there was a question about whether I weighed enough. It was the beginning of a transition period; linemen were getting bigger. In those All-Star games, I probably weighed only about 230 or 235 pounds, although I was about six foot three. Kansas City, which was playing a three-man defensive line, had drafted a kid from University of Southern California in the first round as a center who was about six foot five, 265 pounds. It was right at the point where people saw that the defensive line was going to put a bigger guy on the center, and you therefore needed a beefier guy there. I think if I had weighed 20 pounds more, I might have gotten drafted higher.

SN: *Did you think you would go high or low in the draft?*
KM: I was close friends with the three guys at Oklahoma who were drafted in the first round, and it was easy to see that there was a lot more attention being paid to them than to me. Jim Files was a little bit of a surprise. He came on in the All-Star games. I suspect that he went from maybe a fifth-round to a first-round choice because of his performance in postseason play, and because he grew physically his senior year and was a lot faster than they thought he was. They timed him running some really outstanding times. So, he improved his stock from the end of the season pretty dramatically. In fact, he was drafted ahead of Steve Owens.

Steve Zabel was a can't-miss from the beginning, and everybody told him he was going to be a first-round draft choice. The question was whether he was going to go in the first ten in the first round. He ended up going sixth. Steve was my closest friend on the team, and his wife, Susan, and my wife, Myrlane, and I all went to high school together. We were together all the time in those All-Star games, and I could see that I wasn't going to go anywhere close to where he was as a draft choice. People guessed I'd go between the third and sixth rounds.

SN: *What was the emotional experience of the drafting process like for you?*
KM: I can't really remember what it felt like. My experience was a lot different from guys who got drafted in the first round. The scouts probably hyped those guys into a frenzy. They'd be on the phone constantly with them. If you were a first-round draft choice, you knew you were going to get more money. I don't think anybody got guaranteed contracts. But you knew you were going to be there in the league for a while. If you were a washout, it was egg on their face, and they would keep you for a couple years anyway. But all of our first-rounders had outstanding careers.

So finally the phone rang, and the Atlanta Falcons told me they had made me their number-five draft choice.

SN: *How did you feel about that?*
KM: I felt encouraged. They didn't have a solid performer at center. I think the center they'd had maybe retired. It looked to me like the position was open for the 1970 season.

SN: *Did you have an agent assisting you in your contract negotiations?*
KM: I had an agent, Jack Mills, who signed me to a contract with the Falcons in a hurry. He was the same guy who represented Jim Files, Steve Zabel, and Bobby Anderson, a number-one draft choice out of Colorado. My salary was going to be something like $17,000, $19,000, and $21,000 a year the first three years. But I didn't collect the $17,000 because, as it turned out, I didn't make the team.

SN: *Did you use the same agent in Baltimore?*
KM: No. That was the last time in my career that I had any representation in salary negotiations.

Unfortunately, I was picked to play in the College All-Star game in Chicago, and that jeopardized my making the Falcons. I might have been the only fourth- or fifth-round draft choice there. All the rest of the guys were first- and second-round choices, and they were going to make their teams.

SN: *How did playing in the College All-Star game affect your chances of making the Falcons?*
KM: I wasted time being at the College All-Star game, because I wasn't in Atlanta's training camp learning the plays and their system. When I finally reported to them, as a fifth-round draft choice, I was already behind. A first-round choice could have fallen over his shoelaces for the first ten days, but he was going to be there. That's not the case with a fifth-round choice.

SN: *What was it like, showing up at the Falcons camp and being received by the team?*
KM: The Atlanta Falcons were pretty sarcastic and caustic towards the rookies and not at all encouraging. They saw a rookie as a threat.

SN: *Nobody stuck out his hand and welcomed you?*
KM: No, least of all the coach, Norm Van Brocklin.

SN: *What was your impression of Van Brocklin?*
KM: Guys were pretty fearful of him. He went into some real tirades as a coach. I knew some guys who played for him for a long period of time, and it was the most miserable experience they had had. Because there had been a players' strike, Van Brocklin said we were going to have to make up time. So, we'd get up at five o'clock and have meetings until the first practice. It was really nuts.

When I was training for the College All-Star game, the Falcons had converted a linebacker named Jeff Van Note, who'd been on their taxi squad the year before, to center. When I arrived at the Falcons' camp, he was the starting center. He ended up being a tremendous player, with a fourteen- or fifteen-year career, appearing in numerous pro bowls. He hasn't made it to the NFL Hall of Fame, but I think he will. I just had the misfortune of going to a team that had just converted a linebacker into what became a great center.

SN: *So you got cut at the end of the training camp?*
KM: Prior to our last exhibition game, I got called in and was told that the Falcons had traded me to the Green Bay Packers. I don't even know what I got traded for. It might have been another player or a draft choice. I've never been privy to that information, although I heard later that if more than one team claimed you when they put you on waivers, that they'd try to work out a trade for you.

So with about ten days to go before the last cut, I was traded to Green Bay. I went through a few practices with the Packers, but I had trouble getting the snap to Bart Starr, who was still there. That probably didn't help.

SN: *Why did you have trouble?*
KM: We just had trouble connecting on the snap.

SN: *Is that something you have to work on—a particular quarterback takes the snap differently from others?*
KM: Some might. I'd never had that trouble before. But he was used to the snap being in a different place.

SN: *Did you sense impatience in him?*
KM: No, Bart Starr seemed like a wonderful guy, and he had a little party for the rookies before the final cut. He and his wife had us all over to their home. I know he's had a lot of personal problems since then, but he was a class guy. But I was only at Green Bay for a few practices, and then I was released at the last cut. I came home after that short stay in Green Bay. I was certainly discouraged.

SN: *What did you think you would do then?*
KM: I didn't really know what I was going to do. It was into September 1970 by then. I was living in Enid, and I started to work with the high school team. That was kind of therapeutic. Some of the coaches I had played under were there, and that was fun.

About five weeks into the NFL season, I got a call from the New York Giants, who asked me to come up to New York and go to their game that weekend. They quizzed me a bit about my experience with the Falcons and the Packers and wanted to know why I thought I had been cut. Jim Files, my old teammate at Oklahoma, had gone there as the number-one draft choice and was having a tremendous year. I think he ended up being the defensive rookie of the year. I'd never been to New York, and finally, by luck, I found Jim Files' apartment. The next day I went to Yankee Stadium, where the Giants were playing the Cardinals. After the game, the Giants' director of player personnel asked me to come out to the stadium the next day and run through a couple of agility drills. I did that, and then they told me that they didn't have any room for me on their roster, but that they had a spot open on the taxi squad. It was a reserve role, where you practiced but didn't suit up with the team.

So I agreed to that, and signed with them for next to nothing—maybe $500 a week. Of course, rent for an apartment in New York was very expensive, more than I could afford. Jim Files was very gracious, and said I could stay with him. I had only taken enough clothes with me for a couple of days, so my wife mailed me some clothes.

SN: *You were married by that time?*
KM: Yes, Myrlane and I were married prior to my senior year in college.

SN: *So that must have helped, getting emotional support from her as you were getting cut.*
KM: Yes, I had emotional support from her going through this. It was as difficult for her as it was for me. I met Myrlane in high school in Enid. She was a year behind me at the University of Oklahoma and was a cheerleader there. I was staying with my buddy Files in New York and keeping in touch with her in Enid through long-distance phone calls.

Whatever the Giants thought they had seen in me, they reevaluated. I was with them for only five weeks. They released me from their taxi squad with three weeks to go in the season.

Before I could even get a flight home, I got a call from the Houston Oilers, who told me they had claimed me off waivers. They said they might have a spot for me as a long snapper. So, I flew to Houston and signed a taxi squad agreement with them for even less than I got from the Giants. I think it was for $300 a week.

When they tried me out for long snaps, I didn't do as well as they had anticipated.

SN: *Did you do long snaps in games?*
KM: No, I wasn't activated for the last three games. I went back to Oklahoma and trained hard during the off-season, working out and lifting weights. The next year, 1971, I went to their training camp in Kerrville, Texas, but was released after the first preseason game. Houston in the off-season had a coaching change and they were grooming a big offensive line and were bringing in 300-pounders.

SN: *What did you do after the Oilers released you?*
KM: I went back home to Oklahoma, and that week the Baltimore Colts called me and asked me to report to their training camp. They were the defending Super Bowl champions, whereas the other four NFL teams I'd been with had all been sub-.500 teams. Still, I wasn't real sure about whether I'd report to them. I talked with my dad about it some, and I decided I'd give it a shot.

SN: *What was your impression of the Colts when you joined them?*
KM: I could see that the Colts were different from the other teams I'd been with when I reported to their training camp in Westminster, Maryland. They had been successful, and they were not unfriendly. They were more secure.

SN: *Was any veteran particularly helpful to you?*
KM: My mentor that first year with the Colts was Bill Curry, the number-one center. He had played in the Pro Bowl several times and was a class guy. It was just the opposite of what I'd been exposed to on the other NFL teams I'd been with. When I got to the Colts' camp Bill knew I was really behind on the Colts' playbook. So, he told me to come by his room and he'd catch me up on it. I did that one afternoon, and any question that I had, he would answer. Bill was a good mentor for me, because he was a small center, like I was. I emulated a lot of his techniques. The Colts were a really helpful group of guys, and Bill especially so.

Not long after I'd joined the Colts, Bob Vogel, a ten-year veteran, told me: "You know, for a guy to make the team as a backup, it's important that he be able to play more than one position. You're working out at a couple positions, aren't you?" He didn't know me at all. And for him to make a helpful comment to me like that had never happened to me before in the NFL.

The most significant thing that happened in my professional career relates to my spiritual experience while I was with the Colts. At one of the first team meetings after the final roster had been named, Bob Vogel, an All-Pro tackle, stood up and said, "This week, we're going to start the team Bible study. We've had a rich spiritual heritage with guys like Raymond Berry and Don Shinnick."

Ken Mendenhall of the Baltimore Colts blocking Ray Hamilton of the New England Patriots. Courtesy of Ken Mendenhall.

He continued, "I think undoubtedly, part of the reason for our success is this spiritual strength of our team. I want all of you to know that you're invited to come. And, particularly, you rookies and new players." I later found out that the Colts were the first NFL team to have a Bible study.

After I made the team, my wife drove up to meet me. I knew that Vogel's Bible study group was the very type of thing that she would want to be involved in. I had no interest at all. So, I kept it a secret from her. But she eventually found out about it, and she dragged me to it. As I look back, none of what happened was an accident. It had all been preparation for what was going to happen that first year in Baltimore. I had been humbled and realized that football was a poor God and wasn't worthy of worship.

Anyway, we started attending this Bible study class, and I watched the veterans—Bob Vogel, Jerry Logan, and others—pretty close. I watched them in the locker room, and I watched them on road trips. The guys who were Christians on the team were committed to what they believed in, and their lifestyle was consistent with what they believed. And as a result of what I heard that fall, I accepted Christ and became a Christian.

Another good thing about the Colts was their head trainer, Eddie Block, who was a legend and a great model of courage. He was Jewish and very short. Everybody loved Eddie Block. He was a real character. He would stand up at training camp every year to make a speech, and he'd always say the same words: "Unaccustomed as I am to public speaking, it behooves me on this auspicious occasion . . ." He had his speech written out, and he would go on and on. That was the only time he got in front of the whole team. Eddie was a great trainer, who *really* cared for the players. He epitomized care and concern for the players.

The last year I played for the Colts I won the Ed Block Courage Award, named in Ed's memory. He had had a heart attack in training camp one year, and some of the guys on the team had rushed him to the hospital. On the way, their car caught on fire, and they had to pull Ed from the car and flag down another car to get him to the hospital. His heart was so severely damaged that only a portion of it was working, but he recovered. He was a courageous man, who lived on twenty-five percent of his heart for several more years. The Baltimore Colts named their award for courage for Ed Block because his whole life epitomized courage. The award was voted by your teammates and, because of that, it was very treasured.

The award is a big deal now, and since the Colts moved out of Baltimore, it's become a league award. Now each NFL team names a recipient of the Ed Block Courage Award. They have a huge banquet in Baltimore every year, and they bring in all these players from all these teams. I went several years ago and it seemed like they had more than a thousand people there.

SN: *Johnny Unitas was at the end of his career when you joined the Colts. Marty Domres was the starting quarterback in your early period at Baltimore. How would you describe him as a quarterback?*

KM: Marty Domres replaced Unitas at quarterback when Unitas was benched in 1972. Marty was real heady—he was from Columbia, he ought to be. He knew the things that he did well. But he was limited in his physical skills. His passing arm was very average.

A quarterback has to have a lot of leadership ability, and he has to make split second decisions. He has to be able to read coverages, because every coverage has a weakness. There's going to be a receiver that has drawn one-on-one coverage, so the quarterback has to see that and respond accordingly. Marty could do that; he understood the game. He also understood his abilities and limitations.

SN: *Bert Jones replaced Domres. What was that transition like?*
KM: Bert Jones was a first-round draft choice in 1973, maybe the second guy taken, and the Colts started him at quarterback in 1973. They shouldn't have started him; he wasn't ready. He had a lot more physical skills than Marty, but it was just too quick. We weren't a good offensive line, and we couldn't keep guys off of him as well as we should have. And our receivers weren't as gifted as a team like Pittsburgh's. I'm sure if the coaches looked back on it, they would have said that they should have groomed Bert. There was no doubt that he was going to be the quarterback. It sounds cold, but they should have let Marty take the hits for at least the first half of the season. We weren't a good team in 1973. I think we went 4-10 and had a lot of new starters, including me.

SN: *There's an image of the veteran quarterback in a clutch situation saying, "We're going to score," and everybody feels very confident he's going to bring the team down the field. Does a rookie quarterback show hesitation, lack of certainty reading defenses?*
KM: Nearly all rookie quarterbacks show hesitation and a lack of certainty reading defenses, but it wasn't true of Bert. He had a lot of confidence. His father was a coach for the Cleveland Browns. He grew up with the Cleveland Browns. He was born to play pro football. He was only doing what God had created him for. It didn't take very long for Bert to develop into a great quarterback.

SN: *Great arm, threw a perfect spiral, threw long, threw with accuracy?*
KM: Yeah. He could do everything. They used to set helmets up on dummies thirty yards away and he'd hit 'em. Just on a line. An arm you couldn't believe.

Defenses would lick their chops at a rookie quarterback, thinking they could confuse him. They'd throw some blitzes at him to try to test him out. But you've got to be careful if you've got a guy like Bert Jones, with a great

Ken Mendenhall hiking to Bert Jones. Courtesy of Ken Mendenhall.

arm and running ability. He could take off running or could hit somebody way down the field.

SN: *So you saw Bert Jones develop rapidly in that first year.*
KM: Bert matured during that first season, but the next season we still didn't have much of a supporting cast for him. We had an even worse season; I

think we went 2-12. But later, in 1975, 1976, and 1977, we were able to give Bert time to throw the ball, and we won three divisional championships.

Bert was the franchise. Our offensive line coach, Whitey Dovell, used to tell us that if you give him long enough to throw, he'll carve 'em up.

Bert also possessed real leadership abilities. There's one incident that really illustrates that. There was a play in a game where Bert didn't throw the ball and took a sack. We'd given him pretty good protection, but I guess nobody got open. He started running around and got tackled. Robert Pratt was our left guard, and an excellent player. Offensive linemen don't like for the quarterback to get sacked, because the coaches keep track of quarterback sacks, and the offensive line is judged by how many of them take place. After Bert was sacked, Pratt was screaming at him, "Throw the blankety-blank ball!" He felt he should have thrown the ball away to avoid a sack. Bert got up, and walked over to Pratt, and said, "You ever yell at me again, I'll make sure you never get in another game." Robert shut up.

If we could get Bert enough time to throw the ball and to execute, we knew we had a chance to win. Bert had some great comebacks. We were down one time 28-7 at Buffalo, and we came back and won 45-28. Sometimes when we were down, we were better, because Bert just came out throwing. It's easy to be motivated to protect a guy like that, who you know can win a game for you.

SN: *You saw Johnny Unitas play his last game in Baltimore for the Colts. What was that like?*
KM: One of the great moments I witnessed in football was Johnny Unitas's farewell in Baltimore, in 1972. The Colts during the year had been pretty much dismantled. We'd gone to the playoffs the year before, but we weren't having a good season. It was known that at the end of the season the new general manager, Joe Thomas, was going to clean house. He'd been brought in by the new owner, Robert Irsay. Bill Curry had been the Colts' player representative, and he was later traded to Houston.

SN: *Did that have anything to do with his being player rep?*
KM: Yes. The trading away of the player rep was a phenomenon that happened on innumerable teams.

Johnny Unitas had been benched in favor of Marty Domres, and it was known that at the end of the season he'd be gone. In the last game of the season, there had been some talk that Johnny Unitas would make a cameo appearance in the game, a kind of farewell to Baltimore. But Unitas said that he wasn't going to do anything like that. We were playing the Buffalo Bills, and we were winning convincingly in the fourth quarter. The game was uneventful. I was on the sideline charting the plays with Unitas. He'd see the play from the sideline, and he'd tell me, "That's a red right 72." And I'd write it down. Then, all of a sudden, a plane—the kind that they hire to pull a sign behind, usually to advertise a product—appeared overhead, and the whole stadium just exploded in noise. We looked up, and there was this message that said, "Unitas we stand."

You could tell it was really emotional for him. He just stood there, and they ran a play, and I said, "What was that, John?" And he didn't turn around. He was a pretty unemotional guy, but he was really moved.

Just about the time that the noise died down, we were driving the ball, and Marty Domres ran a bootleg or something and scored. A big cheer went up when he went over the goal line. But a bigger cheer went up when he couldn't get up, because that meant that Unitas was going to come in.

It was like a scene choreographed by Hollywood. We kicked off, and Buffalo ran a few plays, and then punted. And then here came old 19 in his high tops, shuffling onto the field. Everybody was just going crazy. He handed off a couple times. Then on third down, he dropped back to pass. Eddie Hinton was running a pattern along the sideline. John threw up a wounded duck. It had no spiral on it. Hinton saw it floating before the defender did, and he turned around and came back for the ball, leaping in the air and making a tremendous catch. Then he zigzagged and went sixty or seventy yards for a touchdown. He made the play himself. But the whole stadium just went crazy. That was Unitas's farewell in Baltimore.

Unitas was bigger than life. Everywhere you'd go, when they introduced the visiting team before the game, the home fans would boo. How much they booed depended on where you were, but they never cheered the visiting team. But they always cheered Unitas when he was introduced. People looked at him as the guy who took pro football into the modern era.

SN: *In Mark Bowden's* Bringing the Heat *(Knopf, 1994) there's a discussion of offensive line play I wanted to ask you about. The book says that centers are the anchors of the offense. The only other player handling the ball on every play is the quarterback. The center is in the middle of the action. Bowden also talks about the difference in temperament between offensive linemen and defensive linemen. Defensive linemen are more egotistical, hot heads. When they make a tackle their name is announced on the stadium loudspeaker. Of course, blocks are never announced. The book says that sportswriters prefer offensive linemen to the many "strutting peacocks around them." It also states that being an offensive lineman requires humility and tolerance. If you lose your temper, act impulsively, you can be easily knocked off balance. "The ideal is to become impervious, to become 'a blocking stone.'" What are your views on these observations of offensive line play? And did you envy the attention the backfield gets?*

KM: If you play on the offensive line for any length of time, you know that you're not going to get noticed much. You knew that that was part of the game, and it wasn't going to change. To be frustrated with that for any length of time would be silly. The offensive lineman gets his strokes from the success of the team. He's more of a team player.

People who know anything about the game know that you have to have great line play. If you're watching football, watch a back, and see how far he runs down the field before he's touched. If you see a guy running through holes, and he's ten yards down the field before he's touched—virtually anybody can do that. It's what they do after they get hit. We used to tease some of our backs. We'd say we blocked for ten yards, and they'd get eight. You don't have to be too smart to know that when you see big holes and backs running through them for ten yards without getting touched that the offensive line is doing a great job. And if the quarterback can stand back there all day long, then you know you've got great line play.

There is a difference in personality between offensive and defensive linemen. Defensive guys are more freelancers. They're probably more outgoing. You have to be a little more of a team player on the offensive line than anywhere else. The offensive line kind of sinks or swims together. You have one breakdown and the quarterback gets sacked every time, and it's a reflection on you.

The offensive lineman also has to be much more self-controlled than the defensive player. If you become agitated or lose your cool, then you're easily defeated. It's counterproductive to try and knock a guy's head off, particularly in pass protection. By contrast, a defensive lineman's getting angry might cause him to become more effective. He might make more of an all-out effort after the ball carrier.

The defense dictates what you're going to do as an offensive lineman, particularly in pass protection. The offensive lineman is the counter-puncher. You mirror their moves.

SN: *Defensive backs will tell you that some receivers will try to verbally intimidate them, sometimes by trash talking like in a boxing ring, whereas others never open their mouths the whole game. When you're up close to your opponent on the line, does talking go on?*

KM: Defensive linemen will try to use verbal intimidation against offensive linemen during games. Joe Greene would spit in your face and tell you that, if you held him again, he was going to kill you. Joe Greene was a pretty threatening guy. And Pittsburgh had that reputation. They weren't dirty players. But they intimidated. I didn't play against Butkus. He would have been intimidating. Ray Nitschke would be, too—those old middle linebackers.

There was a punter we had on the Colts, David Lee, who just hated contact. His whole game plan was to punt the ball and get off the field without getting hit. David would punt and just run down the field and try to avoid everybody. He said when we played the Bears, Butkus would chase him. David could hear him coming, but he could outrun him, and he'd keep on running all the way to the bench.

You experience a lot of different match-ups as an offensive lineman in pro football, if you were there ten years, like I was. You played teams in your division twice a year. I played against Ray Hamilton, a former Oklahoma player, who played for New England, maybe fourteen or fifteen times. It's not like that in college. But when you got into those match-ups in pro ball, they'd go on for half a decade or more.

SN: *Was there any defensive lineman in the pros who was particularly formidable as an opponent?*
KM: Mean Joe Greene was probably the toughest defensive lineman I faced. In fact, most of those guys in the Steel Curtain are in the NFL Hall of Fame by now. Pittsburgh kind of did a little thing where he lined up between the center and guard, at an angle. He would kind of jump around. Their defense was a little bit different. And, of course, Ray Hamilton was an excellent defensive player.

SN: *Jerry Kramer, in his book* Instant Replay *(New American Library, 1968), says that in practice offensive and defensive linemen go up against each other, and he says that antagonisms would develop. He and Ray Nitschke never really got along. The linemen were pounding each other in practice and were really opponents. Is there more antagonism or rapport between offensive and defensive linemen on the same team?*
KM: It just depends on the guys involved. Personality conflicts can develop. Sometimes what upsets a guy is that his teammate is going against him at a different speed in practice. Mike Curtis, who was a middle linebacker with the Colts, always went full speed in practice, even when guys were supposed to be going half speed or three-quarters speed. Everybody just knew that that was Mike, and he couldn't help it. He and Bill Curry used to really mix it up. They squared off a few times, even though they were roommates. You'd have a guy

like Curtis who didn't have a slower gear, who'd be going all out all the time. But most of the time, practices would be fairly amicable. By the middle of the season, you were so beat up anyway that you didn't want to waste your energy on that. You don't get paid for beating up your own linemen.

SN: *What are some of the differences involved in playing the various offensive line positions?*
KM: The major difference between offensive tackles and guards is not so much size, but that the blocking angles are so different, especially for pass protecting.

SN: *Aren't tackles generally bigger than guards?*
KM: They generally were, but I don't know that they are anymore. It used to be that the guards had to get out and run. You had running guards—Jerry Kramer was a pulling guard.

Generally the center would call the offensive line blocking. A tackle might call the blocking between a guard and a tackle. But, if there was a pattern for the whole offensive line, the center would call that, because of his location. So, you'd have to have a high level of awareness as a center, and experience is always a big plus.

I did notice in the time that I played in the NFL, in the 1970s, that I saw blocking patterns become simplified. I would guess that the cerebral capacities of the players in the offensive line were probably dropping. Maybe it was because I became more experienced and understood the game better. But the guys coming in didn't seem like they could grasp things as quickly.

I did see the responsibility of the center over my career become simplified. It became less of a challenge to me. The most boring thing I went through was sitting in training camp year after year and listening to the offensive line coach go through the classroom work, how we were going to block a particular play, when you'd been blocking it for ten years. The experience you got was always invaluable, but the experience didn't come in the classroom. Once you learned the system, you had the system down. And when it became simpler, then it became even more monotonous.

I was always comfortable doing long snaps as a center, although I never had the type of speed some of the long snappers did. Some people could burn it. Speed is important, because the quicker you got it back there, the quicker the punter would get the kick off. They would time long snaps. A guy who was really fast would be a . 7 second. Well, I was maybe a .9, or even 1 second. Two-tenths of a second could make the difference in blocking a punt.

SN: *I see how complex statistical measurements in football have gotten. You see hang time on punts flashed up on the television screen. Time of a long snap isn't broadcast yet. I would think reliability is as important as speed on long snaps, because a bad long snap is a disaster.*

KM: Absolutely. I was never erratic on long snaps; I never put it over somebody's head. When I was playing professionally and I wasn't starting, I'd come in and do the long snaps. But they'd usually bring in someone else to do them when I was starting. The reason is, if your backup snaps and pursues on punts, it saves a little bit of wear and tear on the starter.

SN: *Did any of your offensive line coaches stand out to you in the pros?*

KM: I had an outstanding offensive line coach at Baltimore, Whitey Dovell, who came in 1975 and was there through 1978. He was a great teacher. All the best coaches are great teachers. He was committed to me personally. There's a lot of politics that go on. The general manager traded for an All-Pro center, Forrest Blue, from San Francisco. I talked to Whitey about it, and he said he didn't care if the general manager traded for King Kong, I was the center. He had that type of personal commitment to the people who played and performed for him.

Teaching offensive line play is pretty fundamental across the board. There are only so many different ways you can learn to pass block. To be sure, you'll have a new coaching staff come in and bad mouth the previous one. They'll tell you, "You were taught wrong."

NFL coaching is the premier example of not so much how much you know, but whom you know. Coaching staffs are like little fraternities. A head coach will surround himself with his cronies. When a head coaching change takes place, they might get rid of an excellent assistant coach, because the new head coach doesn't know him. It's hard to break into the NFL coaching fraternity, no matter how skilled you are.

SN: *What changes have occurred in offensive line play since you retired?*

KM: Offensive linemen in the NFL have changed a lot since I retired. The size of them is just unbelievable. Their bellies can hang completely over their belts. On a team roster now, they've got maybe fifteen guys over 300 pounds. We never had anybody over 300. When I played, nobody could get away with looking like some of them do. That doesn't mean that they're not effective. Nate Newton is a tremendous player, and he's a beast, almost. But he has great strength and agility.

Even when I was playing, I always struggled with being underweight.

SN: The Sports Encyclopedia: Pro Football *(St. Martin's, 1994) lists you at 242.*
KM: I might have weighed 242 pounds at the beginning of the season, but I
played a lot more games closer to 230. Some coaches, like scouts, might be more
concerned with the stopwatch and scales than performance, and I didn't want
them to think I might be too small. So, if my weight dropped below a certain
point, I'd take these old five-pound weight-lifting plates and fit them on the side
of my stomach and then tape them to myself. Then I would weigh in wearing a
loose T-shirt. I'd weigh ten pounds more than I really did.

SN: *Did you ever feel in a big game that if you made a mistake, it would be something you'd have a hard time living with? In sports, your mistakes are magnified
way out of proportion and millions of people can watch them, like if you made
a bad snap on a field goal. I would think this could be devastating, particularly
because athletes are relatively young people.*
KM: I never had a fear of making mistakes when I played the offensive line.
Certainly, a mistake in snapping for a field goal would have been devastating.
But one of the things that's different about football, or basketball, or any sport
that's physically exhausting is that you're so caught up in what you're doing at
that particular moment that you don't feel the pressure. You're not sitting up
in the stands building up all of this emotion and tension. It's all coming out
through your pores. You're tired. Even during those moments that are really
tense, you're physically spent. Things are moving so fast out on the field. To
me, the pressure would be much greater in a game like golf, because you're
walking up to your next shot fifty or a hundred yards away. You've got all that
time to think about it.

The greatest nightmare would be to do something that hurt the team and
do something that would lose the game. Obviously, though, one particular
thing doesn't lose the game. There's a million chances to lose it or win it along
the way.

I think in some high-profile position like quarterback, who has so much
more responsibility than any other player, there's added pressure. Everybody
can see their mistakes, and those really could affect the outcome of the game.

I guess my fears or apprehensions going into a game would be that I was
overmatched physically. When I played against Mean Joe Greene, or Curly
Culp, or somebody like that, I knew that physically I couldn't match up with
him. I didn't have great physical strength and never overpowered anybody.
My strengths as a player were consistency and not making mental mistakes.

A lot of the game is mental. I didn't have many fumbled snaps, which at
any level will kill you in a game. I didn't get the quarterback killed because

I had blocked the wrong guy. I might have gotten beaten on a pass rush, but at least the quarterback could see it coming and would have time to react.

SN: *How often does holding go on on the line?*
KM: Holding goes on all the time. I'm not so sure that it's planned or that it's intentional. The rules are pretty lenient now. What isn't holding now would have been when I played. But holding is a real gray area. Most guys weren't overt in it and didn't intentionally grab hold of somebody. You generally didn't get away with the overt stuff; you'd get picked up pretty easy. You couldn't tackle guys. The umpire would watch the offensive line, but he couldn't watch everybody.

I think holding is the toughest call to make. Some would say interference— that's tough, too. But holding is pretty tough to figure out. Sometimes I'd think maybe they could just give each team so many and go on.

SN: *Jerry Kramer's book talks about coaches attempting to speed up an injured player's recovery pace. How does a player react to that? What goes on when a player gets hurt?*
KM: There's a lot of pressure to play when you're injured. You've got the coaches and the team wanting you to get back on the field. There's a lot of pressure on the trainers, and probably a lot on the doctors, to get you back out there. From reading *Sports Illustrated,* the doctor involved in the case of the player who had his foot amputated in Oakland seemed to be a puppet of management.

But the player is putting pressure on himself to get back as well, since the quickest way to get replaced is to be injured and to have somebody who makes half as much money as you do and is five years younger step in. My offensive line coach with the Colts in 1973 was George Young, who used to always tell us the Wally Pipp story. Wally Pipp was the first baseman with the Yankees before Lou Gehrig. Wally Pipp had a headache one day and sat the game out. Lou Gehrig replaced him and had a fantastic day. And that was Wally Pipp's swan song. I always remembered that: the quickest way to get yourself out of the game is to take a day off.

So, you don't malinger. The player usually wants to play worse than the coaches want him to. I knew guys who would take painkillers so they could play, and probably without the knowledge of the training staff or even the doctors. The Colts' owner, Irsay, accused Bert Jones of malingering at one point, and that was absurd. Bert was trying to play with a separated shoulder, with excruciating pain. He should have had surgery. Bert played one year with, I think, four broken ribs.

Everybody is hurt at one time or another, and they play with it. I mean, you just do it. In a game situation, there's a lot of adrenalin, and that makes a lot of difference in handling the pain. Of course, the adrenalin wears off you after a time.

SN: *Did you ever use painkillers to enable you to play when injured?*
KM: The only time I used painkillers was when I had a turf toe, which is a hyperextended toe. I had a painkiller injected in that toe to play on a particular weekend. I couldn't have done it without it. If I had to do it over again, I probably wouldn't have done it. But it did allow me to play, and there were no long-lasting side effects from it. I don't think there was a lot of danger of the joint being damaged. I never had the idea that they were violating any rules in doing that. With a knee, that would be different.

SN: *What kinds of injuries are most commonly sustained by offensive linemen?*
KM: As an offensive lineman, you don't think of serious injuries as much as you do at some other positions. Offensive linemen probably missed less time due to injuries than players at any other position. You never got the high-velocity collisions, because you're not downfield, and you're not hitting people after running thirty or forty yards, like a lot of running backs or defensive backs or wide receivers. Offensive linemen suffer some leg and knee injuries. Probably the most common are injuries to the upper body—shoulders seem to be most common.

SN: *The Baltimore Colts finished 10-4 in 1975, 11-3 in 1976, 10-4 in 1977, but then went into decline. To what do you attribute that?*
KM: For a number of reasons, the Baltimore Colts went from being a very successful team to a team on the slide. Ted Marchibroda had been a very successful head coach for us, but they fired him after the 1979 season. And the Colts drafted poorly for a number of years in a row. Our number-one draft choices were not playing. Four or five years went by like that. So, we weren't building our team through the draft. And, of course, our fortunes went as the health of Bert Jones went. There's no question about that. We rode his strong arm. Bert was injured in 1978 and played infrequently.

SN: *You get a sense of the Colts being in turmoil.*
KM: It was constant turmoil under Bob Irsay's ownership. Oh, it was wild. Consistency and continuity all start at the top of an organization. Irsay would

overreact to a not-great performance in a preseason game. But a preseason game is really just a proving ground. Of course, there's always the fear that you're going to breed bad habits if you get off on the wrong foot. But the teams that are secure use the preseason games to experiment.

SN: *How did it feel to play in Baltimore, when the Colts had had those great championship teams in 1958 and 1959?*
KM: It always irritated us on the Colts that all everybody would talk about in town was 1958 and 1959. A lot of the guys from those teams still lived in Baltimore; they hung around. They would reminisce probably every time they had a beer.

But it was an unbelievable experience to attend the reunion of all the Baltimore Colt players that they had in Baltimore about three or four summers ago. People there desperately wanted to get a franchise back in Baltimore, and they had made arrangements to have an NFL preseason game in Memorial Stadium on a Friday night between the New Orleans Saints and the Miami Dolphins. The town thought it could show the NFL that the enthusiasm and spirit was still there. They sold out the game, 60,000 seats, within twenty-four hours.

They made provisions for John Mackey to receive his Hall of Fame ring at halftime. I had heard that they had wanted him to come to Indianapolis to receive the Hall of Fame ring, and that he had said, "I wasn't an Indianapolis Colt. I was a Baltimore Colt." And that materialized into a reunion of the old Colt players.

We had eighty guys who came back for that reunion, including five Hall of Famers. There's a lot of NFL teams who don't have any Hall of Famers. At halftime, they started bringing us out of the dugout and lining us up. The sound just exploded when you walked out onto the field. It was unbelievable, the sound of the 60,000 fans cheering. I walked out, and they started introducing Gino Marchetti, Lenny Moore, Ted Hendricks, Johnny Unitas, all Hall of Famers, and John Mackey, who was going to receive his ring.

The Dolphins and the Saints were standing there. They were all looking over at the dugout, at the guys from a different era that they had only heard of.

This was a party with 60,000 fans who'd come to cheer the Baltimore Colts of the past. You hadn't heard a crowd roar that long for a group of guys. Everybody had goose bumps as big as marbles. Here was John Mackey, who'd come to Baltimore to get his Hall of Fame ring. Don Shula, who had coached him for years, was the head coach of the Miami Dolphins. And they had Shula come out on the field. Like my friend Joe Ehrmann said, "This is Field of Dreams."

The only regret I had is that I didn't bring my kids. The guys who lived in Baltimore had their kids with them. You see, my kids missed my career. My daughter went to a couple of games. She was born in 1974, and I retired in 1980. I wish my daughter at least had been able to come, to have seen the appreciation of the fans, and what a big part of my life pro football was.

Sports has never been a priority for my daughter, and my son has no interest in sports whatsoever. He has his own identity, and I don't want him to feel any pressure. You know, somebody coming up, and scruffing his head, and saying, "You're going to be a good football player like your dad." I want him to do what he's good at. My dad was every bit as supportive of my youngest brother, who was a motorcycle rider, and of what he did as he was of me.

SN: *Why did you decide to retire when you did?*
KM: I decided to retire because we weren't winning and, frankly, because I was just worn out. There are some individual honors that go with any position, but the offensive lineman really gets his strokes from the success of the team. And so the team's lack of success was a factor in my decision, along with the coaching changes that were happening.

I was also having some physical problems. I think I had 118 starts in a row. There were seasons where I played every offensive play. My knees were incredibly sore. I suffered some pain during the season. I was not incapacitated, and I could have continued to play. I had not suffered a career-ending injury. But it was very uncomfortable to play.

Finally, the Colts had drafted Ray Donaldson to take my place at center. A week into training camp, I saw the type of abilities he had—strength, speed, balance. He had all the tools. I knew that it was just a matter of time before he put it all together, before he had some experience and learned the system. I knew that they were grooming him to take my place, and in their case, the sooner the better. I probably could have caught on with another team, but I wasn't crazy about doing that.

Still, retiring was a difficult decision. I had decided during my tenth season in Baltimore that that season would be my last. I had decided intellectually, but emotionally it was pretty tough to let go. I think part of it was that it had been so difficult for me to break into the NFL. On my fifth team, I had hung on, and it wasn't until two years later that I finally got a starting position. And I never forgot that. But I could see that I was slipping as a player, that my quickness had begun to go, ever so slightly.

I had played a long time, a lot of games. I never made it to the Pro Bowl, and I wasn't going to the Super Bowl, unless I went to a different team.

SN: *What was it like, adjusting to retirement?*
KM: Adjusting to retirement was easier as an offensive lineman, because the level of adulation that you got when you played wasn't the same as a quarterback, or a running back, or even a defensive lineman or linebacker. It's just not so far to tumble.

I think my faith in Jesus Christ was also a big factor in my ability to make that adjustment, too. My identity was not totally wrapped up in football. Often, a guy's identity gets so wrapped up in being a football player, and he doesn't have a strong sense of self or any transcendent values. Then retiring is like falling off a cliff.

We had lived a modest lifestyle as well; I never made big money in the NFL. For some guys it's a fairy-tale world, the money they make. So, the transition for them is really difficult when the money's not there anymore. Some of them never recover. It was different in my case.

SN: *What kind of money were you making in the NFL during the 1970s?*
KM: I would guess that my average salary for my ten-year pro career was about $45,000. There was a guy I roomed with my last year with the Colts, a journeyman ballplayer. Somebody told me, not too many years after I had retired, that he was making $600,000 a year. And he wasn't even a starter. That's more than I made in my entire career.

SN: *Did any NFL team try to sign you after you had retired from the Colts?*
KM: I did have an opportunity to come back and play the season after I had retired. Ray Perkins, the head coach of the New York Giants, called me early on a Monday morning and asked me to play for him against Dallas that very week. He had gotten a center hurt. It meant playing against Randy White, and on my best days I'd had trouble blocking him. I decided not to accept the offer.

SN: *Where did you move after you retired from football, and what kind of work did you become involved in?*
KM: I came back to Enid, Oklahoma, and worked with my brothers in the oil drilling business for a number of years. I had already been involved with them in the off-season. It was busy, and the company was successful.

In 1987 we moved to Oklahoma City, and I became involved full-time with Search Ministries. I'm an area director, and we have about twenty-five guys around the country. One guy described what I do by saying, "You're kind of a minister to the people who don't go to church." And that's true. I work with a lot of people who aren't involved in organized religion. I lead discussions on spiritually related issues and do Bible study groups, at noon in office settings and in people's homes in the evenings.

SN: *What do you think about the changes in pro football since you retired, like the end zone dancing?*
KM: Pro football has changed a lot in the fifteen years since I retired. I think the showboating you see today takes away from the game. It's unprofessional to draw attention to yourself, to run around, trying to get the fans up. Being from the old school, those things kind of just get under your skin. Do something to get the fans on their feet, instead of waving your hands. The game has lost a lot of class in that way. I'll never forget the statement somebody made about Paul Warfield—that he used to always hand the ball to the official after he scored a touchdown, because he wanted everybody to know that he had been there a lot of times before. Barry Sanders is one of the few who is not a cheerleader and consumed with himself.

SN: *So how do you feel looking back on having been a pro football player?*
KM: I notice a lot of men find pro football alluring. They have that fantasy— it would be their dream to have been a pro football player. The question you always get is, "What was it like?"

Sometimes it seems like your football career was a different life. You get so far removed from it. You don't forget. But it's a lot different from what you do today. Football was such a life-and-death issue at the time. You'd do anything to have success or go to the Super Bowl.

All of my trophies, game balls, and stuff like that are in black plastic trash bags in my attic. That stuff doesn't carry the significance it once did. You would play injured, and you would shoot your foot up to play, like I did.

The Apostle Paul is always using military or athletic analogies. In First Corinthians he was talking about the backdrop of the Isthmian games, which were a prelude to the Olympics. One of the statements he makes is: "Everyone who participates in the games goes into strict training. They do it for a prize that will not last." One translation says, "They do it for the perishable wreath. We do it for the imperishable." He's talking about the transcendency of spiritual things. And I can relate to that.

Only when your career ends at age thirty-two do you have that type of perspective. There are a lot of guys who will be sixty-five when they look back and say, "I sold my soul to this company, or this job, and what's the pay off?" Those comparisons speak very strongly to me. And probably to the other players as well, as they look back reflectively on what you're willing to trade your health and family for, for that brief moment.

The thing that you take out of it, more than anything, is your relationship with people. That's what matters. I don't look back on games, maybe because we weren't in the Super Bowl. But I look back on the people I played with and the pleasure I had in knowing them. There's a deep bond with those guys that couldn't be forged like that probably anywhere else.

GREG PRUITT

RUNNING BACK

—Cleveland Browns, 1973–1981
—Los Angeles Raiders, 1982–1984

Greg Pruitt, the pioneer of small running backs in the NFL, played twelve years with the Cleveland Browns and the Los Angeles Raiders and went to the Pro Bowl five times. He played in the 1984 Super Bowl with the Raiders. Pruitt, who gained over 1000 yards rushing three times in the NFL, was also an excellent kickoff and punt returner. He was an All-American at the University of Oklahoma, where he played for coach Chuck Fairbanks and offensive coordinator Barry Switzer.

Pruitt discusses the influence of his grandparents, who instilled in him a work ethic that contributed significantly to his athletic success. He explores the impact of his grandfather's coaching him in Little League and high school baseball. Pruitt played football on the Houston sandlots, and he explains how he learned his moves as a running back in games staged in the narrow street in front of his mother's beauty parlor. He recalls his experience playing football at a small African-American high school.

Pruitt discusses the college recruiting process, which involved taking his first airplane trip, and the difficulty of adjusting to the University of Oklahoma.

Greg Pruitt with the Clevelend Browns. Courtesy of Greg Pruitt.

He examines the college athlete's academic experience and the strict discipline Oklahoma then maintained over its athletes.

Pruitt explains what separates an excellent from a mediocre running back. He relates what it was like playing for Forrest Gregg at Cleveland, whose coaching was patterned after that of his mentor, Vince Lombardi. After a long career with Cleveland, Pruitt was traded to a veteran Raiders club. Initially bitter,

Pruitt came to view the Raiders as "like football heaven." He describes the excellent rapport owner Al Davis had with the players. Pruitt also explains how playing in the Super Bowl is completely different from the experience of being in any other game.

STEPHEN NORWOOD: *I'd like to start by asking you about your background—where you come from, the community you come from, and your parents, and from that point we'll talk about how you got involved in sports in childhood and adolescence.*

GREG PRUITT: I'm from Houston, Texas. I was born there on August 18, 1951. Television first drew me to sports as a child. We would often watch football, basketball, and baseball, and then go out and play sandlot. We would pretend we were the different athletes that we had seen on TV.

My grandfather, Edward Philpot, was a major influence in my life. He had played professional baseball in an all-Negro league, and so my first sport was baseball.

SN: *How long was he involved in that? Do you know what teams he was with?*
GP: No, but I remember watching him play toward the end of his career. By that time, he was so old that I saw him hit a ball against the fence and get thrown out at first.

My grandfather was a pitcher. So, when I started playing organized baseball, of course I became a pitcher. He taught me all the trick pitching. We didn't concentrate so much on throwing the fastball, because he no longer had the stamina or the strength to overpower batters. Instead he used a lot of different types of breaking pitches, pitches I didn't even know existed.

SN: *Did your grandfather coach you in any other way?*
GP: Oh, yes! My grandfather really made me a much better baseball player. He coached a Pony League team up in Willis, Texas, about fifty miles north of Houston. The team was composed of teenagers, seventeen, eighteen, nineteen years old. When I went up to see him and my grandmother during the summer, I was his bat boy. He made me stand up at the plate, and he'd have these guys throw pitches to me.

SN: *How old were you?*
GP: Probably eight or nine years old. Well, I was scared to death. The ball looked like aspirin. Hey, I didn't have a chance. For a while, I got away with standing up there and closing my eyes. When I heard the ball hit the glove, I would swing. I was afraid to watch the ball.

After a while, my grandfather took away my fear of the baseball. Even when I was crying, he would make me stand up there and try to hit. And eventually, I wasn't afraid of the ball. Of course, I still didn't have any chance in the world of hitting the ball, because it just moved too fast, and I was too young to swing that fast.

SN: *But you could at least stand up to that fastball there.*
GP: I was actually up there thinking I had a chance. And when I went back to play in Little League, with my own age group, and later in high school, it was just easier to hit the ball. I could hit to any field I wanted. I thought the guy was throwing a softball rather than a baseball. And I did real, real well.

If I got my athletic ability from anybody, I got it from my grandfather. He was the athlete in the family. He came to a lot of my high school and college games, and I continued to learn from him. I always looked for him.

SN: *Was your grandfather involved in football in any way?*
GP: My grandfather was from the old school. There was only one sport— baseball.

I remember a high school baseball game where he really helped me. I was a left-handed batter, and I was facing a left-handed pitcher who threw a lot of curve balls. Late in the game, I came up with two out and the bases loaded. I had struck out three or four times. I hadn't even come close to this guy. His curve ball curved so much it looked like it was going to hit you. And you would dodge, and turn right at the umpire, and it would curve over the plate, and the umpire would go, "Strike!" I was up there, and he got two strikes on me. Then I heard a voice say, "Greg, I know I've taught you how to hit a curve ball." I looked, and it was my grandfather. He shouted, "You're sitting so far behind the plate that you're getting the full trajectory of his curve. Get up at the plate with the ball before it curves, and it'll become a fastball to you." So I stepped up and hit a grand slam. That was the only hit I got, but it felt good, because my grandfather saw me do it and the adjustment he helped me make was the reason I did it.

SN: *What else can you tell me about your grandfather?*
GP: He was from Willis, Texas. He was a lumberjack. See, I was probably protected from a lot of things that happened in the inner city, because my grandparents owned a farm. We were always sent there to live during the summers. So, I was more like a country person, because I was brought up by country people with old values. My two brothers and I lived with my grandparents up in Willis during the summers. It was a really small town, with 999 people in it.

My grandparents were stricter than my parents. We used to call my grand-mother "The Warden." If you did wrong, you knew up front that if you got caught, you had to pay the penalty. In Houston, we would get out of line some-times, and all my mother had to do was threaten to send us to our grand-parents. That pretty much kept us in line.

SN: *Did your grandfather or grandmother ever talk directly about what the possibilities would be for you to become a pro athlete? Did they direct you in any way, in terms of your future, towards anything? What did they emphasize that you should be thinking about?*
GP: *Work ethic.* And that helped me develop as an athlete. If you want to be better, you have to work at being better.

SN: *My colleague, Professor David Levy, told me you took his course in African-American history at the University of Oklahoma. Do you remember that course?*
GP: Oh, yeah, I remember that course. I learned so many things about black history in that class that I didn't know about, and a lot of times I was pissed leaving that class learning those things. I told you that my grandparents were farmers. We used to pick corn and peas for them, and I've also picked cotton. The first day that I went out with my grandmother to pick cotton, there was cotton as far as I could see. And that was just one row! (Laughs) There were rows, and rows, and rows of cotton. I assumed that was our land. I later found out that we were sharecroppers, and picked cotton to split with the owners. We did all the work. And it was in that class that I understood what sharecropping was. And I got mad.

SN: *In Houston, what kind of neighborhood were you living in?*
GP: We lived in a low-income neighborhood—not ghetto, but low-income. The guys there, who were all black, played sandlot football, and I was the youngest and smallest to go out for it. I was seven or eight years old. Everybody wanted to be a receiver or a running back; nobody wanted to be a lineman. So, I volun-teered to be the center, which was the most unpopular position. That gave me an opportunity to play. They usually played four guys against four guys, and I made the ninth guy. So, they made me the center for both sides. It got to the point to where they were used to having me, and my age didn't matter. After a while, I got to play other positions, and I did very, very well.

SN: *Was there any involvement by local businesses in sponsoring the teams?*
GP: No. We just got a football, and one street would play another street. Other times we divided the neighborhood, about ten streets, in half, with Eastland

Street as a divide. One half of the neighborhood would play the other half. Every Saturday or Sunday, we would play. No adult supervision; it was just kids.

SN: *You had a good role model in your grandfather and other members of your family. You mentioned your parents. . . .*
GP: My parents separated when I was nine years old, and my two brothers and I were raised by my mother.

SN: *What did your mother work at to support the family?*
GP: She's been a beautician for forty years. Her mother was a beautician in Willis, Texas. My mother's being a beautician actually influenced my development as a football player, believe it or not. She often worked very early in the morning and very late at night, because her customers worked at different times and got off work at different times. My friends and I used to play football in the streets, in front of my mother's beauty shop. She felt safer with us out there playing. There were days when we played out there all day and most of the night. The street was narrow, three yards wide, if that, and that helped me develop a lot of my moves as a running back. Playing in a narrow street, you had to have some kind of move to get by the defenders. When I went into organized football in high school, I was playing on a field fifty yards wide, which seemed like much more room than I needed. A lot of the moves I used as a running back were developed in that little street right in front of my mother's beauty parlor.

SN: *Was your mother ever concerned you would get hurt playing football?*
GP: You remind me—I remember when I started playing organized football in junior high school, I needed five dollars to pay for insurance. My mother knew nothing about the game. She didn't know a football from a baseball. She just knew we played some game in front of her beauty salon. When I approached my mother about the five dollars, she said, "Oh, no. You're not going out there and get hurt!" I gave her a big speech about how I was going to play well enough to win a scholarship, and she wouldn't have to pay for my going to college. I thought I was saying what she wanted to hear, and it worked. She gave me the money, but she told me, "When you get hurt, don't come running to me."

SN: *Did you see much of your father after your parents separated?*
GP: No. After my father left us, I didn't see him again for fifteen years.

SN: *What did he do for a living?*
GP: He had worked at Folger's Coffee Company in Houston. But when he divorced my mother, he moved back to Arizona, where he came from, and remarried.

SN: *Your grandparents you were talking about are your mother's parents.*
GP: Right. Because my father was from Phoenix, I really didn't know my relatives on his side very much.

When I became involved in sports, the coaches served as father figures for me. All of the coaches were the same. They disciplined you when you needed discipline. There was no bending of the rules. You either played by the rules, or you didn't play at all. I don't really know where I would be if there wasn't athletics.

I remember when I was a junior in high school, and football practice was canceled, I didn't know what to do. I didn't know what kids did after school. You either went to basketball practice, baseball practice, or track. You got home at seven or eight o'clock at night.

SN: *What kind of high school did you attend in Houston?*
GP: B. C. Elmore was a very small school. There were only fifty-eight people in my graduating class. But we had a very good football program. We beat a lot of the larger schools.

SN: *This is an all-black high school?*
GP: Yes.

SN: *What was the football equipment like?*
GP: We didn't have much money for equipment. We had to make a lot of our equipment, and we used to sell things to buy equipment. I can't ever recall having a new pair of pants to practice in or a new uniform. Maybe once we had new jerseys. But I never had a new uniform, from junior high all the way through high school.

SN: *What can you say about the quality of coaching in high school?*
GP: We had excellent coaching.

SN: *Did the coaches have contact with major college football programs?*
GP: Well, my high school coach, Wendell Mosley, went on to coach at the University of Oklahoma. He coached me there when I was a junior.

SN: *How important was your high school coach in your development as a player?*
GP: He was a guy who was an athlete all the way around. And you were an athlete from the day you walked in the first time and said you wanted to play for him. For life, you were one of his players. He enforced strict discipline. If he said, "Jump!" the players just wanted to know how high. I've heard that he went into bars to confront players of his who were in there wearing their letterman jackets. He told them to either take the letter jacket off or get out of the bar. He didn't want that kind of reputation for his program.

Everybody respected him. A lot of people feared him. He'd challenge you verbally, and he'd challenge you physically, if you had to be challenged that way. He was offered a coaching position at Oklahoma two years before he went there. But he didn't come to Oklahoma until my high school was closed down, as a result of desegregation, and became a middle school. That disrupted his program. If he was going to leave, that was the time to do it.

SN: *Did he impart any football skills?*
GP: Oh, yeah, sure. Your foundation comes from high school.

We had a winning tradition at B. C. Elmore High School, and athletes were accorded a lot of status. There are traditions among inner city schools where one school just always wins all the time or is expected to win. We were that way. It was a big thing to be a football player. To signify that you played football, you would take your chinstrap and put it in your back pocket. Girls were attracted to guys who did that.

SN: *Did you play all-white schools at their home fields? Were there any tensions that you detected at games like that?*
GP: We played some all-white high schools as well as black schools in Houston and nearby cities like Galveston, Baytown, and Port Arthur. I never detected any tensions when we played the white schools. We were just amazed that high schools were that big. We used to try to count the schools that were smaller than ours. We very seldom found any.

By my senior year I had become a pretty good football player, and a lot of people were telling my mother how good I was and asking whether she'd ever seen me play. So, she began asking me when my next game was and telling me she was going to come see me play. The first game she ever came to, I got hurt and cracked three ribs. I was lying on the field in pain, and I looked right up into my mother's face. She had jumped the fence and run out onto the field to see how bad I was hurt. She was screaming, "My baby! My baby!" Man, that was embarrassing. The whole rest of the season, all I got from other guys was

"Don't hit Pruitt. His mom will come on the field and get you." That was the most embarrassing moment of my life.

SN: *Was there a problem in the high school with violence, drugs, gangs?*
GP: Oh, there were gangs. We didn't have the drug or discipline problem in my high school that you have now. There were a lot of gang fights. But we didn't pack Uzis and ride by and shoot people. We respected adults, and we respected senior citizens. It was just a thing among young men.

SN: *That would be a very different attitude from today, then.*
GP: Night and day. Night and day. These kids today don't respect anybody. I think it's a matter of kids not liking themselves or their situation and not knowing what to do to get out of it. They just revert to what they know, which is violence.

I grew up in a neighborhood where, if you did wrong and a neighbor saw it, he might kick my butt. Today I hear of kids jumping on their mothers. That thought never went through my mind. I can't even conceive of that. I've gotten upset. But back then, if you got upset with your parents, you better go three or four blocks away and say whatever you had to say about them. But they better not hear you. And you better not even have facial or body gestures that you didn't like the discipline they put on you. I think that's gone.

I was brought up in the church, and I think that's one thing that's missing. I was *amazed* to go to church, and I feared God. I was taught that God will punish you for doing wrong. So, when I wasn't with my parents, I always knew that God was watching. My parents, and especially my grandparents, always used to say that. If I did something bad and it got back to them, they'd say, "God don't like ugly. And that's why you got caught." So, I guess I was brainwashed in a sense. That was good for me to think that whatever I'd done, I had to fear that God was there when my parents and grandparents weren't.

Not only would the parents and the neighbors discipline you, but the teachers would, too. The teachers had permission to whip your butt. Now you get more lawsuits from teachers disciplining students that the teachers take the attitude, "We'll teach those who want to learn. Those who don't, we'll forget about." That's the wrong attitude, because the problem hasn't been resolved.

SN: *This was a period when the civil rights movement was developing and becoming influential. What do you remember about that?*
GP: I was really too young to understand what was going on. My mother's and grandparents' attitude was basically not to do anything to get yourself in

trouble. I remember in high school we demonstrated about a levy, or something, that had been passed by the city. We were supposed to get something from it, but we hadn't gotten it. To me, the biggest thing about marching was that we didn't have to go to school. I was also in a desegregation march, to have black students go to white schools. But again, we students were just following the lead of our teachers and parents. They marched, so we did it too. Anyway, that march didn't change my situation very much, because I continued to go to the same, nearly all-black, high school.

SN: *What was the college recruiting process like? Did the recruiters give much attention to your high school?*
GP: We had a really good high school football program, but the white colleges generally hadn't looked at our players, only the black colleges. A few of the white schools were beginning to show interest.

I was a quarterback in high school, a running quarterback, but my coach switched me to wingback my senior year, because he knew it would improve my chances of getting recruited. At that time, there weren't very many black quarterbacks in white colleges. I didn't understand what he was doing, and I was upset. Just to show you how small the world is—the game that I was switched was a game we played against Joe Washington's high school, from Port Arthur.

SN: *Which colleges were interested in you as a prospect?*
GP: I wasn't heavily recruited, in part because I went to a small high school and in part because a lot of people thought I was too small. When I went to Oklahoma, I was only about five foot seven or five foot eight and weighed only about 142 pounds. Still, I had been a good high school player, and four major schools were interested in me: Oklahoma, Wyoming, Arizona, and the University of Houston. Houston became interested because there was a linebacker at Farr High School that they were really after, bad. And when they collected the film to see him, it was film of a game his high school was playing against mine. They said, "Hey, what about this kid over here, Pruitt?" I was local, so they brought me over and tried to recruit me.

SN: *What led you to go to the University of Oklahoma?*
GP: I ended up going to Oklahoma for two reasons. First, my mother wanted me to get out of Houston. She felt that at the University of Houston, I'd be too close to my friends, whom she saw as a bad influence. She thought I was better off being as far away from that situation as possible. And secondly, my

coach, Wendell Mosley, who was also a father figure, said I should go to Oklahoma. I had three teammates from my high school, who had been a year ahead of me, who were already at Oklahoma.

Wendell Mosley was a really good friend of Bill Michaels, one of Oklahoma's coaches, and he worked out a deal with him to recruit me. Michaels had been coaching at West Texas State, or Texas Western, before going to Oklahoma, and still recruited in the same territory in Texas. He was after an underclassman at my school named Gene Sellers, a highly regarded linebacker. My coach struck a deal with Michaels that if Oklahoma took me, he would see to it that Oklahoma would get Gene Sellers.

Texas Southern University, a black school in Houston, was also after me. Their coach had a guy named Mitchell, who had gone to my high school and was then a senior at Texas Southern, come and try to influence me to sign with them. I had pretty much made up my mind to go to Oklahoma, but I went over to Texas Southern to see what their coach had to say.

SN: *What reasons did he give that you should go to Texas Southern?*
GP: He told me they had a winning tradition and that we were losing all our black athletes to the white schools. He admitted that the white schools had better facilities, but he said that Texas Southern had just as good a program as they did. Texas Southern didn't have the financial backing that the white schools had, but they still put a lot of people into the pros. This being a black school, and you being a black athlete, you should consider staying at home. I'd have all the benefits of being a homeboy, homegrown. I was nervous walking around his yard, because I knew I wasn't going to go to Texas Southern. I had really already decided to go to Oklahoma.

SN: *What was Oklahoma's recruiting pitch to you?*
GP: Oklahoma never really recruited me. They got me as a result of a deal cut between two coaches, which in turn had to be accepted by the Oklahoma head coach.

SN: *Were you confident that you could make the starting lineup at Oklahoma?*
GP: Oh, I could play football. I didn't have any lack of confidence in my ability. Still, I was nervous going up there, because I had never flown on a plane before. I remember my mother bought me a new suit for my first airplane trip. When I got on the plane, I pretended that I had always been on planes. I flew to Oklahoma on a Sunday, a sunny day. I was looking down from the plane, and I couldn't see anything. So, I told myself that the reason I couldn't see

cars or anything else was because everybody was in church. When I flew back, I flew at night, which meant that I could see the little headlights on the cars. I said, "Man, I'm glad I didn't tell anybody else that the reason I thought I didn't see anybody was because I thought they were all in church."

Oklahoma hadn't recruited me like a lot of other guys, where they roll out the carpet, and show you all the things that they want you to see, and try to sell you on the program. When I came to Oklahoma, I slept on the floor of a dorm room, with my two high school teammates. Chuck Fairbanks, the head coach, came by and introduced himself to me on his way to the golf course. Oklahoma's freshman coach, Jerry Pettibone, remembered me because I had beaten Joe Wylie, whom Oklahoma had heavily recruited, in a high school track meet. People started to take notice when they put us through various tests like the forty-yard dash and the vertical jump, and I beat Joe Wylie in all of them.

Pettibone kind of took offense to me beating Joe Wylie. He had suddenly become known as "super-recruiter" when he had signed Wylie, with all these other schools after him. He resented my beating him.

Early on, Pettibone treated me unfairly, and I didn't speak to him the rest of the season. Oklahoma had a rule that you had to eat breakfast. You had to at least come down to the cafeteria and tell the guy there, "I'm not eating breakfast today." You had to get out of bed and get signed in. If you didn't, you had to run stadium steps as punishment. One morning, I overslept. When I went down, there were about seven other guys who were late; I was the only black guy. Pettibone told me, "You know the rule. Meet me at the stadium six thirty tomorrow morning." I was more mad at myself, for oversleeping, than anybody. But the next morning, I was the only guy at the stadium. I asked Pettibone about the other guys who had been late. He just said, "Well, they told me about it." I said, "Well, I told you about it, too." He replied, "Well, I'm the coach. You're going to run stadium steps." I got so upset with Pettibone that I ran the stadium steps, and I never got tired. You hear about women picking up cars off their kids, feats that they don't later remember—this was like that. The last thing I remember Pettibone saying was, "Damn, you ran those stadium steps!" I made it a point that whatever Joe Wylie did, I did it better. I did it for the wrong reason, but I think the motivation actually helped me play better.

SN: *Did you have any difficulties adjusting to the football program?*
GP: I was unhappy my sophomore year at Oklahoma. Oklahoma was using a veer offense, with Jack Mildren at quarterback. But Mildren was having a lot of difficulties throwing the football. They brought in the baseball coach to try

to help him throw the ball better. Finally, they decided to go to the wishbone, meaning mostly running. I had been starting as a receiver, and was switched to second-string halfback when they went to the wishbone. When they did that, I was really determined to leave Oklahoma.

SN: *What did you plan to do?*
GP: I decided to transfer to a junior college, but Oklahoma was in a position to prevent that. Oklahoma sent a lot of athletes out of high school whom it wanted, but who couldn't pass the entrance exam, to junior colleges to get their grade points up. The junior colleges were able to get great athletes in this manner, for two years, before sending them on to Oklahoma. So, their allegiance was to Oklahoma. So, when I contacted the junior college coach to say that I was interested in coming there, he turned right around and called Oklahoma. He didn't want any flak from them.

As a result, Oklahoma's head coach Chuck Fairbanks called me in and asked me, "You're not happy here?" I was determined to leave, but I wasn't going to let him know. So, I just sat there and lied, and said I was happy. After I got through lying, he let me know that he knew I was trying to leave there.

My mother was instrumental in getting me to stick it out. I called her and told her I was going to quit. My mother very calmly said, "Well, if that's what you decide to do, that's fine. But you can't come here." I said, "What do you mean?" And she replied, "I didn't raise a quitter. Better call your uncle, or call your aunts, but you can't come here." I started crying about this isn't right, and that isn't right, and I want to play. And she said, "Well, just for me, why don't you just give it some time?"

SN: *This is sophomore year.*
GP: Right. When I came to Oklahoma, I really thought I was a better baseball player than a football player, but I didn't play baseball for two reasons. First of all, there were no black players on the team. That was, of course, not the case in football. And secondly, I was so homesick my first year at Oklahoma that I didn't want to stay there any longer than I had to. That was the first time I had ever been away from home. And Oklahoma's baseball team was always in the College World Series or in some national championship tournament, which meant you had to stay in Norman well into the summer.

SN: *What were your objectives in college? Were you looking to be an NFL player at this point? What ambitions did you have?*
GP: My objective was to be a businessman. But I didn't know what that took to be that. Academically, I had some trouble adjusting. I remember when I arrived at Oklahoma, I was totally lost, coming from a small school.

The football program maintained good discipline on the academic side, and I benefited from that. They automatically put you in study hall, and you needed to make a certain grade point average to get out of it, which I did. If your average went down, they added days that you had to be in study hall. You went there from Monday through Friday, and if there was no improvement, they made you go on Saturday. If there was still no improvement, you had to go on Sunday, too, seven days a week. They also gave you tutoring.

When I first got to Oklahoma, I didn't want to be in study hall, and when I was there, I did everything but study. I threw spitballs and popped people on the head. But I got bored sitting there for two or three hours doing things like that. Then, when I started to read and study, the time went by real fast. So, I chose to study, because then it didn't seem like I was there long at all.

Port Robertson was in charge of the academic side then, and it was when he left that the Oklahoma football program started to get into all this trouble. I think Port had been a marine, and he kind of ran things like the marines. It was discipline. No matter who you were, if you had a problem with your grade, he knew it right away. If you missed class, he knew it. His name was Port G. Robertson, and we used to say that the G stood for God, because there was nothing we did that he didn't know about.

To make sure we were alert, Port told us he was going to call us in the morning, and if the phone rang twice, we'd have to wash dishes. He called me one morning, and I dove out of bed, and I missed the phone, and it rang twice. So, I had to wash dishes. I was leading the nation in rushing. But with Port, it didn't matter who you were. When you washed dishes, all your teammates walked past you, and you got all that joking and kidding. To save yourself that embarrassment, you made sure that didn't happen again.

SN: *What was the atmosphere like living in the athletic dorm? There was the impression from the scandal a few years ago that things had gotten way out of hand. They had guns. . . .*
GP: That didn't exist when I was there. Oh, no. Port was an intimidating figure. There were rumors that he had been a national champion wrestler, along with being a marine sergeant. People said he could take a pair of pliers and break them with his bare hands. He walked around in study hall with a big set of keys, and if you went to sleep, he'd hit you in the head with those keys, Bang! They used to always tell you that if Port opened his desk drawer and closed the door, you were in *big* trouble. They said he had a pistol in that drawer, and he was closing the door so you couldn't get away. So, anytime you went to see Port, the first thing you would check would be to see if he was going to close that door.

You just had a respect for Port. Because of that discipline, and the study hall, and tutoring, I was able to make it academically. It was a struggle at first. I used to sit in classes, especially my freshman year, lectures with 200, 300 students, and the professor would be up there talking, and he might as well have been speaking in Japanese. I had no idea what he was talking about. When everybody else wrote, I would write. When they stopped writing, I stopped writing.

There was only one subject that I didn't struggle with in college and that was English. I hadn't been a very good student in high school. To get out of doing assignments, I would tell my teachers, "We had a game last night in Baytown, and we didn't get back until one or two o'clock, and I'll have it tomorrow." That excuse worked with all the teachers except the English teacher. I hated the English teacher. She'd say, "I don't care how many touchdowns you made, I don't care when you got back, if you don't do my work, I will flunk you." So I had to do her work. And I skated on all the rest. When I got to college, the English class was the one class where I understood what was going on.

Insufficient high school preparation caused me to switch my major from business to journalism, at least unofficially. There was a math requirement for the business major; you had to take algebra. But geometry was as high as the math went at my high school. I never could master algebra. I wanted to switch over to the School of Journalism, but they had a foreign language requirement. My counselor expected that Oklahoma would soon eliminate its foreign language requirement, since a lot of schools were doing so. She advised me to start taking courses as if I had switched my major to journalism. When Oklahoma eliminated the foreign language requirement, then I would officially change my major. But what she thought would happen never happened. So, I ended up having to come back in the off-season, after I had made it to the NFL, to take three semesters of Spanish classes. As a result, it took me seven years to get my degree.

SN: *You'd played freshman year as a receiver. Where were you on the depth chart sophomore year?*
GP: I was a second-string running back, playing behind Everett Marshall. I got my big opportunity three-quarters of the way through my sophomore season, against Iowa State. Everett got hurt during the game. Iowa State hadn't beaten Oklahoma in over thirty years, but they had us down 21-0. It looked like the upset of the decade. I'm telling you, football is *real* important in Oklahoma. At halftime, it was almost like, "We're going to line all you guys

up and shoot all of you, if you lose this game." With Everett hurt, I ended up playing the second half of that game. At the end, we had pulled to within one point of them, and we decided to go for the two-point conversion. A tie with Iowa State was considered as bad as a loss. So, we went for the two points, and I made it.

SN: *From the Iowa State game on, you were a starter?*
GP: Oh, yeah. I think I led all the rushers after that.

SN: *What was the team's national ranking?*
GP: We finished in the top twenty and played Alabama in the Bluebonnet Bowl, where I was the most valuable player.

SN: *What was junior year like?*
GP: My junior year was probably my best year. We ended up ranked number two in the nation and went to the Sugar Bowl. I was a candidate for the Heisman Trophy. We had a great team. We were a running team, and I was a running back, so I got the opportunities and I took advantage of them. I had as good a year as a senior, but I got hurt and missed some games. That injury probably cost me the Heisman Trophy, to Johnny Rodgers of Nebraska. The size thing was always an issue with me. I always went out and played extra hard to prove that I belonged there, that I was big enough to play.

My junior year, I began to imitate Muhammad Ali. He predicted the round he was going to knock people out in. One day in the locker room, the reporters were doing some interviews, and I got up and announced, "I'm going to rush for over 200 yards against Southern California," which was our first game. All the reporters came over. When I got back to my room, I said, "Why did I do that?" I thought I had screwed up. Sure enough, the next day I read in the papers, "Pruitt Predicts He's Gonna Get . . ." Oh, man!

That's when Barry Switzer, our offensive coordinator, came out with the "Hello-Goodbye" T-shirt. "Hello" on the front, "Goodbye" on the back. They took pictures of me with that T-shirt on, saying I was going to get 200 yards against USC. I knew that before the ink even got dry, it was being pinned up in the USC locker room.

USC came in to play us ranked number one in the nation, and we beat 'em. I gained 213 yards. So, now I really had reporters all over me. You'd think I'd learned my lesson. The reporters asked, "Well, what about next week?" And I said, "Yeah, I'm going to get 200 yards next week, too."

I was doing all this talking, and I'd go back to my room, and sit up, and say, "Hey, boy, you're going to put your foot in your mouth one day." And I said, "Well, I'm going to keep doing it until it does happen." But I had a great season that year and was All-American.

SN: *How did the team do that year?*
GP: We only lost one game that year, but that loss deprived us of the Big Eight championship, the Orange Bowl bid, and the national championship. That was the Thanksgiving Day game against Nebraska. I had only five or six carries in that game. Not to sound conceited, but I think that was the difference. I remember getting upset that I wasn't getting the ball.

SN: *When did you start thinking that you could play in the pros?*
GP: My junior year, when I put up the kind of numbers that would draw interest from the pros. I made all the All-American teams and was getting the kind of awards that separated me from everybody else. So, I was pretty confident. I was so happy to be considered for the Heisman Trophy as a junior that I probably should have raised more hell about losing it than I did. I remember commenting, "Well, there's always next year. I'll get it next year." But it didn't work out that way.

My senior year, I was in contention for the Heisman, but I ended up losing out to Johnny Rodgers of Nebraska. Unfortunately, I hurt my ankle the week before we played Nebraska. The Oklahoma-Nebraska game was scheduled for Thursday, not Saturday, so I had very little time to recover. I had thought if I could outperform Rodgers in the same game, I could get the Heisman. So, I was very disappointed. I was only able to play in two or three plays against Nebraska. My ankle was hurt too bad.

When my roommate Ken Pope, a defensive back, saw that I was upset and just moping around, he determined that he would help me. Ken is still my best friend today. I told him, "I blew it. I got a chance to play Johnny, and I can't play, and Johnny's going to have a great game." I got Ken all worked up, and he told me, "Don't worry about Johnny Rodgers. I'll take care of Johnny Rodgers!" Nebraska ran a reverse or something, and Ken hit Rodgers and put him out of the game.

So it turned out that the game wasn't a determining factor. I got hurt prior to the game, and Rodgers got hurt in the game. But Johnny ended up winning the Heisman Trophy. I think one of the factors in Rodgers winning was that his coach, Bob Devaney, had announced his retirement, and he had never had a player who won the Heisman. Devaney had had All-Americans, he had won national championships, he had won the Big Eight, but he never had coached a Heisman Trophy winner. So, there was a sentimental advantage that Johnny benefited from.

SN: *Looking at the coaching at Oklahoma, how would you describe Chuck Fairbanks's style? Was Barry Switzer the head coach your last year?*
GP: Switzer was offensive coordinator. I left when Fairbanks left.

SN: *So how would you assess Chuck Fairbanks's coaching style?*
GP: Well, Chuck didn't have to do very much. What he did was to put together a staff of great assistant coaches. The assistant coaches at Oklahoma, when I played there, all went on to become head coaches at major colleges. That tells you their caliber.

SN: *Were you interacting mostly with Switzer?*
GP: Oh, yeah. The players didn't have much contact with Fairbanks. The only communication you had with him was when you screwed up. When Fairbanks came to practice, he would drive by in a golf cart. They had a portable tower, which they put on the fifty-yard line, and he would go up in the tower to watch the practice. When you screwed up, you had to run over and look up at the tower. And he'd tell you, "You don't do this, and we don't do that."

SN: *He would summon you over and talk down to you from the tower?*
GP: Right. (Laughs) That was it, as far as any contact with the head coach, other than some pep talks and pregame speeches. Fairbanks had such talent at the assistant coach level, that there was really nothing for him to do but just reap the benefits.

SN: *What do you think are the ingredients of a good coach?*
GP: Two things are important. One is your ability to prepare your team and put together game plans for opposing teams. That's the coaching part. Then there's the ability to communicate with your players. You can put together the best game plan, but if you can't get them to execute your game plan, it's no good to you. There's got to be a cohesiveness between the players and the coach. The players have got to believe that the coach will do anything for them and will be there for them. There are some coaches who have the ability to make their players feel at ease around them. Barry Switzer has that ability, Jimmy Johnson has it, Tom Flores has it.

My senior year, I played in the same backfield as Joe Washington, who was a freshman. He tells this story that we ran this play, where he had to block a

250-pound linebacker. And being a freshman, he did as he was told. He told this when they roasted me two years ago. He said he went up, and hit the linebacker as hard as he could, and got the short end of the stick. And he got up real slow, and came back to the huddle. And I looked at him, and saw he was dazed, and said, "Run it again!" So he says he ran it again—runs it about two times. By this time, we had gotten down to the three- or four-yard line, which is the ideal place to run this play. Joe didn't know what day of the week it was, or what time it was, and I said, "Run it again!" And he said, "Okay, if we run it again, I'll run it and you block." And I said, "No, change the play."

SN: *What was the NFL draft like? What did you expect would happen?*
GP: Having been second and third runner-up for the Heisman Trophy as a junior and senior and getting all the publicity and awards, I was pretty sure I was going to be drafted by an NFL team and drafted pretty high. As a journalism student, I also had access to information coming over the teletype. And Chuck Fairbanks had left Oklahoma when I was a senior and gone to coach the New England Patriots, where he had three first-round draft picks. To be sure, there was some question about my size. But I said, "Who knows better about whether or not I can play than my head coach? And now he's sitting up there with three first-round draft picks. Hey, two plus two is four, and everybody knows I'm going to New England."

But draft day didn't go the way I thought it would. I was just waiting for it to be official, going to the Patriots in round one, and I actually went out and bought things for a party. But the first round went, and I hadn't gone. And all of those worries I had about whether my size would be a question mark started to become a reality to me. I couldn't take it any more. So, I went out on the golf course and played golf, not knowing where the draft was.

Some reporter found me and told me I had been drafted by the Cleveland Browns in the second round. So, I went back and Mr. Modell called me, Cleveland's owner, and welcomed me to the Browns. I had no idea where Cleveland, Ohio, was. All I knew was that it was where Jim Brown had played. Jim Brown was one of the players we used to always fuss about when I was a kid. You know, who got to be Jim Brown when we played football. I was a running back, like he had been, and I thought this was a great opportunity.

SN: *What was it like to adjust as a rookie to the NFL?*
GP: I knew a lot of people thought I was too small to play in the NFL. So, when I came to Cleveland after being drafted, before they weighed me I ate all

I could eat and drank as much water as I could drink. Then I got up on the scale and weighed in at 177 pounds. I tell people today, jokingly, that I spent all of my career trying to get to 190 pounds. And now, I'm 225 pounds and trying to get back to 190!

When we played our first preseason game, I was really nervous. We were in the locker room, and the closer we got to the game, the more nervous I got. Regardless of how good you were in college, until something happens that convinces you you're good enough to play on this level, you're just going to have these reservations about yourself. I had done well in practice and in camp. But I was always told it was a different game when it starts to count. We were playing Los Angeles, and I remember saying the Lord's Prayer, and hearing the team pep talk. I got out on the field, and the butterflies were so bad I said to myself, "I'm not ready, I'm not ready." They went out to flip the coin, and I was hoping that we'd lose the toss. If we lost the toss, then we'd kick, and I'd have a little more time to get myself together. So, they flipped the coin, and we won the toss. Oh, boy.

I was one of the kickoff returners, and I was hoping they'd call a return to the other guy. So, the special teams coach calls us over, and he calls a return to me. We went out, and I was hoping, by some miracle, that they kicked the ball to the other returner. They kicked off, and they kicked it to me. I got the ball, and we had a left return on, and I was running left, and all of a sudden, I saw a hole open up in the middle of the field, a hole big enough to put a Mack truck through sideways. And I made the ultimate mistake. I left my blocking and shot for the hole. Some guy hit me with a forearm, and I went down head first, with my feet going straight up in the air. The crowd went, "Ohhhh!" I mean, he knocked the crap out of me. Then he reached down to help me up, and he said, "Welcome to the NFL!" And I went to the sideline and said, "Damn. It's going to be like that every time?"

SN: *You held on to the ball, though?*
GP: I held on to the ball. Later on, we played the New York Jets, and Joe Namath was their quarterback. I was special teams captain, and I was thrilled that I was going to go out and shake Joe Namath's hand. I went out, and they went through "Captain Pruitt and Captain Namath." And they flipped the coin, and then they said, "Captains, shake hands." I had Joe Namath's hand, and I was just saying, "*Joe Namath.* I can't believe it's Joe Namath!" And he said, "Hey! You're one of us now. Turn my hand loose and act like it." I was a player and a fan, too. It was like a dream come true. I still couldn't believe it.

SN: *How did the veterans treat the rookies?*

GP: They used to haze the rookies, make us stand up and sing our school songs, and put on a talent show. Having gone through that as a rookie, you couldn't wait to be at the other end of it. I don't know if that still exists now. Guys make so much money now, that they'll probably have Michael Jackson come in and sing their school song.

As a rookie, I liked challenging the Browns' traditions that restricted rookies. They had a tradition that in training camp, rookies weren't allowed to come up to the second floor, which was for veterans only. I'd come up, and they'd run me back down. On the plane, the seating arrangement was based on how many years you had been in the league, with the rookies in the back. I'd get in first class, and they'd run me to the back. One day I walked into a lounge for veterans only, after I had scored the winning touchdown against Pittsburgh, a big rival. All the veterans were in there, and it got real quiet. It was like, "This is it. We've had it with this rookie." I stood up on a chair and started singing, "They call me Mr. Touchdown." They ran me out of there.

When I became a veteran, I appointed myself the guy who rode the rookies. But I saw these traditions start to change at the end of my career, the way rookies began to come in making so much money. There was just a different air about them.

SN: *You participated in the 1982 players' strike. What were the issues in that strike, and how were you involved in it?*

GP: I was very much involved in the 1982 players' strike, which was much better organized than the one in 1974. Previously, the owners had been able to break a strike because the players had been insufficiently prepared. That's where the union had made a mistake, in not preparing the players the season before, telling them they'd be on strike the next year and to put some funds aside. There were a lot of guys then who weren't making a lot of money. It got to the point where the checks were more than the issue.

The players didn't foresee that one day we'd all be out of the game, and that benefits should be the priority. The attitude was more, "What can I get now?" That was a mistake. The Players' Association has come a long way, increasing the benefits by forty percent. But in comparison to other sports, it's lousy.

SN: *In football you have a shorter career and a career that can end at any moment due to injury.*

Greg Pruitt with the Cleveland Browns. Courtesy of Greg Pruitt.

GP: More physical, life span is shorter, and you're prone to have a lot of repercussions from injuries incurred during your career.

SN: *What was it like trying to maintain solidarity on a team on strike?*
GP: It's difficult being on strike, because the team is divided into a lot of different groups—the backs, the receivers, the linebackers, and so on—and those groups pretty much talk among themselves and not so much with guys

in the other groups. It's hard to coordinate the different groups. You always had somebody trying to lead players this way, and somebody trying to lead players in a different direction. But we always knew we should go with the majority of the league. Other teams were out with us. And, hey, what if we did go back? Who were we going to play?

If you pay attention to player strikes now, the first people to come in are the people making the most money. It really should be the reverse, because the people making the most money should have more staying power. The owners know that, and so they go after those players. They figure that if they can get certain people to come back in, the others will follow.

The NFL Players' Association has made a lot of progress, and they've won a lot of cases, anti-trust lawsuits and things of that sort. I just read in one of the Players' Association newsletters that the people who went out on strike in 1987 are going to get their salaries for the games they missed. They're talking about a couple of million dollars they have to pay the players—more than that, I believe. I won't benefit from that. But if I'd have played in 1987, that would be nice for me now, to get a game check. It would be nice.

SN: *What was it like, adjusting to the NFL as a running back? What about the mental aspects of the position?*

GP: Playing in the NFL involved a big adjustment. When I first walked on to a football field in sandlot, there were no guidelines or rules. There could be guys out there who were thirteen years old, when I was eight. So, I always had to hustle harder, run faster, just to maintain the same level. That was an advantage to me, because as I got old enough to go into organized football, all of a sudden the guidelines eliminated the older guys. The guys I played with were my age, and it was easier to deal with them. So, high school was pretty easy for me. In college, the guys got two or three years older, but never older than that. So, college wasn't really a big effort for me.

But then when I got to the pros, it went all the way back to when I had first started in sandlot. You had guys out there thirty, thirty-five, thirty-seven years old, and I'm twenty-two. And the game is played ninety percent from the neck up. All those little tricks that worked for you in high school and college don't work at this level. Now, it's how well you use your head and how well you prepare yourself.

SN: *When did you start studying other players?*

GP: When I went to the Pro Bowl. I made it to the Pro Bowl my first year, as a kick returner. And because I was a running back, at the Pro Bowl I sat in the meetings and practiced with the running backs. So, I was sitting in with O. J. Simpson, Franco Harris, and Mercury Morris, and they were talking about what they did in certain situations. They're talking to each other, and I was twenty-two years old, and they were my heroes, and I listened to them. And I used those things later, and they worked.

I remember O. J. saying that he would reverse the field if he was playing a team that was fast defensively. The reason he did it was because a pursuing team is not a disciplined team. You have a play where you may run this way, and stop, and then run back that way. So, on any play, the defenders have to take at least a split second to make sure that you're not coming back that way. So, you've bought yourself a second that can make the difference in whether or not you can outrun a guy.

I also learned that on every play as a running back, there is a key block. If the key block is not executed, ninety percent of the time the play is not going to work. When you're running the football, you not only have to know where the key block is, but you also have to know if the person making the key block can make it. You have to adjust your timing accordingly.

Let's say there's a cross block, where the tackle blocks down, and the guard pulls around to get the linebacker. If your guard is great at that, you help him by not being late off the ball, because he's going to be there. If he's there and you're at the right position, that's a big play. But if you have a guard who is having a problem getting around to that linebacker, you have to run it differently. If that's the case, your first move when you get the ball should not be to hit the line real fast. Instead you make a move at the linebacker, to make him think you might be going the other way. When the linebacker hesitates, you've bought time for your guard, and now you go off the block. It's those little things that make the difference.

See, football at the professional level is just experience. What separates a great running back from a so-so back is that the great back makes the right adjustments. You're going to play the teams in your conference twice a year for how many ever years you play. So, every year, you get to know them a little better. And you have to take advantage of what you know. It's like a chess game. I just saw this guy from New Orleans rush for over 100 yards on TV. I said, "Okay, he showed me that he has potential. But now he has to show me that he's a great back, because I now know that the team he's about to play is going to watch him for one week, and they're going to try to shut down all of the things that he did great. The great back will find a way to counter that. If you beat me here, then you expose yourself there. The great backs find a way. That's the difference."

SN: *What about the role of blocking by running backs in the running game?*
GP: Your success as a running back depends to some degree on how well the
other running back can block the linebackers for you. In football, the linebackers make most of the tackles. You might get a great defensive lineman who can
make a tackle. But an offensive lineman doesn't have to look for a defensive
tackle or a defensive end. He's right there. But linebackers flow, so it's hard to
get to them. If you have a play where the tight end comes off on the linebacker, you know you can hit, because that's not that difficult a block. But
when you've got a fullback leading you and his assignment is to block the linebacker, it's another matter. A veteran linebacker is going to take the first gap
that's available to him. Your fullback in front of you is going to have to make
the adjustment.

Cleo Miller was the fullback for me when I played in Cleveland, and every
year that he started, I rushed for 1000 yards. He knew how to block, and
he could make that adjustment very well. Most of my plays came off the
I-formation, where the fullback would either go through the line and block
the linebacker or go around and block him. But when Mike Pruitt was the
fullback, he couldn't do it, and I never got 1000 yards because he made the
same mistake over, and over, and over again. He used to say, "They don't
pay me to block, man, they pay me to run." And I said, "You got that right."

SN: *The fan misses ninety-five percent of that, at least.*
GP: Oh, yeah. On every play, someone has a blocking assignment, some of
which are more difficult than others. You have to know how well each guy
can handle his assignment, and then make the necessary adjustments. Timing
is all-important.

SN: *You were a kickoff and punt returner. What was involved mentally in those
assignments?*
GP: Being a student of the game helped me in returning kickoffs and punts.
I was struggling my first year as a punt returner. The coach would say return
right, or return left, or return middle, but I didn't really understand what we
were trying to do. To relax myself, I would always go to the stadium three hours
before the game. That way I didn't have to get in line and get in that rat race of
trying to get my ankles and wrists taped. If you wait in line too long and are late,
the coach is going to jump all over you, and you don't need that. So, I got there
ahead of time, and got taped, read the program, said my prayers, concentrated
on my plays, or went in the john.

One day before a game against the Houston Oilers, I was in there sitting on the john reading the program, and I came across an interview with Speedy Duncan, which taught me a lot. Speedy Duncan was one of the top kickoff and punt returners in football, and the interview was about his success as a return guy. He said, "What I do is I put the defense on the defensive. When guys come down in a lane, you're trying to return the ball, and they have to respect whatever moves you make. If you get the ball and run right, all those guys are going to run right. You haven't fooled anybody. You're now totally dependent on the execution of your return team. You're not helping them at all. What I do is attack the coverage team. I run right at them. When I do that, they have to stop. Then I can go right if it's a right return and left if it's a left return."

I was sitting there saying, "Man, that makes a lot of sense." And I went out there against the Oilers and applied it. My first punt return, I challenged the defense, and I went seventy-nine yards for a touchdown. I went in saying, "It works!" It's all in being a student of the game.

SN: *Who was your first head coach at Cleveland?*
GP: Nick Skorich. He thought I was too small to make it at running back.

SN: *He thought of you more on special teams?*
GP: On special teams and as a backup running back. That used to just irk me, because Skorich is smaller than I am. He's a little guy, and he'd look up at me and say, "You're too small to play." I constantly was in his face about playing, playing, playing. After it was announced he would not be head coach in 1975, I even went to the newspapers, trying to pressure him to play me. I think he was trying to get back at me when he decided to start me at the end of the season. You say you can play, let's see. In the last game of the season, against Houston, I had a total offense of more than 300 yards. It was a little too late. If he had made the move earlier, I would have benefited from it, and maybe he would have benefited, too.

SN: *Forrest Gregg replaced Skorich as head coach. How would you describe his coaching style? How did he plan to use you?*
GP: Forrest Gregg told me he was going to start me and that I was his running back, so be ready. Fortunately, because I was so excited, I really worked out in the off-season—I mean, really lifted weights—and came to camp in the best shape I had ever been in. I'd hate to imagine what it would have been like if I'd come to camp without seriously working out, as I had the previous couple years. As it was, I came to his camp and almost died. His camps were that tough.

Forrest had played for Vince Lombardi, and he followed Lombardi's approach to coaching. His camps were very physical. When we veterans reported to his camp, the rookies, who had arrived a week before, were all telling us how tough the camp was. We didn't really take the rookies' stories very seriously, because we just figured they had never been in a two-a-day camp on the pro level. But we soon found out they were telling the truth. He had us doing almost 100 up-downs prior to practice.

The up-downs were so brutal, we had guys who wouldn't do them when Forrest turned his back. But they were stunned the next day when we had a meeting. The lights went out, and the projector came on, and to our amazement, Forrest had filmed the up-downs, so he could catch all the guys who weren't doing them when he had his back turned. The next day, those guys had to do the up-downs, plus a different drill, where he just ran them until they just dropped.

Forrest was too tough, because all of that drained us to the point that we lost our stamina during games. We were more physical as a team, but we got so tired in games because of those practices being so tough.

SN: *How about his attitude toward injuries? Do some coaches push you to play more when you're injured?*

GP: Oh, he pushed you to play. When you walked into the training room, you'd see guys getting treatment, and there was a little room for the trainer himself. And Forrest would walk in and ask the trainer to come into that room. The blinds would come down, and Forrest would stay in there for three or four minutes. Then the blinds would come up and Forrest would walk out, looking at everybody. After Forrest disappeared, the trainer would say, "Why don't we try that ankle today, and see if you can run on it?" We knew that Forrest had gotten all over him, because it was the trainer's job to keep guys on the field or to get them back on the field as soon as possible. We always used to say, "Forrest is coming through today, and he's going to pronounce everybody healed."

Forrest's approach was much like that of my high school coach, so even though a lot of guys fought what he was doing, I was used to it. I was the team captain in high school, and I never missed a practice, even when I cracked my ribs. I had thought that having cracked ribs would get me out of practice, but the coach didn't see it that way. I was sitting in the whirlpool, smiling to myself, and thinking, "I got out of practice." All of a sudden, I see that the water level is going down, and the motor that agitates the water is making the sound it makes when the water level gets low. And I look up, and the coach is over next to where you drain the water out of the whirlpool. He asked me, "Aren't you my captain?" I said, "Yes, Sir." He said to me, "I've always told my captains to be my leader. Ain't that right?" I said, "Yes, Sir." Then he asked me, "Can that whole team get in that whirlpool?" I said, "No, Sir." "Can they all get out on the field?" "Yes, Sir." He said, "Well, get out there where the whole team can get!" Forrest was pretty much like that.

One time Forrest really pushed me over the edge, but we ended up a little closer than before. It was the first year that Forrest was there, that my grandfather died. My grandmother had had a stroke, so I was kind of preparing myself for her. When my mother called me and said it was my grandfather, it took me totally off guard. My grandfather died during the week, and we had a game on Saturday. When I told Forrest I was going home to the funeral, he looked at me, and asked, "Do you think you can be back Saturday?" I cursed at him. I just lost it. I told him I didn't know if I'd ever be back to this goddamn—that ain't important to me. And I left. When I came back, we became a little closer. I don't think he had meant it the way I took it. I found out a little later that Forrest was real close to his family.

One time at the end of his second year he got really abusive, and from then on it was downhill. We had finished 3-11 his first year, and we were 9-4 with one game left, against Kansas City on Sunday. Pittsburgh had a better record, and they played Houston on Saturday. If Houston beat Pittsburgh and if we beat Kansas City, we'd win the division. Well, it didn't work out that way. We all had our hopes up real high, but Pittsburgh went out and beat Houston. So, regardless of what we did, it didn't matter. We were going home. And we lost the game in Kansas City. We had gone from 3-11 to 9-5, and you'd think Forrest would be happy. Man, he took us in the locker room and cursed us out. He told us we were so sorry, he didn't even want to pray with us.

The season had ended, and guys had made preparations to fly home from Kansas City. Their wives had already moved back home. And Forrest said, "All you assholes, who think you're going to wherever you're going, you got to think that again. Get your asses back on the plane. I'm taking all you sorry such-and-suches back to Cleveland. And anybody who is not on the plane, I'm going to fine you." That's when he lost the respect of his players. From that time on, any situation that came up that they could make him look bad, they did. Guys didn't play all-out for Forrest after that.

Also, the game was changing in ways that Forrest didn't really understand. He was from the Vince Lombardi days. There was no fooling anybody. If you executed properly, then the other team can't stop it. But with the introduction of computers, teams were getting more prepared. When I first came into the NFL, a game plan consisted of two pieces of paper. It contained a diagram of the other team's defense, with a list of all the starters and their backups, and the two different defensive formations that they ran. On offense, there was a list of the starters and their backups, and a list of a few plays and formations they ran. That was it. By the end of my career, I got a computer printout! It went on for fourteen or fifteen pages. I remember the first day they introduced that, I didn't have any idea of what the coach was talking about. He was saying things like "two percent of the time, they're in this formation." I was looking around, and everybody had the same blank look on his face that I did.

That computer printout was so thorough, that they'd know exactly what the other team was going to do. The computer could compile all the plays run up to that point, separate them, and come up with a percentage of how often they ran them.

I played well with Forrest. He gave me my break despite my size, and he judged you based on what you'd done. Although he was tough, I was already used to that because of my high school coach. But a lot of the players didn't like Forrest. And they raised enough hell that eventually he got fired.

When they finally fired him, I thought that Forrest had learned something, but it was too late. What he learned, he couldn't execute with the Browns. And Cincinnati benefited from it, because they went to the Super Bowl the very next year. I think that was a result of what he had learned with the Browns.

SN: *I notice you've got a Raiders sticker on your door, not a Browns sticker.*
GP: My house too is Raiders colors. It was Browns colors, but they pissed me off. It used to be beige, with brown and orange. When I got traded, I had it painted silver and black, and put that sticker on, and it's been on ever since.

But I'm a Browns fan. I understand now. Trading is a part of the game. I've gotten over it now. When it happens to you, you go through that, "Why me?" and the pity and all that. But, eventually, you realize that if you want to continue to play, you've still got to do what you've always done to play this long. And that's prepare yourself, be prepared, and be in the best condition that you can be in. And that's what I did.

I played nine years with the Browns before getting traded to the Los Angeles Raiders. I got traded in large part because I didn't get along with the head coach, Rutigliano, who succeeded Forrest Gregg. And when I hurt my knee, he got upset.

I really believe the Browns panicked on me when I sustained that knee injury. With my style of running, it took longer for me to come back from a knee injury than, say, a fullback or a lineman. That was because my moves were more lateral than straight ahead, and I had ligament damage on the inside. So, there were certain things I couldn't do. I had done so many things

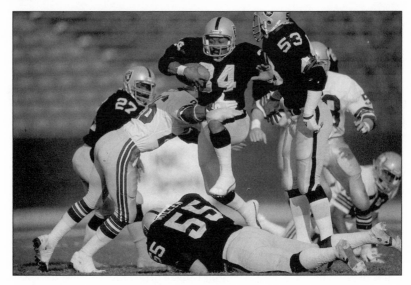

*Greg Pruitt with the Los Angeles Raiders. Courtesy of Andy Hayt/*Sports
Illustrated.

before that, that now that I wasn't 100 percent and couldn't do some of those
things, they just decided I was washed up. Rutigliano used that to sell the
owner on trading me.

SN: *What was it like adjusting to a new team?*
GP: When I first went to the Raiders, I was bitter with the Browns. I really
wanted to end my career with the Browns. After being somewhere as long as I
had been, it was really tough to have to go through the relocating and learning the new system.

I sat in camp really thinking about retiring. I talked to my backfield coach in
Cleveland, Jim Garrett, about it. He told me, "Well, Greg, if you do that, you're
admitting that the Browns were right. They say you're washed up. They don't
want you anymore. The Raiders are saying that you're not. So, to retire, you're
going to make Rutigliano look like he's a genius." And that was the only incentive I had.

I came to peace with myself and decided I would do the best I could with
the Raiders. I said, "Okay, I had over 10,000 yards in the league. Not one yard
with the Raiders. So, that don't mean nothing." My attitude was that I didn't
want to ever have to say, "Well, if I had run a little harder in practice, or if I
had done this, that could have been the difference."

SN: *What was your impression of Al Davis, the Raiders owner?*
GP: I was really impressed with Al Davis when I met him. When I got to the Raiders, he called me into his office and he told me not to expect to play a lot that year. He said, "You don't have anything to prove to me. But if the Browns are silly enough to trade you out here on a conditional draft choice, I'll give them a low draft choice." The only way he could do that was by limiting my play. It worked out real well, because the next year when I started to play more, I went to the Pro Bowl.

Al Davis is like an encyclopedia. You walk in, and he knows your stats from high school. He knows everything about you. Anytime you have a good game against Al Davis, he will eventually try to get you to play for him.

Davis has great rapport with his players, and as a result, he gets more out of them. Everybody asks, "How does Al Davis keep getting these washed up players and getting more years out of them?" The point is it's not that they're washed up. In my case, my stats went down at Cleveland because the head coach wouldn't let me come back and play the position that I played, the way I played it prior to my injury. In a lot of other cases, the players just stopped playing up to their ability because they didn't like the situation they were in. They're trying to force a trade.

If you ask most of the players, especially the veterans, where they want to play, they'll say the Raiders. The Raiders is like football heaven, especially if you're a veteran. This situation with Marcus Allen is probably the first situation I ever heard of where a player was trying to leave the Raiders.

The feeling of closeness that you had with Al Davis was the opposite of what you had with Cleveland's owner, Art Modell. When Modell walked in, it was like, the Boss. Everybody held his breath. And he was really an owner who wanted to be close to his players. But the players couldn't pull up that curtain that said "Owner." Whereas Al Davis, with the Raiders, made it sound like a saloon when he came in, and it sounded like a saloon after he got there. Guys would talk to him about anything and everything. He just had that closeness.

I was with the Raiders during the 1982 players' strike, and Al Davis had very good rapport with us then. He kind of went along with what he thought was in the best interests of the players. I believe he sent word to us to follow what the majority of the team does. The other teams are striking, so we should strike, too. Al Davis is different from the other owners. He's a maverick. He busted the NFL owners himself. He made something like $84 million, through lawsuits and whatever, just making the decision to move from Oakland to Los Angeles.

The Raiders catered to veterans, more than younger players. Al Davis's philosophy was that you win with experience. Other teams look at it the other way. You have a few veterans around to give you that experience, but you win with youth, with the strength and speed of the young players. But the teams that win are generally the ones with the veteran players.

In fact, the Raiders even had days where the veterans didn't have to practice. Al Davis came up to me after practice one day, soon after I had arrived, and asked me if my knees hurt. They were killing me, but I responded, "No, Sir. My knees don't hurt." He said, "Don't lie. If your knees hurt, tell me, and I'll give you a day off." I was worried, and thought, "Uh, oh. They're going to make sure I don't get hurt so they can cut me." But he told me, "We have veteran days off here." Davis explained, "This is a veteran team. You can't keep up with the same pace those other guys do. You ain't got nothing to prove to me. I want you at your best to play. I don't want you hurt and trying to play."

But I still wasn't convinced. I still went, "No, ain't nothing wrong with my knee." And the next day, I actually thought I had been cut. I was putting my clothes on to go out to practice, and the coach came and said, "Greg, don't get dressed." The next thing usually is, "Bring your playbook." I'm saying, "Oh boy." But it turned out that there were about twelve of us who didn't have to practice, simply because we had been in the league ten years. That's the way the Raiders were.

SN: *Some offensive players single out linebackers as radically different in outlook.*
GP: Linebackers are strange people to me. They're *weird*. Very few people on football teams hang out with linebackers. They're a different breed altogether. They think different. They have a strange perspective on life. I can walk up to a guy, I don't care how long he played, and it'll take me only a very short time to determine he's a linebacker. Just the way he acts, the way he talks.

SN: *But the middle linebacker is often the defensive captain.*
GP: Yeah, and he's usually crazy, too. (Laughs) I'll give you a good example. The craziest linebacker to me was Ted Hendricks of the Raiders. His elevator didn't go all the way to the top. I'm serious. He was strange. Matt Millen was another—a great linebacker. The first time I met Matt Millen, I had just been traded to the Raiders. I was sitting there eating dinner, and he walked over to me and started eating out of my plate. He said, "Oh, you're Greg Pruitt, aren't you?" And I said, "Yeah, I am." He was still eating out of my plate, and he said, "Oh, you really know how to pick your food! I'm Matt Millen." And I said, "Yeah, linebacker, right?" They do that kind of stuff.

SN: *You played for the Raiders in the 1984 Super Bowl against the Washington Redskins. What was it like playing in the Super Bowl? How does it feel compared to playing in a regular game?*

GP: The key for the Raiders in getting to the Super Bowl in 1984 was that our starting quarterback, Mark Wilson, stayed healthy long enough that when Jim Plunkett came in to replace him, he was in very good shape and in a position to use his experience to get us there. Plunkett was a great quarterback, but he hadn't been playing well, and they had decided to start Mark Wilson at the beginning of the season. After about nine games, Wilson got hurt, and Plunkett was slated to start the game against Kansas City, which is a big rivalry. I remember Plunkett telling me before the game, "Greg, I have never been this late in the season with nothing hurting." He told me that he felt so good, he would probably throw a bomb on the first play. So, we had the kickoff, and Plunkett went out there and threw an eighty-yard touchdown pass.

I played against Joe Washington in that Super Bowl, and Joe and I have always been very, very good friends. We went out to dinner in Tampa before the game. And some fan saw us together and said, "It's a fixed game." She said, "You're supposed to hate this guy. You're getting ready to play in the Super Bowl." So we told her, "Hey, he's offense, and I'm offense. We're never on the field at the same time. We're friends, and we don't stop being friends because he plays with the other team."

Playing in the Super Bowl is totally different from playing in any other game. During the two-week preparation for the Super Bowl, your biggest concern is, "Damn. I may never get this chance again. I don't want to blow this. I don't want to come all the way through this to lose it." In every game, you get butterflies. Usually, once the game starts, you get hit and your concentration goes to the game itself. Except for the Super Bowl. I was nervous from beginning to end. Even at the end of the game, I was saying, "All right, guys. It ain't over, it ain't over." It was Matt Millen who came up to me and said, "Greg, look at the scoreboard." I looked. He said, "What's the score?" I said, "Thirty-eight for the Raiders, nine for the Redskins." And he told me, "Believe me, it's over. They don't have enough time." And I still didn't believe him. I didn't believe it until I read it the next day in the paper. That's when it came to me that we had won the championship. That was a great feeling.

SN: *Why did you decide to retire when you did?*
GP: I wasn't ready to retire. I wasn't ready. I was looking forward to my thirteenth year in the league. I knew it would be my last year, but I thought it could be my best year. But I couldn't pass the physical. They had put a staple in my knee some time before, when I had gotten hurt, and I wasn't really aware it was there. I was using ultrasound, and it made my knee flare up. The Raiders asked for the records, and they found out I had this staple.

When they removed the staple, the recovery took longer than I thought. I didn't pass the physical, so I retired.

Football is kind of funny. When I thought I was worth more money, I wasn't making it. And then when I didn't think I was worth what they were paying me, they were paying me. I really thought I was much better toward the middle of my career or at the beginning than at the end, but I was making more money at the end. Mentally, I was probably better at the end, but physically, I couldn't do the things I had.

SN: *But you still wanted to keep playing?*
GP: Oh, yeah. Where else can you make that kind of money? (Laughs) I accomplished a lot in my NFL career.

SN: *How many times were you All-Pro?*
GP: I went to the Pro Bowl five times.

SN: *How many times did you gain over 1000 yards in a season?*
GP: Three times. I've always thought I was the pioneer of the small backs. I was probably the first guy to be as small, to play as long. Things have really changed. Emmitt Smith is five foot nine. You've never heard once that he's too small to play.

SN: *Since you retired, you're president of a computer company in Cleveland.*
GP: Yes. I have a lot of rental property. We sell computers and sell parts for upgrading. I have an office in Washington, D.C., which I formed three years ago. Those guys go after maintenance contracts in the Department of Defense. They take existing equipment and maintain it. We ain't raising a lot of hell, but we're making enough to get by.

I have to work. I can't sit around and do nothing. I've got to have all these things going. I have this goal that when I'm fifty-five, then I'll slowly start to enjoy. But I get enough enjoyment now. I've been involved in charity golf tournaments. I fell in love with the game of golf, so I get great opportunities to do what I like to do and see the country, too.

There's a lot of pressure on me, because being a small company, I have a lot of things to do. So, today is a typical day. I just got back. I got all these things to do.

INDEX